# Praise for *Seeing Is Hearing Is Believing*

"Diffrient makes a compelling case for a synesthetic and intersensorial approach to horror, shining the spotlight on extra- and paratextual elements like audio commentaries or subtitling and teasing out the importance of cinematic dis/belief. Compulsively readable and theoretically astute, this book comes to join the ranks of the influential phenomenological studies upon which it builds."

—Xavier Aldana Reyes, author of *Body Horror: Biology, Biopower, Biotechnology*

"I couldn't have written this book. I couldn't have even imagined this book. The vision to do so required David Scott Diffrient. It is always gratifying to read such a book as *Seeing Is Hearing Is Believing*, one that seems simultaneously so improbable and so necessary. Never less than innovative, original, and delightful, this is a book that enriches horror studies. It is certain to be discussed for years to come."

—Murray Leeder, author of *Horror Film: A Critical Introduction*

"With *Seeing Is Hearing Is Believing*, David Scott Diffrient gives us a major intervention in horror studies. His study of the intersensorial is as imaginative as it is significant."

—Gary D. Rhodes, PhD, author of *The Birth of the American Horror Film* and *Vampires in Silent Cinema*

"*Seeing Is Hearing Is Believing* is a fascinating, impressively researched, and much-needed study of the multiple sensory—and intersensorial—experiences involved in watching horror. It offers an unprecedented view of the dimensionalities of the genre as it reaches out to varied audiences."

—Aviva Briefel, Edward Little Professor of the English Language and Literature and Cinema Studies, Bowdoin College

"*Seeing Is Hearing Is Believing* charts a provocative new path into the study of the horror film. By centering the body and the complex relationship between our various senses, Diffrient reframes the relationship between the rational and the irrational and the provocative space that lies between."

—Kendall R. Phillips, Syracuse University

"*Seeing Is Hearing Is Believing* takes a fresh and original look at horror cinema as a deeply intersensorial experience, where sight, sound, and feeling are inseparable. In this engaging study, David Scott Diffrient also demonstrates how subtitles, audio description, and disability perspectives open up new ways of understanding how horror produces meaning and shapes spectatorship. Thoughtful and rich in insight, this book makes a significant contribution to horror scholarship, disability studies, and contemporary debates about film experience."

—Angela Ndalianis, professor of media and entertainment,
Swinburne University of Technology

# Seeing Is Hearing Is Believing

**Contemporary Approaches to Film and Media Series**

*A complete listing of the books in this series can be found online at wsupress.wayne.edu.*

**General Editor**

Barry Keith Grant

*Brock University*

# SEEING IS HEARING IS BELIEVING

## SENSORY HORROR AND ASSISTIVE TECHNOLOGIES

David Scott Diffrient

WAYNE STATE UNIVERSITY PRESS
DETROIT

ISBN 9780814351888 (paperback)
ISBN 9780814351871 (hardcover)
ISBN 9780814351895 (ebook)

Library of Congress Control Number: 2026935510

Cover art © durantelallera / Shutterstock.com. Cover design by Brad Norr Design.

Published with the assistance of a fund established by Thelma Gray James of Wayne State University.

Wayne State University Press rests on Waawiyaataanong, also referred to as Detroit, the ancestral and contemporary homeland of the Three Fires Confederacy. These sovereign lands were granted by the Ojibwe, Odawa, Potawatomi, and Wyandot Nations, in 1807, through the Treaty of Detroit. Wayne State University Press affirms Indigenous sovereignty and honors all tribes with a connection to Detroit. With our Native neighbors, the press works to advance educational equity and promote a better future for the earth and all people.

Wayne State University Press
Leonard N. Simons Building
4809 Woodward Avenue
Detroit, Michigan 48201-1309

Visit us online at wsupress.wayne.edu.

# CONTENTS

**INTRODUCTION:** Irrationality, Intersensoriality, and the Horror Film 1

## PART I.
## Decentering Sight and Synchronizing the Senses: From Disbelief Mitigation to Directors' Commentaries and Audio Description

1. Tricking the Eye, Believing in Bodies: Optical Illusions and Spectatorial Confusions 33

2. (Not) Seeing Is Believing: Ghostly Bodies, Heretical Texts, and Hysterical Failures 67

3. Just for the Smell of It: Offal and Olfactory Awfulness in the Horror Films of Herschell Gordon Lewis 99

4. Taste the Pain, Bro: Horror Film's Masculinist Flavors and Masochistic Mouthfeel 125

## PART 2.
## You Can't Spell "Fear" Without "Ear": Hearing Images and Seeing Sounds Through Assistive Technologies

5. (Not) Hearing Is Deceiving: Deaf Gain, Pleasurable Pain, and the Missing "[SQUISHES]" of *Hush* 165

6. The Unholy Sight of Unsightly Sounds: Horror Film Subtitles for the Deaf and Hard of Hearing 193

7. "Hearts That See": Blind Spectatorship, the Horrors of War, and the Historical Roots of Audio Description 223

8. It Doesn't Follow: Audio Description and Verbal Premonition in Horror's Home-Video and Streaming Presentations 257

CODA: Believing Women and Writing Tomorrow's Histories of the Horror Film 291

*Notes* 303

*Index* 331

# INTRODUCTION

## Irrationality, Intersensoriality, and the Horror Film

Don't tell me you're afraid of witches!

—Tony (Eduardo Capetillo) to his older sister Vicky (Mineko Mori) in Rubén Galindo Jr.'s *Cemetery of Terror* (*Cementerio del terror*, 1985)

We all go a little mad sometimes.

—Norman (Anthony Perkins) to Marion Crane (Janet Leigh) in Alfred Hitchcock's *Psycho* (1960)

Few dates in the history of cinematic horror are as significant as June 16, 1960. On that otherwise unremarkable Thursday, a motion picture that has since become synonymous with the "birth" of modern horror premiered, forever altering the public's perceptions of the genre's most entrenched iconographic feature—the monster—while tapping into the medium's latent ability to shock audiences through sudden eruptions of carefully edited onscreen violence. Debuting with considerable anticipation and ballyhoo-style fanfare at Manhattan's DeMille and Baronet theaters, Alfred Hitchcock's *Psycho* hardly needs any introduction today, now that the low-budget film's reputation as a paradigm-shifting departure from previous US productions has been firmly established. Indeed, most critics would agree that it set the template for subsequent domestic and international productions about human monstrosity, personified by Anthony Perkins's deceptively unassuming character: the "normal-looking, boy-next-door" serial killer Norman Bates.[1] However, at the time of the film's original theatrical release, before it made its way to overseas markets and inspired a host of imitators (in Italy, France, and Hitchcock's country of birth, England), reviewers were far less sympathetic to the director's latest attempt to playfully terrorize viewers—or, as the master of suspense himself liked to say, to play them "like an organ"—with unprecedented levels of nail-biting tension and bloody mayhem.[2] Unlike those initial critics in New York, who wrote "middling-to-hostile" reviews of *Psycho*,[3] audiences around the country seemed to delight in partaking in the skillfully manufactured fright of a motion picture that quickly became a national sensation.[4] Reports of spectators shrieking loudly and cowering in fear, and in some cases even fainting at the sight of the film's ostensible protagonist, Marion Crane (Janet Leigh), being stabbed to death in a motel shower, contributed to its notoriety, as did Paramount Pictures' heavily reproduced publicity photos of long lines of ticketholders snaking outside those venues on Broadway.

To be sure, this standard view of *Psycho* as a landmark example of auteur-driven, studio-financed art-horror, whose affective intensity and psychological complexity cleared the way for even more radical interventions in cinematic form in the years following its debut on June 16, 1960, is such a widely accepted facet of film history that it would hardly be worth noting were it not for the need to constantly remind ourselves—younger viewers in particular—of the continuity between past and present. But that link between Hitchcock's apparently "unprecedented" thriller and contemporary horror (including slasher films of the last few decades that pay homage to it) rests upon a perceived discontinuity between *Psycho* and the earlier generations of studio-produced motion pictures with which it is frequently contrasted (e.g., Universal's classic monster movies of the 1930s and the atmospheric chillers produced by RKO's resident horror specialist, Val Lewton, in the 1940s).[5] In other words, critical focus on its extraordinariness simultaneously conforms to "traditional accounts of genre history," which, as Adam Lowenstein argues, "chart the modern horror film's 'evolution' after its genesis in *Psycho*," and ruptures that history by severing Hitchcock's work from antecedents produced not only in the United States but in other parts of the world by equally talented commercial artists.[6] Such an approach, Lowenstein goes on to remark, has the effect of making it seem as though "the modern horror film emerge[d] not only as a uniquely

American phenomenon, but as a matter of simply adding increased doses of gore to themes and formulae apparently invented by Hitchcock."[7] Nevertheless, *Psycho* continues to be "regarded as a turning point in the history of the genre," when the external threats associated with previous generations (embodied in the uncanny form of the hideously deformed monster) were replaced by the internal mechanisms of barely suppressed sexual desire as well as the close-to-home horrors of family members turning against one another and becoming metaphorical monsters themselves.[8]

Coincidentally, another noteworthy thing occurred on June 16, 1960, not in the United States but in Italy, and from an adjacent sphere of popular culture that was likewise coming into its own artistically. Compared to the theatrical premiere of *Psycho*, it will seem to be of little historical significance. But this relatively minor event is equally telling as a sign of the changing times, when the traditional view of horror as an "ancient" category steeped in supernatural elements and otherworldly beings was giving way to an emerging conception of the genre as a means of confronting contemporaneous anxieties (ranging from the midcentury threat of nuclear annihilation to the breakdown of the nuclear family and the spread of serial killings in the years that followed). It was on that date that the Milan-based publisher Mondadori released its latest weekly installment of the Disney-inspired *Topolino* comics: issue number 508, which featured an eccentric, broomstick-riding witch trying to convince Goofy and a host of other city slickers that she really *is* the supernatural creature she claims to be. Over several colorful pages and panels, artist Luciano Bottaro and writer Carlo Chendi's "Washed-Up Witch" (originally titled "Pippo e la fattucchiera") shows the homely title character, Witch Hazel, growing increasingly distraught by the fact that "twentieth century folk" are so "spoiled by technology" that they no longer fear real magic. "These modern souls are just *too busy* to be scared," Hazel laments in the comic's first large panel, setting the stage for a series of humorous encounters between this relic of the past and a representative cross-section of contemporary society. Comprised of anthropomorphized animals, the members of that society simply will not be convinced that she is a magically endowed spellcaster capable of altering reality, rather than a delusional old crone in need of psychiatric evaluation.

Using a quaintly antiquated form of speech, Hazel wonders aloud, "Doth anyone still believe in witches?" before resorting to a common, if desperate, fright tactic—yelling "Booo!" at a momentarily startled passerby—only to be threatened with a speeding ticket once a police officer arrives on the scene. She repeats her rhetorical question following a run-in with a drawling country dog on the outskirts of the city (someone who mistakes her for a cleaning lady) and then during the lead-up to her first encounter with Goofy, another canine creature not known for his high intelligence. Nevertheless, this latter character—the comic book's disbelieving hero—spends the remainder of the story insisting upon *rational*, scientific explanations for all of the inexplicable events occurring around him. Even after being sent high up into the air as a passenger on her flying broomstick and coming face-to-face with a conjured dragon, Goofy stays true to his naysaying ways, emphasizing that he only believes what he can see. He later modifies that familiar phrase, telling Hazel, "I only believe what I can see . . . and *feel*!" (fig. I.1).

Besides linking belief—that all-important ingredient in both horror and fantasy fiction—to the senses of sight and touch, the lanky dog draws attention to one of the chief technological means through which midcentury "movie magic" was created, telling the witch that the impression of traveling one hundred miles an hour in an enchanted automobile is something that she could only achieve through rear-screen projection. "Thuh background's movin', but we're just standin' still!" the

**Figure I.1:** Goofy's willingness to believe in otherwise unbelievable things hinges on sight and touch, a topic broached in Luciano Bottaro and Carlo Chendi's comic "Washed-Up Witch" ("Pippo e la fattucchiera"), which was published on the same date of *Psycho*'s theatrical release.

oddly savvy simpleton exclaims, before concluding (a few panels later) that Hazel must be a film director, owing to all the movie props that she probably used to create such convincing special effects and optical illusions (fig. I.2).

A more specific cinematic reference occurs a few panels later in the same comic book when the witch teleports Goofy to the Mad Hatter scene from Walt Disney's animated feature *Alice in Wonderland* (1951). He quickly finds himself in the company of the ill-tempered Queen of Hearts, someone who threatens to decapitate our hero before Hazel intervenes and returns Goofy to his home (realizing that, should he find himself headless, he would almost certainly *never* believe in her existence). Tellingly, the comic book wraps up with another intervention, this time featuring a psychiatrist who takes a slightly different interest in the *witch's* head. With notepad and pencil in hand, he consults first with the old woman, who now no longer believes in *herself* and lies exhausted on his couch (as if in desperate need of a "talking cure"). The psychiatrist then interviews Goofy about these recent run-ins with a clearly insane human being. After spending just a few minutes with the disbelieving dog, the shrink—a canine himself (albeit one who is clearly modeled on Sigmund Freud, right down to his Austrian-German accent)—even begins to question his own identity and sanity as a medical doctor specializing in

**Figure I.2:** Goofy surmises that Witch Hazel must be a movie director, given her perceived proficiency in using props and special effects as part of her magic act.

mental health. "We don't believe in witches . . . or psychiatrists!" he and the old woman chant in unison in the final panel as they scurry away from Goofy's house, leaving her magical broomstick behind along with any pretense that these two individuals—one a throwback to a much earlier set of conventions in supernatural horror, the other a more modern figure emblematic of horror in the age of knife-wielding "psychos"—really *are* who they claim to be.

This final scene of Bottaro and Chendi's "Washed-Up Witch" thus forms a strange, unexpected parallel with the concluding moments of Hitchcock's *Psycho*, which culminates with a psychiatrist, Dr. Richmond (Simon Oakland), weighing in on the irrational rationale behind Norman's murderous ways (fig. I.3). However, unlike the Disney-inspired comic book, the film does not end with the mental health specialist succumbing to the same diagnosable problem that the latter's colleagues might attribute to his psychologically troubled subject. Instead, the motel manager, who sits by himself in a local courthouse's detention room and awaits prosecution, gets the last laugh. Or, rather, Norman-as-mother, wrapped snugly in a blanket, flashes a wry smile at the audience in the closing seconds, now that his condition (which today would be clinically classified as Dissociative Identity Disorder, but which was commonly referred to as "multiple personalities" in that era's parlance) has been dutifully detailed by Dr. Richmond in an adjacent room of the police precinct.

**Figure I.3:** During the penultimate scene of *Psycho*, a psychiatrist delivers a lengthy monologue that explains the matricidal killer's motives.

Judging from fans' online commentary as well as the critical consensus surrounding *Psycho*, the doctor's lengthy explanation of what has driven the cross-dressing killer to commit otherwise inexplicable acts (including the "most unbearable crime of all," matricide) leaves many viewers cold. To their ears, his five-minute spiel sounds forced and serves no purpose other than to deliver exposition near the end of the narrative. However, the psychiatrist's comments about Norman's "dangerously disturbed" mind and pathological jealousy toward his mother's suitors underscore the paradoxically negative pleasure built into the genre, which caters to our perverse desire to plumb the depths of human depravity and confront images or ideas that we would otherwise prefer to avoid in everyday life. One wonders if the general dissatisfaction and outright antipathy directed toward that penultimate scene, unrelated to its expositional clunkiness as a heavy-handed wrap-up, reflect an unwillingness on the part of audiences to subject themselves to such mental poking and prodding—to the same intense scientific scrutiny whereby something of the "self" can be discerned in the "other." Perhaps the doctor's diagnosis cuts too close to the bone, revealing as much about our own contradictory urges—particularly in the context of horror film spectatorship (an "irrational" pastime in which comfort comes from crisis and pleasure derives from displeasure)—as it does the main character's confounding set of psychological traits. But his words also provide analytical accompaniment to the *other* voice that can be heard during this concluding scene.

As the camera dollies in and lingers on the murderer's face, an old woman's voice—that of Norman's dead mother—rises on the soundtrack as if it were emanating from inside him. Within seconds, her words, which underscore his "badness" as an inveterate criminal who should have been locked up years ago, appear to get under his skin. "I hope they *are* watching," she says in reference to those "all-seeing" authorities (like the offscreen psychiatrist) who subject their patients to a form of invasive scientific scrutiny and state-mandated surveillance that borders on voyeurism. If not quite cackling with laughter, her creaky intonation throughout these closing seconds of the film sounds like that of a *witch* from some earlier horror movie. It is as if Norman, momentarily "possessed" by his mother, were actually channeling the spirit of an old crone like Disney's Hazel or any of her cinematic sisters from decades past.

The haunting and indeed *haunted* effect of this concluding moment is heightened through Hitchcock's use of a dissolve, which not only shows Marion's white 1957 sedan being towed out of the swamp behind the Bates Motel (with the towing chain appearing to be tethered to Norman's chest), but also gives viewers a quick, almost subliminal glimpse at a skull inside his face. In that split second of visual overlay, when the skeletal remains of the dead mother and the smiling face of the criminally insane son can be seen simultaneously, audiences are given access to the very thing that Dr. Richmond has just made a verbal pronouncement about, but which quickly flickers out of existence only to be replaced by the words "THE END," printed atop that final image of the car being dredged from the swamp to the accompaniment of composer Bernard Herrmann's unsettling score.

On the surface, these two texts—one a feature-length, black-and-white Hollywood production helmed by a legendary fright-master and distinguished by its decidedly Freudian take on Oedipal desire, the other a slim, colorful comic book published in Italy for a presumably preteen readership—share little in common besides a release date (June 16, 1960). But, in their own unique ways, they lay bare one of the central preoccupations of the horror genre—namely, the dialectical tension between rationality and irrationality. The frequency with which those ostensibly warring perspectives proliferated at that historical juncture, when cinematic horror was undergoing a facelift and putting audiences into the shoes of deranged human monsters, is indicative of a general feeling of anxiety or widespread ambivalence surrounding not only the fracturing of familial bonds but also technological and scientific advancements, which appeared to threaten the sanctity of more traditional structures of social life, including religion. If the "unconsciously motivated fear" associated with such foreseeable loss—of control, of middle-class comforts, of presumed safety in numbers, and of the very idea of a Supreme Being upon whom religious adherents depend for their own lives' meaning—came to be a defining feature of these and other midcentury cultural productions, it is only because the context in which they were made was so contradictory in its framing of technology and science as modern-day "saviors" of society that were at least partly responsible for its downfall and eventual destruction.[9] Although the combined wonderment and technophobia that accompanied the introduction of the computer, a "mechanical monster" in Cold War–era America, has traditionally been thought of as a subject best left to the inference-making moves of horror's sister category of science fiction, practitioners of cinematic dread have long used the medium to extrapolate the possibly devastating effects of using machines to engineer alternative realities and new ways of (beastly) being. From Dr. Mirakle (Bela Lugosi) to Dr. Moreau (Charles Laughton), Hollywood's most iconic "mad scientists" from decades past harnessed tools of creation in ultimately destructive ways. Indeed, I am hard-pressed to find a more "natural" setting for the promethean experiments of someone like Victor Frankenstein (Colin Clive)—an irrational rationalist if ever there was one—than those paradoxically old-fashioned yet technologically advanced laboratories in which Tesla coils and other electrical equipment pulsate with an energy that anticipates the computing power of more modern devices.

By the time of *Psycho*'s 1960 release, such iconography—a staple of studio-era horror films made two or three decades earlier—had largely given way to more mundane illustrations of modernity's encroachment on people's lives. However, that replacement of the "extraordinary" with the "ordinary" (reflecting the broader routinization of work and domestic life under new regimes of managerial and organizational disciplining beginning in the 1950s) should not be mistaken as a wholesale rejection of the fantastical during an atomic age when scientific rationality and the instrumental value of machines—their functionality as labor-saving devices—were merely a front for the US military industrial complex to carry out some truly irrational and inhumane actions with computers as weapons of combined mass destruction and mass distraction. As a vehicle through which to allegorically confront if also obscure the nightmarish realities of that and subsequent eras, cinema has continued to serve the seemingly opposing agendas or contradictory needs of different groups. But its primary function might lie in the force with which it compels audiences toward a shared "delusional certainty" in the rightness or wrongness of their own or other people's beliefs. In the words of Patrick Fuery, author of *Madness and Cinema*, as spectators of film "we engage in a certain type of hallucination which . . . demands certainty over reality," making us oddly agreeable bedfellows not only with psychotics like Norman Bates but also psychiatrists like Dr. Richmond, who (speaking with the authority that many laypeople associate with his profession) chalks up his patient's malicious actions and mental derangement to unconscious desires rooted in familial fantasy rather than to the societal pressure to conform to an ostensibly natural yet highly artificial, human-constructed reality.[10]

Mental health specialists have appeared onscreen throughout the history of the genre, from Depression-era and wartime studio productions such as *Dracula* (1931) and *The Wolf Man* (1941) to postwar cult favorites such as *Night of the Demon* (1957). However, it was not until the 1960s—in the years following *Psycho*'s theatrical release—that such figures of "social authority and rationality" rose to prominence.[11] Peter Hutchings attributes this increase in the number of psychiatric representations to the "turn to contemporary settings," which began to be favored over the gothic architecture, ruined landscapes, and cavernous mad scientists' laboratories of previous eras' period films, as well as the public's growing distrust of authority figures in the decades that followed, reflected in both mainstream and independent productions from the 1970s onward—although, as we shall see in this book's early chapters, films such as *The Exorcist* (1973) and *Halloween* (1978) paint a more complicated picture of society's conflicted attitudes. One of the ironic facts of the modern horror film's fixation on mental health issues is that the presence of psychiatrists and other medical personnel whose professional endeavors are organized around the human mind is frequently predicated on their ultimate irrelevance, ineffectualness, or ignorance in the face of some inexplicable occurrence and possibly supernatural or nonhuman entity.

In motion pictures ranging from *Burn, Witch, Burn* (a.k.a. *Night of the Eagle*, 1962) to *Candyman* (1992) and *Gothika* (2003), the rationality of mental health specialists and professorial types is deflated at that inevitable point in the narrative when a strange creature or bizarre event (whose very existence would be brushed off as fantastical or nonsensical in the real world) is proven to be *true* within fictions that ask spectators to momentarily suspend their disbelief and swallow truly preposterous scenarios. To continue Hutchings's line of argument, "Horror films help us in making the transition from a disbelieving 'There's no such thing as vampires' to a credulous 'Look out, it's Dracula!' by dramatizing the overcoming of those beliefs to which, in reality, we might generally subscribe."[12] Notably, Hutchings's choice of words compounds the irony at the heart of so much contemporary horror by suggesting that it is our belief in *disbelief*, or audiences' general insistence that otherworldly creatures and beings such as vampires, werewolves, and witches (in the Disneyesque "Hazel" sense) are beyond imagination in reality, that most firmly delineates the boundaries of the genre. It is what sets it apart from other categories of cultural production, such as dramas, which, if peopled with psychiatrists, are far more restricted to the realm of the sensible and sensical than are the many textually unfettered, psychologically unhinged, boundary-breaching films discussed in the following pages.

## Rationally Irrational: Making Sense of Multiple Senses

> The sense we make of any one sense is always mixed with and mediated by that of others. The senses form an indefinite series of integrations and transformations: they form a complexion.
>
> —Steven Connor, "Edison's Teeth: Touching Hearing" (2004)

To return to Bottaro and Chendi's "Washed-Up Witch," it perhaps goes without saying that the canine psychiatrist whom I have described as having an "Austrian-German accent" cannot *literally* be heard speaking. Nor does the voice of the title character—the old hag whose spoken words remind me of the creaky intonations of Norman Bates's mother in the closing minutes of *Psycho*—produce actual sound waves or pressure variations that enter my ear canals before being transmitted as nerve impulses to my brain. And yet, each time I hold a physical copy of that comic book in my hands, or simply peruse its framed panels via digital technologies (e.g., cellphone, laptop, tablet) that bring their own materiality to bear on my reception of both the story and the medium through which it is communicated, I find myself succumbing to a similar state of "auditory hallucination" as that experienced by the murderous motel owner, and which likely would have been diagnosed as a symptom of mental illness by Dr. Richmond. Still, my tendency to hear voices while reading "Washed-Up Witch," which could be construed as a sign of schizophrenia or some other psychiatric disorder (or at the very least a byproduct of stress or lack of sleep), can more reasonably be attributed to a lifetime of exposure to Disney's animated shorts featuring the distinctive chuckle and prolonged vowel sounds of Goofy (the "hyucks" and hollers voiced by actors Pinto Colvig and Bill Farmer). It can also be linked to the highly subjective yet socially conditioned ways that a person's "structurally and functionally distinct" senses might become interdependent or unified, combining into an integrated whole that makes it possible for someone to imagine and possibly experience "seemingly irrational aesthetic connections" among incomparable perceptual phenomena.[13]

Regardless of whether the internal processing of external stimuli results in the kind of unconscious neurological cross-wiring or coupling of the senses that Sven Hroar Klempe calls "genuine synesthesia" (an aberrant if not abnormal condition present in only a small percentage of test subjects) or is the self-conscious, culturally inflected sort of intersensoriality that drives the central thesis of this book, the metacognitive process by which one undertakes reasoning through such unreasonable or irrational means has tended to be trivialized as being unscientific or highly suspect within the larger medical community. However, in recent years, a number of psychologists, neurobiologists, and anthropologists have called for a more inclusive view of sensory blending, arguing persuasively that most humans display "synesthetic tendencies" whenever they are asked to describe the sight, smell, sound, taste, and touch of perceivable things.[14] According to Lawrence E. Marks, while relatively few people are "vividly synesthetic," or prone to experience an involuntary "breakdown of modularity" when it comes to receiving visual, olfactory, aural, gustatory, and somatosensory impressions of the world (e.g., "colored hearing"), a statistically larger cross-section of society is able to "recognize or appreciate similarities between sensory experiences in different modalities."[15] This is partly owing to the cultural codes and language-based signifying systems that are shared among members of that society.

Providing an example of those synesthetic tendencies, which are often learned over time but might also be "hard-wired" or built into the nervous system, Marks explains that "when asked, 'which is brighter, a cough or a sneeze?', most of us readily acknowledge that sneezes are brighter—perhaps because sneezes are more compact in terms of the distribution of energy over time, 'sharper', if you will, and generically higher in pitch."[16] It is worth pointing out that "brightness," which typically refers to the visual perception of light's intensity (its luminance and "shininess"), is itself a "vivid" signifier, evoking a range of sensations associated not only with the *eyes* but also with the *ears* (e.g., vibrant, clear, high-pitched sounds) as well as the *mind*, since the term also refers to "the quality of being intelligent and quick-witted." This makes *brightness*—or, for that matter, *sharpness*—an especially sensible and, indeed, *synesthetic* way for Marks to underscore the near-universality of sensory blending even among nonsynesthetes who "have linguistic access to the same cross-modal similarities" as those for whom "enhanced neural connectivity" is a genetic trait.

As for the latter group of people, synesthesia is a complex integrative and cerebral process "resulting in simultaneous perception of sensory modalities," one that "is related to changes occurring in the activity of cortical and sub-cortical neuronal networks, especially in the limbic structures."[17] Neurobiologist Jean-Pierre Ternaux reminds us that the brain's integration of "afferent messages from sensory-specialized organs" responsible for the classical five senses is induced by stimuli that are either internal to a living organism ("generated by motor activity in skeletal muscles, tendinous and articular proprioceptors or visceral activities") or external to it (detected by specialized cells enabling individuals to process what they see, hear, smell, taste, and touch, "including thermal, pressure, cutaneous pain and vibratory sensations"). Both the interoceptive and exteroceptive sensory modalities require chemical and physical stimulations, which are "transformed into electrical messages conveyed to the central nervous system via afferent sensory nerves."[18] More pertinent to the present study, "synesthesia can also be considered as a physiological feature belonging to *every* individual, hyperexpressed in some subjects."[19] This accords with Richard E. Cytowic's notion that synesthesia, far from being a hallucinatory state reserved for "attention-seeking kooks" (as some medical specialists of the distant past might have claimed), is, "in fact, a *normal* brain process that is prematurely displayed to consciousness in a minority of individuals."[20] Not only is it normal, but it is also a very *reasonable* way to go about processing lived experiences. Still, the widespread belief that synesthesia runs counter to reason persists.

Scholars such as David Howes, Constance Classen, Allyson C. DeMaagd, and Caroline A. Jones have drawn attention to the long-standing dismissal of this "rare neurological condition."[21] Throughout much of the eighteenth and nineteenth centuries, scientists viewed synesthesia as "evidence of a disturbed mind that forged irrational associations among the senses," causing affected individuals to nonsensically link tastes to sounds or the letters of the alphabet to colors.[22] Within the scientific community, "there was a general feeling that 'the senses have been confused and mingled; what is needed is further purification and segmentation: the nose alone should smell, the eyes should only look, and taste should be reserved for the tongue.'"[23] Responding to the contrary that "cross-modal connections [are] generally shared by *all* humans," Howes and Classen argue that framing synesthesia as either a "pathology" or a "gift" bestowed upon only a few individuals obscures the "ways in which it is socially elaborated."[24] They, like the comparative religion scholar Lawrence Sullivan, the philosopher David Ekdahl, and the psychiatrist Laurence J. Kirmayer, are interested in the "symbolic expressions" of synesthesia as it is imagined in a social world that is culturally constructed.[25] I, too, am drawn to the hermeneutic value of cross-modal association within the humanities and share their belief that synesthesia is "too multifaceted and too culturally important to be left solely to neuroscientists to define."[26] However, I gravitate toward the more broadly encompassing concept of *intersensoriality* as a guiding principle in the interpretation of cinematic horror, a genre that likewise appears to challenge reason while triggering "seemingly irrational aesthetic mental activities" in viewers whose "view" of a grisly scene or terrible thing is often entangled with other senses besides sight.

This book starts from the basic premise that "the senses are multiply related," and that, to quote Steven Connor, "we rarely if ever apprehend the world through one sense alone."[27] Such a thesis is hardly profound. It was probably not even a radical statement a couple of centuries ago. But a key part of Connor's argument, which echoes much of the scholarly efforts to account for the cultural and social import of synesthetic "spillings and minglings" alluded to above, is that "under conditions in which any one sense predominates," as sight/seeing appears to do whenever a person watches a film, "closer inspection may disclose that the predominating sense is in fact being shadowed and interpreted by other, apparently dormant senses."[28] As I emphasize at various junctures throughout this volume, *intersensoriality*, or the simultaneous, synesthetic processing of distinct sense modalities (neurologically and/or culturally), results from the various excitations visited upon viewers' minds and bodies by horror films. Notably, the term "excitation" is itself shadowed by multiple, seemingly contradictory connotations, at once suggesting an arousal or pleasurable stimulation—of nerves, muscles, and sensory end organs—as well as a disturbance, disruption, or loss of stability owing to a sudden gain in excess energy. Following that paradoxical logic, one of this book's central claims is that the negative pleasures of horror are most acutely felt whenever the dormant senses of cinema—those of smell, taste, and touch—are implicated in the acts of seeing and hearing that have long been understood as the primary ways of engaging the medium and its associated technological apparatuses. Sight and sound are themselves difficult to disentangle from one another. They probably should not even be taken as separate phenomena—for, in the words of Tim Ingold, they are "just facets of the same activity: that of the whole organism in its environment."[29]

*Seeing Is Hearing Is Believing* brings two related irrationalities to the fore as it undertakes a series of investigations into the inner workings of cinematic horror. It explores slippages between sight-based and sound-based hermeneutics along with the decisiveness with which a person's *disbelief*—in monsters and other supernatural beings, for instance—shifts into *belief* within scenarios that, on the surface, seem far-fetched. But the stories that horror films tell reveal real-world resonances to anyone with eyes to hear or ears to see. "Seeing" in the synesthetic sense entails a more holistic bodily-filmic conjugation than what a single organ can provide. Moreover, it has frequently been presented in a variety of texts as a prerequisite for any cognitive understanding or comprehension ("seeing" in the epistemological sense) that might occur when someone encounters something deemed too "unbelievable" to possibly be true. Just as listening, as a "mode of acoustic knowing," is both an aesthetic and epistemological phenomenon, according to Thorsten Gieser, so too can the sort of sense-based knowledge that comes from witnessing a visually arresting, potentially terrifying sight—for instance, human remains and desecrated corpses in *The Texas Chain Saw Massacre* (1974)—be seen as a multifold way to frame "belief" as a highly subjective yet socially circumscribed undertaking.[30]

Tellingly, in his exploration of the multisensorial processes through which people come to know noises, Gieser focuses on the chainsaw, an instrument of "brute materiality" whose visceral sound bores down "deeply into our bones" even when it is heard from a distance or through mediated representations.[31] In much the same way I hear Goofy talk whenever I read a comic book in which he appears, so too does the mere sight of Leatherface (Gunnar Hansen), the chainsaw-wielding killer at the heart of Tobe Hooper's nightmarish horror film, produce an unmistakable sound—a sharp, metallic rattle when the engine is revved—that, to lumberjacks and other auditors who are skilled in the practice of tree-felling, conveys subtle information about the generally benign activity for which the object was designed. Safely ensconced in my home and seated in front of a television screen on which *The Texas Chain Saw Massacre* plays, I may not be on the receiving end of that machine's spinning blades. But I still fall victim to its acoustic violence and vibrational rumblings in the pit of my stomach and at the back of my throat. I can also imagine the terror of anyone who might be threatened by the prospect of those metal teeth tearing into their flesh.[32] More to the point, I can perceive the less-obvious threats—beyond those to life and limb—that the noisy, gas-fueled device poses to other sensing organs besides the eyes and ears.

Indeed, my own "acoustemology" of the masked killer and his weapon encompasses *smell*, as I mentally breathe in the poisonous exhaust emitted by the chainsaw, and *touch*, as I can still recall the sensation of holding the slick, greasy handles of the heavy tool many years ago (as a teenager who had not yet been exposed to the film). The latter sensation, detected not only across the skin of my fingers but also in the grip and musculature required to safely swing that tool, as well as the proprioception needed to keep my feet firmly planted to support the chainsaw's considerable weight, seeps into the visceral depths of my body whenever Leatherface, flushed with homicidal fury, exceeds the limits of what is permissible both morally and physically.[33] Thus, the "sensory meshwork" of synesthetic listening, prompted by the seemingly disconnected yet deeply entangled acts of looking and feeling, brings the embodied knowledge and personal memories of the auditor-viewer to bear on fictional representations that, however far-fetched, tap into real-world fears and elicit seemingly irrational responses ranging from amusement to anger, relief, sorrow, and pleasurable fascination with horror's aesthetic forms.

## To Believe or Not to Believe

Horror films assert that not everything can or should be dealt with in rational terms.

—Isabel Cristina Pinedo, "Postmodern Elements of the Contemporary Horror Film"

In her study of the various pleasures experienced by viewers of horror films, Isabel Cristina Pinedo identifies five characteristics of the postmodern variant of the genre, which began to crystallize during the decade-long span of time covered by the theatrical releases of Peter Bogdanovich's *Targets* (1968), George Romero's *Night of the Living Dead* (1968), Tobe Hooper's *The Texas Chain Saw Massacre*, and John Carpenter's *Halloween* (1978):

(1) There is a violent disruption of the everyday world;
(2) there is a transgression and violation of boundaries;
(3) the validity of rationality is thrown into question;
(4) there is no narrative closure; and
(5) the film produces a bounded experience of fear.

According to her, modern horror films distinguish themselves from classical antecedents by intensifying or making explicit the manner in which the first three items on that list leave the body and mind in ruins.[34] The fourth element, related to the open-endedness of many contemporary motion pictures—from *The Thing* (1982) to *The Blair Witch Project* (1999) and *American Psycho* (2000)—speaks to another kind of ruination, whereby cinematic storytelling itself appears to be divested of its comfort-providing function through the removal of that most keystone of narrative elements: resolution. Although the last of those five characteristics "applies to horror in general" and is the only one to relate directly "to the dynamic between the film and the audience," it is central to contemporary productions like *Suck* (2009), *Scream VI* (2023), and other motion pictures that, as discussed later in this book, play on "seen-it-all" spectators' presumed mastery of genre conventions.

At first blush, all five of these characteristics would seem to produce emotional anxiety and mental as well as physical stress rather than pleasure or relief. To be sure, the collapse of once-stable categories and the encroachment of nihilistic thoughts or inexplicable actions on a narrative universe that once promised a superficially comforting return to social order (signified by the defeat of some unnatural "Evil" by the forces of "Good"), but which now only seems to be devoid of traditional morality and meaning, can be upsetting. And yet, because even the most unnerving horror film is a "bounded experience of fear," placed within a comfortably familiar frame that ensures distance between our perceiving bodies and the "spectacle of the ruined body" onscreen, any displeasure associated with the above elements is mitigated by the recognition that no actual harm will come to the viewer—although the same cannot be said about the movie audiences *within* metafictional works like *Demons* (1985), *Popcorn* (1991), and *Cut* (2000), to take just three. I, for one—though I know I am not the only one—continue to find pleasure in horror films and have endeavored to impart something of that hedonic or holistically sensual experience to readers.

This book is divided into two sections. Each section highlights aspects of cinematic horror that have largely gone unaddressed in previous studies of the genre. In the first section (comprising chapters 1, 2, 3, and 4), I delve into some of the persistent ways in which horror "exposes the limits of rationality and compels [audiences] to confront the irrational."[35] Building upon Pinedo's pioneering work in this area, in particular her arguments about the amenability of postclassical narratives to that which is "disordered, ineffable, chaotic, and unpredictable," I seek to illustrate how the breakdown of social order, whether on a small scale (within domestic settings and local communities) or on a large scale (nationally and globally), reflects a general failure on the part of institutions associated with rational thought to make sense of those monstrous forces of disruption with which horror is largely associated.[36] As shown near the end of director Herk Harvey's independently produced *Carnival of Souls* (1962), when a medical doctor and a church minister, accompanied by equally befuddled police officers, are unable to ascertain the reason for the female protagonist's sudden disappearance near a possibly haunted pavilion on the shores of the Great Salt Lake, even faith-based organizations and their leaders lack the means of determining the meaning of metaphysical things whenever the "unpredictable universe that constitutes the underside of life" pokes through the surface of our carefully ordered, physically intelligible world like a knife blade.[37]

Even more so than *Psycho*, this classic example of micro-budget moviemaking—a regional production that Harvey (a Kansas-based industrial filmmaker) made for $33,000—marked an epistemological shift in the history of cinematic horror. Its 1962 release anticipated by at least a full decade the cycle of postmodern films that Pinedo explores in her book *Recreational Terror*. To varying degrees, her examples, ranging from *The Texas Chain Saw Massacre* to *A Nightmare on Elm Street* (1984) and its metatextual descendent *New Nightmare* (1994), reveal how "an unstable, open-ended universe in which categories collapse, violence constitutes everyday life, and the irrational prevails" in narratives centering on women's traumatizing encounters with male monsters came to be a recurring feature of the genre from the 1970s to the 1990s. Not coincidentally, that period witnessed the American people's faith in their country's governing bodies and elected officials steadily erode, although that too had been anticipated by tumultuous events of the 1960s. Developing her argument further, Pinedo states,

> To be efficacious, the protagonist [of postmodern horror] must objectify the monster and subject it to a controlling gaze; that is, she must treat it the way it treats her. Paradoxically, characters who survive in horror films eschew critical tenets of rationality (for instance, that the attacker cannot be dead already), while at the same time they utilize instrumental rationality to objectify the monster and facilitate their own exercise of violence. Postmodern horror compels its heroes, many of whom are women, to both exercise instrumental rationality and to rely on intuition; it requires them to be violent and to trust their gut instincts. As such, postmodern horror defies the Cartesian construction of reason that reduces it to instrumental rationality and pits it against emotion and intuition.[38]

Although it lacks the graphic depictions of violence and bloodshed featured in Tobe Hooper's *The Texas Chain Saw Massacre* and Wes Craven's *A Nightmare on Elm Street*—a film in which the teenaged female protagonist, Nancy Thompson (Heather Langenkamp), is "caught within a closed system from which there is no exit"—*Carnival of Souls* hinges on a decidedly disconcerting form of *undecidability* that Pinedo believes is pronounced in postmodern horror. Centered on the experiences of a young woman who, stuck between two worlds, appears to survive a car accident in rural Kansas (where her vehicle plunged into a river after being forced off the road by another car) only to be haunted by her own presumed death upon moving to Salt Lake City, the film models a particular type of epistemological ambiguity that has become more prominent in the years since its 1962 release, in productions defined in part by the representation of male authority figures' *loss of authority* in the midst of such inscrutable events. In her book, Pinedo notes that "cops and psychiatrists (descendants of the soldiers and scientists of classical horror) are largely absent from or ineffectual in the postmodern genre, despite the latter's insistence on the use of force."[39] The inability of police officers, medical doctors, clergymen, and other individuals to draw any reasonable conclusions about a missing woman's whereabouts or, for that matter, the motives of a monster that only manifests in teenagers' dreams, points to the prescience of Harvey's film. As I will elaborate in chapter 1, with each passing year *Carnival of Souls* looks more and more like a precursor to recently produced works about the paradoxical *irrationality* of rationality as an ultimately punishable mode of "epistemological recalcitrance."

The paradoxes of horror, beyond those that Noël Carroll and other theorists have identified as being relevant to spectators' cognitive and corporeal relationship to negatively valanced emotions (e.g., anxiety, dread, revulsion, shock), tend to emerge whenever the genre's dueling epistemologies—its tendency to leverage belief against disbelief while casting both of those two as embodied forms of "knowledge"—are verbally expressed by individuals representing two often-violently opposed sides. One of the most noteworthy aspects of the abovementioned films as well as more recent examples of the genre (e.g., *Revenge* [2017], *Ready or Not* [2019], *The Menu* [2022], *Scream VI*) comes from the propensity of protagonists to emulate the actions of human and nonhuman monsters—malicious men and creatures of the night who spend much of the narrative stalking their victims as a sort of gendered "sport." Pinedo gestures toward this aspect of postmodern horror, noting that "characters who survive must come to terms not only with the irrationality of the situation but also with their own ability to be as single-mindedly destructive as the monster."[40] While I do not dwell on this violence-engenders-violence facet of the genre, large portions of the first four chapters draw connections among several seemingly unrelated cinematic texts, past and present, to show how horror's "critique of science and rational discourse" not only runs deep but also spreads far beyond the spatial confines of haunted houses and abandoned pavilions.

"I don't have the answers you want," says a paranormal scientist in one haunted house movie, *Amityville 3-D* (1983), informing the mother of a recently drowned teenager that a simple "yes or no" response to the question of her daughter's ghostly existence does not suffice when it comes to coping with emotional pain or identifying the "things that people carry around with them." To Nancy Baxter (Tess Harper), the visibly distressed woman on the receiving end of these comments (and who appears to be on the verge of a nervous breakdown), the doctor's words matter little. Or, rather, they do not dissuade her from the possibility that her daughter Susan (Lori Loughlin)—still dripping wet from the motorboating accident—is alive or exists in some spiritual form, traipsing up and down the staircase of her estranged husband's recently purchased house on Long Island's Ocean Avenue, which, unbeknownst to the skeptical new owner John Baxter (Tony Roberts), sits atop a portal to hell. Notably, Dr. Elliot West (Robert Joy), the scientist saying those words, is initially shown conducting an experiment on another woman in his laboratory, one that forces him to explain his unusual methods to the grieving mother when his test subject suddenly bolts up from a prone position and screams in terror (fig. I.4). As his medical staff attends to the screaming woman, removing the coverings from her eyes and ears, the doctor tells Nancy that his patient has been subjected to nearly fifty-two hours of sensory deprivation. "Once you deprive the mind of the usual external stimuli, it eventually starts to improvise," Dr. West remarks. "So, she's been in some kind of limbo?" Nancy asks, to which the doctor responds in the affirmative, before stating that "there's no sight, no sound, nothing to touch or taste or smell. Under those conditions, reality has no objective meaning for a person." The dialogue in this scene, which hints at Nancy's own in-between state as well as that of her daughter—whose watery death might remind viewers of the cruel misfortune dealt to Mary

**Figure I.4:** In a key scene of *Amityville 3-D*, a paranormal investigator who remains skeptical about the supposed haunting of the titular house conducts experiments on a female test subject, who finally cracks after several hours of sensory deprivation (including the temporary loss of sight and hearing).

(Candace Hilligoss) in *Carnival of Souls*—underlines just how significant the senses are not only as perceptual-navigational instruments but also in terms of simply "being-in-the-world."

The latter phrase, which brings to mind Martin Heidegger's concept of *dasein*, or "there-being" (a kind of consciousness of possibilities based on a person's constantly changing relationship to the world), is especially pertinent to our understanding of horror as an ever-shifting form, both in the moment of spectating and across the history of the medium. Indeed, the genre, perhaps more than any other, keeps audiences on their toes through moment-to-moment "fear-jerking" and by pulling the proverbial rug out from under viewers' feet, just when audiences have let their guard down or they mistakenly believe that they are standing on solid ground. As I have argued elsewhere, the only thing predictable about this category of cultural production is its *unpredictability*, which, from a narrative standpoint, produces feelings of unease even in those of us who have consumed enough horror films to anticipate the sudden eruptions of shocking violence, supernatural revelations, and literal unmaskings that are such an expectedly unexpected part of its paradoxical appeals.[41]

Chapter by chapter, this book charts a path through those paradoxical appeals by steering the discussion of belief toward the bodily senses that Dr. West's test subject has been deprived of, and which—in their absence—intensifies her and presumably other people's fear of the unknown. Chief among those senses, at least according to film theorists whose work betrays an ocularcentrism in keeping with horror's privileging (and punishing) of eyes, is *sight*. Tellingly, visual perception, which is at the heart of horror's uniquely eye-focused belief system (since, to quote a well-known adage, "seeing is believing"), is frequently revealed to be as insufficient as the aforementioned authority figures in making sense of anything that truly tests the limits of rationality.

In the words of Baron von Leppe, Boris Karloff's character in *The Terror* (1963), "You should never believe everything your eyes tell you." He utters these words during an early scene in the film, addressing a much younger man who stands before a painting of a female subject and mistakes her for a woman he claims to have recently glimpsed through a window (but who is the baron's deceased wife, or so the older man insists). Importantly, the recipient of the baron's advice, Jack Nicholson's Napoleonic war veteran André Duvalier, spends much of the film trying to prove von Leppe wrong. Turning his head to-and-fro, André casts frantic glances and quizzical looks upon entering the many rooms of the baron's castle, searching for the source of a ghostly woman's voice and other strange sounds emanating from its inner sanctums. Claiming to be a man in full possession of his faculties, André is almost exclusively guided by his ears (and his heart) but seeks to lay eyes (and lips) on a woman he *did*, in fact, see earlier, and who is later revealed to be a shape-shifting demon. Theatrically released a few months after *Carnival of Souls*'s limited distribution, this Roger Corman–directed film is one of many productions from that era to problematize characters' dependency on sight as a pretext for belief.[42] More importantly, *The Terror* sets up rationality as a strawman: an ultimately *irrational* approach to confronting life's mysteries. But it also exposes, through a series of highly improbable role reversals and character revelations near the narrative's end (including those related to Baron von Leppe's true identity), how overreliance on one or two senses can affect a person's perception of reality or deprive that individual of differently embodied ways of being in the world.

Familiar expressions and commonly uttered colloquialisms, such as "I'll believe it when I see it," indicate how foundational eyewitness accounts and visual perception are to empirical confirmation. Nevertheless, other English-language phrases, including "There's more to this than meets the eye" and "I couldn't believe my eyes," hint at the *insufficiency* of that sensing ability whenever something pushes the limits of reason or requires verification from another of the body's sense-making organs. As personified by Dr. John Lanyon (Holmes Herbert), a close confidant to the human side of the title character in director Rouben Mamoulian's *Dr. Jekyll and Mr. Hyde* (1931) who cannot believe what he has seen and does not understand how his friend can be both man and monster during the final transformation that occurs near the end of the film, comprehension does not always follow perception. The film's source material—Robert Louis Stevenson's 1886 novella, *Strange Case of Dr Jekyll and Mr. Hyde*—places greater emphasis on the mind-altering terror that Lanyon experiences when confronted by the feature-melting physical transformation of the blackened Hyde into the pale-faced Jekyll.[43] But MGM's early sound-era production fleshes out that fear by granting aural and visual access to elements that are left to the reader's imagination. One could argue that, by limiting our ability to hear and see the terrifying thing that prompted Lanyon to remark that "when that sight has faded from my eyes I ask myself if I believe it, and I cannot answer," the author of the original text places us more deeply inside the skin of that diegetic spectator. However, we must remember that Lanyon himself did not *read* about Jekyll's condition; he witnessed it firsthand. That alone makes the film a kind of secondhand sensorial extension of a character whose enunciated disbelief and failure to comprehend are not unrelated to the medium in which this well-known, frequently adapted story is being told.

In many cases, a character's *inability* to believe modulates into an *unwillingness* to believe. This idea is broached in another M-G-M production from the classical studio system era, *Mark of the Vampire* (1935). Directed by Tod Browning and starring Lionel Barrymore as Professor Zelen, a specialist in occultism living in Prague, the film shows the main character not only trying to prevent the death of a young woman whose father has already succumbed to the lethal bite of a vampire but also dealing with "disbelievers" in both senses of that term. This occurs, for instance, when Zelen tells a local baron, Otto von Zinden (Jean Hersholt), that the dead man is no longer in his coffin and now walks among the living in the pale moonlight. "I can't believe that!" Zinden exclaims, then adding, "I *won't* believe that!" The baron's recalcitrance in the face of mounting evidence of supernatural events is in keeping with the attitude of other naysayers populating horror films of the 1930s and 1940s, such as Dr. Seward (Herbert Bunston) in *Dracula*, Dr. Waldman (Edward Van Sloan) in *Frankenstein* (1931), and police detective Lieutenant Shawn (William Demarest) in *Night Has a Thousand Eyes* (1948). However, over the course of the narrative, and through the professor's surreptitious hypnotism of Baron Otto, audiences discover that the disbelieving man is the *real* culprit, having murdered Sir Karell Borotyn (Holmes Herbert, a.k.a. Lanyon in *Dr. Jekyll and Mr. Hyde*) but staging it in such a way that it resembled a vampire attack. As such, his earlier resistance to the idea of a supernaturally reanimated corpse is only natural, for he (unlike the audience) knew the *real* cause of Sir Karell's death. Cultural historian Ken Hanke calls *Mark of the Vampire* along with its source material (Browning's 1927 silent version of the story, *London After Midnight*) "masterful con games played on the viewer," who might retroactively feel foolish once the film's "vampires"—Count Mora (Bela Lugosi) and his daughter Luna (Carroll Borland)—are revealed to be actors hired by Zelen as part of an elaborate charade designed to trick the real murderer into confessing his crime.[44]

Such shenanigans on the part of screenwriters and filmmakers might make audiences feel as Tony Vincente (James W. Quinn) does when, near the end of the supernatural horror film *Witchtrap* (1989), his skepticism finally melts away as surely as the flesh of a Satanic serial killer does. "I'm not sure *what* I believe anymore," Tony muses, casting a deeply confused gaze at the gloppy remains of the monster whose skull now contains *another face* inside it—that of a clairvoyant who was possessed and consumed by the killer—visible below the melted-off skin. One might even say the genre is "two-faced" in its combined sincerity and deceitfulness, aiming for genuine scares but sometimes resorting to sudden plot reversals and narrative ploys designed to fool audiences into believing one thing only to instill a retroactive feeling of shame for being so easily duped. This is an aspect of cinematic horror to which Regan MacNeil (Linda Blair), the formerly terrorized teenager from director

William Friedkin's *The Exorcist*, draws attention during an early scene of that film's sequel, *Exorcist II: The Heretic* (1977), a major case study of chapter 2. Performing a spoon-bending trick for her guardian Sharon (Kitty Winn), Regan castigates the older woman for being so easily taken in by this sleight of hand, saying, "Oh, look, you fool, you believe *everything*," before revealing how the trick was done. The girl's words might just as well be applied to the original film's audiences, who—unlike the less-impressed spectators of the sequel (directed by John Boorman)—were able to momentarily suspend their disbelief and immerse themselves in a vomit-soaked tale of demonic possession that is as farfetched as anything in *Witchtrap*. In his discussion of *The Exorcist*, Matt Glasby notably states that Friedkin used "every trick at his disposal to create the sense that monumental evil has been unleashed before our eyes," thereby relying on Uri Geller–inspired ruses and technological mischief (including special effects by Dick Smith) to show "all hell breaking loose."[45] Calling *The Exorcist* a "full-on assault of the senses," Glasby furthermore suggests that eyes are not the only organs being terrorized by this slimy, foul-smelling, sour-tasting but critically esteemed motion picture.

A couple of additional case studies—director Nicolas Roeg's *Don't Look Now* (1973) and director William Castle's *House on Haunted Hill* (1959)—bookend the second chapter's discussion of the first two *Exorcist* films, so that the conflation of sight and vision might be confronted head-on, with the goal of further unpacking the long-standing association between seeing and belief. Roeg's byzantine film, a literally visionary work about the limitations of sight, highlights how our collective tendency to be seduced by the physical surfaces of the world has only strengthened our "misguided reliance" on what "we only *think* we know." James Palmer and Michael Riley point out in their reading of *Don't Look Now* that "film and the physical world are in some measure analogous in the ways they proffer the primacy of the seen and heard as the repository of meaning."[46] Although I do not attempt to dethrone sight and hearing as the two most privileged senses not only within horror film scholarship but also within the field of cinema studies more generally, I spend much of the first half of this book looking (and listening) for alternative pathways through the perceptual affordances of the medium, which is not only an audiovisual art form tailored to the ears and eyes but also a means to stimulate the spectator's senses of touch, taste, and smell.

In chapters 3 and 4, I offer what might seem to be odd, nonsensical propositions, putting olfactory, gustatory, and tactile approaches to cinematic horror into the mix as alternatives to the predominately visual (and secondarily auditory) rubrics found in most critical studies of the genre. Exploring such notoriously sleazy films as Herschell Gordon Lewis's *The Gore Gore Girls* (1972) and Alfred Sole's *Pandemonium* (1982), the latter one of several comedy-horror mashups from the past fifty years to be centered on the lives and excessively gruesome deaths of cheerleaders—for example, *Satan's Cheerleaders* (1977), *Cheerleader Camp* (1988), *Attack of the 50 Foot Cheerleader* (2012), and *All Cheerleaders Die* (2013)—these chapters of the book illustrate how the convergence of two types of "bad taste" might prompt even the most desensitized audiences to question not only the filmmakers' motives but also their own literal and figurative consumption practices, in addition to the ease with which horror shifts into humorous modes of bodily excess in keeping with the culinary excess at the heart of those films in which food is the focus.

If such talk of the "lower" senses seems irrational or even ridiculous in a book devoted to horror films, it is perhaps because the belated critical "elevation" of the genre in recent years has obscured its history as a "low" cultural form awash in stinky, greasy, disgusting stuff. It might also be due to the fact that tactile, gustatory, and olfactory approaches to the genre have been sidelined for so many years in previous publications, and for obvious reasons (since cinema is still primarily seen, and secondarily heard, as a medium custom-made for the eyes and ears). While I, like most scholars in the field, focus largely on seeing and hearing as embodied activities that serve spectators well (*if* audiences are able to do those activities, which we should never assume), it is imperative that we entangle rather than disentangle those senses as creatively as horror has done over the years. This book therefore mounts an intersensorial critique of the horror film and the literature surrounding it, drawing from published work in the areas of disability studies and translation studies (in addition to both classic and cutting-edge work in genre studies) in hopes of inspiring future scholarship rooted in the language of affect theory and phenomenology.

The latter area of philosophical inquiry, which traces its origins to the work of Georg Wilhelm Friedrich Hegel (although predecessors such as fellow German Immanuel Kant had already laid the foundation for a critical methodology that would be developed into a full-fledged "school of thought" by Edmund Husserl, Alexander Pfänder, Max Scheler, and Moritz Geiger after the turn of the twentieth century), informs several modern-day studies of cinema, including those that are centered on horror as both a technologically mediated form of fright-delivery and an immediate, corporally felt experience. Examples of contemporary scholarship on the subject include Julian Hanich's *Cinematic Emotion in Horror Films and Thrillers* (2010) and Adam Daniel's *Affective Intensities and Evolving Horror Forms* (2020), both of which draw upon earlier books by Vivian Sobchack and Steven Shaviro that were key to the "somatic turn" in film studies in the 1990s.[47] In these and other works, the once-sacred line between "film-as-object" and "viewer-as-subject" gets blurred as the authors explore a fruitful "dialectic of perception" that occurs whenever the two converge. That convergence is neither occasional/sporadic nor a purely theoretical supposition. It is a persistent aspect of cinematic spectatorship, which is always situational and shaped by context-based factors such as the size of the screen, the loudness of the speakers, the darkness of the screening room, and the proximity of other viewers' visible and audible bodies to one's own. Although phenomenological approaches tend to foreground the *object-orientation* of the perceiving subject, whose consciousness is always a "consciousness-of" something, the film scholars mentioned above do not reduce motion pictures to the status of static observable phenomena or treat embodied vision as the sole means through which spectators communicate with the medium—itself a perceiving body capable of making its own "seeing" visible.[48] Instead, they make the case for a more capacious framing of corporeal expression, extended not only to perceivers whose sensory inputs are on the receiving end of a communicative act that makes *them* the "objects" of that transaction, but also to film as a site of intersubjective, intersensorial feeling—a feeling for and through the bodies of others.

After first gesturing toward the phenomenological intentionality of horror films, I spend much of this book stressing the importance of intersensoriality as a theoretical means to consider, for instance, how cinematic images can be seen through the ears, just as I will explore the prospect of hearing horror's many distinctive sounds through the eyes. Aiding me on this journey into the hidden recesses of horror films are some of the many extratextual and paratextual artifacts included on DVD and Blu-ray releases: supplemental features like audio commentaries (in which cast and crew members share newly recorded conversations about the production process while the film plays) as well as accessibility tools such as audio description (AD) (for persons who have blindness or low vision) and subtitles for the deaf and hard of hearing (SDH), both of which are also available on streaming websites such as Amazon, Hulu, Netflix, and Shudder. Anyone who has experienced a loss of one of the two so-called master senses, and is unable to see or hear a motion picture as its production team or distributor perhaps assumed it would be seen or heard, usually calls upon the other fully or partially active sense in a compensatory way when presented with the option of either captioned text or AD services.

As I explain in chapters 5 and 6, SDH captioning options on home-video releases and online platforms make it possible to perceive sounds synesthetically (those that have been transcribed by professional subtitlers) while allowing motion pictures to play upon our bodies in a more sensorially holistic fashion than what is typically described in many accounts of cinematic reception. Chapter 7 presents a sweeping account of the history of AD, which stretches back to theatrical presentations of wartime dramas and "preparedness pictures" during the 1910s that were couched in the visual and verbal rhetoric of "horror," despite the absence of the genre's traditional iconography as well as the (wrongly described) "lack" of sound in "silent" cinema. Chapter 8 moves AD as a historical object of study forward into the contemporary era, so that we might determine its usefulness as a hermeneutical tool through which to hear the most unsettling yet mundane images of horror films, including visual information that is often overlooked by sighted audiences. Before getting to the many irrational, intersensorial aspects of horror that distinguish it from other categories of cultural production, let us start with a more basic set of propositions. First, the question of what a horror film actually *is* demands at least passing consideration, just as we should begin to ask how it is that we "know"—or rather *believe*—that what we are seeing and hearing (when situated before a screen) is an example of the genre. These are questions that propel my discussions of classic and contemporary horror films in the pages that follow.

# PART 1

# DECENTERING SIGHT AND SYNCHRONIZING THE SENSES

## From Disbelief Mitigation to Directors' Commentaries and Audio Description

# 1

# TRICKING THE EYE, BELIEVING IN BODIES

## Optical Illusions and Spectatorial Confusions

How do you know a horror film when you see it?

—Peter Hutchings, *The Horror Film*

Watching a horror film is usually an intentional activity, one for which the viewer is mentally and physically prepared before they sit down in a movie theater or push the play button on a television's remote control. The mind and body are therefore in a ready state, primed to be aurally and visually assailed by sounds and images that, while safely contained within the diegesis, are sufficiently intense—just "dangerous" enough—to provoke perspiration, an increased heart rate, and a tensing of the muscles. The lead-up to such spectatorial activity, which might include reading reviews of a new release, watching TV ads, hearing cast interviews on radio talk shows, and discussing the film with friends in anticipation of a screening, paves the way for the viewer's response and helps to ensure that particular film's fit within the larger generic corpus. Stated simply, there can be little doubt of a motion picture's status as a horror film when so much of its contextual and textual framing is designed to put audiences in place as purposefully thrill-seeking subjects whose gasps, screams, and occasional laughter will later confirm that categorial fit. But what if a viewer's run-in with a horror film is *not* premeditated, happening by accident as a result of flipping through cable TV channels or walking into the wrong auditorium without a clue about what is being projected on the screen? Lacking the kind of preparation that comes from paratextual exposure (e.g., seeing promotional material, such as movie posters and trailers, that clearly indicate a film's genre), how would an audience know that what they have stumbled onto is "horror"?

In more cases than not, horror films announce themselves as such within their first few minutes, either prior to or during an opening credits or title sequence that contains aural and visual markers of the genre. If, to continue our hypothetical scenario, a channel surfer happened to land on a televised broadcast of a motion picture just as it was beginning to air, they would likely be able to discern its generic affiliation within a matter of seconds—especially if it is a horror film, which tends to be more explicit in announcing that affiliation than are other categories of cultural production (with the exception of the Western and the musical). For the sake of convenience, let us say that the channel is Turner Classic Movies (TCM), which caters to fans of multiple genres, and that the first scene of the film (which, following the 20th Century-Fox logo, appears onscreen precisely when our imaginary viewer puts the remote control down) begins with a black-and-white shot of an urban residential roadway with trucks in the distance motoring toward the camera. Nondescript buildings, possibly apartment complexes, line the streets, but nothing leaps out as a particularly noteworthy indicator of this setting's actual location. For a brief moment, based on the bleakness of this introductory image, the viewer might surmise that they are watching a film noir, or simply a hard-edged drama set on the outskirts of an American city. However, almost as soon as the shot fades in, the rumbling sound of the vehicles is accompanied by a plaintive note played on a woodwind instrument, timed to coincide with the panning of the camera. Shifting the viewer's focus from the asphalt road to a stone wall and iron gate on the right side of the frame, the camera continues panning, in the process revealing an overgrown cemetery just beyond the barrier. This is the kind of disquieting place that anyone who is familiar with horror would recognize as a staple of the genre, showcased in everything from *The Iron Rose* (*La Rose de Fer*, 1973) to *The Omen* (1976), *Phantasm* (1979), and *Return of the Living Dead* (1985). With startling efficiency, the still-untitled film provides an early clue about its generic affiliation and, in a single shot that brings the eerie periphery of the frame into the center of our consciousness, hints at the horrors to come.

By this point—a mere half-minute into the diegesis—the musical score, now imbued with the timbral fluttering of nervously plucked harp strings, has already intensified, propelled by the nondiegetic beating of kettledrums. The instrumentation suddenly bursts forth with a cacophonous blast of horns at the very moment when the title of the film, *WITCHCRAFT*, appears in all caps atop this somber, monochromatic backdrop (fig. 1.1). The manner in which that word emerges is significant: It rushes toward the viewer, increasing in size from a small font in the center of the frame to a much larger, notably jagged signifier that blocks our view of the gravestones behind it before being replaced by the names of the film's three main stars: Lon Chaney Jr., Jack Hedley, and Jill Dixon. Those names, superimposed atop a stone angel praying to an unseen god, are also unusual in appearance. Their letters are serrated or spiked in a way that complements the cutting, cacophonous music, which grows darker, more intense, with each shot's fade in and fade out.[1] Still more names appear, including those of composer Carlo Martelli, screenwriter Harry Spalding, producers Robert Lippert and Jack Parsons, and director Don Sharp, whose last name conveys the shrillness of the soundtrack and reminds us of the "pointed" way in which visual and aural elements (from

**Figure 1.1:** The 1964 film *Witchcraft* brings "horror" to the fore within its opening seconds (through a combination of audible and visual cues and clues).

the fonts of the credits to the musical stingers in this opening scene) metaphorically jab at the audience—a lunging move that is relatively rare outside the generic confines of horror.

Putting aside the intertextual connections that might spring to mind when confronted by those famous names, there is enough information in the first two minutes of *Witchcraft* (1964) to confidently establish its generic heritage.[2] The title alone, referring to the practice of black magic by individuals whose unconventional beliefs and paganistic rituals are often attacked or ridiculed by mainstream society, is one telltale sign. Indeed, more than one production after this film's theatrical release would adopt the same title, putting audiences in a frame of mind that recognizes how the culturally stereotyped activities associated with ancient witchcraft (e.g., devil worshipping, voodoo curses, virgin sacrifices) might be conceived of as "horrifying" to some people. Besides its titular reference to a "deviant" form of neoreligiosity (a mainstay of cinematic horror for decades), the film's cemetery setting is another dead giveaway, recalling the opening scenes of influential classics such as *Frankenstein* (1931) and *Night of the Living Dead* (1968) as well as more obscure independent and international productions such as *The Flesh and the Fiends* (a.k.a. *Mania*, 1960), *Fiend* (1980), and *Dracula's Fiancée* (*La fiancée de Dracula*, 2002). Indeed, the credit sequence that kicks off the 1990 Stephen King adaptation *Graveyard Shift* bears more than a passing resemblance to this first scene of *Witchcraft*, from the overgrown weeds creeping up several oddly angled tombstones to the dense fog that hangs ghostlike over the proceedings. That blanket of low-hanging fog, which rolls in just as a bulldozer begins to plow the ground in which a witch was buried alive three hundred years earlier, provides the same spookily atmospheric orientation that has served horror cinema so well over the decades, evidenced in everything from *The Wolf Man* (1941) to *The City of the Dead* (1960), *Assignment: Terror* (*Los Monstruos del Terror*, 1969), *Pumpkinhead* (1988), *Silent Hill* (2006), and *The Mist* (2007).

Moreover, the aggressively orchestrated tune that accompanies these images would hardly be mistaken as the musical score for a light romantic comedy, a feel-good family movie, or a science fiction film. Indeed, few markers are as conspicuous as a motion picture's soundtrack when it comes to indicating its genre. Horror in particular relies heavily on aural signifiers, including dissonant or atonal musical flourishes, to evoke the darkened moods and troubled mindsets of characters while provoking strong emotional and physical responses in audiences. It is obviously true, as Neil Lerner states, that "music in horror film, just as in any other cinematic genre, participates crucially in the creation of the film's meaning."[3] What partially distinguishes horror from other types of cultural production is the "greater freedom" given to composers "to experiment with harmony and instrumentation."[4] Although the classically trained composer Carlo Martelli had spent the first half of his professional life creating melodious, tonal chamber music prior to pursuing a career in film scoring, his work on *Witchcraft* and two other British horror movies made around the same time—*The Curse of the Mummy's Tomb* (1964) and *Catacombs* (1965)—suggests how a "traditionalist" like him might lean "modernist" when tasked with intensifying the frightening effects of cinematic images.

If not quite avant-garde, the musical score of *Witchcraft*, like those of countless other horror films designed to make audiences "feel threatened and uncomfortable through . . . sudden stinger chords and other shock effects," features stylistic elements that can be found in the modern or neoclassical works of early twentieth-century composers like Russian-born Igor Stravinsky and his Austrian contemporaries Alban Berg, Arnold Schoenberg, and Anton Webern (purveyors of atonalism and the twelve-tone technique).[5] Just as Stravinsky's scandalous ballet and orchestral work *The Rite of Spring* (1913), replete with "hideous sounds" and "rhythmic shocks" (or, in the words of *New York Times* critic Donal Henahan, "crunching, snarling chords from the brass and thundering thumps from the timpani"), had been deemed an affront to musical propriety by several of its first listeners, so too would the many horror film scores directly and indirectly influenced by it—from Bernard Herrmann's slashing composition for Hitchcock's *Psycho* (1960) to John Williams's terrifying theme music for Spielberg's *Jaws* (1975)—be cited as a chief source of spectatorial unease in the years that followed.[6] Produced at a pivotal moment in the development of modern horror bracketed by those two better-known films' theatrical releases, *Witchcraft* might seem comparatively inconsequential within the larger history of the genre. But the all-too-familiar visual and aural tropes of this cheaply produced "minor chiller" make it representative of a cultural category that places a number of unusual demands on audiences, asking them to *look at* and *listen to* things that are violently aimed at their *eyes* and *ears*.

Given the centrality of these two perceiving organs to the field of film studies, it should not come as a surprise that our exploration of horror as an intersensorial body genre begins by reproducing some of the ocularcentric and audiocentric proclivities of existing theories. Nor will the reader be shocked to see that *seeing itself*, as the most privileged of all perceptual capabilities (evident in the very language that we use to describe films and other things), occupies a place of hermeneutic significance throughout this book, even in chapters devoted to other physical senses or parts of the human anatomy that, at first glance, do not seem to necessitate looking or the use of one's eyes.

Ever since its origins as a technological marvel that, while reminiscent of optical novelties of the nineteenth century, brought visual culture to unprecedented preeminence at the beginning of the twentieth century, the medium of motion pictures has aroused a host of speculations about the nature of looking and the implications of being seen.[7] From Dziga Vertov's development of a mechanically enabled, all-seeing technique called *kino-glaz* (or "cine-eye") during the 1920s, to theories of the "gaze" and writings about "suture" that became the bedrock of much scholarly activity a half-century later, the history of film has largely been a history of *vision*—or, rather, of the particular "ways of seeing" that cinema has enabled and conditioned spectators to accept as normal (based on continuity editing, point-of-view shots, and other storytelling devices).[8] Among other things, the horror film pushes the medium's latent yet glaringly obvious optical bent to the fore, often by drawing attention to the very organ whose properties are mimicked in the machinic makeup of the movie camera (a lensed apparatus with pupil-like light-focusing capabilities). Perhaps Carol Clover put it best over thirty years ago when she wrote what has since become axiomatic in the minds of many theorists: "Horror privileges eyes because, more crucially than any other kind of cinema, *it is about eyes*."[9]

That oft-quoted passage—one of many from her book *Men, Women, and Chain Saws: Gender in the Modern Horror Film* that I will ruminate on throughout the present study—prompts me to ask what gets left behind in our rush to accept the ocular orientation of both the genre and the medium (in addition to the critical discourses surrounding them) as a truism or taken-for-granted fact that is beyond reproach. Like Tony Perrello, who has written about Clover's "metacinematic turn," or her rhetorical framing of horror as an inherently reflexive genre (one that is "about eyes watching horror"), I find much of value in her pioneering work.[10] Since its publication in 1992, Clover's book has inspired numerous attempts to unpack contemporary demonic possession films, rape-revenge films, and teen slasher films (as well as the latter's "classier" forerunners from 1960: *Psycho* and *Peeping Tom*) with the same sophisticated understanding of horror's contradictory appeals that she brought to once-derided case studies like *I Spit on Your Grave* (1978), *Hell Night* (1981), and *Witchboard* (1986). One of her major contributions concerns the "mirroring effect" of the genre, which turns the sight of characters screaming or shuddering—often while they are watching scary scenes on a screen, as in *Videodrome* (1983), *Demons* (1985), and *TerrorVision* (1986)—into a reflective image that shows the audience their own fear. Putting his own spin on that effect, Perrello notes that "the final cause of horror" in movies like those cited above lies not in the "thing" that initially draws out a scream or induces a shudder (such as a monster or a mangled body part) but rather in the act of viewing itself: "Horror takes effect when a viewer watches a viewer watching horror."[11]

Rather than dispute her claim, I wish to take up this metacinematic aspect of Clover's argument and apply it in a way that acknowledges a broad range of specular possibilities for audiences who might "look" at screens differently than what is generally encouraged. Far from suggesting that eyes and their sensing proficiencies cease to matter in this age of increased disability awareness and neurodiversity, I argue that they should be placed in dialogue with other anatomical and sensorial features in hopes of arriving at a more full-bodied, critically reflexive assessment of the genre. Additionally, by directing one's attention toward heretofore overlooked or understudied aspects of cinematic horror, including the digital technologies and delivery systems that make it possible to listen to and watch movies through the assistance of AD and subtitling services as well as DVD/Blu-ray commentary tracks, I seek to promote an oblique approach to horror film hermeneutics, a kind of "listening-anew" and "looking-askew" view of texts that can be *seen through the ears* and *heard through the eyes*. Before teasing out the interpretive possibilities of such sensorial entanglements and eventually returning to Clover's foundational approach to the genre (which complicates the different gaze structures embedded in slasher films and other horror subgenres), let us consider how *Witchcraft* and other motion pictures produced in the wake of *Psycho*'s and *Peeping Tom*'s 1960 release—including those that mount a "savage assault on the audience and its belief systems"—foreground *belief itself* as a precondition for seeing and hearing the world differently.[12] What I am referring to here is not a "belief in rationality," which comes under attack as frequently and as fiercely as do those two faculties of perception, according to Stephen Prince, but rather a belief in *irrationality*. It is, in other words, a radically altered view of the world—metatextually embedded in several examples of modern horror, where monsters are gazed upon by otherwise rationally minded characters—that might prompt a similarly subversive or unconventional approach to spectatorship in the coming years.

## I Do NOT Believe

Following on the heels of the 1962 British horror film *Night of the Eagle* (with which it shares similar themes), the aforementioned *Witchcraft* made its way into theaters already preloaded with the associative baggage of its titular subject, which that earlier black-and-white production—directed by Sidney Hayers and written by Richard Matheson and Charles Beaumont, who adapted Fritz Leiber's *Conjure Wife* (1943)—had broached with even greater dramatic flair. In fact, the various objects that partially comprise the iconography of this supernatural subgenre, chock full of "charms, amulets, voodoo candles, grave dirt, and locks of hair [that] are believed to ward off evil spirits and spells," were verbally referenced in *Night of the Eagle*'s stateside release (retitled *Burn, Witch, Burn* by US distributor American International Pictures [AIP]), during a tacked-on pre-credits prologue that warns the audience of the many frights to follow. Spoken over a black screen by voice actor Paul Frees (who, with tongue planted firmly in cheek, announces that "the motion picture you are about to see contains an evil spell, as used by practitioners of witchcraft for centuries"), this offscreen narration lasts nearly three minutes and is reminiscent of the sort of ballyhoo with which B-movie gimmick specialist William Castle is famous. Punctuated by an incantation in which Frees sets about "to dispel all evil spirits that may radiate from the screen," it is followed by an opening title sequence that, to paraphrase Paul Mavis, exudes a spookily hypnotic quality.[13] Notably, the film's credits and title appear as white text next to a close-up of a woman's eye, which is frozen in a state not of fear but of something potentially more terrifying. Creepily, her unblinking stare gradually seems to change somehow, "becoming meaner, more demonic . . . until you realize it's just your mind playing tricks on you after staring at an object too long" (fig. 1.2).[14]

Another modern-day critic with a fondness for the film, Douglas Buck, likewise notes the unsettling effect of staring at that "slightly twitching female eye," which gives "little clue to the emotional state of its . . . owner (terrified? fascinated? insane? or worse . . . condemning?)"[15] The manner in which that eye is framed, suggestive of the opening image of Michael Carreras's Hammer-produced thriller *Maniac* (1963) and some of the imagery subsequently included in Roman Polanski's British psychological horror film *Repulsion* (1965), seems less like the low-budget stuff of William Castle or AIP than the kind of auteur-driven art cinema that was beginning to attract international attention around the time of *Burn, Witch, Burn*'s theatrical release.[16] That literally *optical* illusion near the beginning of *Burn, Witch, Burn*, following an audio-only preface in which viewers are asked to "see" things with their ears while

**Figure 1.2:** The 1962 film *Burn, Witch, Burn* foregrounds one sense—that of seeing—above all others in its opening title sequence, which also invites audiences to question if the sight of the unblinking eye is a still frame or a moving image.

listening to an invisible, baritone-voiced speaker doing a spot-on Orson Welles imitation, could be interpreted as a "proper metaphor for the entire film," which pivots thematically on the conflict between scientific rationality and neoreligious belief and pits a nonbelieving skeptic against a demonic force that becomes terrifyingly real during the narrative's concluding moments.[17]

Believing in the existence of an unseen demon, as this film's spell-casting female protagonist Tansy (Janet Blair) does to the consternation of her initially incredulous husband, sociology professor Norman Taylor (Peter Wyngarde), necessitates moving the audible threats posed by the creature, which can be heard shrieking outside the couple's English cottage during a particularly spinetingling scene, into the realm of the *visible*. As a man of science, Norman is a familiar figure in paranormal tales: someone who searches for reasonable explanations for otherwise inexplicable occurrences (e.g., attributing the strange banging on the front door of their house to the storm winds outside), and whose eventual willingness to suspend his disbelief signals that crucial moment in the narrative when even the most farfetched ideas can stand up to scrutiny and be supported by empirical evidence. The latter, thought to arise from the stimulation of a perceiver's sense organs, puts a scientific gloss on matters that at first appear more metaphysical than physical, but which materialize into observable, verifiable phenomena at various points in a horror tale when the audience's own disbelief must be suspended if the intended effect—fear, dread, or disgust, for instance—is to be achieved. While the earlier *Night of the Demon* (1957)—a Jacques Tourneur–directed British production with which *Burn, Witch, Burn* is often compared—"tipped its hand and showed the physical manifestation of sorcery and Black Magic in its opening scenes," Hayers's film builds slowly, atmospherically, "from a stance of open disdain for belief in the supernatural to a terrifying acceptance" of the dark arts.[18] And it culminates with the death of Flora Carr (Margaret Johnston), a modern-day witch who, seeking to kill Norman because he opposes her professor-husband's departmental promotion, animates a large eagle sculpture perched atop a campus building only to be flattened by it in a flash of cosmic comeuppance. Near that literally crushing, gravity-filled ending (if readers will excuse the pun), the protagonist, utterly shaken by what he is seeing, is brought to his knees by a spectral force that assumes the same physical form as that giant stone bird. It is a moment of clairvoyant reckoning that conveniently occurs in the college classroom where he had earlier proselytized to his students about the need to remain vigilant against occult superstitions and had written the statement "I DO NOT BELIEVE" on the chalkboard, with the word "not" underlined and the word "believe" circled for emphasis (fig. 1.3).

Regardless of whether they are spoken or not, those words—the first that are uttered by this seemingly doomed main character immediately following *Burn, Witch, Burn*'s opening credits—are the bedrock upon which many horror narratives are constructed. Indeed, one of the recurring rhetorical strategies employed by creators of literary and cinematic horror is "disbelief mitigation," a foregrounding of rationally minded, often scientifically inclined characters whose initial skepticism toward the supernatural world is tested and finally undermined by the presence of spirits and other liminal beings that materialize within the world of the living and, most importantly, can be *seen* by those same doubting individuals.[19] One such person appears in Universal's 1931 monster movie *Dracula*. However, as an expert in "obscure diseases" who specializes in vampirism, he has already cast off his recalcitrance toward unscientific hokum and learned to accept the supernatural as a natural part of life

**Figure 1.3:** A staunch rationalist who refuses to believe in supernatural entities or events, college professor Norman Taylor eats his words in this scene of *Burn, Witch, Burn*, when a giant eagle prowls the campus in pursuit of human prey.

(and death) by the time we pick up his thread of the narrative. Loosely based on Bram Stoker's 1897 novel of the same title, this film—directed by Tod Browning and starring Bela Lugosi as the vampiric count from Transylvania—features a scene in which Professor Van Helsing (Edward Van Sloan) discusses one of the patients at a sanitarium with the director of that institution, Dr. Seward (Herbert Bunston). Importantly, Seward's patient, a "raving lunatic slave" of Count Dracula named Renfield (Dwight Frye), who traveled from Transylvania to England with his master but got separated from him and has since been locked away in the madhouse, started this story as a disbeliever himself, calling all the talk about the undead just a bunch of local superstition in the village near Dracula's castle. But, even more so than Renfield's transformation into a bloodsucking creature of the night, it is Van Helsing's conversion into someone who, during his talk with the sanitarium director, openly declares that "the superstition of yesterday can become the scientific reality of today" that secures a place for audiences to follow the vampire-hunting professor's lead and become "believers" themselves.

Subsequent horror films likewise followed *Dracula*'s lead in attempting to mitigate spectatorial disbelief in this way. Examples are too numerous to cite in their entirety, although they range across historical periods, national contexts, and subgenres: haunted house stories like *Amityville 3-D* (1983), Japanese ghost-and-goblin tales like *Yōkai Hantā: Hiruko* (1991), urban legend films like *Candyman* (1992), coming-of-age werewolf allegories like *Ginger Snaps* (2000), and Indian demonic-possession hits like the Tamil-language *Pizza* (2012) and its Hindi-language remake of the same title. In some cases, survivors of freakish phenomena are shown pleading their cases to medical and psychiatric staff who are asked, point blank, "Do you believe me?" This is the question that Kirsty (Ashley Laurence), the bedridden protagonist of *Hellbound: Hellraiser II* (1988), puts to a doctor after recounting her recent run-in with a group of extradimensional demons—a traumatizing experience depicted in this film's 1987 precursor, writer-director Clive Barker's *Hellraiser*. Refusing to call her "crazy," which is not a word that people in his profession typically employ, the psychiatrist to whom Kirsty opens up and shares her eyewitness account also declines to weigh in on its truth claims, taking an agnostic or neutral position that, for all intents and purposes, suggests incredulity. With time, however, he is made to feel the full brunt of the demonic Cenobites' might and adjusts his position accordingly, in much the same way that Detective Mike Denver (Omar Epps) is forced to question his own skepticism when chasing down a possibly indestructible or superhuman murderer in the more recent theatrical release *Trick* (2019).

Taking its title from the nickname of that masked serial killer ("Trick"), who stabs his victims every Halloween only to escape police capture and disappear until the next year's deadly festivities, this homage to 1980s slasher films (directed by Patrick Lussier from a script that he cowrote with Todd Farmer) has been widely criticized for asking audiences to suspend their disbelief and to overlook its many narrative contrivances, not to mention its glaringly obvious nods to previous cultural productions that might be deemed "superior" by comparison. But disbelief is something that the film's perpetually questioning protagonist must *also* suspend if he is to follow every lead during his dogged pursuit of the slayer, whom he gradually begins to suspect is the Devil incarnate after coming into physical contact with him. Explaining to a colleague that he has "never been a believer," and lumping everything from "ghosts, Bigfoot, aliens, God, [and] Satan" together as fictional bugaboos best left to children's fantasy tales rather than forensic investigations, Mike nevertheless admits that Trick is "beyond abnormal"—a force of "pure evil" that exceeds the limits of rational thought and human psychosis. That this "most grounded cop on the planet" (to quote a group of copycat killers who, as the most egregious of Lussier and Farmer's many narrative "tricks," are revealed to be the *real* culprits near the end of the film) can be made to believe in the existence of supernatural events and otherworldly entities is significant, as is his earlier claim of trusting in the existence of only "what I can *see* and what I can *touch*."[20] That comment calls attention to two sense modalities central to the acceptance of previously unbelievable scenarios or fantastical beings as "real."

Between those two modalities, the sense of sight stands out as the operative—but certainly not only—means of forging an affective bond between character and spectator. After all, viewers are frequently forced to see the same things that characters see, although the technological means and mediating screens through which we access such horrific visions can hinder that bonding by coming in between our bodied selves and those fictional figures. Indeed, the latter, as disembodied forms flickering across a two-dimensional surface (e.g., cinema screen, television monitor, handheld tablet), might seem as phantomlike as the ghosts that so often haunt those characters. When sight is combined with other senses, however, or is shifted to bodily organs besides the eyes (including ears and skin), fictional characters begin to gain the material solidity and phenomenological presence that they so frequently attribute to previously unseen spectral forms and monsters of every stripe—big-screen baddies that are claimed to be real, but are not yet *really real* until they are *seen*, *heard*, *felt*, and sometimes *smelled* by those individuals most firmly set in their scientific ways or committed to logical, rational explanations.

Along those lines, the William Castle–directed film *House on Haunted Hill* (1959) features a passage of dialogue between eccentric millionaire Frederick Loren (Vincent Price) and Dr. David Trent (Alan Marshall), a psychiatrist specializing in hysteria, in which the latter explains that there must be some rational explanation for the seemingly supernatural events occurring in the titular mansion. "I don't believe in ghosts, nor in frightening women," David tells Frederick, moments after Nora Manning (Carolyn Craig), another guest trapped inside the purportedly haunted house, finds a decapitated head in her suitcase. Although David is later revealed to be behind many of the extraordinary events (including the faked beheading) that are meant to drive the other guests mad, as the supposed "voice of reason and logic" he ultimately slips into a state of madness himself, allowing his "illicit passion" for Frederick's wife, Annabelle (Carol Ohmart), to cloud his judgment.[21] Undertaking an "insanely convoluted murder plot," the good doctor, who is actually the bad guy behind all the spookings leading up to his and Annabelle's fatal fall into a vat of acid in the film's penultimate scene, thus descends to an irrational state befitting the genre's tendency to push people to their limits.

One might reasonably assume that, since there are not any paranormal phenomena in *House on Haunted Hill* (i.e., no strange apparitions or walking corpses save for the skeleton being animated by Frederick in his own puppet-string-pulling attempt to scare his cheating wife to death), the psychiatrist has been proven right by narrative's end. However, because he has done the very thing that he professes not to "believe" in (i.e., "frightening women"), doubt can be cast on his *other* doubt—his abiding skepticism toward supernatural entities. Ultimately, it matters little if the latter are real or not, or if the inexplicable happenings within this or any other horror tale have been produced by some higher power or engineered by mere mortals (as revealed near the end of the aforementioned *Trick*), so long as our spectatorial alignment with characters distinguished by their scientific disposition is forged early on in the narrative. The presence of people like Norman (in *Burn, Witch, Burn*) and David (in *House on Haunted Hill*) is thus vital if audiences are to swallow the many implausibilities that set the genre off from other categories of cultural production (though fantasy and science fiction are horror-adjacent bedfellows) and that require compensating degrees of verisimilitude in order to ground its fantastical scenarios and otherworldly creatures in something resembling reality.

In the real world, of course, multiple senses work together and sometimes compensate for one another so that people, not unlike detectives, can gather information about their social environments and, importantly, interpret that information. The spaces that people move through and take up temporary positions within during their everyday lives "mold their sensory experiences," though, as Devorah Kalekin-Fishman and Kelvin E. Y. Low point out, we tend to take those commonplace, quotidian experiences for granted and think of seeing, hearing, smelling, tasting, and touching as uniquely individual impressions of the world made possible by neurological, physiological, and psychological mechanisms located in the human body and brain.[22] What these and other theorists call for is a broader, socially expansive understanding of perception as being culturally constructed, going beyond the conventional framing of the senses as strictly subjective processes of stimuli-response to account for the ways that *inter*subjective feelings—for and with other bodies and brains within a shared location or across time and space—shape our thoughts, behaviors, and perhaps even our personal memories of particular places.[23]

In addition to intersubjectivity, the entwining of those deeply social processes might result in "intersensoriality," a term used by David Howes and Constance Classen to describe the "manifold relations among the different senses."[24] Akin to synesthesia, a cognitive and corporeal phenomenon that has long been associated with "superstition, irrationality, and primitive cultures" (and which is sometimes dismissed as "fanciful thinking" in Western culture), intersensoriality points toward human beings' capacity to perceive things outside the "tight physiological boxes" that have for too long separated the experiences of seeing, hearing, smelling, tasting, and touching into self-contained categories tethered to specific bodily organs (respectively, and reductively, the eyes, the ears, the nose, the tongue, and the skin).[25] Notably, in their book *Ways of Sensing: Understanding the Senses in Society*, Howes and Classen briefly refer to motion pictures and other forms of mass communication as being "sensorially-limited but culturally and psychologically powerful representations of the world," and that modern media's "pairing of sound and sight" makes *sense* (in both "senses" of that word), whereas "olfactory-visual or audio-gustatory pairings would hardly seem as convincing."[26] In upcoming chapters, I will ask the reader to entertain some rather odd, "nonsensical" propositions, putting tactile, olfactory, and gustatory approaches to cinematic horror into the mix as alternatives to the predominately visual (and secondarily auditory) rubrics found in most critical studies of the genre. Additionally, in the second half of the book I will circle back to the idea of intersensoriality to consider how cinematic images can be seen through the ears, just as I will explore the prospect of hearing horror film's many distinctive sounds through the eyes. For the time being, let us plunge deeper into the concept of disbelief mitigation and consider why, in this particular genre (but in adjacent categories of cultural production as well), sight is often privileged over other sense modalities as a perceptual precondition for *belief*, which, as the philosopher John Heil reminds us, is itself a "potential knowing" that sometime arises from "hunches and intuition."[27]

## "What Are We (Not) Seeing?": Comprehension, Confusion, and Negative Pleasure

I don't know what's worse: seeing them or not seeing them.

—Susan (Blanchard Ryan) speaking to her partner, Daniel (Daniel Travis), as they float in shark-infested waters, in *Open Water* (2013)

Among the genre's many contradictory appeals, including its ability to instill a feeling of "negative pleasure" in audiences who are drawn to shocking or suspenseful scenes of violent mayhem and unrelenting dread (discussed at length by Noël Carroll in his 1990 book *The Philosophy of Horror, or, Paradoxes of the Heart*), is the fact that viewers are frequently asked to suspend their disbelief and adopt an apprehensive stance toward things that many of us know (or, dare I say, *believe*) do not exist: vampires, werewolves, zombies, and other beings that lie "outside our standing conceptual schemes."[28] In fact, those paradoxes are not unrelated, for our confrontation with the once-unthinkable but all-too-real "thing" that makes us quake with fear or shake with laughter (or both)—mediated though it is by those onscreen surrogates whose reactions we are meant to share in moments of affective congruence—entails more than just an attitudinal adjustment on the part of the disbelieving audience. More profoundly, it involves some amount of abnegation or self-reflection for spectators who find themselves caught up in the emotional and cognitive bivalency of this body genre, one that not only runs viewers through a gauntlet of negative (and positive) feelings but also asks them to doubt their own disbelief or to momentarily reside in that liminal space between knowing and not-knowing.[29]

With regard to "negative pleasure," Katerina Bantinaki poses a critical intervention that is worth exploring, for she challenges Carroll's and other theorists' long-standing claims that the physiological symptoms of horror emotions (including, but not limited to, accelerated heart rate, queasiness, skin conductance, a spike in adrenaline, and a tensing of the muscles) are essentially painful or unpleasant. She argues that a more hedonically expansive understanding of the genre is needed to account for spectators' enjoyment of fear or disgust.[30] And that enjoyment, according to her, is perhaps not even paradoxical in the first place. Bantinaki maintains that consuming fictional horror, or what Carroll refers to as "art-horror," is both beneficial and rewarding, granting audiences a reassuring sense of control and safety that they are often denied whenever they are confronted with real-life horrors (since, in her words, we can always "decide to shut our eyes, or walk away" if a movie becomes too disturbing). The intense yet positively valanced *pleasure* of the genre therefore stems from the chance it affords us to "learn to master our responses to fear and even to test the limits of our endurance to frightening stimuli" within a safe environment.[31] But it also emerges, as I think Carroll would contend, whenever the heretofore mysterious or perplexing aspects of a horror tale, including the nature of the threat posed by a monster that gradually reveals itself or discloses something about its unholy (or quotidian) origins, are rendered in such a way—a satisfyingly *surprising* way, one hopes—that our initial curiosity or confusion is replaced by comprehension if not "cognitive mastery" by narrative's end. For that to happen, though, some amount of attitudinal affiliation between the audience and the resident skeptic of a horror film needs to have occurred, so that their change of heart in the face of incontrovertible evidence of the creature's abject state and very existence stirs a comparable spectatorial sensation. Hence the reason why people like Norman populate stories like *Burn, Witch, Burn*, which trade on our familiarity with genre conventions (including those related to witchcraft) but nevertheless surprise us by framing the characters' own shocked reactions as a "reasonable" outcome of having laid eyes on something hideously grotesque, unnatural in size, or simply beyond the bounds of normality.

Norman's horrified reaction to the rampaging eagle, which can finally be *seen*—rather than just heard—smashing through the doors of the medical university (an institution reserved for scientific inquiry and rational debate, where cadavers as well as living test subjects are in ready supply), notably occurs in his own classroom at night. It would be easy to say, based on this setting alone, that the teacher has become the student and must be taught the error of his naysaying ways. Indeed, his own words ("I DO NOT BELIEVE"), still visible on the chalkboard from the previous day, serves as self-mocking commentary throughout this scene, as risible as the spoken prologue that kicked off *Burn, Witch, Burn*. But if we laugh too heartily at the heavy-handed irony of this otherwise terrifying encounter, or—to use the kind of ableist language that suffuses the genre—view it simply as a means of condemning the professor for his previous "blindness" to the monstrous thing whose audible presence, just offscreen, would have been difficult to refute by anyone who relies more heavily on their non-ocular senses (owing to vision impairment), then we find ourselves implicated in an equally myopic worldview. We might also miss other objects within the mise-en-scène that flesh out Norman's fear, including a poster-sized illustration of the human brain, which can be seen in shots that ironically point toward that part of the body where thought is housed. This anatomical image, a standard feature of medical school classrooms showing the "meat" of cognition, is visible to viewers who are at once attentive and distracted, casting their gaze in a focused yet frantic manner, not unlike the way that the once-uncomprehending character scans his surroundings in search of the horrible thing that will deliver him (and us) into full comprehension. If this embedded representation of a cross-sectioned brain were to catch the viewer's eye, then the doubly denotative act of "seeing" would crystallize around Norman's confrontation with the monster, whose presence is now visually confirmed and rendered comprehensible to the audience.

Of course, when we finally see the winged beast, barreling down school corridors and wreaking havoc on an institution committed to scientific inquiry, we might respond in a way that is *not* congruent with the character's terrified reaction. To be sure, the excessively large eagle makes for a formidable foe. But there is also something funny about the thing, whose incongruity within this setting as well as its enormous size—a somewhat unconvincing special effect hamstrung by the low-budget production's cost-cutting measures—are likely to generate laughter or a condescending smirk among contemporary audiences who perhaps look back at horror films made decades ago with a mixture of nostalgia and ironic detachment. If, from that detached vantage, the unintended humor of the scene obscures its intended effect, and in case we find ourselves snickering when a more "appropriate" response (shuddering, for instance) would have better enabled suspension of disbelief, it is still possible to *believe*—if not in the monster, then in *belief itself*. Specifically, our belief would be that of the now-enlightened character who, eyes wide open and mouth agape, needs no further convincing of the creature's existence. Indeed, witnessing the horrified reaction of a character like Norman, his face a jumble of contorted features, is often more effective at striking the intended chord than actually seeing the thing that prompted that reaction.

The confluence of humorous and horrific tones near the conclusion of *Burn, Witch, Burn* contributes to the onset of a third experiential aspect of the film, leaving audiences in a state of confusion only moments after comprehension through visual perception has occurred. Paul Mavis speaks for several viewers when, slightly bemused, he asks, "Are we seeing what we think we're seeing? And if so . . . *what are we seeing*?" Here, "sight" brings forth cognitive as well as perceptual connotations, carried over into the critic's next set of questions:

> What exactly is going on in *Burn, Witch, Burn*!? Is it a beautifully stylized fable of ancient witchcraft delivered via modern

> innovations (a nice metaphor for Norman and Tansy's relationship: she believes in magic; he believes in technology and science)? Are Norman and Tansy being stalked by a demon that inhabits their phones and their tape recorders and even their black cat, conjured up by a vengeful colleague bent on destroying Norman? Or are they being hypnotized through subliminal noises and prompts over their phone and tape recorder (that grating sound on the tape and phone that only Norman and Tansy seem to hear)?[32]

Posing these inquiries, Mavis puts more than a rhetorical spin on his earlier question of whether or not the woman's unblinking eye at the beginning of the film might have been moving imperceptibly. Following the film's lead, and reminiscent of the way that Nicolas Roeg's metaphysical murder mystery *Don't Look Now* (1973)—a case study in chapter 2—places ocular stumbling blocks on the audience's path to narrative comprehension, the critic offers no answers. Instead, he leaves his readers with the same comically inflected uncertainty and polysemic potentiality that characterize the best, most unsettling horror tales.

Another example of narrative ambiguity, or what Simin Nina Littschwager refers to as "epistemological uncertainty," is director Herk Harvey's *Carnival of Souls* (1962).[33] Notably, it was released the same year that *Burn, Witch, Burn* encouraged audiences to question what they were seeing while paradoxically planting the seeds of *belief* rather than doubt in horror's well-tilled soil of sight-based fright. Like that British production, this low-budget American effort is sure to leave even the savviest viewers confused about the very things that they have seen leading up to the narrative's denouement. In what can accurately be described as a "twist ending," *Carnival of Souls*'s traumatized protagonist—a young church organist named Mary (Candace Hilligoss) who has recently survived an automobile accident in Lawrence, Kansas, and made her way to a new job two states over in Salt Lake City—is revealed to be *dead* (or undead). As such, her many encounters with other people throughout the lengthy, dreamily disorienting middle section of the film can retroactively be understood as either a stretched-out figment of her imagination in the seconds before her watery demise (a kind of waking dream of the soon-to-be dead) or a "purgatorial fantasy" whereby non-flesh-eating zombies peacefully coexist with the living.[34] It is difficult to say which one of these two (or possibly other) interpretations offers the most reasonable explanation for the film's otherwise unbelievable events. Contemporary audiences accustomed to the mendacious storytelling techniques of narratively complex "puzzle films" (or what Littschwager and other scholars call "mind-game films") might see that plot twist—a big reveal pivoting on the protagonist's "unconscious death," not unlike the surprise endings of M. Night Shyamalan's *The Sixth Sense* (1999) and Alejandro Amenábar's *The Others* (2001)—coming from a mile away.[35] But its effects extend beyond the localized surprise that arises from a final-reel revelation to encompass a more profoundly unsettling sense of global *unknowing*, derived in part from our inability to piece together *Carnival of Souls*' narrative puzzle through the simple act of "looking back" at previous scenes.

From the moment, roughly five minutes into the film, that she staggers shell-shocked from the muddy river where two fellow car passengers (also young women, victims of a drag race gone wrong) have just drowned, Mary embodies our spectatorial confusion. For much of the narrative, she wears a haunted, bewildered expression on her face while striving to make sense of why her actual senses (of sight and of hearing, especially) are failing her at crucial moments. That visible bewilderment—her eyes at once vacant and searching—only intensifies when she finds herself in the presence of department store clerks and shoppers who do not appear to see or hear her when she steps out of a dressing room, and whose own spoken words and physical noises are momentarily removed from the soundtrack (leaving only the nondiegetic organ music audible). Moments later, after exiting onto an eerily silent yet pedestrian-filled sidewalk and traipsing into a nearby park, the gently rising sound of birdsong and the swoosh of wind through the trees becomes perceptible, bringing a look of comfort to her face. But that relief is fleeting, a rare occasion when the certainty of audibly and visibly perceived things in the natural world distracts Mary from her own existential uncertainty and allays her growing suspicions that another (unheard, unseen, and unknowable) world beckons, not from afar but from a nearby pavilion on the shores of the Great Salt Lake.

It is from a distant vantage, while driving through Utah on her way to her new job, that Mary first spots the abandoned pavilion, which, according to a gas station attendant (Dan Palmquist), was once a bathhouse and then a dance hall before it was boarded up. Not long after arriving at the church where she has been hired to play the organ, an elderly minister (Art Ellison) asks if she would like to get a closer view of the pavilion and kindly drives her to its empty parking lot. However, he cautions her against going onto the actual premises, which "the law has placed . . . off-limits" and which is no longer "safe" to enter. "It wouldn't be seemly for a minister to break the law," he says, delivering a line laden with sexual subtext (if not intentional innuendo). Unable to suppress his curiosity as to why the old place should exert such a powerful "attraction" on the young woman, this man of God gives her a disapproving look when she notes how easy it would be to step around the barrier separating her from it. "Maybe I want to satisfy myself that the place is nothing more than it *appears* to be," our potential lawbreaker says, casting her forlorn gaze toward the crumbling buildings that will draw her back just as surely as she will be forced to return to her watery grave in Kansas by narrative's end. Notably, before driving her to the pavilion for a closer look, the minister catches this newly hired organist gazing at a stained-glass window in his church, as if she were fixated on its beautiful yet unsettling representation of a religious scene—a "casting-out-of-the-devil" image (seen from her point of view) that might remind contemporary viewers of *The Exorcist* (1973) and other films about demonic possession. "What do you see?" he asks, approaching Mary from behind, to which she responds, "*Nothing*, nothing at all."

That simple question-and-answer between the minister and the protagonist, who will later refer to herself as a "reasonable" person (meaning: someone who is generally not prone to let her imagination run wild), forms the basis for the sensorial privileging or centering of sight in the first third of *Carnival of Souls*, even when there is nothing really *there* to be seen. That is, there is no farfetched idea or supernatural phenomenon that has to be believed before the uncanny effects of horror take hold. Gradually, though, as the film builds toward its ambiguous, inconclusive conclusion, other senses are called upon to do the work of the eyes, and the distinctive sounds of *Carnival of Souls* (at least as much as its images) are what make it possible for us to finally "un-see" Mary just as the people around her have begun to do. Nevertheless, we will continue to look at the increasingly strange objects and people populating the main character's environment from *her* ocular perspective, and our forced attachment to her dying or undead vision(s) is what ensures spectatorial confusion even when we finally comprehend her situation.

In addition to being transfixed by the sight of the abandoned pavilion, Mary begins to have recurring visions of a pasty-looking man (played by the film's director, Herk Harvey), who first zooms into view as a kind of roadside distraction during her westward drive in the dead of night. Later, after Mary has reached her destination—a three-story house where she is renting a room from a woman named Mrs. Thomas (Frances Feist)—he is briefly visible through the open window, but only *she* can see this menacing stranger standing silently outside. Significantly, when she advances toward the window to have a second look, the man has disappeared, and her reflection is the only thing that can be seen in the pane of glass (fig. 1.4). Importantly, the woman's reflection is doubled and distorted, suggesting a cleaving of the self into physical and spiritual parts as well as the dualizing of someone who appears to be stuck between two worlds.

**Figure 1.4:** When Mary, the possibly dead protagonist in *Carnival of Souls*, peers through the window, her reflection appears distorted, as if her ghostly double has a double of its own.

The next day, that same unnamed figure (identified only as "The Man" in the film's credits) pops up inside the house, first on the staircase landing and then, most terrifyingly, within her bedroom. His ghoulish features are framed by the mirror above her chest of drawers as if he were a reflection of her own abject fantasies or deathly desires. While the presence of this proverbial "beast in the boudoir" is not explained, and although he disappears as quickly as he appears, it is clear that the two share something in common, and their combined attraction-repulsion adds to the sexually charged atmosphere.[36] It also points toward Mary's own strangely *discarnate* carnality, which has been drawing the unsolicited attention of another of the house's tenants, an equally creepy man named John (Sidney Berger) who lives across the hall, and whose amorous advances become more aggressive whenever she is at her most vulnerable. In fact, it is John's reflection in the mirror that Mary mistakes for that of the monstrous other, suggesting that the two men are really one predatory figure split into corporeal and noncorporeal forms.

In the words of one critic, *Carnival of Souls*' female protagonist appears to be "flickering in and out of existence," moving between this world and a "parallel universe" much like the pale-faced man does.[37] That element, combined with the film's "funereal tone and odd pacing," anticipates the work of David Lynch, including the similarly themed *Eraserhead* (1977) and *Lost Highway* (1997), by several years.[38] It also brings to mind the aforementioned supernatural thrillers *The Sixth Sense* and *The Others*, which, although more straightforward than Lynch's films, are perhaps more radical in bestowing "a sense of epistemological uncertainty upon sight" throughout a diegesis that has been carefully crafted to "trick" its audience.[39] More fundamentally, the existential in-betweenness of the main character reflects the ontological features of the cinematic apparatus, which presents spectators with an optical illusion (that of movement) and masks the intermittent darkness between "flickering" still images through the perceptual phenomenon of persistence of vision.

Something of cinema's own liminality as a *medium's* medium—a means of casting a "spell" over the audience (similar to what occurs in the first three minutes of *Burn, Witch, Burn* and in the hypnosis-themed, eyeball-filled Spanish production *Anguish* [*Angustia*, 1987])—is even conveyed in a comment that Mary makes to John. Looking out the window and musing about how different the world is in daylight compared to nighttime, she remarks that, "in the dark, your fantasies get so out of hand." "Let's have no more nights," she declares, putting a damper on the lecherous man's eagerness for a date that evening while hinting at the way that one half of the motion picture medium's light-dark dyad is concealed through deceptive "illuminations." Indeed, cinema can be thought of as a waking dream in which the black screen appears as frequently as do projected images, though our eyes, which play tricks on our brains, do not perceive it as such.

When Mary tells Mrs. Thomas about these unnerving encounters with the pale-faced man, the older woman thinks that she is simply letting her imagination run wild and attributes her skittishness to the sound of creaking floorboards. "I didn't *hear* him, Mrs. Thomas. I *saw* him," is the protagonist's reply, emphasizing the idea that one sense modality offers more legitimate claims to truth than do the others. But *Carnival of Souls* is similar to *The Sixth Sense* in that it hints at the *limitations* of vision, thereby calling into question the "culmination of the eye as the center of human subjectivity and meaning, the receptacle of truth" itself, which Littschwager (quoting theorist Judith Mayne) links to "the long-standing foundation for the ocularcentric paradigm of the 'ideal spectator of the motion pictures', the legacy of psychoanalytically inflected film theory of the 1970s."[40] Like Shyamalan's much-discussed blockbuster, famous for having its audience share the same sensing capabilities of the dead-people-seeing Cole Sear (Haley Joel Osment), Herk Harvey's comparatively amateurish production, noted as much for its technical deficits (such as poorly looped dialogue and obvious foley effects) as for its artistic merits (drawing unlikely comparisons to the critically adored films of Jean Cocteau and Ingmar Bergman), and initially released in drive-in theaters rather than multiplexes, "does not disparage vision as such." Instead, if I may adopt the words that Littschwager reserves for *The Sixth Sense*, "it undermines only a mechanical and disembodied notion of vision, one that claims primacy over the other senses as a means of knowing the world." In this way, *Carnival of Souls* "sensitizes us to other modes of perception, reminding us of their epistemological capacities as well as of the fact that the traditional hierarchy of the senses is all but a fixed biological order of perception."[41]

In keeping with historical precedents, Mary eventually seeks help from a medical professional in hopes of either confirming her sanity or determining how to reconcile disbelief with what she has seen. Although he readily admits that he is not a psychiatrist, Dr. Samuels (Stan Levitt)—a skeptic himself—informs her that the fantastical sightings and bizarre occurrences are all in her head, symptoms of the emotional shock that resulted from the previous week's car accident. The doctor's words bring no comfort, though his comment that the old pavilion has something to do with her mental hang-ups prompts Mary to revisit it, this time on her own. Breaching the physical barrier that marks the threshold between what is permissible and what is "off-limits," she explores the pavilion grounds thoroughly, strolling past giant bells, piles of plywood, and a dance floor littered with moldy party decorations. She casts her gaze to and fro across a scene that is desolate and empty yet filled with material remnants of the pavilion's festive past.[42] As this four-minute sequence comes to an end, Mary is once again in the presence of the mysterious man with the pallid expression, only this time she does not see him lying below the surface of the water nearby—his submerged body and closed eyes foreshadowing her own fate. One might be tempted to say that her metaphorical "blindness" in this moment is the "cure" to a condition that she had sought counsel for in the doctor's office, and that she has finally been spared a vision of the monster. But, arriving at the midpoint of the film, this sequence is just the beginning of the end for Mary, who will eventually cross over another barrier—that between the world of the living and the world of the dead—and lose other faculties besides her sense of sight in making that crossing.

Indeed, the next scene, which occurs later that night, shows her succumbing to the same dark "fantasies" that she had spoken to John about and features an extended performance at the church organ, whose spectral sounds, reminiscent of the live music that often accompanied movie screenings during the 1920s, are momentarily silenced (though her hands continue to move atop the instrument's keys, as do her bare feet atop the pedals).[43] After a minute of silence, the metallic warbling of the carnival music returns to its normal volume, initiating a series of visions that take hold of Mary, as if she were possessed or under a sonically induced spell. Intercut with her playing the pipe organ are shots of the same stained-glass window depicted earlier as well as inserts of the pale-faced stranger back at the pavilion, opening his eyes and rising from the murky water to join a host of other walking dead to dance the night away. Expressionistic lighting effects and close-up shots exaggerate the largeness of her own eyes, like those of a windup doll mechanically pumping out a tune that is now excessively loud and deeply offensive to the ears of the minister (who has been listening to this profane bit of "sacrilege" the whole time). As Julie Brown notes in her exploration of the organ music that suffuses *Carnival of Souls* from beginning to end, much of this film's disorienting effects originate in the uncertain placement of that music within the narrative. Indeed, "we are not always sure where it belongs within the soundtrack's 'geography'" and cannot be certain if Mary "hears it or not."[44] While it is "clearly linked with Mary's subjectivity by virtue of her fictive performance of most of the obviously diegetic music within the film," there are times when she is a *listener* rather than performer (as when those same carnivalesque sounds transmit over her car's radio).[45]

It is unclear precisely what her unusually large eyes communicate in this scene, though a mixture of emotions—from surprise to skepticism and perhaps even anger—seems to flit across her facial features, including one raised eyebrow and one slightly lowered eyebrow along with glossy pursed lips curled up almost imperceptibly at the edges (rather than an open mouth to let out a scream), all of which express something other than outright terror. In a humorously exaggerated way, that close-up shot can be said to reflect the spectator's mounting feeling of confusion as the film builds toward its inconclusive conclusion. If not an actual mirror like the object propped atop her chest of drawers, and if not the same type of figuratively and literally reflective surface witnessed in an earlier scene (when Mary stands before a window looking outside her rented bedroom), this image throws the audiences' own bewilderment back in their faces, intensifying any discomfort that might have been part of their earlier attempts to make sense of a narrative that, as Brown asserts, is "completely disassociated from reality."[46]

That unsettling uncertainty only increases once *Carnival of Souls* reaches its final sequence, which shows the medical doctor and the minister—the two men in Mary's prematurely ended life who might have lured viewers toward different interpretations of, or explanations for, her inexplicable visions—together for the first time, each one casting a questioning gaze at the other. What prompts their quizzical yet strangely accusing looks is the woman's disappearance. Only her footprints and a single handprint in the sand outside the pavilion attest to her earlier presence. Exploring the abandoned carnival grounds in the company of a police officer, who directs their attention to her car parked nearby, this man of science and this man of religion have no words for what they are seeing, or *not seeing*. Their speechlessness at hearing this man of the law (who represents a different sort of authority, one distinct from their own) say, "And then . . . *nothing*" as he points out how Mary's tracks in the sand just end (going nowhere), magnifies their inadequacy, and perhaps that of the audience as well. Notably, the policeman's final spoken word in this penultimate scene of the film, "nothing," echoes its earlier occurrence, when Mary (prompted by the minister's question "What do you see?") used that same casually annihilating word to describe the creepy religious image depicted in the church's stained-glass window. Facing one another, these stern-faced, patriarchal embodiments of horror's dueling epistemologies—the genre's tendency to leverage belief against disbelief, spiritual credulity against skeptical agnosticism—are left as defeated in the end as the spectator is. In this light, *Carnival of Souls* is all the more remarkable as a film that not only refuses pat answers but also undermines those most vaunted of cinematic sensing abilities—seeing and hearing—in its embrace of a gut-punching, spirit-crushing *nothingness* that exceeds our perceiving abilities, if not our imaginations.[47]

## Commentary of Souls

In her analysis of *Carnival of Souls*, Bernice M. Murphy highlights its narrative ambiguity, stating that the black-and-white horror film "can potentially be read in any number of ways."[48] It can be interpreted, for instance, as a story about "the paranoid fantasies of a repressed young woman unable to fit into the world around her; as a representation of hell as a kind of bespoke ordeal tailored for each individual sinner; or as a subtle indictment of the conformity and conservatism of the Eisenhower era." Going deeper into *Carnival of Souls*' hermeneutic possibilities, and referring to the shell-shocked, walking-dead protagonist played with wide-eyed bewilderment by Candace Hilligoss, Murphy adds that "Mary's fate . . . resonates with powerful anxieties related to the very-mounting road accident death toll" in the United States at the time of the film's release.[49] This latter interpretation, predicated on the idea that midcentury mass automobility and the construction of the US Interstate Highway System brought not only greater freedom but also heightened levels of social panic as a result of increasing numbers of car-crash fatalities, is one of the most original, historically informed takes on this film to emerge since its 1962 theatrical release. But Murphy's reading is hardly the last word on a motion picture that, six decades removed from its original context, continues to attract horror fans *because* it lacks the superficially comforting type of narrative closure traditionally associated with other genre productions (e.g., the happy endings of romantic comedies and musicals). Indeed, *Carnival of Souls*' elusiveness as a text—its vagueness with regard to what *really* happened to Mary (even after concluding shots back in Kansas suggest that she has apparently been dead the whole time)—is one reason for its enduring appeal. Of course, other factors have contributed to this unassuming sleeper's late success, from its televisual "reincarnations" during the 1970s, when it was on heavy late-show rotation, to its theatrical rerelease at the end of the 1980s, when it was promoted as "the movie that wouldn't die" and raked in considerable coinage at arthouse and revival theaters in forty-seven cities.[50] That expression is the title of a documentary about the 1989 reunion of the film's cast and crew: *The Movie That Wouldn't Die!*, one of several supplemental features included on the Criterion Collection's lovingly packaged DVD of *Carnival of Souls* that was published a decade after its theatrical rerelease.

Anyone hoping for simple, straightforward answers to this film's lingering mysteries in the documentary or any of the other paratextual materials on the Criterion release will be disappointed. This is not because the cast and crew, including director Herk Harvey and novelist/screenwriter John Clifford (who share speaking duties on the disc's audio commentary), have been tightlipped about such things, guarding *Carnival of Souls*' secrets so as to maintain its mystique as a belatedly appreciated "cult classic" (to borrow Harvey's own words). Rather, they themselves are unsure about *what it all means*, saying as much whenever pressed to provide clarifying clues or definitive statements in response to the question, "What actually occurred when [Mary] went in the river and came out?" In the commentary track that graces the Criterion DVD, and which was ported over to the same company's digitally restored Blu-ray edition in 2016, Harvey puts that exact question to

Clifford as a summary of the many inquiries he has had to field from fans over the years (e.g., "Is Mary a poltergeist, or did she really come back and live, or was this all imagination?"). The screenwriter's spoken response—"I hate to admit to people that I don't know the answers to these things"—coincides with one of the film's darkest passages, the pitch-black nighttime scene (around the fourteen-minute mark of the eighty-three-minute extended director's cut) in which the female protagonist silently drives toward her destination in Utah and passes by the main setting, a haunted pavilion, for the first time. It is an appropriately nebulous visual accompaniment to these two collaborators' admission of being perpetually "in the dark" about their own film.

Notably, the Criterion Collection, a world-class home-video distribution company celebrated for its high-quality transfers and "definitive editions" of landmark films packed with value-boosting bonus features, prides itself on shedding *light* on various aspects related to the production and reception of those films and in giving viewers the opportunity to "look at [them] 'with a new eye.'"[51] The company's Blu-ray edition, sporting a 4K digital transfer and a new interview with comedian-fan Dana Gould as well as a new video essay by film critic David Cairns, on top of deleted scenes, outtakes, English-language SDH, a visual history of the Saltair Resort in Salt Lake City, and excerpts from movies made by the Centron Corporation ("an industrial film company based in Lawrence, Kansas, that once employed Harvey and Clifford"), is how many of today's connoisseurs of world cinema first encounter or rewatch *Carnival of Souls*. This means that the film's place in the cinephilic canon—with Criterion spine number 63, sandwiched humbly between Carl Theodor Dreyer's *The Passion of Joan of Arc* (*La Passion de Jeanne d'Arc*, 1928) at number 62 and Carol Reed's *The Third Man* (1949) at number 64—is firmly secured and well supported by paratexts like these. One of the other bonus features on that Criterion release is the aforementioned audio commentary, which, despite not offering any trenchant insights into the underlying themes or meanings of the film, is enlightening as an entrée into its production history, the logistics of shooting on a limited budget, the mixed reception at its premiere in Lawrence, Kansas, the filmmakers' troubles with stateside distributors and bounced checks, its pairing on drive-in double bills with *The Devil's Messenger* (1961), and its gradual transformation into an "accidental masterpiece."

On the commentary track, Harvey talks about how he and his small crew—primarily assistant director Reza Badiyi, cinematographer Maurice Prather, and sound recorders Ed Down and Don Jessup—managed to stick to a three-to-one shooting ratio (meaning that they were not able to do many retakes) and achieved some fairly rudimentary practical effects on a budget of $30,000 (with deferred salaries of $13,000 for himself, Clifford, and Prather, leaving just $17,000 for all shooting and distribution-related costs on their end). After discussing the challenge of syncing the sound of Mary's clicking shoes on the boardwalk (an effect that he foleyed himself with high heels and a piece of plywood), the director chuckles about his film's "amateurishness," one of many self-effacing remarks that he makes on this track. Here Harvey's comments recall the way that other filmmakers with limited budgets—from James L. Conway (director of *The Boogens* [1981], released on Blu-ray by Olive Films) to Kevin S. Tenney (director of *The Cellar* [1989], released on Blu-ray by Vinegar Syndrome) and Stevan Mena (director of *Malevolence* [2004], released on Blu-ray by Mena Films)—have modestly called out the technical mistakes (e.g., camera reflections, continuity errors, visible boom mics) and even artistic failings of their own work in similarly self-deprecating audio commentaries. Like many of today's younger horror filmmakers, Harvey seems to understand that the various "shortcomings" of his picture, from its poorly looped dialogue and obvious lip-syncing to its many glaring continuity errors, are endearing in the eyes of hardcore fans. Moreover, as Kenneth George Godwin states in his review of both the film and the Criterion Blu-ray release, such gaffes actually complement the epistemological uncertainty of *Carnival of Souls*, "a case of technical limitations (perhaps inadvertently) becoming valuable creative elements" in the filmmakers' attempt to "emphasize the unnaturalness of the world Mary finds herself in."[52] In contrast to his and Clifford's graceful sidestepping of the question of what *Carnival of Souls* ultimately "means" or how one might interpret its dream-logic narrative, Harvey's forthrightness about perceived deficiencies in the script or imperfections in his handling of that material strikes me as an opportunity to rethink how we usually go about analyzing horror films.

In one of the most illuminating, if seemingly trivial, passages of the audio commentary included on the Criterion DVD, Harvey notes that Sidney Berger, the only member of the film's cast besides lead actor

Candace Hilligos to have professional theater training (which he brought to bear on his convincing performance as the creepy neighbor across the hall), had, in his words, a "false eye." The director references this when Berger's obnoxious character, John, first appears onscreen and peers through a crack in Mary's partially open door to ogle her as she gets dressed. Cutting to an extreme close-up of the prosthetic, the filmmaker makes a point of showing how the female protagonist, who has just gotten out of the bathtub and now hurries to clothe herself in the presence of a stranger, is ensconced within a world that, if not explicitly hostile toward her, presses down on her with the surveillant force of a predatory male gaze. "Actually, he couldn't see *anything* with it," Harvey says about the actor's glass eye, a remark that paratextually anticipates one of the strangest moments in the text: a scene when Mary appears to disappear in the presence of clothing store shoppers, who can neither see her nor hear her despite her increasingly desperate efforts to have her existence be recognized as such.

That scene likewise anticipates a lengthier sequence filled with watery, vision-blurring dissolves near the end of the film, leading up to her disappearance: Mary once again realizes that no one around her seems to notice her, and in voice-over muses to herself, "They can't *see* me. Why can't they see me?" after flashing her now-customary look of wide-eyed surprise. On the surface, this sets up the revelation, provisional though it is, that she is a ghost who has been flickering into and out of existence ever since the automobile accident back in Kansas. But, on a deeper level, this emphasis on seeing and not seeing in *Carnival of Souls*, brought to light in the director's audio commentary, poses a dilemma for audiences who—seeking to make sense of a motion picture as willfully vague as this—rely upon the falsely superior perceiving power of the eye to the exclusion of other sensing organs. Moreover, the commentary itself, as a kind of prosthetic vision of what happened during the making of the film, stops short of resolving narrative ambiguities or settling viewers' questions about Mary's ontological status, underscoring once again the compromised value of sight when *nothing* can be believed.

The extreme close-up shot of the man's eye—an organ at once capable of sight (invasively so in the context of the film's narrative) and incapable of sight (an artificial implant prosthetically filling in for the missing body part in the context of the film's production)—is highly suggestive and overdetermined within the larger context of horror film hermeneutics, given the preponderance of such imagery across the history of the genre. Reminding her readers that "eyes are everywhere in horror cinema," no less an authority on the matter than Carol Clover has weighed in on the supertextual suggestiveness of a perceiving organ that suffuses not only individual texts but their promotional materials as well.[53] But by putting so much emphasis on ocular iconography and the *visual* rather than *aural*—or, for that matter, tactile, olfactory, and gustatory—appeals of cinematic horror, we miss opportunities to reflect on a wider set of corporeal and sensorial demands placed on audiences who are expected to "feel" everything that the characters experience at their most terrified or repulsed moments, when death, decay, or damnation is only a hair's breadth away. Besides shifting focus from the visual plane to the aural plane, audio commentaries like the one that *Carnival of Souls*' director Herk Harvey recorded for his movie's home-video release hint at how the most frightfully insightful clues to a horror film's effectiveness as a body genre, if not to its underlying meanings, derive not from sight but from the sound of someone taking his or her listeners by the ear and whispering something truthful about that film's production, which has perhaps placed an even more disturbing amount of corporeal and sensorial demands on its cast and crew for the sake of entertainment.[54]

# 2

# (NOT) SEEING IS BELIEVING

## Ghostly Bodies, Heretical Texts, and Hysterical Failures

To see only with one's eyes is hardly to see at all.

—James Palmer and Michael Riley, "Seeing, Believing, and 'Knowing' in Narrative Film: *Don't Look Now* Revisited"

The adage "Seeing is believing," which dates back to the writings of seventeenth-century clergyman Thomas Fuller and possibly to earlier texts that emphasize the primacy of sight over other senses, has been uttered by characters on more than one occasion throughout the history of cinematic horror, fantasy, and science fiction, in films as varied as *Don't Look Now* (1973), *The Company of Wolves* (1984), *Species* (1995), *Final Destination 3* (2006), and *The Eye* (2008). It has even found its way into a few films' promotional materials, including the trailer for Darren Aronofsky's biblical allegory *Mother!* (2017) and the one-sheet poster for Joe Wright's *The Woman in the Window* (2021), a Hitchcockian suspense thriller reminiscent of that most metatextual of mid-twentieth-century studio releases, *Rear Window* (1954). It is therefore not surprising that the expression lends itself so readily to critical discussions of the genre, especially given what Steffen Hantke refers to as the "scopophilic demand in horror films for the audience to *see* the monster."[1] Indeed, Hantke himself uses the phrase "Seeing Is Believing" as the title of an introductory section of his essay about the challenges faced by filmmakers—in particular industry personnel who worked on motion pictures prior to the widespread use of CGI beginning in the 1980s and 1990s—in visually rendering the presence of ghosts onscreen, despite the apparent commensurability between these liminal beings (situated between the world of the living and the world of the dead) and cinema as a spectral medium well suited for such phantasmatic representations. In his words, the ghost's "impossible ontological liminality" as a visibly invisible sign of ethereal uncanniness presents a problem when it comes to arresting or fixing it in place as a "stable cinematic image," though the technological tools through which to achieve that effect have developed to a point where even the most unbelievable of premises can be believed.[2]

Inspired by a line spoken repeatedly by Donald Sutherland's character John Baxter in director Nicolas Roeg's *Don't Look Now*, Marsha Kinder and Beverle Houston likewise use "Seeing Is Believing" as the title of a cowritten essay that compares that film to another critically lauded work from that same year, director William Friedkin's *The Exorcist*. Although both of these motion pictures "deny psychological explanations of the supernatural and accept the metaphysical nature of good and evil," Roeg's experimental occult thriller is deemed the more radical of the two in its merging of the banal and the extraordinary and in finally dissolving the Manichean binaries that structure Friedkin's Oscar-nominated stomach-churner.[3] Based on a 1971 short story of the same title by Daphne du Maurier, *Don't Look Now* asks audiences to "see in new ways and confront the problems of interpretation."[4] This is something that John too must do as he gradually (if unwillingly) learns to accept his "non-ordinary" gift of second sight and to follow a blind psychic's lead in "seeing" his dead daughter. Although the young girl, Christine (Sharon Williams), accidentally drowned before John and his grief-stricken wife, Laura (Julie Christie), relocated to Venice, he catches brief glimpses of her in what can only be described as clairvoyant flashes: She pops up, pixie-like, around the canals and dark alleyways that he traverses, each time wearing what looks to be the same red raincoat that she wore the day she died. It is also there, in the appropriately nicknamed floating city, where he meets the unseeing yet all-seeing psychic (Hilary Mason), an eccentric middle-aged English woman vacationing in Venice and accompanied by her more conventionally sighted sister (Clelia Matania), whose otherwise perfect vision is momentarily impaired when a speck of dust gets in her eye. This, Kinder and Houston point out, is one of several instances in the appropriately titled *Don't Look Now* when conventional notions of present-tense "looking" (tied to one's sense of sight) give way to alternative ways of envisioning past and future events, brought together in the person of the strangely intuitive woman whose various insights into the grieving couple's personal tragedy are met with skepticism (by John) and acceptance (by Laura).[5]

The blind psychic's combined *dis*-ability and *super*-ability further demonstrate the film's commitment to blurring the lines between phenomenological states, including that between physically embodied perception and mystically endowed intuition. A smattering of flashbacks and flashforwards, some of which lack context, interrupt the diegesis, thereby extending John's own visionary power—his unsettling premonitions—to the spectator, who becomes "clairvoyant" of an impending fate awaiting this tragically doubting and therefore doomed (if not damned) character. In the end, comprehension comes too late for the protagonist. John's failure "to recognize and believe in the nonrational, visionary world" and misinterpretation of the signs pointing toward his own death (at the hands of a small-statured serial killer wearing the eerily familiar red mackintosh) are finally spelled out to him and the audience when the diminutive murderer pulls out her meat cleaver and slashes his throat.[6]

As James Palmer and Michael Riley state in another cowritten article about *Don't Look Now*, "John's narrow insistence that 'seeing is believing,'" which runs counter to religious teachings across various faith communities, makes him vulnerable to "deceptive appearances."[7] The other phrase that he repeats (but seems to forget) over the course of the film, "Nothing is what it seems," should have made him more skeptical of his own skepticism and might have spared him from joining his daughter in death. What is revealed in that fateful run-in with the Venetian killer is that, rather than being haunted by memories of his dead child reaching out to him from beyond the grave, John has been having prophetic visions of his own demise. By asserting the primacy of sight over vision, or rather by "turning a blind eye" to *other* types of seeing embodied by the literally sightless psychic woman (who uses her hearing and sense of touch to engage the physical world while harnessing the power of her mind's eye to peer into the unknown), he joins a long list of rationally minded movie characters doomed to repeat the mistakes of their scientific forebearers on the silver screen. On a metatextual level, his actions, which parallel the failures of the Venice police "to discover the elusive killer preying on the city," and which lead him, almost willfully, to that decisive moment when he is blindsided by the truth, reflect our own investigatory spectatorial drive.[8] In searching for meanings of texts or for answers to mysteries that have already been revealed to us in an untold number of previous horror films where there is *another world* (a different reality "beyond what one conventionally sees and hears"), we follow in John's footsteps, though the consequences of our disbelief are less fateful than those that bring his pursuit of truth to a sudden end. If we find ourselves questioning what we have seen by the end of *Don't Look Now*, it is perhaps because we have forgotten the second half of Thomas Fuller's famous aphorism, "Seeing is believing, but *feeling is the truth*."[9]

Both the inner and outer forms of "feeling," connoting emotional and tactile sensitivities (i.e., the abilities to "think" with the heart and to "see" through touch), are palpably present in several horror films, including the second of the two case studies discussed by Kinder and Houston in their aforementioned essay "Seeing Is Believing." Written for the screen by William Peter Blatty (author of the 1971 novel on which it is based), *The Exorcist* is concrete, confrontational, and explicit where *Don't Look Now* is abstract, elusive, and inscrutable, though its lessons about the dangers of misinterpretation are no less powerful than Roeg's film. This much-discussed adaptation, which Friedkin made on the grime-caked heels of his equally successful crime thriller *The French Connection* (1971), has continually appeared in "best of" lists of the greatest horror films ever made, a sign that the young director managed to skillfully balance expressionist and realist aesthetics while successfully exploiting the medium's latent capacity to "manipulate feeling."[10] Notably, in his four-star review of *The Exorcist* (published in *The Chicago Sun-Times* on the date of its theatrical premiere, December 26, 1973), film critic Roger Ebert uses the words "feel" and "feeling" five times, apparently unable to shake off the shock of witnessing Linda Blair's twelve-year-old character, Regan MacNeil, being possessed by an evil spirit and suffering all manner of physical and psychological abuse (which some characters in the film attribute to "a severe neurological disorder"). Ebert was not alone in experiencing those negatively charged yet positively interpreted emotions: Contemporaneous reports indicate that audiences who saw the film upon its initial release "routinely fainted, vomited, and even suffered heart attacks."[11] In the words of Charles Derry, "Seeing *The Exorcist* was a rite of passage," and only those viewers who passed out or puked up their lunches were the "winners," reaffirming "man's ability to be revolted, his ability to *feel*."[12] Putting aside the strong possibility that such accounts are slight exaggerations (which have only grown more sensationalistic over time), Friedkin's graphically violent, obscenity-laden film—which Ebert called a "frontal assault" on the senses—was framed by the press and the distributor (Warner Bros.) as something that had to be *seen* to be believed.[13]

It is for that reason that Kinder and Houston single out *The Exorcist*, noting how makeup, prosthetics, sound effects, and other tricks of the trade are deployed to transform, "before your own eyes," an adolescent girl into a "yellow-eyed, thick-lipped, scarred and growling monster, who spews out jets of bright green bile."[14] The puke-inducing physical evidence of Regan's demonic possession, including her memorable 180-degree head-turn (which radiates "authenticity" through makeup artist Dick Smith's use of plastic molds of the young actress's body), might be all that is required for audiences to momentarily suspend their disbelief in mythological creatures like Pazuzu (the film's unholy intruder, an Assyrian demon later identified by name in the 1977 sequel *Exorcist II: The Heretic*). But the abject fact of Pazuzu's hold over the girl's ravaged body, which performs actions that defy the laws of physics, is counterbalanced by the medical diagnoses supplied by Regan's doctors, who refuse to validate her panicked mother's account of the events. Worst of all, they attempt to explain away inexplicable phenomena as well as the girl's "abnormal strength [and] accelerated motor performance" as "pathological states." Exasperated by their medical jargon, Chris MacNeil (Ellen Burstyn) grows further incensed upon hearing the doctors' claim that an exorcism might finally work on her daughter "only because the patient believes [she's] possessed . . . purely by force of suggestion." Having witnessed what Chris has seen (in earlier scenes), audiences might share her outrage, which finally bubbles over when she screams, "Jesus Christ!" before asking the men: "Did you *see* her or not?"

In posing that question, Chris—whose first name is one letter shy of a reference to the Bible's foremost figure of faith (the savior whom religious adherents believe to be the son of God)—stresses the evidentiary power of the eye to behold that which *cannot literally be held* or even cognitively grasped by men of science. Capping this pivotal scene in

*The Exorcist* with the sarcastic conclusion that a "witch doctor" might be better equipped to handle her daughter's dire predicament, she shifts her rhetorical inquisition into these medical specialists' suitability for the job at hand away from "Christ" (a faith-based healer in holy scriptures) toward one of the horror genre's most commonly recurring personages: a stereotypically "othered" specialist in the dark arts (the very practices that lend the 1964 film *Witchcraft*, which I discussed in chapter 1, its title). Of course, what Chris has in mind are not the kind of indigenous folk figures showcased in earlier films, ranging from Depression-era classics like *White Zombie* (1932) and *King Kong* (1933) to postwar jungle exotica like the *Captive Girl* (1950) and *Voodoo Woman* (1957) and regional curios of the mid-1960s like *Moro Witch Doctor* (1964) and *Death Curse of Tartu* (1966), which, to varying degrees, reflect deeply embedded racist fears or white colonialist fantasies of "natives" whose superstitious beliefs contrast the scientific advancements of American and European "civilization."[15] Instead, she turns to the Western world's version of the witch doctor, a Jesuit priest named Damien Karras (Jason Miller). Trained in psychiatry, Damien is initially shown struggling with his faith, but eventually—as the right-hand man to the ill-fated Father Lankester Merrin (Max von Sydow)—he plays a pivotal role in saving the physically and mentally scarred Regan from her unseen, unholy assailant.

Another psychiatrist—this time a nonreligious specialist in mental health—appears in *The Exorcist*'s 1977 sequel, *Exorcist II: The Heretic*. Directed by John Boorman, this critically damned *film maudit* continues to pop up in "Worst Of" lists, even though time and lavishly packaged collector's edition DVD and Blu-ray sets have given its harshest reviewers the opportunity to reconsider their initial reactions upon subsequent viewings (a kind of "second sight" affordance of contemporary media culture whereby what was once derided can now be appreciated). The doctor in question is Gene Tuskin and, as played by Louise Fletcher—best known for her portrayal of the cold-hearted Nurse Ratched in *One Flew Over the Cuckoo's Nest* (1975)—she is every bit the unimpassioned scientific rationalist we would expect her to be (from having encountered other onscreen representatives of her profession attempting to explain away paranormal phenomena through logic and reason). Monitoring Regan's condition at a children's psychiatric institute in New York and speaking to Father Philip Lamont (Richard Burton), a Catholic priest whose religious doubts remind one of the struggles faced by Father Damien in the first film, Dr. Tuskin insists that the residual effects of her patient's painful experiences can be chalked up to "mental illness," not to the presence of "evil."

In an effort to help Regan confront her repressed guilt for her role in Father Merrin's death four years earlier, Dr. Tuskin hooks the teenager up to a medical device outfitted with strobe lights and EEG biofeedback electrodes, one that allows patient and doctor to coordinate their brainwaves and perceive the same recollections of past events through synchronous hypnosis. Connected to Regan in this way, Father Lamont comes "face to face with the evil that's inside her" and calls the so-called "Synchronizer" a marvel of modern science, capable of proving *scientifically* that "there there's an ancient demon locked within her." Casting a condescending gaze at the priest, the psychiatrist responds that "the machine is simply a mechanical device to penetrate psychological states," and that what he saw "could just have easily been a dream, a fantasy, a hallucination, *not* a memory." "We make our own 'demons' up *here*," she insists, pointing at her head. She will later eat those words when she sees firsthand the continued effects that Pazuzu has not only on Regan but on all those who come into her orbit and care about her safety. By the end of *Exorcist II: The Heretic*, Dr. Tuskin is ready to make amends for her earlier mistrust of Father Lamont's wild assertions and apologizes to Regan, telling her, "I understand now, [but] the world won't. Not yet."

At first glance, the psychiatrist's journey from disbelief to belief, propelled by the twin engines of an audiovisual machine (cinema) that privileges sight (first) and sound (second) as operative means of adducing the "truth" of such claims, is not all that remarkable. Indeed, one can discern a similar movement away from skepticism toward acceptance and outright fear of the unknown in innumerable examples of the genre, from *Gothika* (2003), which likewise features a clinical psychologist, Dr. Miranda Grey (Halle Berry), who describes herself as a "rational person" before admitting that she was wrong to deny the existence of ghosts (and might actually be possessed), to *The Skeptic* (a.k.a. *The Haunting of Bryan Becket*, 2009), which virtually repeats that dialogue in the voice of yet another doctor who states flatly, "I don't believe in anything supernatural," only to see the error of his ways by narrative's end. What sets *Exorcist II: The Heretic* apart from these and other films, however, is its introduction of a Synchronizer machine that binds people together, fusing their (potentially conflicting) views of the world—their "altered states"—into a single vision. In that respect, it makes for a fitting allegory of the cinematic apparatus, which, positioned between filmmaker and spectator, unites two forms of embodied perception and encompasses not only the "film body" but also its "enabling mechanisms" (including, but not limited to, the motion picture camera and projector).[16] In his summary of Vivian Sobchack's phenomenological approach to what she calls "instrument mediation," Sean Cubitt reminds us that the experience of film is "simultaneously human and mechanical."[17] But this utopian intersubjectivity extends further into the realm of magical thinking (farfetched to some readers, but believable to this author) when we consider how the "technologies of vision" that are locked together during moments of cinematic perception create more than just a feedback loop.[18] They constitute a "regime of seeing" that disciplines the gaze as much as it enables new ways of looking at the world (outside of one's own subjectivity, through other people's eyes).

With respect to the Synchronizer, the scene that best brings this hypnosis machine's allegorical resonances to light occurs a mere fifteen minutes into the narrative. Regan and Dr. Tuskin don the linked headsets in an effort to better understand what actually happened to her and to Father Merrin during that fateful encounter four years ago. When a lab assistant asks the girl if she can recall the traumatic event, Dr. Tuskin, who is seated across from her subject, suddenly gasps in horror, for she has been granted a vision of Regan as she once looked: a physically and spiritually ravaged pawn of Pazuzu who suddenly springs up on her left side (in the girl's bed back in Georgetown but also in the clinic where this experiment in cross-consciousness is taking place). Or, rather, a ghostly palimpsest of the demonically possessed child materializes, as does the similarly transparent body of Father Merrin, who—situated on the psychiatrist's right side—performs the dispossession that occurred during the climactic scenes of the original film (leading up to his death). By this point, Regan has already removed her headset and Father Lamont has put it on, so that he might see with his own eyes what, until this moment, had been taken on faith. With Regan now standing behind her and placing her hand atop the older woman's breast in an attempt to ease her paralyzing fear (while the phantom version of Regan reaches into her chest to fondle her fibrillating heart), Dr. Tuskin is surrounded on all sides by figures who are either physically or metaphysically present. Significantly, our view of this image is from Father Lamont's ocular perspective, seated across from the woman who, like him (and similar to a moviegoer sitting before a screen), appears to be in a trance, her mouth agape as she casts a distant yet terrified gaze (fig. 2.1).[19]

Although they are not the same kind of liminal beings alluded to by Steffen Hantke in his essay about Hollywood's pre-CGI ghosts, these apparitional projections of the dead priest and the demonically possessed girl have a "spectral presence" similar to the spirits on view in earlier studio productions such as Paramount's *The Uninvited* (1944). Like that classic ghost tale, which also revolves around possession and dramatically reveals the previously unseen culprit during its climactic scene, *Exorcist II: The Heretic* achieves that otherworldly special effect through old-fashioned means. However, rather than rely upon the "trick photography" of double exposure, cinematographer William A. Fraker and his camera crew used a light-sensitive semitransparent mirror, which allowed a 50 percent transmission of the scene set up behind the surface while reflecting another scene, occurring simultaneously and staged adjacently to the action. Colloquially known as "ghost glass," the

**Figure 2.1:** In *Exorcist II: The Heretic*, the spectral presence of the dead priest Father Merrin and an earlier version of Regan as a demonically possessed girl was achieved through a device known in the special effects community as "Ghost Glass."

device, which has been employed by filmmakers since the silent era, gives the uncanny impression "that the action happening within a single shot [is] taking place in two separate locations and times," since the camera catches the reflection of one scene while shooting through the semi-transparent mirror to record another scene.[20] When asked how this elaborate effect was achieved, Fraker explained that the actors involved in the two scenes (Burton, Fletcher, and Blair in Dr. Tuskin's office, Max von Sydow and a double for Regan in a recreation of the original exorcism in Georgetown) were arranged on two adjacent sets and asked to perform their roles at the same time, with "the camera shooting through [the ghost glass] to record both images on the same strip of film" and the light levels being adjusted to either strengthen or weaken the visibility of one scene relative the other.[21]

In harnessing the practical effect of ghost glass, which creates the appearance of double exposure during the *production* stage rather than the postproduction stage (when most final editing takes place), Boorman's film relocates the "site of abjection from something existing prior to, or separate from, the cinematic apparatus to the site of *the cinematic apparatus itself*."[22] Mechanically rather than optically superimposing two images, which together show the stunned face of scientific rationality being beset on either side by the forces of "good" and "evil," this thirty-second effect gives us two ways of looking at supernatural phenomena, which are simultaneously "there" and "not there" in a single shot. Thus, the moral binaries of this and the preceding film—two texts that are likewise joined together by name/title (with one, the original *Exorcist*, being championed as a believably "real" horror film, and the other, this sequel, being chastised as an unbelievably "bad" cash grab on the part of Warner Bros. executives)—are extended to their aesthetic framing of *supernatural* phenomena such as second sight as "*cinematic* phenomena."[23]

In fact, dichotomies pile up in and around *Exorcist II: The Heretic*, which is itself a doubly "heretical" text, a film with two different endings: one capping the original 118-minute version, the other a reworked climax to a much shorter version that was released in theaters following the initial wave of negative reviews (including that of *The New York Times*, which called it "second-rate").[24] Within both versions there are split-screen effects as well as two immolation scenes involving young women, both of whom meet untimely ends as Pazuzu's temporary playthings and thus serve as bookending reminders of the life-or-death stakes faced by the demon's principal target, Regan. And, as pointed out by the *New York Times*' critic who reviewed the film one day after its theatrical premiere, the first half of *Exorcist II: The Heretic* employs "a fancified exercise in what might be called 'simultaneity', which simply means it contains lots of crosscutting between scenes of simultaneous action, in this case involving characters who are supposed to be in telepathic communication."[25] The second half of the film divides its time between two periods and two places, oscillating between present-day scenes in New York and past events in an unspecified location in Africa, a "strange mud city" called Jepti (to borrow Regan's words) where Father Merrin had lent his skills in exorcism to a young boy named Kokumo years ago.

Rather than depict those events in Africa as a standard flashback, the film shows Father Lamont, once again hooked up to Regan via the Synchronizer, gaining mental access to them as if he were able to share the young girl's supernaturally evolved channeling ability. When he follows in Merrin's footsteps and makes his own journey to the African continent to see if the adult Kokumo (James Earl Jones) might hold the key to defeating the demon Pazuzu (who takes the form of locusts), Lamont finds that the man is both scientist and witch doctor, someone who is simultaneously "advanced" and "primitive" according to the film's starkly dichotomous, stereotype-laden representational schema.[26] Though Lamont initially cautions Dr. Tuskin that the groundbreaking experiments she and her team are conducting (and which point ahead, toward future discoveries) might lead people to "look in the wrong direction, *toward Satan*," the film ultimately makes the conciliatory gesture of requiring *both* empirical evidence and embodied belief before the various people involved—those who remain alive at the end—are able to overcome past traumas and move forward.

In that respect, the film "speaks" in two voices at once, not unlike Regan near the end, after she and Father Lamont have returned to the Georgetown residence where it all started (in the previous film), and she finds herself once again in the thrall of a demon. In the seconds leading up to Lamont's successful attempt to banish Pazuzu from earthly existence by ripping out the heart of Regan's succubus-like doppelgänger (who had earlier seduced him into her bed), the teenaged girl opens her mouth to speak, but her voice is joined by that of Kokumo. They say in unison that she is the “Good Locust” who will “break the chain reaction” of demonic possessions that have resulted in other lives lost. Then, Regan speaks in Father Merrin’s voice, overlaid with her own, as they together instruct Lamont on how to break the spell (by tearing out the succubus’s “evil heart”). This sonic superimposition emulates the visual effect described above, in which the ghost glass makes it possible for audiences to see two events at once. Eventually, the demon’s hold over Regan weakens to the point that she is free. At that point, the brick house where the penultimate scene’s cataclysmic events have been playing out (but which go entirely unnoticed by anyone else in the neighborhood, confirming the suspicion that all of this is happening in a parallel world or collective mind-space) splits in two, a literalization of the heretical break that prompted Lamont to get involved in Merrin’s case in the first place. As the building’s foundation shifts and the structure collapses, viewers are left with parting shots that further suggest how everything that William Peter Blatty and William Friedkin had built in *The Exorcist* was being torn asunder by this critically derided “secondary” text.

## *Exorcist II*: The Version You’ve Never Heard

Sometimes, *hearing* is believing.

—Adam Nayman, “The Best Horror Movies of 2021 (So Far),” The Ringer (April 28, 2021)

In his 2021 online article about some of the most noteworthy horror films of that year (four months in), Adam Nayman argues that “horror films don’t have to be plausible, logical, or even necessarily coherent to be great. Some are at their best when they leave all three of these adjectives in the dust.” No one would accuse *Exorcist II: The Heretic* of being plausible, logical, or even coherent throughout much of its globetrotting yet hermetically sealed-off narrative, which treats the potentially earth-shattering demonic possession of Regan as a personal trauma best left to a few interested parties and suggests that the events of the story are of little consequence to anyone outside her immediate vicinity. To many audiences, this sequel to William Friedkin’s truly horrifying film (made four years earlier, at a time when the novelty of witnessing a twelve-year-old character stabbing her vagina with a crucifix while screaming "Fuck me!" was unparalleled in its shock value) did not measure up to its predecessor. After all, *The Exorcist* was, in Nayman's words, "convincing" in the way that it turned even the most skeptical among us into "believers." He states, "We watch Father Karras's skepticism melt away and realize ours has evaporated as well."[27] It is something that has been much slower to come for those of us who watch Dr. Tuskin undergo a similar spiritual transformation, to the point where she finally says the word "Pazuzu" when asked to name the source of Regan's traumatic childhood experiences near the end of the film. But just as the psychiatrist has a change of heart during the penultimate scene, so too do several critics and commentators now seem to be ready to evaluate the sequel not only on its own merits but also through tools unique to the present-day media convergence and digital technologies.

Now that it has been made available as a special collector's edition Blu-ray release from home-video distributor Shout Factory in 2018, *Exorcist II: The Heretic* is finally being reappraised as a misunderstood entry in the *Exorcist* franchise (which currently includes six films released by Warner Bros. Pictures and 20th Century-Fox). This has resulted in another "split" in the form of divided opinions on the film, which seemed to generate only negative feelings throughout much of its life as a universally reviled work that not only verges toward but also crosses over into camp.[28] In fact, the (unintentional) campiness of *Exorcist II: The Heretic*, magnified by the sight of James Earl Jones decked out in a flamboyant locust costume and Linda Blair performing an eye-rolling tap-dancing number, is perhaps better received today than it was at the time of its original theatrical release. Indeed, several reviewers of the recent Blu-ray release have warmed up to the sequel's ambitious attempt to replace what Daniel Humphrey refers to as "the first film's rather simple good-versus-evil, literalist theology with a more complex, progressive, almost 'new age' theology inspired by the heretical writings of French Jesuit Pierre Teilhard de Chardin."[29] Shout Factory's supplement-packed collector's edition of this "spectacular failure" reveals its counterintuitive *success* in riling up the original film's fan base and extending the franchise's mythos into uncharted territory. It also provides access to an assistive technology—specifically subtitles for the deaf and hard of hearing (SDH)—in addition to now-commonplace features such as making-of documentaries and bonus audio commentaries from filmmaking personnel that make it possible to *see* and, perhaps more importantly, *hear* the film in a new light.

As I will elaborate in the second half of this book, SDH is "assistive" in more ways than one. Besides making both spoken dialogue and nondialogue audio elements (including noises and music) accessible to anyone who can see printed text, it provides an interpretative lens through which to perceive the relationship between a film's images and its sounds. Sound, in fact, becomes *part of the image* to the extent that the printed text, usually located near the bottom of the screen (unless other onscreen words would be obscured by that subtitling), can be seen by the eyes. But the exigencies of cueing the audience to important sonic elements while keeping pace with a motion picture's moment-to-moment unfolding also means that several sounds drop by the narrative wayside and go "unheard." That is, not *all* of the noises and musical elements are textually translated for viewers reliant on sight to "hear" things that other audiences—those who have not experienced hearing loss (or deaf gain)—can access through their ears and a decent set of audio speakers. Besides narrowing in on just a few of the many facets of a much larger acoustic field, filled with ambient, background, or environmental noises and the layering of voices in an ebb and flow of modulated variety, SDH frequently deprives the audience of those properties of sound, such as pitch (or frequency), intensity (or amplitude), and color (or timbre), that might impart clarifying clues about the sometimes-mystifying nature, source, and/or effect of terror or revulsion in horror films; such that the *form* of speech and other sounds is often ignored in favor of their *content*. Even more egregiously, translation errors sometimes go undetected through the proofreading process during the production of DVDs and Blu-rays, resulting in odd—sometimes oddly appropriate—subtitles. For instance, Synapse Film's 2017 home-video release of the 1991 slasher-comedy *Popcorn* features a scene in which an audience member attending a screening of one of the three fictional films within the film (the giant insect movie *Mosquito*) yells, "Bring on the *bugs*!" though the line is miscaptioned as "Bring on the *boos*!" And yet, for all of its built-in "deficiencies" (a word that is troublesome in the context of disability studies), SDH can enliven spectators' engagement with a cinematic text by emphasizing certain types of sounds and linguistic descriptors over others while drawing intertextual parallels between other captioned films that would not be apparent to the naked eye otherwise.

Viewers who watch the Blu-ray of the original cut of *Exorcist II: The Heretic* with its SDH feature enabled will see that the first captioned text, flashing onscreen right as John Boorman's name appears in the opening credits, is "[woman moans]." Within a few seconds, another parenthetically bracketed signifier, "[woman screams]," appears, followed by "[demon howling]" and "[woman shouts]." At this point, the only other images are the names and job titles associated with the film's above-the-line creative talent, printed as blood-red text atop a black background. Before the narrative has even begun, the audience is thrust into a darkened world where three distinct vocalizations—at this point, unattached to any one person (or possibly more people) and unmarked by descriptors that might indicate whether the moan, scream, and shout are of ecstasy or terror (or a different emotion in between those two extremes)—provide little in the way of orientation. However, by *not* signaling the emotional characteristics of those vocalizations, the captioned text allows for the possibility that *other* sensations *besides* fright might be latent within the film, which notably builds toward concluding scenes (some ninety minutes later) that show Regan's temptress-like doppelgänger in bed and which bring this eroticizing potential full circle. To take three radically different motion pictures as objects of comparison, the SDH services provided by the on-demand streaming video platform Kanopy for the blaxploitation horror film *Blackenstein* (1973), the Italian giallo film *The New York Ripper* (*Lo squartatore di New York*, 1982), and the feminist horror-comedy *The Love Witch* (2016) deploy the words "(moans)" and "(moaning)" frequently during scenes filled with either frank sexual content or barely sublimated desire. Even when the threat of violence is apparent, as happens near the end of *Blackenstein*, which shows the title monster (played by Joe De Sue) carrying his latest victim in his arms—a woman squirming to get free even as she voices a perverse pleasure in her predicament—to the accompaniment of the parenthetically transcribed words "(woman moans)," the sadomasochist underpinnings of that particular sound are exploited to put the viewer on shaky ground.

Audiences with the ability to hear those individually bracketed introductory sounds during the title sequence of *Exorcist II: The Heretic* will likely ascertain the ensuing scene's emotional cadences. Those cadences are soon revealed to hinge upon the demonic possession of a woman who is surrounded by a "[crowd chattering in foreign language]" and joined by Father Lamont, armed with a vial of holy water but ultimately unable to prevent her death—the first of the film's two immolation scenes (sparked by her clothes brushing up against candles). Refusing to specify what that "foreign language" is or hint at where this opening scene (peopled with Latin American women) might be located, the SDH confronts deaf and hard-of-hearing audiences with the same kind of Eurocentric view of other cultures deployed later in the film, when an unspecified country in "darkest Africa" is spoken of in a generalized way and exploited by white characters as a source of information about the nature, source, and/or effect of Pazuzu's power. Here, a vaguely Central American or South American context, signaled by elements in the mise-en-scène rather than the SDH, fleshes out what is otherwise left to the imagination of viewers who have little or no hearing.

Notably, another Blu-ray of *Exorcist II: The Heretic*—one published in 2014 by Warner Home Video—was introduced into the home-video market four years prior to the Shout Factory release, and it features a different set of captions as part of its own SDH option. Besides reminding us that such work is contracted out to different companies and assigned to different individuals, the presence of alternative subtitles means that viewers who are deaf or hard-of-hearing—and who are able to buy, borrow, or rent the discs (another "accessibility" issue tied to socioeconomic factors) have more than one hermeneutic pathway through this text. It also means that certain sounds will assume varying degrees of significance (based on how and when they are printed on the screen as *literal text*) across the range of options available. The first caption to appear in this Blu-ray release is the all-caps statement "[WOMAN WAILING]." In fact, this is the *only* subtitle to flash onscreen during the opening credits of this Warner Blu-ray release (in place of the "moans," "screams," "howling," and "shouts" that appear in the Shout Factory Collector's Edition). Despite its simplicity, the captioner's verb choice, rendered as a present participle, more accurately reflects the emotional cadences of a scene in which an unsettling mix of mournful lamentation and shrieking terror is audibly expressed by the aforementioned pawn of Pazuzu. Though the older women surrounding her can be seen-heard "[CHATTERING]" (similar to how they were described in the other Blu-ray version of the film), they can also be seen-heard "[SPEAKING IN SPANISH]," as can she, when she sobbingly asks, "¿Por qué?" between deep guttural voicings that seem to belong to someone else. As the voices of the women, who beseech Father Lamont for help, climb to a crescendo, he puts a stop to the cacophony by adopting their native language and yelling, "Silencio! Silencio!" That repeated word is itself silenced by this disc's SDH, which renders it as "[SPEAKS IN SPANISH]," one of the few instances in which the *form* rather than the *content* of the dialogue is stressed by an "outsider"—the person responsible for the subtitles (beyond the control or oversight of the film's production staff yet weirdly "inside" the text) and whose choices impact how deaf and hard-of-hearing audiences understand narrative events.

"Ghostly" in his or her own right, the captioner is discarnate yet strangely present as an interpreter of the text, remaining invisible save for the subtitled audio that appears onscreen while lending an ear to the proceedings, as if that person were a prosthetic extension of the viewer's body. Steering the spectator toward certain sounds while ignoring others, this otherworldly entity flickers in and out of existence with each appearance and disappearance of onscreen captioning. Although it is a stretch of the imagination to suggest that physical media such as DVDs and Blu-rays are "possessed" by the spirits of those whose presence outside the text assumes metaphysical connotations whenever their disembodied words appear to float atop the cinematic images, the SDH captions that can be accessed on these home-video releases remind me of the way that messages appear to be written on the inside of Regan's stomach in one of the most unsettling scenes of *The Exorcist*. Displaying the words "Help Me," which suggest that "the 'real' Regan is trapped inside her own body," that scene anticipates how messages both beyond and within the body of a film can flicker into existence in this age of assistive technologies and greater accessibility opportunities, the affordances of which are not unlike the Synchronizer machine that makes it possible to take hold of otherwise inaccessible experiences.[30] Once again, "synchronizing" can be taken to mean a number of things, including aligning oneself with the embodied experiences of others. And this can occur either in the physical company of fellow moviegoers or in the virtual presence of those who speak or write to us from the "other side" of the film.

For an individual spectator, the metaphorical yet materially real process of synchronization might also imply adjusting one's attitudes toward a critically derided work, putting aside one's preconceptions, and embracing (if not always resolving) the contradictions that arise between different, potentially conflicting versions of a single film. Just as there are numerous discrepancies between the original theatrical cut of *Exorcist II: The Heretic* and the shorter alternative version of the film that Boorman prepared for release soon thereafter (including different music cues, voice-over narration, deleted dialogue, newly added footage, still frames, and reedited scenes), the differences between the two SDH transcriptions productively highlight thematic preoccupations and render the heretical position of nonbelievers or doubters within a faith community in appropriately "schismatic" ways. For instance, in the closing moments of the film, when Pazuzu returns to Georgetown in locust form, the swarm of insects flying toward Regan's former home produces a "[buzzing]" sound on the Shout Factory disc (which also alerts us to the "[groans]" and "[growls]" of the teenaged girl), whereas the Warner Home Video version indicates a "[CHIRPING]" noise rising up against the character's "[moaning]" and "[grunting]" sounds (figs. 2.2 and 2.3). While this might appear to be an insignificant point of distinction, it not only highlights the rhetorical elasticity of verbs commonly employed by critics in their own written assessments of this and other horror films (including words that do not accurately reflect those films' sounds), but also hints at the irreducible otherness or radical alterity of nonhuman creatures whose bodily presence frustrates our epistemological efforts to lay claim to them as metaphors for human predicaments.

Besides the film's opening and closing scenes, the aforementioned synchronizing scene, in which the hypnotically transfixing biofeedback device is hooked up to Regan and others who wish to see and hear what she experienced during her initial encounter with Pazuzu, is rife with discrepancies in terms of how it is subtitled for deaf and hard-of-hearing audiences with access to SDH. Whereas the Warner Home Video version of the scene offers nine bracketed words or phrases highlighting the "[GROWLING]" and "[GASPING]" of characters caught in the grip of a monstrous force confined to their own technologically linked minds, including Regan (who notably speaks "[IN DEMONIC VOICE]" and "[IN NORMAL VOICE]"), the Shout Factory Blu-ray presents twenty-three captions throughout that same scene. Among those captions are indicators of Dr. Tuskin's deep inhalation of air and "[loud heartbeat]," which—despite its volume and the fact that I have not experienced significant hearing

**Figures 2.2 and 2.3:** Depending on the platform or home-video version of the film being viewed by deaf and hard-of-hearing audiences, the locusts that dot the sky in this scene near the end of *Exorcist II: The Heretic* produce either a "buzzing" or a "chirping" sound, both of which bring their own set of cultural connotations based on viewers' previous experience of hearing, or *seeing*, those noises in other horror films.

loss—is something that I had not heard during previous viewings of the film. Or, rather, if I had heard her fibrillating heartbeat and sonorous breathing, I did not give them any thought. In other words, I had not tuned myself biorhythmically to her body in quite the same way that I do now, when listening to the film's sounds through my newly attuned eyes.

Subtitles for deaf and hard-of-hearing viewers are assistive in much the same way that a director's commentary track on a DVD or Blu-ray can be, nudging audiences to use their eyes or ears differently or (for people without the sense of sight or hearing) to draw upon the affordances of today's viewing and listening technologies as part of their bodily engagement with a genre that is so often celebrated for its palpably real special effects and sticky prosthetics. Importantly, the "stickiness" of horror—the gooey, syrupy, viscous "stuff" of the genre, so palpable within *The Exorcist* (and to a lesser extent *Exorcist II: The Heretic*)—is something that SDH can help to bring to the surface as a *sonic* rather than strictly tactile or visual element. However, in many cases the captioners responsible for transcribing those "squishy" noises opt not to explicitly spell out this auditory aspect of horror, and in the process wring out much of the wetness that contributes to its affective power and distinguishes it as a body genre. One significant exception to that "drying-out" tendency of captions can be found in the various online and home-video iterations of director William Castle's *House on Haunted Hill* (1959), a film that was briefly discussed in chapter 1, but which deserves a lengthier consideration here, as we draw this exploration of seeing (and hearing) as the basis for believing to a close.

## "[SOUNDS DIFFERENT]": Captioning Hysteria

Dust and dirt everywhere, the water barely trickles.

—Annabelle Loren (Carol Ohmart), complaining to her husband, Frederick (Vincent Price), about the decrepit state of the cobweb-filled mansion where they and five other guests must stay overnight, in *House on Haunted Hill* (1959)

Written by screenwriter Robb White and brought to the screen with trademark relish by William Castle, postwar Hollywood's greatest ballyhoo artist, *House on Haunted Hill* requires considerable suspension of disbelief if audiences are to accept its basic premise: an eccentric millionaire with a macabre sense of humor and an axe to grind with his possibly unfaithful wife invites five strangers to stay overnight at a haunted house that he has rented, promising ten thousand dollars to anyone who survives until the next morning. It is a challenge that is in keeping with Castle's own brand of big-screen showmanship—his much-hyped spectatorial solicitations to play the "game" of horror inside movie theaters equipped with fake skeletons hanging by wires (throughout this film's initial release) and electric seat buzzers (for that same year's *The Tingler* [1959]). According to their droll host, Frederick Loren (Vincent Price), the five guests in *House on Haunted Hill* were selected because he wanted a group of people from different walks of life who nevertheless share a desire for wealth: the deeply skeptical psychiatrist David Trent (Alan Marshal), the levelheaded test pilot Lance Schroeder (Richard Long), the sarcastic newspaper columnist Ruth Bridges (Julie Mitchum), an impressionable young worker at one of Frederick's companies named Nora Manning (Carolyn Craig), and the current owner of the house, Watson Pritchard (Elisha Cook Jr.), who has never stayed overnight at the place for reasons that are made abundantly clear during the first seconds of the film. The latter character, knowing that the previous owners' lives were cut short there, has been driven to drink and is already a bundle of nerves before he meets the people with whom he will share his own home.

Significantly, Mr. Pritchard is the first character to appear in the film, even prior to the narrative's beginning. Against a black background, his face floats into view at a far distance from the camera but quickly zooms in to a close-up, with everything below his neck cut off (as if his head has been optically decapitated). As described on the first page of White's script, Watson appears to be "in his late forties," a "timid, moody man, given to consoling himself for his many failures." After introducing himself to the audience, he proceeds to inform us that seven people, including his brother, have already been killed inside the house, built a century ago. "The ghosts are moving tonight, restless, hungry," he intones gravely. His words are accompanied by the offscreen sounds of creaking floorboards, ghoulish laughter, rattling chains, and a woman's ear-piercing screams. Those loud noises are the first things that can be heard in *House on Haunted Hill*, and the fact that they rise up against a black background in the seconds before Watson's face appears suggests that genre-defining sounds will be as instrumental as the film's visuals in communicating its themes and in helping spectators to determine its success as a comically imbued, hysterically terrifying tale prone to milking the seemingly contradictory meanings of "hysteria" for all of their worth.

Of additional interest is the elaborate—dare I say, hysterical—manner in which White describes this opening shot, using an array of sonic signifiers to put the audience in place as *auditors* as much as viewers. His screenplay (or, as Castle would have it, "screamplay") reads as follows, with all of the typographical features intact:

> As the house lights go down, the screen remains dark. This darkness lasts in silence until you begin to fill restless. Then, without any warning, there is a WOMAN'S SCREAM. Silence returns for a few seconds and then, almost inaudibly, we HEAR a confusion of SOUNDS, with only a STEADY, HARSH, BREATHING SOUND being completely recognizable: we HEAR GROANS, GRUNTS, TINY SQUEAKS AND SQUEALS, TINKLINGS with this HEAVY BREATHING GROWING LOUDER AND LOUDER. the SOUNDS COME UP TO A CRESCENDO and then, as they FADE, A SPOT OF LIGHT IN LEFT, LOWER CORNER OF THE SCREEN APPEARS AND MOVES TOWARD US. AS THIS SPOT OF LIGHT TAKES THE FORM OF A HEAD, THE SOUNDS FADE and the face of WATSON PRITCHARD RUSHES FORWARD to almost fill the screen.[31]

It is worth pointing out that only one of my descriptions of the opening shot's noises (the woman's scream) can be found in White's script, suggesting that Castle had other sound designs in mind during production and/or postproduction than what the screenwriter had intended. Nevertheless, both sets of words—my own and White's text—are "accurate" to the extent that they convey what he refers to as a "confusion of SOUNDS." Preceding that phrase are the words "We HEAR"—one of two instances where White adopts a rhetorical move that is often discouraged by screenwriting experts, but which underscores the importance of one of the two sensorial activities most frequently associated with cinematic spectatorship (the other being conveyed a bit further down the page: "*We see* the face of a man in his late forties . . . *we see* that he is a timid, moody man").[32]

Many other screenwriters besides White have broken the much-debated "rule" of *not* using "We hear" and "We see" in their film scripts. To take one example, the first page of David Robert Mitchell's shooting script for his 2014 horror film, *It Follows*, includes the scene text, "We hear the screen door open and close again" and, a few lines down, "We see nothing." On the surface, this is not dissimilar from what the Duffer Brothers do throughout their sixty-four-page pilot episode script for *Stranger Things* (Netflix, 2016–present), which spills over with rather pedestrian statements such as "We move down a long windowless corridor." But the tendency to put the sensing activities associated with ears and eyes at the forefront of a reader's spectatorial imagination hints at their centrality to the horror film experience as well as to the disbelief mitigation that has been an indelible part of the genre since its beginnings over a century ago. Moreover, by literally spelling out and—in accordance with standard screenwriting formatting—capitalizing the kind of sounds that he had in mind for *House on Haunted Hill*'s opening shot ("GROANS, GRUNTS, TINY SQUEAKS AND SQUEALS, TINKLINGS with this HEAVY BREATHING GROWING LOUDER AND LOUDER"), White undertakes a kind of prefilmic captioning of the text, hinting at the textual transcriptions that would take place decades after he wrote his script in the late 1950s.

After Mr. Pritchard has said his piece in the opening seconds of the film, the camera appears to zoom out from his head, which is immediately replaced by that of another person, Frederick Loren, who likewise speaks to the audience (against a shot of the rented house rather than a black screen). Loren establishes the narrative conceit of this motion picture, explaining that, to help his "amusing" wife throw a "haunted house party," he has rented the venue for the evening and expects there to be "food and drink and ghosts . . . and perhaps even a few murders." Imbuing Frederick with a mixture of levity and malice from this opening scene going forward, horror legend Vincent Price brings his customary taste for arched-eyebrow theatricality to the role, ensuring that nothing—not even the prospect of foul play—will be taken too seriously by the audience. The critical distance that derives from the film's comedic framing of Frederick's game situates the spectator on the side of Dr. Trent, the humorless psychiatrist who sees no reason to believe in things (such as ghosts) that cannot be proven through scientific processes. Compounding that irony is the fact that David, a specialist in psychoneurosis who is quick to label Nora's increasingly frenzied behavior—as someone who claims to have witnessed supernatural occurrences firsthand—as "hysteria," is partly responsible for all the mayhem, threatening his fellow guests with falling chandeliers and bloodstained ceilings so that he and his secret lover, Annabelle, can drive the panic-stricken young woman to kill Frederick and collect the total reward of fifty thousand dollars for themselves.

After Annabelle initially appears to die from a hanging—her body swaying from a rope in the hallway outside her bedroom—but who staged her death to throw suspicion of guilt upon her innocent husband, David tells the others that, in his professional opinion, Nora "has been driven to the brink of absolute *hysteria*." That latter term carries a sexist subtext, owing to its colloquial usage as a reference to the kind of emotional excess and psychological disturbances that are commonly attributed to women. Rooted in the Greek word for uterus, "hysteria" was long thought to manifest in the bodies of women whose irrational, incomprehensible behavior offered proof of an internal problem, an abnormality in the womb that could be repaired through marriage, sexual intercourse, or childbirth. Elinor Cleghorn, author of *Unwell Women: Misdiagnosis and Myth in a Man-Made World*, explains that the Greek physician and "father of medicine" Hippocrates played a large part in medically constructing hysteria as a uniquely feminine pathology when he and his followers claimed that women who had stopped having sex and bearing children might suffer from wandering uteruses. "Empty and dry" because they were not being filled, those uteruses—not unlike monsters in a horror movie—went creeping toward livers and other internal organs "in search of moisture."[33] By listening to an afflicted woman's belly "for the gurgling sounds of the womb" being fed by phlegm and "returning to its rightful place" (an audible sign of sufficient "moistening"), the physician monitored her recovery from an illness that could only be diagnosed through his *senses*, but in the most *nonsensical* way imaginable.[34] Besides placing his ear just below the stomach of the infirmed, the doctor could only otherwise interpret that patient's hysterical convulsions "through what [he] could see and feel," a reminder that the medical misdiagnoses of the ancient past (when human dissection was prohibited and knowledge of the body was only skin deep) are not unlike the mistakes made by contemporary horror films' many disbelieving skeptics. Notably, the senses of young women during Hippocrates's day were thought to be poisoned by the backflow of blood spilling out every month, their "overly wet" bodies needing the same thing that the "overly dry" bodies of older women needed: to be opened up through intercourse and a resulting pregnancy.

While all of this misogynistic talk of migrating sexual reproductive organs might seem unrelated to a film about murder and mayhem inside a (fake) haunted house, it is important to bear in mind Mr. Pritchard's description of the cellar, where he and the guests of Mr. Loren gather not long after stepping foot into the titular structure. "My, it's dry and dusty down here," he says, not long after showing off the cellar's main attraction, a large vat of acid located beneath a carved-out section of the floor. Long ago filled with wine by one of the house's previous occupants, the bubbling vat is now menacing in its wetness, a threat to life and limb that will surely come back to haunt the characters at a later point in the narrative. In fact, it even "gurgles," to borrow the word that Cleghorn uses to describe the sound of a hysterical woman's return to so-called normalcy under the male scientific gaze (or stethoscope). Not surprisingly, the acid's "splashing," "bubbling," "fizzing," and "gurgling" noises, which are captioned as such on streaming platforms and on the dozens of DVD editions of *House on Haunted Hill* that have been released over the past twenty years (capitalizing on the film's public-domain status), come to the fore in the penultimate scene, when David drags Frederick's seemingly lifeless body toward the vat after the latter has been shot in self-defense by Nora (the resident "hysteric"). For no apparent reason, the lights shut off at the precise moment when the doctor is about to dump his slain host into the liquid below, with scuffling noises accompanied by the sloshing of liquid emerging on the soundtrack. Those noises are captioned as "[SOUNDS OF STRANGLING AND SPLASHING]" on the Kanopy streaming version of the film, clarifying the action for viewers who might otherwise be left in the dark. Holding on the black screen for a full ten seconds, this shot recalls the opening (non)image of the film, which was similarly accompanied by disturbing sounds whose sources were left to the imagination of spectators.

Other captioned versions of this public domain film, including the Warner Bros. DVD release and the legally posted free viewings available on YouTube, feature different renderings of that "splashing" sound of the body hitting and then dissolving into the acid under the floor, using "(liquid fizzes & bubbles)," for instance. Though similar to the "splashing" and "gurgling" that can be seen-heard on the Kanopy version of *House on Haunted Hill*, the "fizzing" and "bubbling" sounds of these other versions suggest a slightly different physical reaction to wet death and hint at the possibility of there being another text below this text—or, rather, multiple untapped ways of hearing those sonic properties of a film that hit the ears (or eyes) differently depending on one's own physical reactions to the materiality of the medium (which includes the platforms or technologies through which one accesses the film). The many doors that open and close over the course of the narrative, highlighted by a passage of dialogue in which Lance remarks to Nora, "I've never seen so many doors," in addition to the fact that no other word appears more frequently than "door" does in the nondialogue subtitles, serve as architectural metaphors of the different hermeneutic paths into and out of particular scenes provided by SDH. Tellingly (and almost humorously), the captioning that was accessible through Kanopy in 2020 includes the bracketed words "[SOUNDS DIFFERENT]" during the scene in which Lance, noting the many doors inside the house while holding a candle to light his way in the dark, taps on a wall inside a secret chamber, which indeed produces different sounds depending on where it is tapped (fig. 2.4). Hardly of much use to anyone who is deaf or hard-of-hearing, that unusual subtitle nevertheless assumes metatextual significance as

**Figure 2.4:** The question of how useful certain subtitled sounds might be is prompted by this unusual moment in Kanopy's streaming version of *House on Haunted Hill*.

a marker of the textual variability with which anyone seeking to make sense of cinematic horror through SDH must contend.

Of course, there *is* a reason for the lights to go out near the end of *House on Haunted Hill*: Castle is obviously trying to make audiences believe that Frederick rather than David has dropped to his demise in the liquid. The film's last big surprise arrives when Annabelle, looking for her lover down in the cellar, is trapped inside that "dry and dusty" place only to be confronted by a skeleton rising from the vat of acid. Viewers are led to suspect that this skeletal apparition is the spirit of her husband. In fact, he is very much alive, pulling the bony thing's strings from offscreen. Advancing toward the terrified woman, who finds every exit door locked, the skeleton forces her to retreat toward the bath of acid. With each backward step, Annabelle emits a high-pitched scream, as if she has inherited the overwrought emotions of the hysterical younger woman (whose earlier shrieks of terror were similarly shrill, and whose gun only fired blanks at Frederick, a man impervious to her ineffectual attacks). Those screams end abruptly once Annabelle takes a spill, joining her lover in a fittingly "wet death" that further suggests how his supposedly scientific specialization in hysteria is rooted to the history of Hippocratic "uterine pathologies" that she—a woman locked in a dry, loveless, sexless marriage to a vengeful husband—had come to embody.

In this way, she demonstrates how "the psychical becomes physiological" not only within the hysterical symptomology of medical discourse but also through the cultural stigmatizing of "bad" women within a genre that frequently associates irrationality with femininity.[35] Throughout the history—or, borrowing Elaine Showalter's term, "hystory"—of cinematic horror, from the pre-Code B-movie *The Monster Walks* (1932) to the postwar creature feature *Konga* (1961) and, more recently, the *Nightmare on Elm Street*–inspired fan film *Don't Fall Asleep* (2016), men in positions of power (and with the support of the scientific community) have verbally described women as being upset to the point of irrationality. Prone to nightmares and caught in the grips of a condition apparently "unique" to their gender, female characters shoulder a narrative weight that is not shared by their male peers, including those—think Guy Woodhouse (John Cassavetes), father in name only of the titular satanic offspring in *Rosemary's Baby* (1968)—who conspire against their own wives while chastising them for evincing an emotional state that they have secretly engineered. Roman Polanski's film, referred to by *The New Yorker*'s Penelope Gilliat as an example of the "gynecological gothic," is perhaps the most obvious case of spousal gaslighting, expressed in Guy's comment, directed toward his wife, Rosemary (Mia Farrow), that she has suffered "some kind of a hysteria. . . . You were really *kapow*, out of your mind," not to mention her own physician, Dr. Hill (Charles Grodin), who states flatly, "I don't believe in witchcraft, but there are plenty of crazy people in this city." However, additional instances of this pejorative framing of women as objects of ridicule and pity can be seen and heard in other films made around the time of *House on Haunted Hill*'s theatrical release, including one—writer-director Edward D. Wood Jr.'s independently produced *Plan 9 from Outer Space* (1959)—that illustrates how the two principal meanings bound up in the word "hysteria" sometimes bleed into one another; especially in a genre where laughter is nearly as abundant as screams.

I will leave my thoughts on the cross-pollination of humor and horror for the next two chapters. However, it is useful to call out a particular scene from Wood's film, the granddaddy of "so-bad-it's-good" cinema (according to his biographers and many other commentators), so that the question of a character's "badness" relative to the double-meaning of hysteria gets fleshed out in advance of forthcoming discussions of hysterically funny horror films.[36] The scene in question revolves around a police investigation into the mysterious deaths of two gravediggers, in addition to a recently filed complaint from Paula Trent (Mona McKinnon), a woman who lives near a haunted cemetery, that "spirits" are responsible for those murders. When a younger patrolman (Carl Anthony) tells his supervising lieutenant (Duke Moore) that Mrs. Trent was "hysterical," and therefore not to be trusted as a witness, the older man agrees that she did, indeed, appear to be frightened, or "in a state of shock." But he also reminds him that her nightgown was torn and her feet were scratched—physical signs of some wrongdoing that, however unbelievable, attains a degree of plausibility simply from these men having laid eyes on those signs. The fact that she had been sleeping in her bed when she was attacked by a ghoulish figure from the cemetery (played by Bela Lugosi and his posthumous stand-in, Tom Mason) makes the police officer's hesitancy to believe her report indicative of the problems inherent within a representational system where the horror of sexual violation—emblematized by the many scenes throughout the genre's history of male monsters entering bedrooms and hovering over scantily clad female victims in repose—is frequently exploited for the sake of titillation. Importantly, another person who filed a similar report with the police, a local farmer named Calder (Karl Johnson), is believed to have been *intoxicated* rather than hysterical when he too claimed to have seen "spirits," just as another patrolman is near the end of *Plan 9 from Outer Space* (someone who, in calling for help after encountering the cemetery's undead, "sounded drunk," according to an assisting officer). In keeping with the rhetorical tendency that I have elaborated throughout the first half of this book, that patrolman tells his fellow officer, "If I didn't see it with my own eyes, I would never have believed it." And yet, as another character says during an earlier scene of this most internally inconsistent of sci-fi-horror films, "there comes a time in each man's life when he can't even believe his own eyes."

*Plan 9 from Outer Space* contains what Christine Cornea calls "internal incongruity," meaning that its various parts "do not fit or harmonize together as might be expected," prompting audiences to laugh at things that were meant to elicit a different affective response.[37] The multiple embedded discourses around the topic of belief in this film are indicative of that incongruity, which also helps to explain why audiences are not able to suspend disbelief in the face of so many "contradictory declarations" and "bewildering inconsistencies in the scripting."[38] Thus, the problem of believability is not strictly reserved for the characters of horror films to grapple with and pontificate about; it extends to the people who make and spectate upon such works with the hope of either creating or enjoying an immersive experience untarnished by textual anomalies or "badfilm" distractions. Like the more expensive, studio-backed critical flop *Exorcist II: The Heretic* several years after it, Ed Wood's "patchy and amateurish" film plays like an unintentional parody of genre conventions. This is one reason why a devoted cult following of fans responds favorably to its "shortcomings," which, to paraphrase Bartłomiej Paszylk, are so funny as to become a *strength* of the film, a sign of its oppositional aesthetics.[39]

At once heretical and hysterical, critically disparaged, laughably "bad" works are as deserving of analytical attention as *Don't Look Now*, *The Exorcist*, or any other positively reviewed horror film discussed in this book, and not only because they shift the burden of belief determination from the characters to the audience. Their very *badness*, which is as much a social and cultural construct as *hysteria* is, reveals the extent to which critics—even those who are sympathetic to monsters as "deformed and destructive beings"—can be implicated in the otherizing/pathologizing tendencies of the genre's most skeptical scientists and hardened disbelievers.[40] Indeed, by hewing to formulas for "success" or asserting the need for evaluative criteria that might help audiences to tell the difference between a "good" movie and a "bad" one, as George Ochoa does in his book *Deformed and Destructive Beings: The Purpose of Horror Films*—arguing that *The Bride of Frankenstein* (1935) is an example of the former while *The Fly II* (1989) is an example of the latter—is to make *monstrous* those productions that do not fit a rather narrow conception of artistic excellence or aesthetic worth.[41] Although books such as *The Golden Turkey Awards* have labeled the output of William Castle as "bad films," few genre enthusiasts "would describe the skeleton in *House on Haunted Hill* or the wonderful plastic-tendrilled lobster-thing that is the tingler as 'failed monsters,'" as Murray Leeder points out.[42] Like the extradiegetic gimmicks that accompanied Castle's films' theatrical releases (including *Emergo*, which entailed the dangling of skeletons above the heads of theater patrons during *House on Haunted Hill*'s initial run), these diegetic figures of abjection blur lines and cross boundaries that many audiences would prefer remained intact. And, like the title creature in director Chris Walas's *The Fly II* (which was described by critics as being as "messy" and "repulsive" in its "slime-ridden, glob-oozing" wetness as the film that contained it), the gooey decapitated head that Nora finds inside her suitcase and which sends her into a prolonged fit during an early scene of Castle's 1959 film is doubly "hysterical," prompting excessively emotional reactions both within the narrative and within the sphere of reception where, in the words of Noël Carroll, "thunderous laughter" frequently accompanies the screening of a "very bad horror film" (figs. 2.5 and 2.6).[43]

For every wet and gooey sequence that is transcribed faithfully in a horror film—as, for instance, the captioners for the region 1 DVD release of *The Fly II* do when they indicate a "[Squishing Sound]" and a "[Gurgling Sound]" during an especially messy childbirth scene, or when "[squelches]" or "[squelching]" pops up in the captions for Brian Yuzna's

**Figure 2.5:** With dramatic flourish, Nora embodies the hysteria so often associated with female fear in this scene near the end of *House on Haunted Hill*.

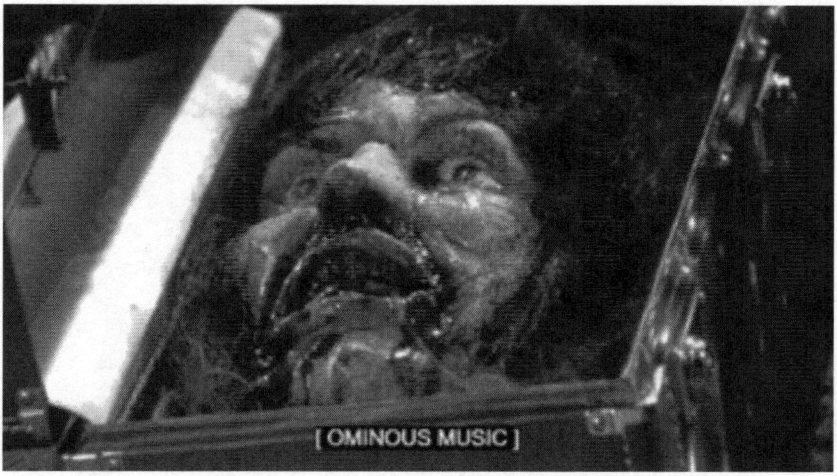


**Figure 2.6:** At once hideously grotesque and humorous in its excessiveness, this moment in *House on Haunted Hill*, scored to "ominous music" (according to the SDH), is just as likely to prompt giggles and guffaws as it is to generate screams from audiences mimicking Nora's terrified reaction.

*Silent Night, Deadly Night 4: Initiation* (1990), Julia Ducournau's *Titane* (2021), and Jordan Peele's *Nope* (2022)—there are dozens more that get "dried out" through SDH. From the Australian horror film *Next of Kin* (1982), in which blood spurts up from a water fountain, to the slasher film *Sleepaway Camp* (1983), in which a pedophilic cook gets horribly scalded when his head is dunked into a vat of boiling water, moist liquidic images thrust themselves onto the viewer's eyes, and are made all the more disturbing by the *noises* (e.g., splashes, splatters, squelches, squishes) that lend them a material presence. The fact that those noises are often excluded from the subtitles that accompany DVD and Blu-ray releases and online streaming versions of the films has potentially far-reaching implications in terms of how audiences with different abilities perceive of horror as a body genre and, ironically, might be "disabled" from doing so because of the captioning choices that are made on their behalf. This is an idea that will reemerge in the second half of this book, which is devoted not only to the representation of deaf and hard-of-hearing characters in horror films but also to the assistive technologies that are ostensibly designed to put audiences with different abilities on equal footing, but which could be blamed for "wrong-footing" those same viewers based on what *is*, and what *is not*, transcribed onscreen.

# 3

# JUST FOR THE SMELL OF IT

## Offal and Olfactory Awfulness in the Horror Films of Herschell Gordon Lewis

The bloodletting in Lewis's films gives off a distinctly disturbing stench, a whiff of long-festering retribution.

—Charlie Largent, in his 2017 review of *Blood Feast* (1963), for the website Trailers from Hell

The smell of rotting meat is not a pleasant smell at all!

—Herschell Gordon Lewis, speaking to Something Weird Video's Mike Vraney during his audio commentary for the Arrow Video Blu-ray release of *The Gruesome Twosome* (1967)

Today, over sixty years after Herschell Gordon Lewis made his directorial debut, his name remains synonymous with the kind of legendarily atrocious cinema that appeals to lovers of "so-bad-it's-good" filmmaking. This is due primarily to his low-budget productions' cheap-looking yet crudely effective special effects and flagrant violation of the formal rules of traditional storytelling, on top of which are sprinkled excessive amounts of exposed flesh, graphic violence, and nauseating gore. That combination of stylistic impoverishment and representational excess—on view in everything from his earliest nudie outings *Living Venus* (1961) and *The Adventures of Lucky Pierre* (1961) to his final stabs at the splatter subgenre before his passing in 2016, *Blood Feast 2: All U Can Eat* (2002) and *The Uh-Oh Show* (2009)—brings a certain degree of spectatorial "difficulty" when it comes to sorting out our potentially conflicted feelings about his body of work's cultural and historical "worth" as well as our own bodies' phenomenological and sensorial relationship to the screen.

In many cases, scholars who have weighed in on either of those two matters resort to an ocularcentric formula whereby the value of a groundbreaking gross-out movie like *Blood Feast* (1963) resides in its observable differences from the comparatively tame horror films that preceded it—differences that would form the iconographic, or *carnographic*, core of his most popular gore films, including *Two Thousand Maniacs!* (1964), *Color Me Blood Red* (1965), *A Taste of Blood* (1967), and *The Wizard of Gore* (1970). Those recurring features, such as the glistening intestines, hacked limbs, and flayed skin that Lewis and his small crew fashioned from the external and internal organs of butchered animals (e.g., chicken skin, fish eyeballs, lox, pig intestines, a sheep's tongue), would be nakedly apparent to anyone with the ability to see, and one way to avoid their disturbing effect is to simply close our eyes or turn away from the screen. Such a sight-centered approach to the visible grossness of Lewis's films fails to account for their audible distinctiveness as recordings that are both literally and figuratively "dirty," according to Kristina Pia Hofer, one of several scholars in recent years to shift the study of 1960s and 1970s exploitation cinema away from vision-oriented interpretations of texts toward a more holistic, hearing-inclusive hermeneutics.[1]

Just as Hofer has done with Lewis's *She-Devils on Wheels* (1968), a biker film filled with "excessive sound textures," or what she calls "sonic dirt" (e.g., distortion, noise, and other "affective-meaningful resonances"), I seek to expand the critical vocabulary that scholars might apply to the director's work, albeit in a more unconventional manner so that other senses besides seeing and hearing come to the fore.[2] While there is much to say about the tactile and gustatory elements at play in Lewis's sticky, gristle-filled films, which can be said to make one's skin crawl and leave a bad taste in one's mouth, this chapter principally explores the cultural construction of those films' awfulness and offensiveness through olfactory means, letting the nose and its neural receptors guide us toward the real-world sources of this trash auteur's inspired takes on "bad death." Indeed, his and his creative team's practical solutions to achieving unprecedented gross-out effects and depicting mortal predicaments onscreen imbue works like *Blood Feast*, *Color Me Blood Red*, *A Taste of Blood*, and *The Wizard of Gore* with an almost palpable aroma that sets them apart from earlier, more tastefully appointed examples of horror cinema. And yet those same deathly elements anticipate the special effects of subsequent motion pictures reliant on remainder animal parts as substitutes for human limbs and skin, including Tobe Hooper's *The Texas Chain Saw Massacre* (1974), Juan Piquer Simón's *Pieces* (1982), and George A. Romero's *Day of the Dead* (1985). Like Lewis's films, these latter productions are reputed to have made cast members and crew members nauseous once those raw pieces of offal became rancid on fly-infested sets.

From the stomach-churning odor of spoiled meat and rotting entrails to the acrid stench of melted asphalt and burning gasoline, several aromatically intense sensations are likely to flare up when consuming Lewis's films. Indeed, a person's previous encounters with certain conventionally bad odors are likely to spring to mind during such a screening, detonating pungent explosions of personal recollections like so many stink bombs. A spectator's memories of, for instance, stepping into a manure-filled feedlot, using a filthy public toilet, driving up to a gas station awash in petrol fumes, or dropping off discarded items at a garbage dump (the setting of one key scene in *Blood Feast*) might get mixed into the intersensorial soup of feelings that his body of work stirs up, making the aforementioned films oddly relatable to even the most casual moviegoer precisely because they, like our own lives, are so smelly. How to sort out those often-contradictory feelings—the combination of identification, excitation, and disgust that constitute horror's negative pleasures or paradoxical appeals—is a question I take up in the following pages. But this chapter is equally invested in the challenge of bringing seemingly trivial production-related details into reception studies, a field of academic inquiry that has largely remained indifferent if not oblivious to the perceiving power of smell.

The latter sense ability is often more *receptive* to a perceiver's surroundings than those associated with eyes and ears, making olfaction a useful and therefore doubly "sensible" alternative to sight- and hearing-based hermeneutics. Because movie audiences are not able to *literally* sniff the figures, objects, and settings that appear onscreen, as film phenomenologist Vivian Sobchack reminds us in her pioneering book *Carnal Thoughts: Embodiment and Moving Image Culture*, the perceiver's body receives the "rebound" of his or her own projected sense memories when confronted by images that, in the final analysis, are only *metaphorically* aromatic.[3] As such, a person's bodily investment in a given motion picture's fictions, aside from any suspension of disbelief that might be required for his or her immersion in a far-fetched narrative, is at least partially dependent on prior exposure to real-world odors that are hard to shake off, or which lie dormant inside the nasal brain until an especially intense image—for instance, an Egyptian caterer gripping a sheep's tongue in *Blood Feast* or a demented painter squeezing blood from butcher-shop entrails in *Color Me Blood Red*—triggers memories of those smells. In Sobchack's words, cinematic aromas, including those that were physically incorporated into public screenings through historically dated technologies like "Smell-O-Vision" (in the 1950s and 1960s) and gimmicky supplements such as "Odorama" scratch-and-sniff cards (given out to audiences of director John Waters's *Polyester* [1981] decades later), can only be "subjectively felt," insofar as a viewer's sense memories and sensing abilities will almost certainly differ from those of other moviegoers.[4] And yet, even though it is nearly "impossible to describe how something smells to someone who hasn't smelled it," as essayist Diane Ackerman claims, certain things—say, freshly baked bread, fried bacon, and the pong of wet dog—have been aromatically arranged across a spectrum of hedonic values, from "good" to "bad," within ostensibly odor-free cultural productions over the years.[5] This suggests that a consensus about their positive or negative associations has also embedded itself inside our nasal brains and infuses the very language we use to feebly describe the indescribable. Our chemical and physical reactions to molecular volatility, in other words, are *ours alone*, though any attempt to interpret smells "beyond the nose" necessarily rests on culturally biased assumptions and is hindered by a linguistic deficiency that contrasts the "exquisite complexity" of this most receptive of sensing organs.[6]

As with the critical evaluation of motion pictures or any other expressive art form, labeling a specific odor as "good" or "bad" is insufficient when so much of the subjectively felt experience of that encounter relies upon complex chemical and physical interactions (those of receptor cells and odor molecules) and is hardly ever only "pleasant" or "unpleasant" to the person on the receiving end. If smells cannot be so easily summed up or made sense of outside the olfactory system that received them (and which sends electrical signals to other parts of the brain for further "translation"), then movies, too, test the paucity of spoken and written language through their textual complexities and sensorial overload—their abundance of signifying "stuff" directed toward the spectator's eyes, ears, nose, skin, and tongue. Nevertheless, the sparsely designed yet richly textured, odor-laden films of Herschell Gordon Lewis, perhaps more than most other directors' work, have inspired knee-jerk criticism and rhetorically unsophisticated commentary from those who reduce his output to a set of familiar tropes and trot out their own hackneyed expressions, often concluding that his movies simply "stink." That was Grady Hendrix's take on the this and other exploitation filmmakers' "crappy" work, which, according to the author, has inspired "misplaced" affection from people who are either too young and naïve or too old and clouded by nostalgia to remember how "nasty" grindhouse theaters and other venues catering to gorehounds were during their heyday (the 1970s).[7] If online reviewer Dennis Schwartz is correct in his summary of Lewis's *Moonshine Mountain* (1964) that "everything about the film stinks," then—based on dictionary definitions of that verb—one must accept that this hillbilly-themed drive-in movie is thoroughly contemptible or at the very least unpleasant not only at the level of narrative, characterization, performance, and direction but also in terms of its *very material existence* (i.e., "everything").[8] Significantly, prior to Arrow Film's digital restoration of *Moonshine Mountain* (the original 35 mm negative of which has been lost), existing prints contained "extreme levels of dirt, scratches and debris as well as many instances of torn or missing frames," splices, and color fading, as if their physical degradation was not only the result of critical disregard over the years but also a manifestation of the malodorous scents that saturate its story of heavily perspiring bootleg whiskey distillers in the backwoods of South Carolina. That is, just as odorants can be said to arise from particular images (e.g., close-ups of dead fish, dog poo, lit cigars), so too does the visual-material state of a motion picture manifest the inner and outer discourses of "badness" that might prompt some viewers to hold their noses in disgust.

Such rhetoric cuts both ways, of course. Just as many admirers as detractors of Lewis's films have called out the irredeemable loathsomeness of certain types of cultural production, including mainstream, big-budget commercial cinema that so often serves as the antithesis of his "do-lots-with-little" credo (despite the fact that Lewis's inveterate business skills as an "exploiteer" who admitted to making motion pictures for monetary rather than artistic reasons accords with the profit-driven philosophies of bottom-line-minded Hollywood types). For instance, in a tribute to the director posted on the website Mondo Exploito in 2012, Dave Jackson readily admits that "Lewis made garbage," but maintains that the "soulless Hollywood tripe" that passes for entertainment these days "are the true bad movies." And yet, even as this reviewer insists that "the worst b-grade stinkers" hold "real value" for anyone who, like himself, believes that "the line between good and bad films has always been irrelevant," Jackson and other critics ultimately reinscribe that line, retaining the hierarchical division between two evaluative terms that say very little about the formal, stylistic, and thematic elements that might contribute to a motion picture's high or low cultural standing. Notably, in using the reductive word "tripe" to trash Hollywood productions, the reviewer brings another, perhaps unintended meaning to bear on his counterbalancing affection for the films of Lewis, who was not above repurposing cow and sheep stomachs (i.e., tripe) as pungent props on set. One lesson that can be learned from watching, and metaphorically *breathing in*, Herschell Gordon Lewis's films is how much the discourse surrounding them—that gaseous cloud of critical commentary which persists in labeling them "gross," "sleazy," and "stinky"—seems to emerge from the noxious odors *within* them.

In contrast to our nasal relation to the screen, there was nothing metaphorical about the odors smelt by cast and crew members during the *making* of Lewis's films. As such, those contributors' written and oral accounts of having to cope with unpleasant physical sensations along with suboptimal working conditions (e.g., equipment shortages, limited rehearsal time, rushed shooting schedules) should be taken into consideration as we try to account for our own mixed feelings as spectators drawn to yet repulsed by the humorously horrible things for which he is best known. Despite the olfactory demands placed on them, frequent collaborators such as Allison Louise Downe, Daniel Krogh, and Ray Sager enjoyed working with their mentor, a former English professor and advertising executive whose self-deprecating wit, gentle sarcasm, and soft-spoken patience in guiding his actors toward compelling if not always believable performances were among his many admirable traits. One such glowing testimony is included as a supplemental feature on Arrow Video's seven-disc Blu-ray box set of fourteen Herschell Gordon Lewis–directed films—a 2020 home-video release discussed at greater length in the second half of this chapter. In a videorecorded interview that accompanies the set's sixth disc, second unit director-turned-actor Ray Sager, who appeared in eight of the director's features (most famously as the endearingly inept yet creepily effective title character of *The Wizard of Gore*), fondly reminisces about how "fun" everything with Lewis was, both in front of and behind the camera, where an atmosphere of joviality and gut-busting humor offset the films' dark, necrofetishistic fixation on busted guts. But Sager's appreciative commendation comes only minutes after he complains about the *actual atmosphere* or air quality of those films' pig-intestine-filled sets, which, in his words, "reeked." Although anecdotal, such behind-the-scenes information not only suggests that bad smells can produce good memories, but also helps to ground spectators' otherwise-groundless speculations about the material properties of onscreen stimuli.

Over the next few pages, I map out the strangely familiar yet hellish smellscape of Herschell Gordon Lewis's films with an eye—or, rather, *nose*—to both the rhetorical and somatic work involved in moving from the hermeneutic practice of "meaning-making" to the corporeal experience of "sense-making." In doing so, I am building upon earlier scholarship concerning horror cinema and the human sensorium to propose a relatively unorthodox mode of critical analysis.[9] It is one that, even within the arenas of film phenomenology and affect theory, might seem comically absurd or simply counterintuitive as a means of discerning the resonances of onscreen representations, including those for which Lewis gained notoriety over a half-century ago: scenes of gut-busting mutilation and physical torture that, for all their grossness, are risible in their fakeness or when seen from the vantage of contemporary audiences casting condescending looks back on metaphorically "musty" or endearingly "cheesy" productions of the distant past. However, when viewed through the nose, and when furthermore brought to the tongue (a body part I will return to in chapter 4), those moments that might strike us as "sick" or "silly" in their excessiveness are only awful to the degree that they bring us into dangerously close proximity with our own animal essence.

## Productive Odors, Putrescent Flesh, and the Sweet Smell of Excess

Yuck! I never smelled anything so terrible!

—Sherry (Judy Clerto) to her boyfriend, Jack (Wayne Ratay), explaining that a night out at the theater would be preferable to another stinky sporting event (his preferred pastime), in Herschell Gordon Lewis's *The Wizard of Gore*

As befits an olfactory tour of critically derided motion pictures directed by someone who, to borrow Jonathan Crane's phrase, excelled at "scraping bottom," it behooves us to start with the tail end of Herschell Gordon Lewis's filmmaking career—or, rather, with the first of two endings and then work our way back to his initial forays into cinematic splatter made a decade earlier.[10] Tellingly, *The Gore Gore Girls* (1972), the last film Lewis gifted the world before leaving the profession behind (at least until his return to directing thirty years later), features a scene in which someone literally scrapes another person's exposed bottom, using an instrument of slow torturous death that is more commonly associated with meal preparation. It occurs inside that area of the home where tastes and smells are expected to intermingle hedonically and the sometimes-bloody business of cooking takes place. The most disgusting demonstration of the filmmaker's pleasure in doling out spectatorial punishment occurs midway through *The Gore Gore Girls*, when a black-gloved serial killer attacks a stripper named Lola "Pickles" Prize (Nora Alexis) in the kitchen of her small apartment. The intruder sneaks up behind her at the refrigerator, forcibly bends her over the dinner table, removes her panties, and repeatedly hammers a meat tenderizer against her bare buttocks before salting them liberally as if preparing steak for the grill. It is a notoriously difficult scene to watch in its entirety. Though "tasteless" and hard to stomach, this scene, culminating with shots of the killer extracting his (or her) victim's eyeballs from their sockets with a knife, are not without "flavor" or stomach-churning astringency, insofar as a discernible twang bleeds through the images and sits heavily upon the tongue, as does the bitter taste of acid reflux (for those of us prone to vomiting). Indeed, the scraping and pounding of the tenderizer against the woman's backside brings forth the tart, metallic taste associated with raw meat. That weirdly savory and unsavory sensation is intensified by her piercing screams, the incongruously upbeat marching-band music on the soundtrack, the harsh incandescent lighting, and the kitchen setting itself, where, seconds before the attack, Lola takes out a pickle from the refrigerator, preparing to sexually pleasure herself with the vinegar-preserved vegetable (distinguished by its briny sourness).

The oral and nasal underpinnings of this scene are further highlighted in the one that immediately follows it, once police officers and crime-scene photographers descend on the dead woman's apartment. Joining them is the film's main character, private investigator Abraham Gentry (Frank Kress), who had visited the pickle-loving woman earlier that evening to inquire about two murdered strippers in the Chicago area, both of whom were employees at the same gentlemen's club—the tellingly named Tops and Bottoms—where Lola worked. When Lieutenant Anderson (Russ Badger), who is leading the investigation, confronts Gentry about his relationship with the victim, he does so while gripping the murder weapon, as if he were interviewing the dapper, cane-twirling private dick with a blood-smeared microphone in hand. After confirming that the circumstances of this latest crime are consistent with the previous murders, Gentry turns his attention to the phallic object that Anderson holds in front of him. Curiously, the protagonist leans in to dab his index finger into the bloody spikes of the meat tenderizer. Even more unexpectedly, he puts his finger to his tongue, tasting the murder evidence in the manner of a TV detective who orally tests white powder to see if it is cocaine (fig. 3.1). The police lieutenant casts a quizzical look at Gentry before bringing the spiked mallet to his nose, sniffing the same stuff that the private investigator has just sampled (fig. 3.2). In swift succession, two sense-based activities—tasting and smelling—have taken place inside a space crowded with other characters who stick to more traditional methods of detection (i.e., taking photographs and gathering physical evidence that might lead to the identification and capture of the apparently psychopathic killer). Grimacing and recoiling from the stench of the blood on the tenderizer, Anderson might just as well be an onscreen surrogate for the audience, who likely shares his combined dismay and disgust at the actions of not only the film's offscreen antagonist but also those of the unflappable protagonist, who (in this and other scenes) shows no sign of alarm or physical revulsion whenever he sees, smells, or tastes the remains of murder victims.

**Figures 3.1 and 3.2:** Within a matter of seconds, the taste and smell of blood—that of a female victim of a maniacal killer—is treated as unofficial evidence during a homicide investigation near the beginning of Herschell Gordon Lewis's *The Gore Gore Girls*.

This scene in *The Gore Gore Girls* recalls a slightly less bizarre moment in Lewis's *A Taste of Blood*, a film unleashed on drive-in audiences five years earlier that likewise shows someone putting a blood-tainted object to his nose and breathing in its unholy essence. That person is John Alucard Stone (Bill Rogers), a Miami businessman who has just received a letter from England informing him that he is the "last descendent of

Baron Vada Khron, Royal House of Khron of Moldavia," and thereby the "Master of Corfax," a sizable estate in a posh suburb of London. Accompanying the letter are two heart-shaped bottles of Slivovitz brandy, one of which he pours into a glass before sniffing the plummy, jammy sweetness and almond-oak undertones of the eighty-year-old beverage and making a toast to his European ancestors. Or, at least, that is what some viewers might imagine this ceremonial wine's aroma to be like (prompted by Stone's comment that it smells like "old brandy"), only to learn that, in keeping with the film's title, it is in fact the metallic tang of *blood* rather than the sugary fragrance of plums that he nasally imbibes in the seconds before literally ingesting the ruby-red drink (and having his own blood tainted as a result). Now that the main character, who is eventually revealed to be a descendant of Count Dracula, has his famous ancestor's taste for blood in his system, his gradual transformation into a vengeance-seeking vampire can take place. But it is his combined act of first smelling and then tasting the tainted stuff, along with his comment that its flavor is "sweet and salty at the same time," that sets the narrative in motion, sending him out into the world in pursuit of the distant relatives of Abraham Van Helsing (Dracula's slayer) but also preparing audiences for the strange mixture of feelings (from disgust to satisfaction) that his murderous exploits might provoke.

Besides that of blood, other, sweeter flavors and taste sensations can also be discerned while watching *A Taste of Blood* and *The Gore Gore Girls*. The latter film includes a murder scene in which another of the serial killer's female victims—a stripper nicknamed "Candy Cane"—chews bubblegum in the seconds leading up to her equally violent death. The fact that she lives above a restaurant (a seemingly trivial detail relayed to Gentry by an informant outside her apartment) is significant, as is the bright pink bubble that sits on her lips after she is knocked out by the mallet-wielding intruder. Once the attacker brings another weapon—a kitchen knife—to her neck and slices it open, blood flows from the cut onto the bed that will be her final resting place. But the gum's bubble remains intact, perched on the victim's still-open mouth and nestled below her nose. As he (or she) will later do to "Pickles," the gloved attacker begins hacking up Candy Cane's face and then grabs bits and pieces of it into mushy clumps, in the manner of a child mashing up squishy playdough or making mud pies. The redness of the unpopped bubble visually rhymes with that of the dead woman's mangled visage and popped eyeballs, though the awful stench and acrid taste of offal now sit atop the fruity/floral sweetness of the gum, a chewable substance that might evoke memories of childhood owing to its minty undertones, pleasant sugary aroma, and cultural associations with innocent youth. There is, of course, nothing innocent or harmless about the killer's brutal act, and the combined gustatory-olfactory elements of this early scene establish the uneasy mix of playful invention and painful destruction that characterizes *The Gore Gore Girls*, not to mention other Lewis-directed efforts to entertain gorehounds through limited means and cheap practical effects.

When Gentry and a young newspaper reporter, Nancy Weston (Amy Farrell), arrive at Candy Cane's apartment, he exhibits the same coolly detached demeanor that he will later adopt during the investigation of Lola's murder. Specifically, he nonchalantly pops open a can of 7-Up and sips the lemon-lime beverage as he surveys the crime scene, bringing yet another set of seemingly hedonic flavors into the proceedings. Unlike her unflappable companion, who remains cool as a cucumber through the scene, Nancy promptly faints, falling to the shag-carpeted floor before being revived and brought back to her feet by a splash of the carbonated soda to her face. A chemical concoction comprised of citric acid, sodium citrate, and high-fructose corn syrup, the 7-Up stings her eyes, forcing her to wipe away tears out of physical irritation rather than sadness at the sight of the dead woman on the bed. As she does so, the not-so-intrepid reporter puts her hands to her face, covering her eyes and nose as if to shield herself from the considerably more upsetting image and odor of the victim's bloody remains. Notably, the sweet-and-sour intermingling throughout this and the preceding bubble-gum scene puts a literalist, lemon-lime, candy-flavored twist on the idea that Nancy had earlier "sweetened" the newspaper's initial twenty-five-thousand-dollar offer to Gentry, convincing him to investigate the brutal murder of a stripper nicknamed "Cream Puff" by adding an extra twenty-five thousand dollars to his payout should he solve the case.

The sweet smell of success spells monetary gain, then, and later scenes of *The Gore Gore Girls* show Gentry waving ten- and twenty-dollar bills in the faces of anyone who might be tempted to spill the beans or offer up information at the sight of cash, under the pretense that the private eye will likewise be handsomely compensated in the end. In one noteworthy moment, a bartender at the strip club where the ill-fated women had earned their own payments by dancing and disrobing (prior to their run-in with the killer) is tempted in this way. Loudly announcing that he needs to step away from the bar to "take a shit," Barney (Ray Sager), the liquor-slinging employee in question, joins Gentry at a nearby table, segueing into a conversation about one of the patrons at the strip club: a mentally disturbed war veteran named Grout (Alex Petrovic) who is fixated not on the women onstage but, rather, on the basket of tomatoes, squashes, and melons that he has dumped out onto the bar, drawing faces on the fruit before mashing them into a pulp. When the private investigator flashes a ten-dollar bill, the bartender snatches it and holds it up to his nose, breathing in its inky aroma before quickly stuffing the payment into his pocket and filling Gentry in on the ex-marine's backstory.

At first glance, this fleeting moment does not appear to be directly related to the film's serial-killer storyline, though the introduction of the fruit-smashing man at the bar presents Gentry with a possible suspect (eventually revealed to be a false lead). Nevertheless, the fact that Barney can be heard sniffing loudly throughout this scene, and not just in reaction to the flashed cash, is significant, for it suggests the persistent presence of odors (even if the bartender is simply dealing with an allergy or just needs to blow his nose). The action of the informant furthermore calls back to the previous scene in which Lieutenant Anderson put the meat tenderizer to his nose, suggesting a link between blood and money as a possible motive for the killer's otherwise inexplicable behavior. More importantly, it hints at the film's intersensorial mix, whereby an audible element on the soundtrack activates a sensing ability other than hearing and nudges spectators to do their own "sniffing" for clues, nasally, through a kind of olfactive ratiocination. Sounds beget smells, in other words, just as the synesthesia wrought by the film's haptic visuality—roughly textured and slickly slimy all at once—induces taste-based sensations along with feelings of disgust located in our own rumbling guts.

The film's synesthetic potency can be felt in yet another disgusting scene set inside a kitchen, this time within the home of two women who each receive unusually cruel forms of physical abuse at the hands of the killer. The latter individual, whose identity and whereabouts are still unknown to the police, sneaks up behind a dancer as she divides her time between cooking French fries on the stove and ironing clothes in the adjoining room. A knife slice to the throat ends her life, but it is what the intruder does to her face and breasts after death that is most disturbing. First, the killer presses the steam iron against her cheeks, charring the skin around her eyes, nose, and mouth until everything melts into a single pulpy orifice. The smell of burnt rubber or plastic rather than flesh might be sensed wafting up from the image like so much sulfuric steam, as the obvious fakeness of the woman's "face"—a mask placed on top of a mannequin's head—distinguishes this oddly humorous display of cheap prosthetics from less jokey, more skillfully shot scenes in today's effects-driven horror films. Next, with a flick of the blade, off come the woman's equally fake-looking nipples. As if from a faucet, milk streams from her breasts—one side white, the other side chocolate—as the killer collects the unpasteurized runoff into margarita glasses. At this point, audiences might groan or guffaw rather than grimace at the sight and imagined smell of this ludicrously "bad" death, but Lewis leaves the most gruesome fatality until the scene's end, when the victim's roommate arrives home. Shoving the unsuspecting woman's face into the pot of boiling oil, the killer literalizes the many figurative food-based horrors that preceded this scene. With as many shots of the sizzling French fries—awash in blood, oil, and pus—as there are close-ups of the woman's greasy, swollen face, the bitter tang and taste of this moment are as palpable as any feeling of dread or terror that one might vicariously experience while watching such scenes (fig. 3.3).

Not coincidentally, that shot of the French fries atop the stove, cooking in a see-through bowl filled with blood, oil, pus, and various pieces of the woman's liquefied face (including at least one eyeball), seems to have inspired the cover art for Arrow Video's seven-disc Blu-ray box set of Herschell Gordon Lewis–directed films (the 2020 home-video release mentioned earlier). A cartoonish illustration of the grinning filmmaker also graces the box, with a spoonful of that culinary concoction hovering just below his nose. It is an appropriately "inappropriate" image, highlighting the combined humor and horror that characterizes his oeuvre while distilling the paradoxically alluring yet distasteful ingredients of his most physically nauseating films.

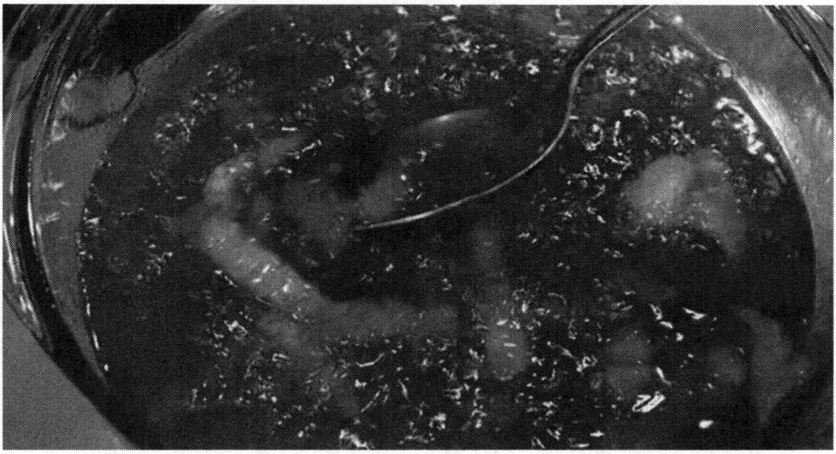

**Figure 3.3:** A bowl full of oily French fries, awash in the partially liquefied remains of a woman's face, flashes onscreen during this grossly aromatic kill scene of *The Gore Gore Girls*. This image recalls the cover art of Arrow Video's Blu-ray box set, which plays up the humorously preposterous, literally distasteful elements for which trash film auteur Herschell Gordon Lewis is famous.

In a *Chicago Tribune* article published a few months prior to *The Gore Gore Girls*' theatrical release (in the fall of 1972), Allison Louise Downe, one of the central members of Lewis's creative team, was interviewed about her role in devising special-effects sequences on the cheap. As someone who had worked behind the scenes as a writer (on *Blood Feast*, *The Gruesome Twosome* [1967], *The Girl, the Body, and the Pill* [1967], and *The Alley Tramp* [1968]) and in front of the camera as a performer (on *Boin-n-g* [1963], *Scum of the Earth* [1963], *Goldilocks and the Three Bares* [1963], and *Suburban Roulette* [1968]), Downe was well versed in the many challenges of low-budget filmmaking and was happy to share humorous anecdotes about her fruitful collaborations with the "Guru of Gore." Having earned her own nickname ("Miami's Sadistic Queen of the Films") through that decade-long collaborative work, Downe long ago had learned to overcome any squeamishness she might have felt about bringing animal parts, including chicken bones and whole sides of beef, onto the set. Looking back at the past with a mixture of pride and wistfulness, she waxes nostalgically about the practical merits of using mortician's wax along with other "goopy" tools of the trade. Besides recounting how she and fellow crew members had come up with a new type of cherry-flavored stage blood on the set of *Blood Feast* and figured out how to quickly fashion fake fingers and other appendages for the mutilation scenes of subsequent films, Downe alludes to some of the various odors that permeated these regional productions, including those that tested her otherwise-desensitized gag reflex and strong stomach.

For instance, during the making of Lewis's 1970 film, *The Wizard of Gore*, one especially disgusting object—the decapitated head of the main character, stage magician Montag the Magnificent (fashioned from a combination of calf brains stuffed into a rubber face mask)—was left to fester in the prop closet for two weeks before it was found by production personnel. "That smell, combined with the formaldehyde from the mortician's wax," according to Downe, "was a stopper," forcing Lewis to temporarily shut down the film's already-short shooting schedule (eight days of principal photography) until the main office could be aired out. When the prop man on that same production was unable to find pig intestines for a scene that was to show a punch press crushing one of Montag's victims, he came back to the set (in the suburbs of Chicago) with a bag of Polish sausages he had purchased from a local butcher and which he proceeded to stuff into a fake abdomen as pretend viscera. Minutes later, when the camera was rolling, the sight of the magician pulling out kielbasa from a human corpse not only "cracked everyone up" but also nearly made Downe sick, owing to the strong garlic smell that wafted across the area.[11]

On the director's commentary track included on Arrow Video's Bluray release of *The Wizard of Gore*, Lewis does not regale his listeners with that food-related anecdote. However, he alludes to another instance in which strong odors delayed shooting and created headaches (and possibly stomachaches) for himself and other members of the small crew. Describing it as the "one thing that went wrong on this picture," Lewis discusses the time when he forgot to dispose of all the "meat and junk" that he had piled into the trunk of his automobile, which he had been using to transport ad-hoc props to and from the set. Because that rotting organic matter left behind such an unforgettably bad stench—so appalling that he was apparently unable to shake it off years later—the filmmaker had to take a momentary break from shooting to seek advice from a used-car dealer, who recommended replacing his Air Wick with burnt coffee grounds. "I could not get that smell out," Lewis remarks on the disc's commentary track, as if he were speaking not only about his car's interior upholstery but also about his mind, which had been forever imprinted with that indelible sense memory.[12] From a production standpoint, the filmmaker's retrospective complaint likely would have resonated with Downe and other collaborators who knew well how budgetary limitations could lead to encounters with literally unsavory elements under his directorial leadership.

Along with the *Chicago Tribune* piece from February 1972, supplemental materials like a director's audio commentary track, cast and crew interviews, and "making-of" documentaries (all of which are included in the Arrow Video "Collector's Edition" release) offer more than just trivial bits of behind-the-scenes information tailored to fans who feed on such details with the same feverish glee that Lewis displays on the brightly colored cover of that Blu-ray box set. In her article "Undoing the Magic? DVD Extras and the Pleasure Behind the Scenes," Nicola Jean Evans argues that such paratexts "reconfigure how we imagine and what we consume as the film text."[13] They not only make it possible for audiences to gain "secret" or "forbidden" knowledge about the illusions upon which so many fictional narratives are predicated, but also gesture toward previously overlooked aspects of the sometimes-horrific "Real" lurking within those fictions. Citing the work of horror film expert Carol Clover, Evans notes that the genre grants considerable power to that paratextual "fleshing out" of texts, since so much of its thematic preoccupations pivots on the consequences of characters' often-terrifying pursuit of truth and/or confrontation with things beyond their imagination.[14] If a newspaper interview or recorded audio commentary can be said to pull back the proverbial curtain and show how the "magic" of moviemaking is achieved (even on a shoestring budget), such revelations only become truly "eye-opening" once other sensing organs (the ears, the nose, the skin, and the tongue) are called upon to imagine that which *cannot be seen*. Short of being on a film set to witness firsthand—to actually *hear*, *smell*, *touch*, and *taste*—the things that were put to creative use during the well-documented making of a film like *The Wizard of Gore* (some fifty-five years ago), cultural historians and horror enthusiasts would do well to draw upon such documents to supplement what little they *do* see on the screen, and to search for meanings beneath the visual excess of texts that beg to be perceived through senses other than sight.

## Fakeness, Realness, Toxicity

The amateurish "magic" for which Lewis is wildly if not widely celebrated—his ability to dazzle audiences through sheer audacity if not technical artistry while relying on sleight-of-hand stagecraft befitting a charlatan like Montag—makes his work especially ripe for paratextual analysis, given how frequently his films function as *documentaries of themselves*, unwittingly bringing the "behind-the-scenes" labor of moviemaking onto the screen. As exemplified by his 1967 exploitation film, *Something Weird*, which includes a fleeting glimpse of a crew member sticking his arm into frame and pouring fake blood onto actor Ted Heil (who, playing a policeman by day, serial killer by night, is gunned down during a climactic scene set in a railyard), Lewis's films are paradoxically honest about their falseness. Though frequently held up as evidence of a filmmaker's incompetence, such mistakes, on top of all the scratch marks, cigarette burns, discolorations, and other celluloid artifacts that are left intact on otherwise pristine home-video releases (like the ones that litter *Something Weird*), reveal something truthful about the materiality of the motion picture medium by shattering the illusion of narrative. Something as simple as a boom mic dipping into frame or an actor fumbling his or her lines of dialogue can make it seem as if we, the audience, are right there on set, watching, hearing, and smelling a film's production firsthand (like honorary cast members or crew members). Supplemental materials on home-video releases along with interviews published in newspapers and magazines merely enhance a feature already present in Lewis's films, giving further access to the inner workings and imagined odors of productions in which onscreen talent and offscreen personnel were known to have switched positions (in front of and behind the camera) just as frequently as animal parts were used in place of human anatomy and real odors intruded into those films' fictional worlds.

Although none of the characters in *The Wizard of Gore* reacts visibly to the stench of the title character's all-too-real stage illusions, which entails pulling entrails from female volunteers on stage, one young woman—an audience member named Sherry—makes a passing reference to bad odors verbally, during a scene in which she and her boyfriend, Jack, discuss the relative merits of magic acts versus sports competitions. Occurring midway through the film, after Montag has demonstrated his knack for faked mutilations that become all too real once his victims return home from a night at the theater, the scene takes place inside Jack's white convertible, where the couple talk about all the baseball, basketball, football, and hockey games he has made her sit through. Trying to leverage this against her obstinate (or, as she says, "pig-headed") partner's unwillingness to go to another magic-show performance, Sherry tells Jack that the intercollegiate wrestling tournament they recently attended was especially onerous, given how offensive the body odor of the sweaty, writhing, nearly naked male bodies was. Prefacing her bizarre comment "I never smelled anything so terrible" with the exclamation "Yuck!," and telling Jack that it wouldn't "kill" him to see Montag on stage one more time, she articulates an underlying theme of *The Wizard of Gore*, which revolves around the dialectic of reality and perception and illustrates how the latter means of identifying, organizing, and interpretating information about the former depends on sensory inputs or abilities that differ from person to person. Indeed, the power of the stage magician's gimmicky show, like that of the film itself, depends on its audience's willingness not to suspend disbelief but to hold two contrasting positions vis-à-vis the illusion of cinematic/theatrical death and dismemberment, which can be gut-wrenching to witness even as their obvious fakeness mitigates against full immersion into that apparently spellbinding illusion. In a related way, Sherry, according to her boyfriend, is said to have "drooled" while watching those yucky wrestlers a few nights earlier, suggesting that she, like Montag's and Lewis's respective audiences, was simultaneously drawn to yet repulsed by what she beheld and smelled.

The tight grouping of sweaty bodies in this and several other films directed by Herschell Gordon Lewis, including *Moonshine Mountain*, *Just for the Hell of It* (1968), *She-Devils on Wheels*, and *Suburban Roulette* (which show, among other things, several characters dancing, destroying property, fighting, sunning themselves at the pool, and making out en masse, their skin oily with cosmetics or glistening with perspiration), would surely have sickened Sherry, based on her comments about the excessive body odor of wrestlers. Viewers, too, might behold something like bromhidrosis or halitosis whenever an extreme close-up of someone's armpit or open mouth flashes onscreen. An example of this occurs in *The Gruesome Twosome*, when another young couple sits in an open-top car at a drive-in theater, watching a film in which a man (played by Ray Sager) ignores his girlfriend while stuffing potato chips into his mouth (fig. 3.4). Besides echoing an earlier scene in which a group of young women in nightgowns scarf down a bucket of Kentucky Fried Chicken, the lingering shot of the salty snacks spilling out from his pie hole brings audiences uncomfortably close to someone whose behavior, like the briny, vinegary odor of his breath, could be perceived as being noxious.

Even more toxic is the close-up of smalltown sheriff Asa Potter (Adam Sorg, a.k.a. Gordon Oas-Heim), the main antagonist of *Moonshine Mountain*, who momentarily interrupts his crooked dealings with two feuding Appalachian families to focus on a young blonde woman from New York City. Grinning devilishly and gazing lasciviously at the well-to-do outsider, who has driven to the Carolinas with her country-and-western singer fiancé but now finds herself unaccompanied in the presence of the leering lawman, Sheriff Potter is practically a caricature not only of hillbilly culture and rural communities in the Deep South (the subject

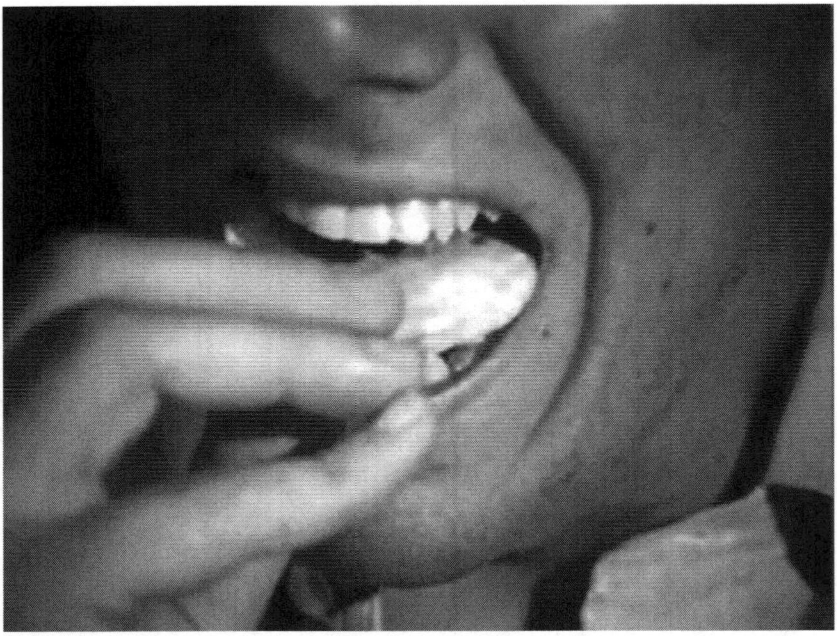

**Figure 3.4:** In Herschell Gordon Lewis's films such as *The Gruesome Twosome* and *Moonshine Mountain*, extreme close-ups of men's faces—drenched in sweat and hovering close to the camera—might trigger olfactory responses from viewers who can practically smell the food on these characters' breath.

of this and other "hicksploitation" movies) but also of cult film audiences and fan communities whose overstimulated zeal in consuming "dirty pictures" (i.e., exploitation movies) has itself been stereotyped over the years. The menacing, morally corrupt sheriff's face looms large in the frame as he bears down on Della (Marilyn Waters), having forced her to slide over into the passenger seat of her white convertible so that he can take control of the situation and possibly manhandle her into submission. The sudden interjection of that close-up shot makes the man's unsolicited overtures all the more aggressive and *oilier* in the literal sense, as his flop sweat and whiskey-scented breath lend additional moistness to a film already drenched in corpse-flavored moonshine, sweltering heat and humidity, and nondeodorized B.O.

Whenever moonshiners uncork jugs of white lightning in this and other Lewis-directed films set in the Deep South (*Two Thousand Maniacs!* and *This Stuff'll Kill Ya!* [1971]), the skunky, gamey flavor and smell of that bottled rotgut are likely to hit the tongue and nose just as sharply as the bloodied knives that press down upon victims' skin in his more widely seen horror films. But that whiskey-triggered assault on the senses is considerably less stomach-churning and "offensive," from a cultural standpoint, than the olfactory and gustatory sensations stirred up by his most shocking, physically nauseating work. Much has been written about the director's initial foray into knife-slicing horror, *Blood Feast*, which effectively kicked off the modern era of over-the-top mutilation scenes and splatter effects by killing off the first character to appear onscreen—a nameless, naked woman alone at home—in graphically violent fashion (a bathroom scene that parodies the one in Alfred Hitchcock's *Psycho* [1960] by adding dollops of chromatically intense gore to the proceedings). With so much discourse already published about this commercially successful film's landmark status as well as its considerably less groundbreaking representational politics, I see little need to say much about it or to contribute to a critical consensus that sees it as the "best" or most representative of Lewis's large body of work. However, it is worth noting that the filmmaker's habit of subbing in offal (the lowly, protein-packed parts of butchered animals) for human organs and flesh began with *Blood Feast*, a film with a title that hints at the bounty of foodstuff awaiting audiences whose consumption is thereby equated with a kind of masochistic mastication, an ingestion of unsavory (yet flavorful) ingredients.

The centerpiece of the film's titular feast is a bloody stew of sundry body parts, gathered from innocent victims by a machete-wielding follower of the goddess Ishtar who believes that he can resurrect the long-slumbering deity through human sacrifice. One such ingredient is the tongue of a young woman who has been captured and tortured by Fuad Ramses (Mal Arnold), the psychopathic food caterer whose main objective, aside from the resurrection of Ishtar, is to make the celebratory blood feast as "authentic" as possible. This is something that Lewis and his crew also sought to do, crafting scenes of gruesome, "realistic" torture, including one of such unprecedented directness and oral invasiveness that audiences would be forced to turn away from the screen. As I have written about in a previous book about horror films, information about the shooting of that scene, in which a sheep's tongue was used in place of actress Astrid Olson's ripped-out tongue, alleviates some of the emotional and physical stress placed on spectators who are able to swallow animal deaths more easily than they can human deaths.[15] The bonus audio commentary track included on Arrow Video's Blu-ray release of *Blood Feast* features a brief conversation between director Lewis and producer David F. Friedman as they reminisce about this scene, which necessitated buying not only a sheep's tongue from a local butcher's shop but also bottles of Pine-Sol, a household cleaning product in which the gloppy appendage was doused so as to cover up the stench of rotting meat.[16] This and other production-related tidbits, though trivial within the larger history of cinematic horror, prompt a recalibration of the senses, including that of *smell* and its sister sense, *taste*.

## A Smell of Honey or a Swallow of Brine?

Look, if I prepare a gourmet feast of monkey brains for vegetarians, I deserve to go out of business because I have totally misread the people who are supposed to be my targets.

—Herschell Gordon Lewis, quoted in Andrew J. Rausch's *Gods of Grindhouse: Interviews with Exploitation Filmmakers* (2013)

The far-from-pleasurable interactions of odors and flavors stimulated by the scenes that I have singled out partially distinguish Herschell

Gorden Lewis's body of work as intensely *body-related work* for the spectator, who is asked to endure one entrail-strewn set piece after another and breathe in their putrescent perfumes while consuming motion pictures that test gag reflexes as surely as they strain credulity. Nevertheless, a more holistic assessment of his film's aromatic suggestiveness would account for other, less repulsive moments, including those scenes in which traditionally fragrant or sweet-smelling objects (for instance, bouquets of flowers in *How to Make a Doll* [1968] and *Just for the Hell of It* and vanilla-frosted birthday cake in *Blood Feast 2: All U Can Eat*) appear before the lens. Across the hedonic spectrum, a variety of scents between "bad" and "good" impress themselves upon our nasal imagination. Still, Lewis's gravitation toward the horror genre—and toward the gore/splatter subgenre more specifically—means that his films lean more heavily to one side of that spectrum than the other, favoring blood cakes over birthday cakes. Moreover, the grisly stuff that so many of his films' characters are shown sniffing, such as the bloodstained shirt of a man who has just been drawn and quartered and which a redneck holds up to his nose in *Two Thousand Maniacs!*, leads us to conclude that the stench of death, far more than any breath of fresh air or fragrant bouquet, pervades Lewis's work. The fact that the latter film—an unofficial adaptation of Alan Jay Lerner and Frederick Loewe's 1947 musical *Brigadoon* set not in a mythical village of the Scottish Highlands but in a rural community in Georgia (full of muddy, bacteria-filled quicksand marshes, along with equally dangerous-looking Confederate flags)—shows townspeople chowing down on another victim's charred arm (which, spinning on a barbeque spit, emits a smoky, charcoal stench) only strengthens the intersensorial bonds between smell and taste. And those two modes of bodily ingestion, when combined, "give us the rich array of flavors we love and loathe."[17]

In his book *The Anatomy of Disgust*, William Ian Miller notes that the physical feeling of revulsion that lends his book its title would be hard to conceptualize without the nose and its neural receptors to guide us toward the sources of our own animal essence—that is, the "feces, urine, decay and sweat" that make life itself so "yucky" and "disgusting."[18] And yet despite, or perhaps owing to, its centrality to the human condition, humbly reminding us of the biological functions that make us kissing cousins or distant kin to so-called less-evolved species, "smell ranks low in the hierarchy of senses."[19] So low, in fact, that we can hardly be bothered to expand our otherwise limited vocabulary of terms for specific olfactory sensations, leaving us with simple adjectives and similes derived from the nouns they describe as shorthand: "Excrement smells like excrement, roses like a rose, rotting flesh like rotting flesh." As such, any developmental advancements that might be chalked up to humankind or attributed to our species' ability to adapt to dangerous encounters in the world are inversely proportional to our *lack of progression*, culturally and linguistically, with regards to smell (an important sense in our defense against such dangers). Unlike the fine gradations of tactile sensations comprising our lexicon of touch (measured "along qualitative axes of temperature, viscosity, texture, movement, adhesion, and so on"), which enables us to make subtle distinctions between "squishy, oozy, gooey, gummy, mucky, dank, and damp" things, odor qualifiers, Miller argues, are usually abstract near-synonyms "expressing either the pleasantness or unpleasantness of the smell, most of which merely mean bad or good smell: fetid, foul, stink, stench, rancid, vile, revolting, nauseating, sickening."[20] Whereas "routine tactile sensation spurs language to inventiveness . . . the olfactory and gustatory reduce us to saying little more than 'yum' or 'yuck.'"[21]

With their reliance on "squishy, oozy, gooey, gummy, mucky, dank, and damp" practical effects, motion pictures such as *Blood Feast* encourage audiences to view offal—the organ meats of animals—as something awful, a food source-turned-movie prop whose low cultural standing is not unlike that of the films in which it appears. Notably, the origins of the term "offal" (*off-fall*, meaning "the bits that fall out when an animal is cut open," but encompassing everything from "putrid flesh [and] interior fish" to "refuse in general") remind us that Lewis's films, like so much "offscouring" or "scum of the earth," have long been cast aside and derided by critics whom the director called "blue noses"—individuals who might fancy themselves gourmands when dining on exotic morsels like Moroccan lamb heart kebabs, barbecued chicken gizzard yakitori, and grilled lamb liver meatballs.[22] What celebrity chef Anthony Bourdain once called "those wonderful tough little bits" are therefore right at home in remainder-like films such as *The Gore Gore Girls*, which not only stage clearly fake yet noxiously disturbing kill scenes inside kitchens but also bring sundry textures, odors, and flavors to bear on the question of "taste." Just as most consumers of food have a "limited definition of meat" and, according to Tony Federico and James Phelan, rarely stray from "safe," culturally and morally acceptable animals to eat (e.g., chickens, cows, salmon, pigs), mainstream movie audiences generally stick to comforting fictions, preferring the familiarity of bloodless, nonoffensive genre films to discomforting gore and other offenses to the senses.[23] A little cinematic offal, in the literal and figurative sense, might be just what is needed for those audiences to follow Allison Louise Downe's lead and overcome their squeamishness about such things, expanding their diets in the process.

Open many a modern cookbook or recipe guide (at least those aimed at nonvegetarians) and one sees just how significant offal is not only from a dietary perspective (since, in the words of Federico and Phelan, "eating from the whole animal provides a tremendous diversity of nutrients," including the amino acids glycine and proline, which most people miss out on if they limit themselves to lean muscle meat), but also from a cultural standpoint.[24] Jeremy MacClancy, author of *Consuming Culture: Why You Eat What You Eat*, makes this argument as well, noting that the "exaggerated squeamishness" many middle-class Americans feel when confronted by gastronomical concoctions comprised of livers, lungs, mesentery, spleens, and other viscera is not widely shared by people in most parts of the world.[25] Claudia Roden echoes that sentiment in her historical overview of ethnic dishes popular in several North African and Middle Eastern countries, where centuries ago and in recent years it was not unusual for people to dine on sheep's head, cow's udder, pig's feet, and other delicacies. In *The Book of Jewish Food*, Roden paints detailed descriptions of "poor food" morsels such as Tunisian *aakode* ("a stew of stomach, tripe, stuffed intestine, testicles, and penis with harissa, cumin, paprika, and tomato paste"), Algerian *faad d'agneau* ("the lungs, heart, liver, esophagus, and entrails of a lamb, cooked with garlic, tomato, onion, and parsley"), and Moroccan *tagine del guezar* ("stewed liver, spleen, heart, lungs, head, feet, and beef-intestine sausage filled with liver"). The pleasure this food expert seems to derive from describing how one goes about preparing a New Year's dish—splitting a lemon- or vinegar-soaked lamb's head in half and removing its eyes and ears (but leaving the tongue and brain intact)—is not unlike the giddiness that Lewis brought to big-screen murders and mutilations, using trotters, sweetbreads, intestines, eyeballs and other parts of dead animals to achieve something of cultural if not culinary significance.

The cultural significance of the motion pictures discussed in this chapter can be measured by the large number of other directors' films—produced before and after his retirement from filmmaking in the early 1970s—which used offal as a practical gross-out effect or ingestible/edible prop. From Roman Polanski's *Rosemary's Baby* (1968), which depicts Mia Farrow's devil-impregnated title character eating raw liver, to Ridley Scott's *Alien* (1979), which features a giant xenomorph's egg made from a cow's stomach-lining (for the membrane) and sheep intestines (for the tentacles),[26] numerous examples of costlier, more critically acclaimed horror and science fiction cinema owe a debt to Lewis's pioneering efforts to, in the words of cult film enthusiast Joe Bob Briggs, "put red meat into the American cinematic diet."[27] Although he did not live long enough to witness its publication, one suspects that the filmmaker, a specialist in what Lorna Piatti-Farnell refers to as "abject orality" who was known for his good sense of humor on set and during interviews,[28] would have welcomed the recent publication of John Dieringer's *Horror Caviar: A Cookbook*, which showcases feasts, delicacies, and drinks inspired by dozens of horror films ranging from Mario Bava's *Blood and Black Lace* (1964) to Andrzej Żuławski's *Possession* (1981), Amy Holden Jones's *The Slumber Party Massacre* (1982), Mary Lambert's *Pet Sematary* (1989), Takashi Miike's *Audition* (1999), and Julia Ducournau's *Raw* (2016).[29] The mind spins—and the stomach churns—at the thought of another, less appetizing, more aromatically intimidating assortment of published recipes based on his *own* films, which were themselves blueprints for what many of today's horror auteurs have been cooking up in recent years.

# 4

# TASTE THE PAIN, BRO

## Horror Film's Masculinist Flavors and Masochistic Mouthfeel

Mmmm, just what I like: fresh cheerleader—sounds like a new Ben & Jerry's flavor.

—The anonymous axe-wielding killer of *Head Cheerleader Dead Cheerleader* (2000), chuckling as he speaks over the phone with the soon-to-be "final girl," Heather (Tasha Biering)

Mmmm, tastes like jellybeans. I'm like the cookie monster up in this bitch! I hope that shit was gluten-free!

—High-school jock Terry Stankus (Tom Williamson), seconds after swallowing a "magic stone" that makes his raging misogyny truly monstrous, in *All Cheerleaders Die* (2013)

Taste is a topic that pops up frequently in studies of cinematic horror, with more than a few scholars weighing in on the lack of tact or discretion that characterizes many so-called low examples of the genre. For instance, in her exploration of horror films produced by the major studios in Hollywood during the Great Depression, including Universal Pictures' *Murders in the Rue Morgue* (1932) (which, prior to being critically reevaluated along with other works by director Robert Florey, was heavily censored and received harsh reviews upon its theatrical release, in part because it contained shocking scenes of "inter-species miscegenation"), Elizabeth Erwin reminds us that such motion pictures "pushed the boundaries of good taste by creating storylines extreme enough to interest a cash-strapped audience."[1] Along the same lines, Xavier Aldana Reyes argues that several recent horror films rooted to a gothic tradition, including those that have been labeled "torture porn," such as *Saw* (2004), *Hostel* (2005), and *A Serbian Film* (2010), "transgress boundaries and play with decorum." In going "too far" in their depictions of gratuitous violence, mangled bodies, nonnormative sexuality, and other signifiers of textual excess, such films are said to cater to spectators wallowing in "puerility and bad taste" (a widespread misconception that Aldana Reyes rightly challenges).[2]

Writing about the buxom, "monstrously curvy" female bodies that figure heavily—*top* heavily—in expensive studio productions like Terence Fisher's *The Curse of the Werewolf* (1961) and schlocky exploitation films like director Al Adamson's *The Possession of Nurse Sherri* (1977), André Loiselle likewise notes that the "cheap, easy thrills" many audiences associate with cinematic horror are thought to be best appreciated by members of the "uneducated lower classes," whose "bad taste" rivals or surpasses that of the films themselves.[3] In other words, the "unwashed masses"—be they the legions of horny teenagers or sexually repressed moviegoers from decades past who, enticed by the promise of exposed flesh, flocked to screenings of the latest Hammer production for reasons other than having a good scare (which Loiselle alludes to in his discussion of the genre's big-breasted guilty pleasures), or today's hardcore horror fans who seek out the "sickest," most physically or morally revolting works with the highest body counts—have a taste for *tastelessness*, a predilection for things of such low cultural standing as to be devoid of anything remotely appealing to more discriminating consumers.

As suggested by the titles of numerous publications, from Gerry Coubro's slim volume *Hammer and Horror: Bad Taste and Popular British Cinema* (1991) to Jeffrey Sconce's edited volume *Sleaze Artists: Cinema at the Margins of Taste, Style, and Politics* (2007), copious amounts of luridness, offensiveness, and vulgarity are to be expected in motion pictures that contravene socially accepted standards of aesthetic beauty or moral duty (i.e., the obligation to be "good"). To take even a small measure of satisfaction in watching a film like *Head Cheerleader Dead Cheerleader* (2000), writer-director Jeff Miller's sleazy metatextual take on the slasher subgenre, is to flaunt one's inability to make discerning judgments about matters of artistic or cultural worth. Even worse, to actually *create* such a homophobic, misogynistic, and racist motion picture (one spilling over with "general bad taste-ism," to borrow the expression of one Letterboxd user who, in his two-and-a-half-stars review, laments the political incorrectness of Miller's film but seems oddly unperturbed about a scene showing one woman "getting her tit chopped off") is to traffic in the kind of "sick-making" that, according to Harmony Wu, "produces corporeal sensations of disgust."[4] Or so goes the conventional wisdom that not only holds filmmakers accountable to audiences defined in part by the latter's lack of refinement, but also asks that they abide by certain "codes of conduct" or "standards of decency" lest they and their otherwise irredeemable work be forever consigned to the trash heap of history.

The kind of "taste" that I have thus far described is rooted to a philosophical tradition stretching back several centuries, past Bourdieu, Hume, and Kant to some of the earliest writings about aesthetic judgment and the apprehension of formal beauty introduced in the works of Augustine, Aristotle, and Plato. Conceptually, it encompasses everything from "cultural capital" to "critical discernment" and has been theorized as being both deeply *social* (a product of one's class affiliation or educational background) and highly *subjective* (a personal feeling or individual predilection). In their exploration of the playful "unproductiveness" of games, John Sharp and David Thomas state, "Your taste is just that—your subjective opinion and not a declaration of anything more substantial. And yet individual tastes . . . conjoin and connect into community standards—all of which reflect back and are influenced by the larger aesthetic and ethical standards of the overlapping communities in which the games exist."[5] Although they focus on a different sort of "idle" pastime than that of film viewing, Sharp and Thomas's comment that "taste is never in isolation and is always layered and complex" pertains as much to the mediated experiences of consuming conventionally "bad" movies as it does to the various procedural and rhetorical activities involved in directly or indirectly engaging in tabletop, online, and console game play.

When someone has a taste or appetite *for* something, that person is inclined toward it, perhaps owing to external (societal) pressures or internal (psychological) drives that produce additional feelings of pride, guilt, or any of the other positively and negatively valanced "meta-emotions" that Carl Plantinga and other scholars have written about in recent years. Plantinga argues that those second-order emotions, which emerge whenever spectators respond emotionally to their own or other audiences' responses, thus coexist alongside—are layered *atop*—the first-order physical reactions (e.g., crying, laughing, retching, shuddering, screaming) that are such an ingrained facet of the moviegoing experience.[6] Of course, the traditional moviegoing experience, which occurs inside a specific type of venue (i.e., a darkened movie theater auditorium) alongside other people (i.e., fellow audience members), and which might not correspond to how today's media consumers actually engage horror "content," adds another layer of emotions and sensations, including that which has nothing to do with the images flickering on the screen or the sounds issuing from the speakers. From the familiar fragrance of buttery popcorn drifting into the nostrils to the flavor and effects of soda or some less-sugary beverage sitting on the tongue and entering the bloodstream, the affective dimensions of the theatrical experience are easy to overlook, especially when spectators are so thoroughly immersed in a story as to forget their surroundings. In fact, for several years those sensorial aspects have been largely neglected by scholars writing about film exhibition and reception.[7] Yet, as stealthily invasive as those smells and flavors are—stealing into our bodies with all of the slyness of an invisible killer sneaking up behind his next victim—they are also hard to ignore once we become attuned to the contextual and metaemotional factors impinging on our reception not only of films but of *our own reception*. Any claim about the strict subjectivity of personal tastes can be easily contested once we see (and hear) how powerfully the very *publicness* of traditional spectatorship affects the degree of "guilt" or "pride" (or any other metaemotion) that one might feel when sharing the laughter or screams (or any other physical reaction) of fellow audience members. Indeed, a different sort of satisfaction or comfort can be derived from the shared experience of witnessing one's own tastes (for particular types of humor or horror, for instance) being validated by the laughter and screams of strangers.

Besides having a taste *for* something, most people—those of us who have not been affected by the rare medical condition known as ageusia—experience the taste *of* things as well. This latter understanding of the word "taste" is what I wish to explore in the pages that follow. As a noun, "taste" denotes not only a fleeting experience or a small portion of a larger substance (as if one has merely sampled it), but also the ways that our minds and bodies perceive the bitterness, saltiness, sourness, sweetness, and umami of comestibles. As a transitive verb, "to taste" refers to the act of putting food, beverages, and other substances past the lips, into the mouth, and onto the palate and tongue, as well as the resulting perception of flavors that, routed through the thalamus, links various organs of the body (including, of course, the brain) along the alimentary tract, all the way from the mouth, the throat, the esophagus, the stomach, and the small and large intestines to the rectum and the anus. Taste in this "sense" is less a property of potentially edible and digestible objects than a *perceptual phenomenon* located across the eater/digester's body. It is a sensation that, like smell, is likely to trigger memories of previous gustatory experiences and can be stimulated through audiovisual means—especially so by the kinds of horror films that depict figuratively and literally distasteful moments of human consumption and sometimes leave a bitter aftertaste long after the closing credits. In this way, two types of "bad taste" converge during viewings of stomach-churning, nausea-inducing movies like *The Human Centipede* (2009) and its two sequels, which stimulate our *mental* taste buds (if not the actual receptor cells located on the tongue, the upper esophagus, and the various tissues of the mouth) as surely as they do those parts of the lower bodily strata from which food and liquids suddenly come up—like so much of the creamy white stuff in writer-director Larry Cohen's *The Stuff* (1985)—whenever *moral disgust* assumes the shape or form of *physical disgust*.

It is worth mentioning that the word "disgust" is etymologically tied to the sense of taste, or gustation, making it possible for us to close the gap between morality and physicality and to argue for a more literal understanding of critical discernment as being a fully *corporeal*, rather than strictly intellectual, activity. Notably, some of the most disgusting scenes across the history of cinematic horror depict characters ingesting something that is not just unappetizing but unfit for consumption: For instance, a "sausage" pizza topped with human flesh in the 1989 slasher film *Offerings*, and the titular dishes in the 2004 Hong Kong horror film *Dumplings*, which contain the ground-up remains of unborn fetuses inside their delicately molded dough. In these latter cases, looks are deceiving, and a given food item's "immoral" nutritional content is masked behind an alluring presentation or a pleasant aroma that corresponds to its tastiness, the pleasurable sensation that it gives to characters who hungrily scarf down or slurp up the nasty stuff while remaining oblivious of its actual ingredients (which merely supplant animal meat with something less tolerable: human meat). Along with our superior knowledge as spectators, which distances us from the characters' cluelessness even if we are sympathetic to their predicaments, that incongruity between the food's *form* and *content* creates a comical effect. As such, chuckles come as swiftly as the need to upchuck, if only because the affective reactions and metaemotional feelings elicited by cinematic horror are so closely joined, and because our "shame" from having been taken in and physically affected by such a fantastical fiction—especially in the company of other grossed-out audience members—must be purged, "laughed off," as surely as do our fears that those unbelievable scenarios *could* actually transpire in the real world. *Purgation* in the form of laughter and possibly even vomit is part of the genre's "mouthfeel," or the perception of tactile differences in the humorous and horrific properties of a given motion picture based on the way that those properties metaphorically materialize and make contact with our mouths.

Because our actual mouths—the oral cavities that we use for eating and speaking—are called upon to do the seemingly dissimilar kinds of work involved in the two types of "taste" mentioned above, it is possible to conceive of movie-viewing (and movie-reviewing) as a type of mastication. Before swallowing the formal and representational "foodstuff" of a film and then letting that film's story and themes sit in the pits of our stomachs, we experience its relative creaminess, graininess, juiciness, oiliness, silkiness, stickiness, and viscosity. The rheological features of the horror film, which frequently deforms or shape-shifts into comedy while we chew on it, are what make our actual mouths *also* change shape, forming "Ahhhs" and "Ohhhs" and panoramic grins or grimaces as wide as an anamorphic lens. Even while seated silently before a screen, as spectators our lips sometimes move with the same spastic elasticity that characterizes the physical flow of chewed food past the mouth and down the alimentary tract toward its final destination. The transformation of that physical material into human waste—from one end of the body to the other—parallels the movement of horror film as a cultural object through hierarchical aesthetic thresholds of "goodness" and "badness" (or, to adopt the rhetoric of many online commentators, "shittiness").

On a related note, it also reminds us that, however "elevated" certain examples of the genre might be, cinematic horror largely concerns moral and physical *descent* and remains a lowly, coarse type of discourse in the eyes (and mouths) of audiences with the "good sense" (and better taste) not to stoop to such disgusting things.

## Mad, Bad, and Dangerous to Chew: Unsavory Stuff, from *Thankskilling* to *The Menu*

It matters to the halibut, Mrs. Leibrandt. And to the artist whose work turns to shit inside your gut.

—Chef Slowik (Ralph Fiennes) to a restaurant patron who questions why it matters that someone might confuse one type of fish for another on his immaculately prepared plate, in director Mark Mylod's *The Menu* (2022)

Portions of my previous book, *Body Genre: Anatomy of the Horror Film*, gestured toward the figuratively and literally "slimy" aspects of motion pictures that revolve around gross acts, including those that leave audiences feeling an assortment of seemingly contradictory emotions: from revulsion at the sight and suggested smell of someone soiling himself (or others) in the presence of a demon (as in *Rawhead Rex* [1986]), to giddiness at having witnessed something either breathtakingly "bad" in its "flouting of stylistic norms" or transgressively "mad" in its button-pushing treatment of subject matter (violence, sexuality, gender representation) that more restrained motion pictures handle with greater care, often for fear of offending audiences.[8] As I. Q. Hunter has argued, even the "worst" motion pictures—those whose creators set out to make "sick, offensive, and disgusting exercises in bad taste"—can be thought of as being "good" in the sense of occasioning not merely a feeling of outrage on the part of an offended spectator (itself a potentially productive response) but a broader recalibration and even "cancellation" of the kind of "ineffective descriptors" that qualitatively distinguish a worthy object of study from one that appears at first blush not to justify such consideration.[9] Though seemingly bereft of the kinds of "awesome moments" discussed by Jeffrey Sconce in his essay "Explosive Apathy" (when the spectator's "enthrallment to the artistry and power of the awesomely executed" set piece, action scene, or individual shot might lead him "to shit and/or piss his pants and, moreover, to be glad that his pants have been thus soiled"), horror films singled out for their badness have given us plenty of awesomely outrageous flashness of mad genius, fueling a social media feeding frenzy through scenes that have become internet memes.[10] Here I am thinking of films such as *Silent Night, Deadly Night Part 2* (1987), which shows its mentally deranged antihero Ricky Caldwell (Eric Freeman) following in his dead brother's murderous footsteps and yelling "Garbage day!" before killing a neighbor who is taking out his trash; and *Deep Blue Sea* (1999), which shows a corporate executive (played by Samuel L. Jackson) in mid-monologue being devoured by a leaping shark and dragged to a watery grave.[11]

Less well known, but no less preposterous, are the events that take place in Lucio Fulci's *Demonia* (*Liza*, 1990). Over a seven-minute stretch that occurs midway through this nunsploitation gore-fest set in the village of Santa Rosalia, Sicily, the following four events, spread out over past and present-day scenes, take place: (1) during the late 1400s, a young man lying in bed, sweaty and spent after having hot, heretical sex with a nun, is stabbed in the neck by the knife-wielding woman as part of a ritual sacrifice; (2) a newborn baby is taken from its mother (that same nun) and dumped into a fire by a wet nurse at a local convent; (3) back in the present day, the decapitated head of a man is dredged up on the tusk of a boat anchored off the island's southern coast; and (4) a librarian is attacked by a clowder of cats, who gouge her eyes out and claw her skin until she collapses in a bloody heap. This sickening sequence of events follows earlier scenes showing (1) a medieval crucifixion; (2) the naked, headless ghost of a nun shooting a harpoon through the stomach of a fisherman; and (3) two members of an archeological team falling to their deaths in a spiked pit inside the ruins of the monastery that is this film's main setting. Fulci saves his ghastliest set pieces for the end, though. *Demonia* culminates with two grisly illustrations of his morbidly humorous taste for distasteful ways to die: (1) a local butcher, stepping into the freezer of his shop, is overtaken by an unseen assailant, who swings a meat hook into the victim's neck before driving a stake through his tongue; and (2) another archeologist is strung up with rope and suspended between two trees, part of an elaborate trap that is triggered by his own son (who accidentally trips the cord) and rips him in half like a wishbone—the dead man's intestines spilling to the forest floor in a slick rubbery heap. Anyone familiar with Fulci's body of work will not be surprised by the fact that he and his effects team are not able to sustain the illusion that these painful eviscerations are really happening, owing to the low-budget film's "hokey-looking" puppets and "blatantly false" prosthetics (whose fakeness stands out all the more once we know that the many skeletal remains that appear inside the Sicilian church where much of the film was shot are *actual corpses* dating back several decades).[12] Nevertheless, *Demonia* is unnerving not despite but *because* of our awareness of the film's artifice, as well as the amount of time and effort required by a labor force largely unknown to most of Fulci's biggest fans (save for above-the-line creative personnel, such as the cast of actors, cinematographer Luigi Ciccarese, editor Otello Colangeli, and composer Giovanni Cristiani).

Produced the same year and directed by the same filmmaker, Fulci's self-reflexive meta-horror film *A Cat in the Brain* (*Un gatto nel cervello* [*I volti del terrore*], 1990) foregrounds that otherwise invisible labor force even as it privileges himself as the fount of inspiration for all involved—a progenitive storyteller from whose brain such bizarre horror films spring. It begins with a two-minute scene that shows an Italian movie director (played by Fulci as a mock-version of himself) sitting at his desk and drawing up a list of the many grisly ways that he has killed or harmed his characters in the past. He writes and says (in voice-over) the following: "A woman hacked to death with an axe. Her face cleaved in half. Another strangled. Yet another hanged. Someone chopped to bits by a chainsaw. Or drowned in boiling water. Or throat torn up by a maddened cat. Burned alive. Buried alive. Tortured. Scarred. Stabbed. Sawn in two. Crucified. Decapitated."

As the fictional Fulci speaks (alluding to some of the murderous acts depicted in the nearly fifty films directed by the *real* Fulci prior to *A Cat in the Brain*'s theatrical release), the overhead camera zooms in to a tighter shot of the balding filmmaker until his head is shown in close-up. A racking of focus blurs the shot and then a cut to an equally blurry image, now red and glistening, appears onscreen. Slowly bringing this new shot into focus, the camera lingers on the soft tissue of the titular organ, a bright, jelly-like mess of stuff that pulsates slightly and looks too wet to be an actual brain, but which we are supposed to imagine is inside the skull of the man we have just seen. The other half of the film's title—a snarling cat—suddenly leaps onto the brain, ravenously clawing at the meat and growing feistier with each lip-smacking taste. John Kenneth Muir states that this literalization of "cat-scratch fever," in which an obviously "fake-looking feline puppet" scrapes its paws through "juicy brain-matter" before devouring it, is "ridiculous."[13] But the gore, he adds, "has a point," especially since it comes after a spoken and written litany of bodily traumas for which Fulci claims full responsibility, and which he appears to be genuinely haunted by (so much so that he eventually seeks the advice of a psychiatrist to work through his issues, which have "infected him"). More than anything, his psychiatric sessions, which are themselves sprung from the same squishy organ that was shown in that cranium-plunging zoom, extend *Cat in the Brain*'s reflexivity into more incriminating territory for the audience, who might be led to suspect that the metaphorical mirror which Fulci holds up before himself is really directed toward them.

Equally absurd and fake-looking is the misogynistic bird named Turkie that terrorizes a group of college students in the independently produced black comedy-slasher film *Thankskilling* (2007). Although everything—including the killer turkey's rape and murder of a young woman—is played for a metatextual laugh or treated as a lark within its far-fetched narrative, the coarse type of discourse that typifies this and other low-budget attempts to shock audiences leaves me as cold as refrigerated leftovers. An example of that coarseness, which comes across as rough or unrefined particulates on the tongue (like the residue of poorly filtered coffee), occurs during a scene in which Sheriff Roud (Chuck Lamb), the aging smalltown lawman in the film's fictional setting of Crawberg (who will eventually become one of the many victims of the homicidal turkey), sits down for breakfast and complains to his wife that her recently brewed coffee "tastes like shit." When asked if she took a "dump" in it, Sheryl (Pat Love), who has been itching for a divorce, responds, "As a matter of fact I did." She proudly shows him the large brown stool inside the coffee pot, which prompts him to spit out the vile liquid in slapstick fashion.

*Thankskilling*, which not only thrusts viewers' noses into uncomfortable proximity to that sniffable poo but also conjures intersensorial memories of seasonal meals involving less deadly turkeys, stuffing, cranberry sauce, and other mainstays of the Thanksgiving holiday, is just one of several "excremental" productions to make such a perverse play to our taste buds. Other horror films, including the Norwegian slasher movie *Christmas Cruelty!* (*O'Hellige Jul!*, 2013), do much the same thing, although the effect will likely differ based on relative degrees of sadistic violence dispensed prior to or after such a gross gustatory scene. Written and directed by Magne Steinsvoll and Per-Ingvar Tomren, who—along with their other writing partners Eline Aasheim, Anita Nyhagen, and Janne Iren Holseter—also play major roles as heavy-drinking, hard-partying friends picked off by a serial killer dressed as Santa Claus, *Christmas Cruelty!* features a scene in which a trio of characters is invited to sample some Dutch cheese that a Christmas tree salesman has made. Biting into the slices, each of the three men makes a face, before one of them, Magne, describes the peculiar taste as "ass-crack mush and sour gym socks." On the surface, his comment is funny in the same way that Gale (Courteney Cox)'s remark to Deputy Hicks (Marley Shelton) that her recently baked "lemon squares taste like ass" is humorous in *Scream 4* (2011). The film's humor is carnivalesque, drawing upon a long tradition of cultural productions combining the cognitive delight of incongruity with the physically nauseating fright of having one's nose and mouth forcibly placed in the vicinity of another person's nether regions, that area of the lower bodily stratum from which the strongest odors and sourest tastes emanate.

However, the odd *specificity* of Magne's analogy stands out, as does the way that it is rhetorically grafted onto images of bro-like bad behavior on the part of men who act like boys. Besides triggering a gag reflex and anticipating a later moment when they sample a vomit-inducing alcoholic concoction that "tastes like seagull cum," Magne's comment about the nasty flavor of the cheese readies the audience for even less appetizing, more revolting displays of the film's titular cruelty. The worst of those actions—Killer Santa's sexual assault of a woman, whose genitals he stabs before performing cunnilingus on her and finally smothering his unconscious victim to death—are difficult to even imagine, much less witness onscreen, thereby putting any prior food-based shenanigans (including the poo-tainted coffee from *Thankskilling*) into perspective as comparatively benign instances of antisocial bad behavior.

Indeed, reprehensible acts like the one just described are not equivalent to someone saying that biting into the neck of a wino is like drinking the Volga River at low tide (in *Love at First Bite* [1979]) or comparing the taste of blood to nail polish remover (in *Vamperifica* [2012]). My point, however, is that such rhetorical flourishes on the part of screenwriters and characters, far from being morally objectionable, exist on a continuum of grossness where questions of those two types of taste might lead to slippery conflations of the truly vile versus the mildly juvenile.

In a considerably more refined way, director Mark Mylod's 2022 horror-comedy, *The Menu*, conflates the two meanings of "taste" broached above just as surely as it mixes two genres that are sometimes thought to be mutually antithetical. As a dark satire of the class-based privileges that partially define the world of haute cuisine, where upscale restaurant patrons partake in elevated dishes (like rock oysters draped in seaweed and algae, or what a less sophisticated diner might call "pond scum") while waxing pretentious on the rich cherry, oak, and tobacco notes of a Pinot Noir, this film draws attention to the ways in which coarseness and refinement are as much properties of food and drink as they are discursive constructs whereby lines are drawn and distinctions are made by people with the power to define what is "good" and what is "bad." In *The Menu*, those people include not only amateur gastronomes and professional "foodies" whose reputation for culinary connoisseurship precedes them (as restaurant critics), but also a trio of "tech bros"—three athletic, party-loving, obnoxiously wealthy young men (played by Arturo Castro, Mark St. Cyr, and Rob Yang)—who have made the trip from Silicon Valley to a private island owned by celebrity chef Julian Slowik (Ralph Fiennes). And they have done this not because they love the taste of Julian's lavishly prepared dishes, but rather because it provides them with a way to flaunt their class and gendered privileges in the company of other rich and famous patrons. Like so many spoiled college students in other horror films, these characters perform an especially toxic type of frat-house masculinity prior to and following their deadly run-in with Julian's kitchen staff and the maître d'hôtel Elsa (Hong Chau).

Reviewing *The Menu* for the food website Eater, Amy McCarthy notes that the film's critique of entitlement and masculinity extends to Julian's tyrannical behavior in the restaurant's well-stocked kitchen, full of boot-licking lackeys who, in order to appease their ruthless leader, will lay down their lives and blow out their brains, as one gun-toting sous-chef, Jeremy (Adam Aalderks), does as part of the show-stopping fourth course of a meal called "The Mess."[14] Inspired by the Cornelius Sjømatrestaurant in Norway, Noma in Denmark, and other three-Michelin-starred eateries around the world, Jeremy's restaurant is a microcosm of a global hospitality industry that caters to the rich but is known to exploit workers of lesser means through systems of inequality and precarity (e.g., long shifts, unpaid hours).[15] Sexual harassment, McCarthy elaborates, is also prevalent within that industry, as denoted by a later scene in the film in which another sous chef, Katherine (Christina Brucato), is given the floor to explain to the restaurant's increasingly alarmed and captive clientele that she has been ignored for months because she refused Julian's advances. Dramatically, she plunges a pair of kitchen scissors into his thigh before the two characters embrace as apparent equals under the watchful eye of Elsa. Though one might interpret this moment as a justified if excessively bloody act of feminist revenge, one that sparks a show of contrition from Julian (who, grimacing from the stab wound, tells Katherine, "I'm sorry"), she was only able to do it—to perform this show of resistance with theatrical flair under the title of "Man's Folly"—with *his* permission, as part of an elaborate multicourse meal that further solidifies his power over the staff. It is the kind of scenario "that workers who have been abused by their bosses and coworkers might fantasize about to some extent."[16] Nevertheless, any satisfaction that viewers might derive from this "discomfiting and tense moment"—later visualized in the look of contentment that washes over the face of the main character and sole survivor at the end, Margot (Anya Taylor-Joy), when she bites into a juicy cheeseburger that Julian has made for her—is problematized by the way that he exerts even greater control by seeming to relinquish it and by gradually relaxing his impossibly high standards so that his overworked underlings (including second-in-command Elsa) can do his bidding while he keeps his own hands clean.

Because this scene "feels like an especially pointed critique of the way the restaurant industry uses stunning spaces and beautiful dishes as a way to hide its abuses," McCarthy is quick to call *The Menu* "a sharp, biting critique" of that industry "masquerading as a stringent, slow-burning horror film."[17] And yet, as Julian pushes his VIP guests "to increasingly extreme levels of discomfort" even as they are invited to take masticatory pleasure in fat, salt, sugar, protein, bacteria, and fungi on carefully prepared plates that contain "entire ecosystems" of plant and animal life, "horror" is very much what comes to mind while watching the film. Indeed, the horrifically bad deaths that occur throughout its second half (including Margot's plunging of a knife into Elsa's throat) stand out by virtue of the "laughably good" food that preceded them.

"*Taste*, don't eat," Julian instructs his wealthy restaurant patrons during an early scene of *The Menu* (not long after the have arrived on the remote island), before telling them that the titular list of dishes swimming in their own "foams and gels and emulsions" is "too precious" for anything so base as mindless ingestion. The fact that his most precious dish—the lovingly prepared cheeseburger that he gives to Margot before allowing her to safely leave the island—is also the least pretentious reminds us that something as "lowly" or "cheesy" or "meaty" as a horror film can also be savored and relished, but also sharply critiqued, with "every morsel that [we] place inside" our mindful mouths (fig. 4.1). With that in mind, let us turn now from cheeseburgers to cheesecake—from the juicy squish of cooked ground beef or a vegan patty (sandwiched between two poppy seed buns) to the less literal sensation of seeing scantily clad women being reduced to food (and visually sliced into "boobs" and "buns")—as we consider particular cycles of cinematic horror that are as distasteful as they are flavorful.

**Figure 4.1:** Margot savors the taste of a juicy cheeseburger near the end of *The Menu*.

## Cheesecake, Cheerleaders, Bottom-Feeders

Men can eat their psychosexual cake and have it too.

—Carol Clover, *Men, Women, and Chain Saws: Gender in the Modern Horror Film*

We're having cake?

—Johnson (Paul Reubens), the assistant to Canadian Mountie Reginald Cooper (Tom Smothers), in the cheerleader-themed slasher parody *Pandemonium* (1982)

More than a few horror movies from the past twenty-five years, especially those set on college and high-school campuses, or which explore the sex lives of twentysomethings and teenagers, foreground young men behaving like prototypical "bros," in addition to featuring young female characters fending off the attacks of killers while being labeled "bitches" and "hos." For instance, in writer-director Jake Helgren's *Varsity Blood* (2014), several members of a high-school football team exhibit toxic masculinity, with Blaine (Blair Jackson) being the most offensive of the bunch: an egotistical, muscle-flexing bully who only wants sex from girls (referring to one fellow teenager as the "tightest piece of ass in high school") and who brushes off his own girlfriend's complaints about such misogynistic behavior as "just bullshit locker-room talk." The fact that one of the most disgusting scenes in the aforementioned *Head Cheerleader Dead Cheerleader* occurs outside any act of physical violence and involves four varsity-jacketed high-school jocks sitting in a circle, tossing back beers, high-fiving one another about the size of their penises, and casually joking about "fags" as well as girls who do not "put out" (all while riffing on horror films, à la *Scream*), says much about the horrible stuff that comes out of—rather than goes into—mouths. Any imagined gustatory pleasure or hedonic experience that might come from watching (or mentally munching on) a broad range of horror films, including those that have generated considerably less critical coverage than *The Menu*, is thus leveraged against the decidedly unpleasant homophobic, misogynistic, and sexist representations that, unlike a bottle of fine wine, will age poorly in the coming years. The unsavory aspects of several recently produced motion pictures, including those that show large groups of teenaged or college-aged girls being reduced to "cheesecake" or turned into "meat" under the piercing gazes and sharper knives of misogynistic men, are worth considering here. Ostensibly framed as eye candy, many of the conventionally attractive, sexually objectified female characters populating today's cheerleader films—a strain of horror cinema that has been popular since at least the early 2000s, when Jim Wynorski's *Cheerleader Massacre* (2003) was released amidst the "rampant misogyny" of the decade—would appear to be as "disposable" as the movies themselves.[18] In that sense, they constitute a seemingly powerful yet subjugated class of characters who, like the wealthy patrons of Chef Slowik's Michelin-starred restaurant, are believed to be deserving of any cruelty delivered to them (owing to their beauty, popularity, and shallowness).

Although cheerleading-themed horror films have been around for a half-century, the past two decades have witnessed an explosion of such works. This is due partly to the commercial success and widespread popularity of the *Bring It On* series of teen comedies initiated in 2000 by the film of the same title (which inspired a half-dozen direct-to-video sequels, including director Karen Lam's 2022 horror film, *Bring It On 7: Cheer or Die*). But it can also be attributed to a growing post-*Scream* nostalgia for slasher movies over the past twenty years, with numerous filmmakers—including women with a vested interest in deconstructing genre conventions—revisiting and in some cases comically *revising* the tropes introduced in classic examples of the subgenre such as director John Quinn's already-comedic *Cheerleader Camp* (1988). As showcased in the intentionally schlocky 3-D throwback *Attack of the 50 Foot Cheerleader* (2012), the subversively postfeminist satire *All Cheerleaders Die* (2013), the low-budget indie film *Virgin Cheerleaders in Chains* (2018), and the unsettling Lifetime movie *Who Is Killing the Cheerleaders?* (2020), horror cinema's many spirit squads of late have demonstrated an impressive resilience in the face of both diegetic and real-world threats to their existence. That, along with the frequency with which cheerleaders appear in contemporary productions, would be noteworthy on its own. However, as B. J. Colangelo argues in a recent article for *Fangoria* magazine, what makes this trend especially significant is the strange affinity between cheerleading and horror, an "oft-misunderstood [genre] . . . with a rabid fanbase desperately and consistently trying to defend its relevance in a society that deems it lesser than."[19]

In her article, Colangelo emphasizes both the datedness of Reagan-era film representations and the paradoxically enduring appeal of slashers and teenpics from the 1980s, when "boys were meant to be football stars and girls were meant to provide their undying support and blind loyalty to them" on the literal sidelines. It was a socially conservative period, she states, when "the standard slasher movie formula" contributed to the perpetuation of similarly retrograde "morality standards" ("hacking to bits any teenager that dare defy the unwritten rules"), "which makes cheerleaders, and other members of spirit squads like color guard and majorettes, the perfect vessel for all things horror."[20] One could go a few steps farther, though, in underlining how the frequently violent competitive antagonism so endemic within chill-inducing cheerleader cinema is offset by the narratively motivated need for young women to overcome their differences and work together toward a common goal (or for the sake of survival). This diegetic emphasis on *cooperation* alongside competition, with multiple opportunities for adolescent girls and teenagers to "bond as a squad" (as one of the characters in the 2009 film *Spirit Camp*, who is trying to defuse a combustible confrontation between two other cheerleaders, says), suggests a strangely comforting "balancing act" that is mimicked in cheerleading formations. While this is furthermore indicative of the affection that many filmmakers have for characters who continue to be stereotyped in US popular culture as brainless "bimbos" and reduced to "boobs" and "butts" (in cleavage- and ass-revealing down-shirt and up-skirt shots), it is important for viewers to move beyond authorial intention as well as onscreen representation so as to arrive at a more reflective set of sense-based speculations about corporeal *reflux* and critical *reflexivity*. By mining the built-in intertextuality of cheerleader horror films, which cater to contemporary viewers' similarly paradoxical "fascination and revulsion with violence," and by staging their homages to earlier slashers as a series of metatextual "winks" to an audience already well versed in its tropes, today's cultural producers perhaps unconsciously reveal something important about the genre: namely, its autocannibalistic tendency to *feed on itself*.

As suggested earlier, despite their seemingly recent vintage, cheerleading-themed horror films can be traced back to a much earlier generation of cultural productions, including director Greydon Clark's *Satan's Cheerleaders* (1977) and director Alfred Sole's *Pandemonium*

(1982). Both films are comedic in tone, though the latter, distributed by United Artists, was part of a wave of slasher parodies that studios rushed through production following the box-office success of *Friday the 13th* (1980). Promoted by distributor Dimension Pictures as being "Funnier Than *The Omen* . . . Scarier Than *Silent Movie*" (ad copy that ran at the top of its movie poster, which was reproduced as the cover image of Sconce's aforementioned book *Sleaze Artists: Cinema at the Margins of Taste, Style, and Politics*), *Satan's Cheerleaders*, in contrast, revolves around a backwoods cult whose hooded members look upon the titular group of high-school girls as potential sacrificial lambs. However, the cultists soon discover that one of the girls—the level-headed feminist Patti (Kerry Sherman)—is a witch who wields greater Satanic power than any of their own. Welch D. Everman points out that the cheerleaders in this low-budget film "are products of the sexual revolution," so much so that their active libidos are what spare them from being sacrificed to Satan. In a plot twist that anticipates Karyn Kusama and Diablo Cody's *Jennifer's Body* (2009), no one who is "soiled" can be sacrificially laid atop the altar.[21] And to be a cheerleader, the film emphasizes, is necessarily to be sexually promiscuous.

This is a theme that *Satan's Cheerleaders* solidified in the late 1970s, but did not establish on its own, since it picked up on the recurring motifs of earlier sex comedies and teen comedies like *The Swinging Cheerleaders* (1974), *The Pom Pom Girls* (1976), and *Revenge of the Cheerleaders* (1976). In fact, the amount of time spent dwelling on relatively innocent teenaged mischief (e.g., water-balloon fights, TPing the football field, pre-*Porky's* locker-room voyeurism) surpasses the few signifiers of outright "horror" that gradually emerge throughout the film's second half, once the question of the girls' virginity has been laid to rest and the cult's devil worshipping begins in earnest. Pausing momentarily on this notoriously sleazy grindhouse movie in his book *Cinema of the Occult: New Age, Satanism, Wicca, and Spiritualism in Film*, Carrol Lee Fry remarks that the "nubile nymphette[s] who jiggle their way through the film, both in and out of their micro-mini skirts," clearly indicate Clark's primary focus as an exploitation auteur who gravitated toward sex rather than horror.[22]

On an even lighter and slightly less salacious note, *Pandemonium* likewise associates promiscuity with spirit squads. However, an early scene of this parodic film establishes the fact that young women's desire for freedom (from the restrictive religious teachings and disciplining of their repressive parents) is a very *normal* pursuit, albeit one that might, in rare circumstances, bring them into the orbit of men with a very *abnormal*, homicidal fixation on cheerleaders half their age. Nevertheless, since this, too, is a humorously infused horror film, everything about its premise and characters is exaggerated or caricatured for comedic effect. For instance, when Candy (Carol Kane), an obvious clone of Sissy Spacek's Carrie (from the eponymous film released in 1976), stands her ground against her domineering mother, who has insisted that she *not* board a bus for cheerleading camp, the telekinetic teenager sends the older woman up into the air with a laser-beam zap of her eyes and responds, "I'm going to that cheerleading camp and I'm going be like everybody else. I'm going to make friends. I'm going to have fun. I'm going to wear makeup. I'm going to go out with boys. I'm going to sleep with truck drivers and get crabs. And I'm going to finally get to use my diaphragm!" In a scene following Candy's verbal explosion, audiences learn that parents are not the only ones seeking to protect their sexually curious offspring from harm. The entire town of It Had To Be, Indiana, where the grisly deaths of several cheerleaders took place in the winter of 1963 (after the hometown football team won the National Championship game), constantly reminds outsiders of their bad decision in coming to this small community. In fact, everything about the town is "bad," if the two no-nonsense waitresses at a greasy spoon called House of Bad Pies are to be believed. When asked by a group of soon-to-be-murdered newcomers, menus in hand, "What's bad today?," twins Crystal (Candi Brough) and China (Randi Brough) respond in unison that "the meatloaf looks pretty bad," though they also "recommend the roast chicken, [because] it's *horrible*." At this point, a hungry patron inquires, "What comes with the roast beef?" They give him a full rundown of what initially seems to be a very wholesome meal: "Homemade mashed potatoes with gravy. A hot roll. Two garden-fresh vegetables steamed to perfection. And an oven-fresh pastry." However, when Candy tells the waitresses that it sounds delicious, they call out the woman's order to the cook in the back, yelling, "One piece of shit!"

*Pandemonium* is awash in such seemingly tasty but terrible (food) stuff, literally so during a scene involving an older woman—a survivor of the 1963 murder who now coaches the next generation of cheerleader-victims—stepping into a bathtub full of milk and chocolate-chip cookies (fig. 4.2). In a recent interview, Candice Azzara, the theatrically trained actor who played the part of Bambi, discusses the day-long shooting of that scene, noting that it was "the hardest thing in the world."[23] Telling her interviewer that director Alfred Sole forced her to eat those cookies, despite there being "bits of dirt and hair in the bathtub" (which, rimmed with cartons and bottles, was filled with real milk instead of some less sour-smelling prop liquid), Azzara can only laugh today at what must have been difficult experience then, when the filming of her "Esther Williams-inspired death scene" demanded a strong stomach and rugged taste buds. It is not necessary to hear from the actor's own mouth what that day of shooting the scene must have smelled and tasted like, as both ingredients are commonly ingested foods that usually pair well with one another (just ask Santa Claus). But when milk goes "bad," signs of spoilage can be detected in the air or in the dairy product's color and texture (e.g., chunkiness, sliminess, yellowness). "Spoiling" things in more ways than one, the film's unidentified stalker sneaks into the bathroom in a manner recalling the stealthy movement of Norman Bates (Anthony Perkins) as "Mother" in *Psycho* (1960), initially thrusting a knife toward

**Figure 4.2:** In this scene from the horror parody *Pandemonium*, the coach of a cheerleading squad spends the last minutes of her life in a bathtub filled with milk and chocolate-chip cookies—props that had turned disgustingly rancid by the time the scene was completed during production (according to actor Candice Azzara).

Bambi before grabbing her cookies. That sexually suggestive action quickly gives way to him dunking Bambi like a human cookie into the tub of milk until she drowns, her death a symphonically orchestrated flourish befitting an MGM musical.

On the surface, there is nothing scary or terrifying about this broadly comedic yet disturbing set piece. But the way the faked/choreographed violence pairs with real/perceived flavors, odors, and textures—that of the familiarly comforting yet strangely disgusting food—contributes to an intersensorial feeling of uncanniness that I imagined tasting, smelling, and touching when I first laid eyes (if not literally hands and tongue) on *Pandemonium* years ago. Although multiple viewings of the film have prepared me for this and other unconventional kill scenes, including one in which a cheerleader named Mandy (Teri Landrum) is attacked in her bathroom by the same killer (who, this time, inserts a toothpaste covered drill bit into the girl's mouth until she expires under the weight of the foamy, phallic shape), I still wince whenever I witness such brutal acts. To say that they leave a bad taste in the mouth would not be inaccurate, as I imagine the aroma, piquancy, and tang of each ingestible thing shown in *Pandemonium*, a film that, not coincidentally, was promoted as "a movie that is totally *taste-free*." Those words, which graced the posters accompanying the film's theatrical release, are simultaneously correct and incorrect, insofar as its "badness" or "tastelessness" as a cultural production is partially borne out of its heavy use of foods as consumable things that activate the taste buds.

Anticipating the weapon used by the tracksuit-wearing killer in the 1984 slasher film *Fatal Games* as well as the poster image for the 2014 slasher film *Varsity Blood*, the most unusual murder in *Pandemonium* involves a line of cheerleaders who are speared to death by a javelin. Occurring during the film's opening sequence, it begins with the black-gloved killer, his face hidden from the camera, hurling the sharp, phallic plaything from inside a track-and-field team's locker room. Then, from the javelin's perspective, the camera follows its detour-laden path through high-school hallways. As it flies toward its target, our view widens to reveal a large outdoor stadium where five young ladies are lined up in a tight formation, each carrying a curiously oversized vegetable (e.g., tomato, mushroom) onto the football field in place of pom-poms. Like audible dominos, their individual screams pierce the soundtrack, one after the other, as the javelin rips through their bodies. Not until the local press and police investigators arrive at the crime scene are we granted a view of the dead cheerleaders. Their corpses, shown from an elevated angle, appear like the speared meat of a shish kebab (fig. 4.3). To drive this analogy home, a newspaper reporter who is at the crime scene responds to a colleague taking photos of the girls' dead bodies that only a "maniac" or a "very large chef" could have done something like this.

The overhead shot recalls an image from the 1979 comedy-horror film *Microwave Massacre*, which shows a man running a shish kebab through his dead wife's hand along with assorted vegetables. Moreover, arranged in this fashion, the victims of the sadistic killer, who is eventually revealed to be none other than the all-American high-school football star Blue Grange (the hero who had scored the championship-winning touchdown in 1963, played by Tab Hunter), might remind some genre enthusiasts of a similar formation of bodies in a more recent, far more unsavory example of gastrointestinal horror, *The Human Centipede*. Written and produced by the Dutch satirist-provocateur Tom Six, the film, unlike the sillier *Pandemonium*, has received its fair share of critical commentary ever since its theatrical debut at London's FrightFest Film Festival in August 2009. Since that time, it has become a springboard for several accounts of self-reflective or hyperaware spectatorship, not

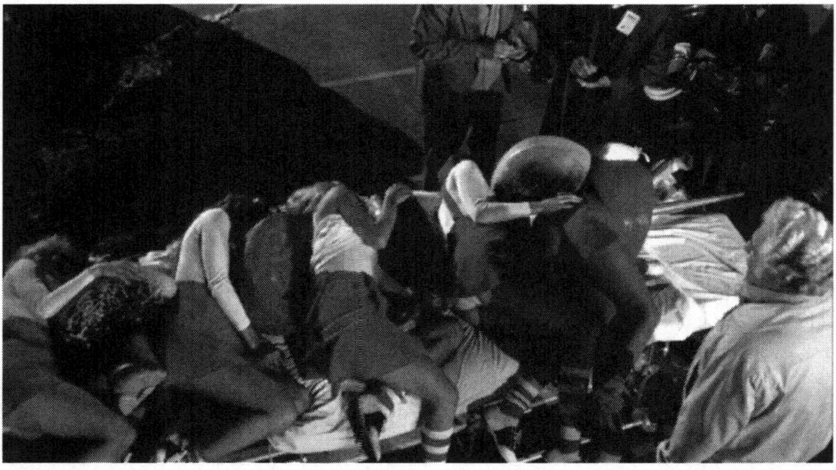

**Figure 4.3:** Like meat on a shish kebab, the impaled bodies of teenage cheerleaders are linked together as a collective sign of the killer's twisted sense of over-the-top humor in the film *Pandemonium*.

only among innumerable critics writing for pop culture websites but also within academia, where attempts to theorize what makes *The Human Centipede* so simultaneously captivating and repulsive have been hampered by the scholarly tendency to privilege the brain and its objectivity/rationality over the gut as an equally relevant if subjective means of getting at what the film "means."

In one of the most thoughtful and "gutsy" readings of *The Human Centipede* yet offered, Laura Wilson, author of *Spectatorship, Embodiment, and Physicality in the Contemporary Mutilation Film*, describes her literally retching experience of encountering the scene in which the titular monstrosity—made up of three naked people who are digestively "attached to each other by their mouths and anuses"—first appears onscreen.[24] "Rocking back and forth, scraping [her] nails across [her] desk, [and] moaning" the words "I don't want to, I don't want to" before vomiting, Wilson felt the greasy surfaces, unpleasant flavors, and noxious aromas of that scene intensely, as if she had been made to *taste* the human waste that flows from the backside of one defecating character into the mouth of another. To be more precise, the "burning taste" that she experienced in that moment was one of "bile," which—combined with the "unnerving tremors of [her] stomach"—made visible to her "those organs that ordinarily escape consciousness," including the small intestine and upper colon. More than merely a "gut reaction" to the film, Wilson's physical response, against her own strong desire to "maintain a divide between [her] subjectivity and [her] throat, stomach and bowels," reveals how "the viewer's corporeality is constituted by and constitutive of the text." In other words, more than two types of transgression distinguish *The Human Centipede* as both a morally and physically disgusting work of gustatory horror in which "anus meets mouth and feces becomes food." A third transgression, which likewise "points to the illusory nature of a stable and defined body," occurs as the physicality of the film's viewer is constructed in the moment of film-viewing, as if she too had been caught in the grips of a mad man—the lab-coat-wearing Dr. Josef Heiter (Dieter Laser)—who terrorizes his surgically conjoined test subjects through forced coprophagy. Like Wilson, I have experienced a "strong reluctance to accept myself as gut" not only while watching this Tom Six-directed Dutch production, awash in "wet, tactile sound effects," but also whenever I encounter a very different but no less sordid mix of signifiers in US horror films in which, to quote a character in *Cheerleader Camp* (1988), "there's something eating at *everybody*."[25]

At this point, it should be clear that the high-school cheerleader's comment is not just figurative. Indeed, *something*—some pervasive form of cultural monstrosity—was not only "eating Raoul," to cite the title of a more fondly recollected "cannibal comedy" that premiered one week prior to *Pandemonium*'s theatrical release in April 1982 (and which, to borrow the words of Roger Ebert, was notable for its "transcendent breaches of taste"), but also devouring other horror film victims around the same time. In the years leading up to the 1982 release of director-star Paul Bartel's *Eating Raoul*, several productions from various corners of the world turned the once-uncommon sight of cannibals and zombies feasting on human bodies and brains into a prevalent feature of the genre. From modern classics and enduring cult favorites such as George A. Romero's *Dawn of the Dead* (1978), Lucio Fulci's *Zombie* (1979), Ruggero Deodato's *Cannibal Holocaust* (1980), and Kevin Connor's *Motel Hell* (1980) to Z-grade trash films such as David Burton Morris's *The Meateater* (1979), Charles McCrann's *Toxic Zombies* (1980), Joe D'Amato's *Antropophagus* (1980), and Umberto Lenzi's *Eaten Alive!* (1980), horror was broaching a new type of fear at that time. In the words of Erin E. Wiegand, "The fear of being food for another—of being the one on the table—[which] is linked to a fear of not being human," came to the fore in several "cannibal-savage" films of the 1970s and 1980s, including those like *Last Cannibal World* (1978), *Mountain of the Cannibal God* (1978), and *Cannibal Ferox* (1981) that exaggerate the savagery of the "uncivilized" and "untamed" Other within distant jungle settings.[26] But middle-class American households were also home to some of the most disturbing scenes of human ingestion prior to and following *Pandemonium*'s theatrical release. To borrow Vivian Sobchack's expression, horror filmmakers were "bringing it all back home" during that period, not only by pitting demonically possessed or supernaturally endowed children against their parents in movies as diverse as *Carrie* (1976) and the aforementioned *Pandemonium*, but also by situating the alienating/foreign figuration of the cannibal within the familiar environs of the nuclear family.[27] In doing so, the limits and contradictions of that family as a cultural construction or social imaginary were exposed, thereby demonstrating a larger crisis in bourgeois patriarchy and helping to unleash a reactive anti-feminism that we are still living with today. Importantly, as the old Oedipal configurations of horror have given way to *edible* reimaginings of the genre's political unconscious, the idea of "Eating the Other" (once largely framed as a form of cultural appropriation on the part of white supremacist patriarchy, which sets its sights on possessing and "taming" primitive cultures) has since transformed into a literal practice whereby anyone who might stand in the way of such appropriative/possessory moves is punished, dehumanized, by being consumed *as food.*

To get a clearer picture of how one especially conservative or politically reactionary strain of horror films attempted to "resolve the contemporary weakening of patriarchal authority" during the 1970s and 1980s, let us turn our attention to an unusual yet strangely representative example of cannibalistic cinema from that period: Wayne Berwick's *Microwave Massacre*.[28] Shot on a shoestring budget, this production, which received a Halloween-night premiere in Austin, Texas, in 1979 before getting a wide domestic release four years later, revolves around a construction worker schlub named Donald (Jackie Vernon). Feeling like he is trapped inside a loveless, sexless marriage, and growing increasingly frustrated by his wife May (Claire Ginsberg)'s insistence on serving fancy gourmet food each night (when what he most craves is a simple sandwich), Donald finally "snaps." More specifically, he bludgeons May to death with a pepper grinder and disposes of her chopped-up, aluminum-wrapped remains in the basement refrigerator. After accidentally biting into her hand and finding it to be delicious, he proceeds to put her recently purchased microwave to use, cooking portions of her body for daily caloric intake. He even shares pieces of the tough but tasty human meat with his coworkers at the construction site, where a buxom young woman—one of his future victims—stops by to show off her "assets." Before this ill-fated woman supplies Donald with fresher meat, she appears during the film's opening credits in figuratively "chopped-up" form, with the camera framing her bouncing breasts and curvy backside in tight close-up shots before she is groped by one of the men who will later unwittingly eat cooked portions of her body (after Donald commits postcoital murder once more). As she is being manhandled, her boobs get stuck in a fence's large knothole, making them appear like a "mammary meal" to her ogling audience on the opposite side of the fence. Such representations accrue their own "flavor" and "mouthfeel" over time, as audiences witness the male protagonist repeatedly dine on the physical remains of his victims' bodies, pulling at the connective tissues, ligaments, and muscles with his teeth as those imagined tastes and textures emanate from the screen into our own mouths.

Looking like a softcore Borscht Belt mashup of Herschell Gordon Lewis's stylistically impoverished "hick-pics," Lloyd Kaufman's schlocky Troma productions, and the throw-everything-at-a-wall-and-see-what-sticks approach to sketch comedy associated with *The Kentucky Fried Movie* (1977), *Microwave Massacre* is hardly "horrific" in the way that contemporaneous films like *Dawn of the Dead*, *Zombie*, *Cannibal Holocaust*, and *Motel Hell* are. Compared to it, another relatively low-budget movie preoccupied with people-as-food—director George A. Romero's *Creepshow* (1982)—looks positively polished, owing mainly to cinematographer Michael Gornick's success in replicating the bold visual style of its source material (EC horror comic books of the 1950s) and to the A-list actors who populate its episodic collection of tales, which traffics in overt Freudianism but lacks the sexploitative tackiness of Berwick's film. Adapted from a Stephen King–penned screenplay that was itself a winking homage to *The Haunt of Fear*, *Tales from the Crypt*, *The Vault of Horror*, and other EC publications from the postwar period, this motion picture adopts the piecemeal structure of the anthology film, recalling earlier efforts to combine multiple stories within a single feature, such as Amicus Productions' *Dr. Terror's House of Horrors* (1965), *Torture Garden* (1967), *The House That Dripped Blood* (1971), *Asylum* (1972), *Tales from the Crypt* (1972), *The Vault of Horror* (1973), and *From Beyond the Grave* (1974). Taking a page out of the Amicus playbook, *Creepshow* chains together five blackout stories bookended by a prologue and epilogue. The prologue shows a young boy named Billy (Joe King) reading a fictional variation on those formerly banned comics, which his abusive father promptly tosses into the garbage in the opening minutes. This initial glimpse into domestic strife and parental disciplining sets the stage for *Creepshow*'s first episode, "Father's Day," which furthermore foregrounds the patriarchal elements that Sobchack identified in that era's home-situated horror films. Coupled with a regressive *Taming of the Shrew*–style attitude toward gender relations, that aspect imbues this work of fiction with something approaching factuality with respect to the often-disrespectful attitudes and behaviors of men toward women.

Indeed, the toxicity of that relationship could sometimes be conjured intersensorially, through the signifying elements specific to the genre, which (beginning in the 1970s and 1980s) tended to rely on the putrefying *exterior* of physically decomposed beings—awash in nauseating odors and slimy textures—to symbolize the equally repugnant *interior* of man.

One such being appears near the end of "Father's Day," a "deliberate EC pastiche" (according to King) in which a zombified creature—the grisly remains of Nathan Grantham (Jon Lormer)—crawls out of his grave to exact revenge against his money-hungry family (whom he once called "vultures"). Tony Williams notes that the aggressive behavior of the entire Grantham clan, both prior to and following the patriarch's death, "takes the form of verbal sniping and humiliating remarks against each other," a pattern that can be metaphorically linked to cannibalism.[29] In fact, Nathan had been full of avarice himself before he was knocked off seven years earlier, having accumulated considerable wealth through bootlegging, extortion, fraud, and murder-for-hire. Perhaps the worst of the sour old man's offenses was his constant belittling of his daughter Bedelia (Viveca Lindfors), who was forced to toil for hours each day in the kitchen perfecting a cake recipe to satiate his hunger for conventionally sweet concoctions. As depicted in flashbacks, the emotional abuse that Bedelia suffered drove her to madness, leaving her no other option but to bash his head in with a marble ashtray. Since that time, she has been coping with the combined guilt and pain through alcohol. In a remarkably silly turn of events, it is whiskey from Bedelia's bottle—spilling onto her father's headstone—that wakes Nathan from his deathly slumber near the end of this story. Once "possessively jealous" of his "fucking bitch" of a daughter (going so far as to kill her elderly suitor), Nathan is now committed to ensuring that no one will ever taste the cakes she once baked for him. Maggot-ridden and tangled in moss, the creature embodies the creepiness of incestuous attraction once he emerges from the grave and unleashes misogynistic fury upon her and her own daughter, Sylvia (Carrie Nye)—the person who had initially thought of staging Nathan's killing as an accident so that she and the rest of the Grantham clan could steal his fortune. This brief plot synopsis of the film's first episode, which can be boiled down to Sylvia's snide comment that her grandfather Nathan's death was "good riddance to some extremely bad rubbish," lends credence to critic Robin Wood's dismissive assessment of *Creepshow* as a whole: "A series of nasty anecdotes in which nasty people do nasty things to other nasty people, the nastiness being the entire point and purpose."[30]

The nastiest of the film's comically grotesque events is reserved for the end of "Father's Day," which culminates with Nathan's walking, talking, dirt-covered skeleton strangling Bedelia, killing his former cook Mrs. Danvers (Nann Mogg), and finally lumbering into the kitchen, where he gleefully holds a platter on which Sylvia's severed head sits. Covered with cake frosting and lit candles, the decapitated body part makes for a comically absurd yet distressingly sexist confectionary item. Colored like candy, in garish primary hues befitting a comic-book panel, the shot of the dead woman's head puts a literalist spin on the "just desserts" morality tale that EC Comics had cornered the market on during the 1950s, but which was ripe for further exploitation in the politically and socially conservative context of 1980s popular culture. But it does so by making it appear as though revenge is a dish best served both *cold* and *hot*, as the competing blue and red colors of the mise-en-scene blend into a purplish mix of emotions and imagined flavors for audiences who might recoil in horror at the sight of a mutilated woman turned into a visual punch line, yet also giggle with delight in recognition of the humorously exaggerated manner in which Romero and his special effects team (including makeup artist Tom Savini) show the dead man finally receiving the "oral satisfaction" he has been demanding all along.[31]

At once morbid and mirthful, this capping moment—one of five in a film comprised of that many stories—hearkens back to a storyline in the October 1952 issue of *Tales from the Crypt* ("Taint the Meat . . . It's the Humanity!" by Jack Davis and Al Feldstein). In that story, a housewife exacts revenge against her husband (whom she blames for the death of their child) by killing him, carving him up, and selling his body parts at the butcher shop where he worked before his demise. However, in flipping genders and presenting Sylvia's chopped-up remains as a visually if not morally palatable alternative to seeing the abusive patriarch receiving his own "just desserts," this final scene of "Father's Day" brings the questionable taste of cinematic horror to the fore even as it obscures the genre's masochistic (mouth)feel—its tendency to sit as heavily on the heart and tongue as her head does atop that silver platter.

## *Scream, Stab, Suck, Swallow*

> When the knife went in her, it's like . . . she wasn't a human anymore. Just an animal. And every time I went in, she was less . . . less human. And then? She was . . . just meat.
>
> —Jason Carvey (Tony Revolori), speaking to someone on the phone moments after killing his film professor, in *Scream VI* (2023)

The past twenty years have witnessed a resurgence of cannibalism-themed horror films, with examples ranging from director Brett Leonard's *Feed* (2005) to Sofian Khan's *Destined to Be Ingested* (2008), Matthew Roth's *The Man Who Collected Food* (2010), Jimmy Weber's *Eat* (2014), Patrick Brice's *Corporate Animals* (2019), and John Migliore's *Creature from Cannibal Creek* (2019). In many cases, these motion pictures regurgitate familiar generic conventions, making it seem as if present-day cultural productions are so firmly rooted to the past that they offer little in the way of commentary on today's most pressing sociopolitical issues, including those related to the Black Lives Matter and #MeToo Movements. However, a few examples to the contrary stand out as demonstrations of the genre's enduring relevance as a vehicle for imagining alternatives to the sociopolitical status quo. Writer-director Carlo Mirabella-Davis's *Swallow* (2019) is one such film. Although it is not, strictly speaking, about cannibalism, this modern-day variation on 1960s horror films such as *Repulsion* (1965) and *Rosemary's Baby* (1968) centers on a young woman's eating disorder—her compulsive consumption of nonfood objects (including a battery, a marble, a push pin, and even more dangerous things)—as a result of an existential ennui unique to the station of a middle-class housewife. That ennui comes from being dependent on her husband and forcibly confined to the domestic sphere, where much of the film's action takes place. But the unrestrained ingestion on view in *Swallow*, which might suggest a feminist unwillingness to abide by the dictates of an equally compulsive heterosexuality or subservience to man, explodes beyond the female protagonist's home to convey a real-world context where the "strange old guard of patriarchy and sexism" (which Mirabella-Davis saw as "being revitalized by the Trump administration") presents an equally restrictive space or inhospitable environment for women like Hunter Conrad (Haley Bennett) to simply be themselves.[32]

Similarly, writer-director Rob Stefaniuk's 2009 horror-comedy *Suck* travels "a road that has been explored in numerous other films before," though it manages to breathe life into the perennial subgenre of vampire fiction by focusing on a once-struggling rock band fronted by a female singer whose taste for blood brings the group newfound success, if also moral dilemmas concerning the acquisition of fresh meat.[33] Jennifer (Jessica Paré), the vocalist in question, spends much of the story not only searching for blood but also staying a few steps ahead of vampire hunter Eddie Van Helsing (Malcolm McDowell), all while traveling from gig to gig and building up a following of groupies who are transfixed more by her pale visage and slinky outfits than by the mediocre music that accompanies her onstage performances. While this might suggest a conventional framing of the female protagonist as an object of desire for heterosexual male audiences, *Suck* goes out of its way to show Jennifer asserting her agency and self-determination as well as her ability to assume leadership responsibilities, which she gradually takes away from the band's nominal leader, Joey Winner (Rob Stefaniuk, the writer-director himself), whose last name serves as the group's name (the Winners). She even has her own Renfield-like minion—a fly-eating roadie named Hugo (Chris Ratz)—do her bidding. Like the deranged and devoted servant of Count Dracula, Hugo mostly does grunt work, rounding up dead bodies and cleaning up his master's messes whenever Jennifer's appetite gets the best of her.

An especially memorable scene from *Suck* occurs early on, when Hugo first realizes who, or *what*, she really is, having accidentally stumbled upon her drinking a deli attendant's blood through a straw (fig. 4.4). Reminiscent of a few earlier films in which the combined humor and horror of cannibalistic or vampiric ingestion is visualized by way of straws inserted into brains, necks, plasma bags, and other fleshy, gooey, or plastic containers—as seen, for instance, in *Blood Sucking Freaks* (1976), *A Polish Vampire in Burbank* (1983), and *Killer Klowns from Outer Space* (1988)—the shot of Jennifer deriving liquid satisfaction from a man who had been all too eager to see her undressed moments earlier brings a salty, metallic taste to spectators' lips, though recognition of the action's artifice might also place the sweet, sugary flavor of red-dyed corn syrup (a.k.a. "movie blood"), with its notes of vanilla or cocoa, on the tongue as well.

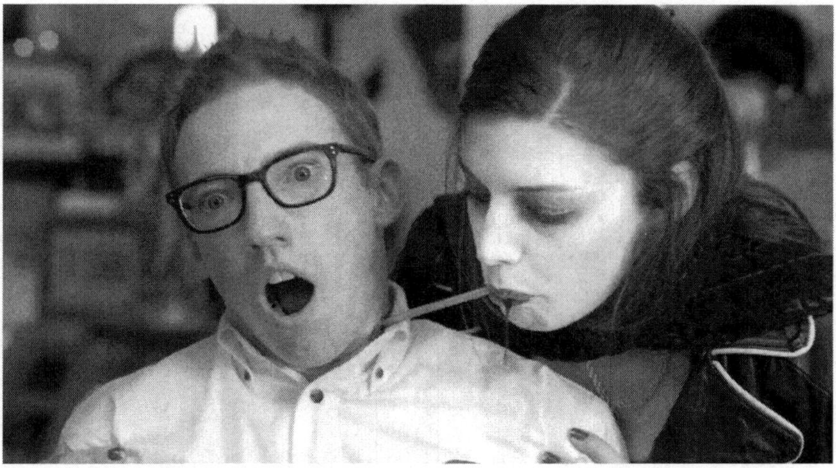

**Figure 4.4:** Jennifer, the vampiric lead singer of a Canadian rock band in the film *Suck*, literalizes the film's title when she plants a straw into the neck of a deli attendant and drinks his life away.

In February 2023, as part of the promotional push to whet audiences' appetites for the impending release of *Scream VI* one month later, Paramount Pictures and Spyglass Media Group partnered with the LA-based pop-up restaurant Chain to create an unusual, nostalgically imbued marketing campaign, albeit one that seems only fitting given all of the food-based horror being produced in recent years. Putting a slasher-film twist on the McDonald's Happy Meal, Chain—the brainchild of chef Tim Hollingsworth and actor-writer B. J. Novak—introduced the "Stabby Meal," giving hungry customers in West Hollywood the opportunity to sink their teeth into an "Extremely Medium-Sized Bone Marrow ChainBurger" topped with American cheese, pickles, onions, ketchup, mustard, and the company's special umami seasoning (fig. 4.5). Accompanying the all-beef patty were "Throwback Fries" and a "Woodsboro Orchards Warm Apple Pie," which, like McDonald's Baked Apple Pie, was packaged inside a handheld cinnamon-scented cylinder.[34] Rounding out this "elevated" version of a fast-food meal (featuring higher-quality ingredients than what would typically come at a lower price point), one of four collectible pins depicting narrative elements and characters from the film, including a bloody buck knife and a subway car as well as likenesses of two of the actresses who star in it (Jenna Ortega and Melissa

**Figure 4.5:** A promotional ad for the "Stabby Meal," a culinary tie-in to the theatrical release *Scream VI* that the LA-based pop-up restaurant Chain unveiled in February 2023.

Barrera), could be added to hardcore fans' collections of *Scream*-related merchandise and memorabilia.

Reviewing the Stabby Meal for the horror website Bloody Disgusting, Matt Donato raved about the decadent tenderness of the "flavorbomb ChainBurger," which, "dripping with greasy goodness," melted in his mouth. In his words, the bone-marrow-infused meatiness was "obscene," making it one of the critic's most memorable dining experiences since he moved to Los Angeles a few months before lockdown.[35] Donato practically salivates when regaling his readers with descriptions of the front-to-back goodness of the meal, which diners could wash down with "signature cocktails like the tasty Sunset Presidente blood orange mezcal margarita with a deep crimson topper"—a beverage that was "like a fresh Ghostface victim spilled into my glass." Ultimately, the restaurant's innovative approach to food-based movie marketing not only successfully generated interest in *Scream VI* but also skillfully combined "culinary craftiness" with "childhood comforts" and, in Donato's words, was a "must-eat for horror fans who also dabble in foodie adventures."[36] One wonders if the delectable flavors of that gustatory experience carried over into the viewing of the film, which marinates in a different sort of "meatiness" and is practically saturated with both savory and unsavory ingredients.

From a narrative standpoint, it is telling that this most recent iteration of the *Scream* franchise, directed by Matt Bettinelli-Olpin and Tyler Gillett, begins not in a suburban middle-class home, a movie theater, or some other hangout spot in the fictional town of Woodsboro, California, but in an upscale restaurant located in New York City where a young college professor who specializes in slasher films nervously waits for her blind date to arrive. Named Laura Crane (a nod to the character played by Janet Leigh in Hitchcock's *Psycho* [1960], Marion Crane) and played by Samara Weaving (recognizable to many horror fans as the tall blonde star of *The Babysitter* [2017], *Mayhem* [2017], and *Ready or Not* [2019]), this woman is already an intertextual palimpsest of past and present-day film references before she opens her mouth to speak or to sip from a cocktail that sits on the bar. Text messages appear on her phone, indicating that the man she was supposed to meet, and whose name, Reggie, is visible on the fake texting app Flirtr, has gotten lost on his way to the restaurant. Reading his message, Laura flashes a smile and tosses back another shot of vodka before texting him back, indicating her approval through laughing-so-hard-I'm-crying emojis. When she accepts his request for a phone call (giving him a thumbs-up on her iPhone) and the two begin talking, she discusses her interest in slasher films, but with some degree of awkwardness. She tells him that "you can really examine the culture of the moment by looking at the tropes of the time. Like the masked killer, the final girl, the different rules: Don't split up, don't have sex. . . . It's all cliché, but out of those clichés comes an opportunity for outsider art, a voice for the voiceless." The crowded restaurant, which the speaker on the other end of the line claims he cannot find, is an appropriate venue in which to have this telephonic, cinephilic conversation, since so much of what made the earlier sequels of the original *Scream* "meta" has since been replaced by "meat." Indeed, *food* culture as much as *film* culture infuses *Scream VI*. Besides being occasionally uttered by characters—including suspects in the most recent Ghostface-attributed slayings—over the course of this multicourse meal of a movie, the word "meat" is literally fleshed out in this and subsequent scenes.

When Jason Carvey (Tony Revolori), the person who has been pretending to be Reggie and who returns to his apartment after stabbing Laura to death in an alleyway outside the restaurant, recounts these recent events to another male college student on the phone, he tells his accomplice, "When the knife went in, she wasn't a person anymore, just an animal, like meat." Soon, Greg, the person on the other end of the line, convinces Jason to tear himself away from a screening of *Friday the 13th Part VIII: Jason Takes Manhattan* (1989), which plays on his TV, so that he might take part in a "game" of "Warmer-Colder." "Find me, and then we'll go and cut up the Carpenter sisters," the menacing voice on his cellphone growls. As Jason approaches the refrigerator, "warmer" gets replaced by "you're on fire," and a tentative opening of the door reveals the butchered, decapitated body of his friend Greg—the person to whom he thought he was talking—inside (fig. 4.6). Shocked by the sight of his bloodied friend inside the refrigerator (a throwback to the sliced-up wife of *Microwave Massacre*), Jason has no time to protect himself from the killer who has suddenly snuck up behind him, another man wearing a Ghostface costume. Repeatedly plunging a knife into the other killer's stomach, this new Ghostface turns his earlier comment against him, asking Jason, "Do you feel like an animal? Like *meat*?" before letting his body slump to the kitchen floor. Jason's dying words, "But we have to finish the movie," is met with the killer's rejoinder, "Who gives a *fuck* about movies?" That line is a rhetorically brutal yet humorous way to cap this pre-title sequence, which began with the murder of a film professor (whose body was left to rot among the dumpsters and garbage outside a restaurant) and ended with the death of her own killer, whose apartment is a mini-shrine to classic horror films such as *The Phantom of the Opera*

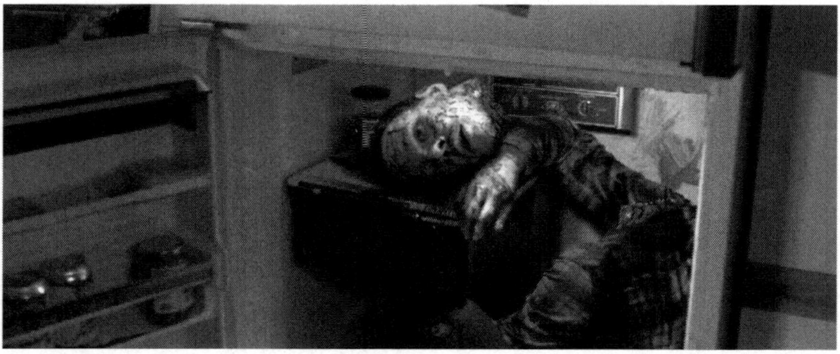

**Figure 4.6:** An early scene of *Scream VI* shows the chopped-up remains of a college student inside his refrigerator—an appropriate location given the film's foregrounding of food-related killings and meat-based metaphors.

(1925), *Dracula* (1931), and *Psycho* (1960), as well as the fictional *Stab* movies that have been a part of this franchise going back to the original *Scream* (1996).

An actual shrine to the *Stab* franchise—and, by self-referential extension, to the *Scream* franchise—is where the final scenes of *Scream VI* take place. It is also where the aforementioned Carpenter sisters, Sam and Tara, take down a family of Ghostface killers, including the patriarch (whom Sam stabs in the eye) and his son (whom Tara stabs in the mouth). Tellingly, the latter character, Ethan Landry (Jack Champion), had earlier been referred to as a "snack" by one of his bros at an alcohol-soaked college party. "You're . . . practically an entire meal all on your own," his friend had remarked (trying to build up his confidence and encouraging him to talk to a girl at the party)—a comment that plays off the opening scene's meat-based metacommentary and anticipates the penultimate scene's depiction of Ethan receiving his "just desserts" orally, after his identity as one of several Ghostface killers has been revealed. As Tara's knife twists mercilessly in his mouth, carving up his tongue and driving down deeper into his throat until he expires, audiences too might open their mouths to let out screams, though the satisfaction that comes from witnessing an abusive male victimizer of women being held accountable for his actions surely offsets any physical unease or discomfort on the audience's part.

In a recent article for *The Los Angeles Review of Books*, horror film expert and *Scream* enthusiast Kartik Nair ruminates on the political subtexts of this sequel to a remake (or "requel"), noting that fans of the franchise "may sense something repressed returning in the shot of the New York skyline" that kicks off *Scream VI*.[37] Following an image of the Paramount Studios logo, which shows "stars gathering around alpine peaks," the city's skyline not only establishes "the much-hyped (re)location of the franchise outside Woodsboro for the first time," but also returns the film series "to where it all began." He points out that the original *Scream* opened with a logo for Miramax studios, "which pictured a New York City skyline by night." Nair writes,

> No other studio was as associated with New York as Miramax. It was in Buffalo that Bob and Harvey Weinstein founded the studio in the late 1970s, before relocating it soon after

> to Manhattan. Around the time Disney purchased Miramax in 1993, Bob Weinstein created Dimension Films, a subsidiary label for the production and distribution of commercial genre films. [Kevin] Williamson's spec script for *Scream* was first faxed to Dimension's New York office, then delivered to Weinstein's apartment from there. The Weinstein brothers left Disney in 2005 and took Dimension Films with them to their next venture, The Weinstein Company (TWC).

He goes on to note that in 2017, one of the stars of the original film, Rose McGowan (who played Tatum Riley, the best friend of Neve Campbell's Sidney Prescott), "alleged that Harvey Weinstein had sexually assaulted her in 1997—mere weeks after the release of *Scream*, and as the film was growing at the box office—at the Sundance Film Festival." In the time that has elapsed since McGowan publicly shared her experiences, other women (including actors Lena Headey, Lauren Holly, Angelina Jolie, Ashley Judd, Romola Garai, Lupita Nyong'o, Gwyneth Paltrow, Mira Sorvino, and Lucia Stoller) have stepped forward with allegations about Weinstein's unwanted advances and abusive behavior (verbal and physical intimidation as well as rape), "leading to his eventual conviction as well as the bankruptcy and closure of TWC and Dimension Films." In 2019, Paramount Pictures purchased the bankrupted company's film library, thus keeping the *Scream* franchise alive but with it the history of abuse for which its founder—the toxic epicenter of Hollywood's most notorious sexual harassment scandal of the modern era—will forever be remembered.

Those events from the past half-decade put any fictional horrors and food-based fears referenced in this chapter into proper perspective, as relatively minor issues that pale in comparison to the real-world horrors visited upon McGowan and countless unnamed women. Nevertheless, something valuable can be gained from assessing the representational patterns of genre-based storytelling, which often allegorically addresses and sometimes directly *redresses* grievances of a significant portion of the population—individuals and communities that might otherwise be "voiceless" or feel that they will not be heard whenever they open their mouths to speak truth to power. In other words, horror's compensating function as a rule-bound yet taboo-breaking corrective to what actually ails the world can serve socially progressive ends, but only if we first acknowledge its politically conservative roots in a patriarchal culture that will be far harder to dislodge than a knife from a monstrous man's throat. Tellingly, as Nair perceptively acknowledges, Laura Crane—the familiar sacrificial "first kill" of *Scream VI* (a staple of the franchise ever since Drew Barrymore's character Casey Becker was murdered in her kitchen while making popcorn, the most "meta-" of movie-based foods)—is dressed in "a bright yellow, high-neck dress" that resembles the clothing worn by McGowan's character, Tatum, in the original *Scream*. As such, Samara Weaving, the actor who plays Laura, brings with her the spectral remembrance of someone who, even in her absence, is as palpably present in this most recent entry in the series as Neve Campbell—the person whom Weinstein claimed was one of the only two people who ever "stood up to [him]"—is. If horror films really can provide a "voice for the voiceless," as Laura insists only minutes before her death at the hands of a young giallo fan who has himself been added to another person's kill list (and is murdered in equally brutal fashion), then we must attend to those figurative ghosts from the medium's recent and distant pasts who are deserving of our consideration or some other, more literal form of compensation so that future generations do not fall victim to abusive men and the monstrous institutions of power that protect them.

# PART 2

# YOU CAN'T SPELL "FEAR" WITHOUT "EAR"

## Hearing Images and Seeing Sounds Through Assistive Technologies

# 5

# (NOT) HEARING IS DECEIVING

## Deaf Gain, Pleasurable Pain, and the Missing "[SQUISHES]" of *Hush*

I have heard a man, suddenly struck stone deaf, describe his experience. First, he senses fiery wheels going round and round in his bursting head—the whole world turning upside down. Then the curtain of absolute silence. He finds himself living in a world of puppets, making senseless, witless gesturings in his stony silence.

—Boris Karloff, explaining why deafness is "the most horrible thing that could happen to me," during a 1940 interview published in *Modern Screen*

In January 1940, Martha Kerr, a contributor to the American fan magazine *Modern Screen*, published an interview that she had conducted with four of the silver screen's most iconic avatars of cinematic fright. They were actors whose careers in Hollywood ran parallel to several industrial changes and technological innovations that would have been terrifying to anyone whose career had begun in the silent era of the 1910s and 1920s. Kerr's interviewees—Lionel Atwill, Boris Karloff, Bela Lugosi, and Basil Rathbone—were each asked to provide their own definitions of "horror," a term that had circulated for many years prior to the coming of sound, but which did not crystallize into a discursively formed motion picture category or genre until a decade prior to her article's publication, around the time that *Dracula* (1931) and *Frankenstein* (1931) were released in theaters.[1] Their answers, when read today, provide valuable insights into the minds of the men behind the masks (or makeup) as well as the broader cultural anxieties that had been brewing throughout the Depression era.

Atwill, who had just appeared in Universal's *Son of Frankenstein* (1939) opposite his fellow interviewees, speculated that nothing—not the loss of a limb or any physical pain that might stultify conscious thought—was more horrifying than paralysis, the absence of movement and possibly feeling in which the brain becomes overactive while the body becomes inactive. His costar Rathbone, perhaps acknowledging the very real horrors occurring in Poland and other countries at the time, screamed "War!" when Kerr put the question to him. The actor, famous for his turn as that most logical of fictional detectives, Sherlock Holmes, elaborated that a different type of paralysis—born of the petrifying fear that accompanies any military soldier's call to arms—was "a monstrous, gigantic, inconceivably barbarous trap," one that turns individuals into the unthinking cogs of a "mass machine."[2] Lugosi, best known for playing the title character in Tod Browning's *Dracula* (a role that the Hungarian actor had already perfected on stage a few years prior to that film's 1931 release, as the star of a Broadway adaptation of Bram Stoker's 1897 novel), had a more humbling, heartbreaking response to Kerr's question, saying that "horror, to me, comes not from the other world but from this one." Specifically, Lugosi referred to the two years of joblessness that he had endured in the late 1930s as a self-described "down-and-out actor" whose services were no longer needed in Hollywood. For him, sitting by the telephone and waiting for a call that did not come while watching his money dry up and losing his home (into which he had put all of his family's savings) was an experience that surpassed any onscreen moment of fright. "Horror," Lugosi mused in a soliloquy as powerful as any he ever spoke while in character, "is the reptilian sting of the knowledge of my own stupidity, my own lack of foresight," which might result in his loved ones going "hungry . . . cold . . . homeless."[3]

A different sort of perceived "lack" lay at the heart of Boris Karloff's feelings on the matter. As the man most responsible for making movie monsters both terrifying and sympathetic in the 1930s, this British-born actor had carved out a unique space in Hollywood as the industry's most dependably sensitive interpreter of roles in which emotions had to be communicated under thick layers of makeup. His archetypal performance as Frankenstein's monster helped to spur an industry-wide expectation for "gruesome realism" in the pre-Code era, thanks primarily to the assistance of makeup artist Jack Pierce (who, while working on director James Whale's *Frankenstein* in 1931, came up with the idea of "bolts in the neck to conduct electricity; clamps in the forehead to secure the top of the skull which had been sawn open to allow the replacement of the brain; stitches around the wrists where new hands had been sewn on to the arms and so on").[4] By the time he appeared in *Son of Frankenstein* at the end of the decade, Karloff had played an assortment of abject figures, from exotic "others" such as the mummified Egyptian priest Imhotep and the Chinese supervillain Dr. Fu Manchu to surgically deformed characters like the murderous convict Edmond Bateman in *The Raven* (1935), illustrating in the process what historian Jon Towlson calls that period's "turn to gruesomeness."[5] Kerr herself expected Karloff—his face "seamed from eye to chin" while seated for a makeup session—to respond to her question of what "horror" is by acknowledging how his own body had become one with the monster's, speaking "with horror's twisted tongue," reaching out "with horror's gruesome gestures," and limping "as horror limps, maimed and mutilated."[6] "No," Karloff replied, "living with the macabre" (by which he meant playing "scarred, seamed, crippled or misshapen" figures on screen) "does not induce in me the morbidities you may suppose."[7]

Giving his interviewer an example of the kind of "abnormalities, disfigurements, distortions and mutilations of the flesh and brain" that might be thrust upon the body and mind of an actor such as he, Karloff explained: "If you play a man with a third ear growing out of his forehead, you've got to . . . figure out his reactions to a world not composed of men with third ears."[8] What makes this rather bizarre anecdote—itself suggestive of the various excesses of cinematic horror as well as the outsider status of the monster as a figure of abject difference—all the more remarkable is that Karloff went on to state that the most terrifying thing he can imagine is "stone *deafness*." Compared to people who were born without the ability to see or who have experienced significant vision loss, a condition that, in Karloff's words, "automatically demands and gets attention and sympathy," deafness "does not manifest itself and induces impatience and annoyance."[9] Using even more questionable language to describe the difference in disposition between someone who is blind and someone who is deaf, Karloff observed that whereas the former is "habitually sunny and gay and high of spirit and ready of laughter" (owing to the "constant attention" a person with blindness receives), the latter is "liable to be petulant, morose, low of spirit, because their trouble is not sweetened with sympathy."[10]

The actor's comment, while unnuanced and problematic in setting ableist parameters for understanding the inner life of individuals based on their outward appearance, accurately reflects early twentieth-century attitudes toward people who were either born without the ability to hear or experienced significant hearing loss (through illness or injury). Throughout the 1900s, 1910s, and 1920s, deafness in the United States was viewed largely as a public health issue, one that required vigilant efforts on the part of physicians and other medical staff (in newly created hearing clinics) if it was to be combatted as an invisible, preventable "handicap" rather than as an "issue of education or communication."[11] Several of the nation's top thinkers spoke of deaf people as being "outside the mainstream who needed to be brought into the fold," an assimilative mandate whereby various facets of oral education ("speech development, lip-reading, and aural comprehension practices") nudged out other skills that would have served this increasingly marginalized group better.[12] Indeed, "an intense campaign against sign language" had been launched in the United States throughout the early part of the twentieth century, and "the Deaf community perceived this attack as an assault on their right to exist as a linguistic minority."[13] One of the so-called problems of deafness, besides the question of "how to best integrate the hard of hearing [and] the deafened . . . into society," was the idea that it was a "disability without outward signs." To quote one otologist, Wendell C. Phillips, who wrote in 1930: "The deafened person uses no crutch, no black goggles, no tapping staff."[14]

Of course, not everyone at that time shared Karloff's feelings, and it bears mentioning that in 1930, the same year that Phillips penned his "Reminiscences of an Otologist" for the health magazine *Hygeia* (published by the American Medical Association), the deaf artist and former silent-film actor Albert Ballin wrote a fictional memoir that anticipated more recent efforts to "challenge dominant ideas about spoken language approaches in deaf education."[15] Viewed today by Octavian E. Robinson and Jonathan Henner as an early instance of "campaigning for disability rights and social justice activism," Ballin's *The Deaf Mute Howls* (1930) called for the widespread adoption of signed language and manualism more generally, running against the grain of oralism (lipreading and audible speech) that had become an indelible part of cultural and educational life by the time of the book's printing. Russell J. Johnson points out that the privileging of oralism in public schools and other American institutions, which contributed to the disabling of Deaf populations in the late 1920s and early 1930s, ran parallel to the film industry's transition to "talkies"—a shift that Ballin had been witness to from the inside (as a performer who was trying to find work in Hollywood). What distinguishes *The Deaf Mute Howls*, a book whose title anticipated one of the most pervasive sounds in 1930s horror films (made by wolves and werewolves), is the author's commitment to bringing his own corporeal knowledge to bear on a subject that had largely been "colonized" by a phonocentric culture fixated on "fixing" deafness. Rather than simply diagnosing and then treating individuals for an incurable "ailment" that was responsible for those *other* afflictions (the ones that Karloff mentioned in his interview: petulance, morosity, and low spirits), society should be prepared, Ballin insisted, to make changes not simply to accommodate but to *learn from* deaf people, to reconceptualize deafness as a *gain* rather than a hindrance.

As an early advocate for deaf epistemology, Ballin was careful to distinguish between impairment and disability and furthermore maintained that sign-language learning, even in—or *especially* in—non-Deaf communities, would not only increase accessibility and inclusion but also prompt greater interdependence of *all* people within society. He also believed that the best silent movies were those that "limited their use of textual insertions and relied on pictures, motion, action, and actors to tell their stories."[16] In his own words (but echoing the sentiments of everyone from Vachel Lindsay to H. L. Mencken), intertitles were a "criminal waste" of film footage, and the "most illiterate" of movie audiences would understand a cinematic story through "better gestures" on the performers' part.[17] Boris Karloff, who had ten years of acting experience under his belt before he (and the industry in which he worked) transitioned to synchronized sound production at the end of the 1920s, was among those few performers to have pioneered innovative *gestural* approaches to screen acting, using his body as an expressive instrument through which to communicate the emotions and mental states of his characters. And he brought those silent film techniques into the sound era, as evidenced in his star-making turn as Frankenstein's monster, a role that earned him plaudits from the first reviewers of that 1931 classic (who singled out Karloff's "restraint" and "intelligent simplicity of gesture").[18] In the words of Peter Hutchings, "Despite the handicaps of cumbersome makeup and having no dialogue," Karloff's performance conveys "the essential humanity of the monster through gesture and facial expression alone."[19]

Even more "handicapped" by a lack of dialogue (to borrow Hutchings's term) is Karloff's facially scarred manservant Morgan in director James Whale's *The Old Dark House* (1932), a Universal production that combines elements of drawing-room farce and clutching-hand thriller. First appearing onscreen in a terrifying close-up, Morgan slowly opens the front door of an old house in the Welsh countryside when three strangers—Philip Waverton (Raymond Massey); his wife, Margaret (Gloria Stuart); and their talkative friend, Roger Penderel (Melvyn Douglas), all seeking shelter from a raging storm outside—come knocking. He also opens his *mouth*, uttering "low, guttural grunts" that are as confusing to this waterlogged trio as his scarred face is unsettling.[20] "Even Welsh ought not sound like that!" remarks Roger, making the first of several derisive comments about the butler's noncommunicative countenance that will become something of a running gag in the film. Eventually, once they are let in to dry off, Philip, Margaret, and Roger learn from the house's eccentric owners, Horace Femm (Ernest Thesiger) and his elderly sister, Rebecca (Eva Moore), that Morgan is mute. Or, rather, the Femms explain that he is "dumb," employing a word that was still being used interchangeably with "mute" at the time of this film's theatrical release (though it has since fallen out of favor, owing to the term's offensiveness as a synonym for "stupid"). Although the butler shows no signs of congenital deafness or an inability to hear, which was widely thought to be the reason for a person's muteness or inability to speak, a few contemporary scholars have described him as being "deaf-mute."[21] Interestingly, it is *Rebecca*, the grouchy, neurotic proprietress of this crumbling manor, who is hard of hearing, a condition that her effete brother also makes a point to point out (as if it, too, will be a source of recurring humor).

For much of the film, Rebecca can be heard asking questions concerning everyone else's talk (e.g., "What did they say? What do they want? What are they doing here? What's all the fuss about? What?"). She is also made to appear physically monstrous in an early scene, when she escorts Margaret to her upstairs bedroom and then volunteers unsolicited information about her godless, wanton family's torrid affairs. Referred to by Harry M. Benshoff as a "rather butch deaf religious zealot obsessed with 'the sins of the father' that she feels have damned the house," the old woman casts a castigating look up and down the shapely body of her undressing guest, only to be transformed into a hideously grotesque figure whose haggish features are reflected in a series of vanity mirror shots (fig. 5.1).[22] At this point, director Whale, working with cinematographer Arthur Edeson and editor Clarence Kolster, strings together a series of horrific images that show Rebecca's "already pudgy and misshapen visage" from multiple angles before suddenly interjecting a close-up of Morgan's "damaged face," as if she and he were one and the

**Figure 5.1:** Like that of the heavy-drinking, "dumb" butler Morgan, the face of Rebecca—the proprietress of the titular manor in *The Old Dark House*—appears distorted in this mirror shot, making her seem like a nightmarish apparition whose otherwise invisible hearing impairment is being visually expressed as a physical deformity.

same, bringing deafness and muteness together in a scene that—putting the viewer "inside the head of a panicked Mrs. Waverton"—does "figure-eights around objective and subjective reality."[23] According to Randy Rasmussen, this is one of a couple of instances in *The Old Dark House* when a psychic link between the hulking figure of the butler (who is revealed to be a "frequent drunkard prone to violence and rape") and the diminutive figure of the bitter old woman (the "tyrannical superego" to his "occasionally unrestrained id") is suggested through cinematographic means.[24] Yet they are both nightmarish apparitions whose literally or figuratively battered exteriors bring to the surface—make *physical* and therefore *readable* to deaf and hard-of-hearing viewers—those "impairments" that were thought by many people to be invisible.

In her book *Hideous Progeny: Disability, Eugenics, and Classic Horror Cinema*, Angela Smith warns against assuming "that any visual marker of disability or deformity—a limp, a misshapen face, a missing arm—functions in the same way as any other marker."[25] Mobilizing examples ranging from "the degeneracy of Dracula, the 'visual disruption' offered by Frankenstein's monster, [and] the deformities and cripplings of mad doctors," Smith observes that by shepherding these and other figures of radical alterity (as prototypical "monsters") into a culturally cordoned-off space alongside individuals at least partly defined by their sensory impairments (including the "insightful and virtuous blind characters" in *The Bride of Frankenstein* [1935], *The Invisible Ray* [1936], and *The Devil-Doll* [1936]), one runs the risk of essentializing embodied difference and eliding "the textually specific manner in which it operates" in a given film.[26] The point that I am trying to make with reference to Rebecca's optically "deformed" representation in this early scene of *The Old Dark House* is that the "hidden" quality of deafness is deflected onto the visual plane and made monstrously manifest with the same frequency that typifies cinema's eugenic conflation of "physical or mental impairment with moral failing."

In contrast to Karloff's and other commentators' description of deafness as a "disability without outward signs," this scene in *The Old Dark House* thus illustrates a countervailing tendency discernible across the genre's history, albeit with decidedly fewer examples than those provided by films featuring blind characters. Even if she is not literally disfigured in the manner that Morgan is, this puritanical, ungracious host is presented to the audience from the inside out, her twisted psyche expressionistically fleshed out for all to see while her hearing loss is monstrously physicalized in the process. Anticipating a similar representation in Arthur Lubin's 1946 horror film, *The Spider Woman Strikes Back*, which generates frisson from the shocking sight of a mute manservant named Mario (played by Rondo Hatton, a character actor who had been diagnosed with acromegaly at a younger age), the twinned images of Rebecca and Morgan manifest one's inability to hear or inability to speak in the ghastly figure of someone who departs radically from the constructed norm of physical beauty (which, in this film, is embodied by Gloria Stuart). Notably, Eva Moore's portrayal of the partially deaf Rebecca marked one of the first instances in a major Hollywood film when a character with significant hearing loss was featured, making *The Old Dark House* doubly significant as a text that both visualizes and trivializes that "invisible disability."

Although deaf actors such as Albert Ballin, David Marvel, Granville Redmond, and Eduardo Romero (who would later be instrumental in developing an early prototype of onscreen captioning, a "precursor of today's subtitles") had appeared in films during the 1910s and 1920s, the characters they played were rarely designated as being deaf or hard of hearing.[27] Whenever deaf "characters" did appear onscreen, it would typically be in educational shorts and fundraising curios like Ballin's *His Busy Hour* (1926), a comedy two-reeler that—while made for the general public—was "never officially released" beyond its limited showing at a school for the deaf in New York City. At first glance, this might seem strange, given how much film producers and exhibitors seemed to value deaf audiences throughout the silent period. As early as 1910, George William Veditz, a writer for the trade magazine *The Nickelodeon*, noted that when the motion picture medium first emerged (little more than a decade and a half earlier) "none were more directly appealed to or felt greater personal interest in its development than the deaf."[28] "It was drama addressed directly to the eye," Veditz continued, "and if anything, they [deaf viewers] had the advantage over the rest of the audience." If contemporary readers bristle at the critic's reductive description of deaf individuals as "a people of the eye" who, "deprived of hearing," enjoy a "limited" range of information relative to other audiences, we might pause to consider his suggestion that the former group has "advantages" over the latter group.[29] Far from being disadvantaged, and hardly confined (as Veditz claimed) to the "scope of their vision," deaf viewers frequently attend to screen signifiers in a way that models a more deeply observant, haptically sensitized spectatorship beneficial to anyone who might follow their lead. This alone offers one reason why perceptual *gain* rather than hearing *loss* or sensorial "lack" should be at the forefront of any attempt to graft deaf epistemology onto the embodied experience of film viewing.

Such is the foundation I wish to build upon in this and the next chapter, which are devoted primarily to the hermeneutic benefits that come from watching horror films with captioning services, including SDH. Although Ballin was among the silent era's most vehement opponents of intertitles, or the use of printed text on inserted cards containing dialogue and expository information (when so much of the art of cinematic storytelling could be better conveyed through actors' gestures and other visual elements such as lighting and camera movement), the various aural elements that comprise a film's soundtrack—from noises to musical cues and spoken dialogue—can be rendered intelligible through SDH, albeit in ways that call attention to the "unspoken" biases of the captioners and perhaps to a more generalized set of preconceptions concerning the horror genre. Simply foregrounding those biases and preconceptions can be enlightening, and reason enough to study what has thus far been a largely ignored topic among film scholars. But the greater "gain" to be had from such an approach reveals itself in the newfound interest that some readers will take in listening to sounds with their eyes (not unlike how modern AD services enable some audiences to hear images with their ears—a topic that I will touch upon in a later chapter).

Before focusing on specific applications of SDH to horror films, as viewed through online streaming services such as Netflix, Amazon Prime, and Kanopy as well as home-video formats such as DVD and Bluray, it will be helpful to consider the troubling manner in which deaf characters figure in the genre, which has long exploited tropes associated with disability for the purposes of intensifying its affective power. To be clear, deafness is only a disability to the extent that institutions and societies discriminate against or place constraints on individuals whose embodied experiences are viewed as "less than" a perceived (and perceiving) "norm." Film is one means through which deaf people have been disabled, and not only through its often-demeaning representations of characters who are pathologized as being either weakened/imperiled or hostile/adversarial as a result of their physical impairment. The medium has also done this through an audist centering of the cinematic experience, one that can be traced back to the motion picture industry's transition to synchronized sound production in the late 1920s (when it essentially turned its back on one of its most dependable demographics: the Deaf community).

As Russell L. Johnson points out, that period, "famously proclaimed a time for 'normalcy' by President Warren G. Harding," gave rise to "an increasingly phonocentric modern American culture bringing, in the words of another scholar, 'the first large onslaught of auditive mass media' to the United States."[30] Besides motion picture "talkies," other, slightly older forms of mass communication, including telephones, phonographs, and radio, came to the fore as never before, occupying a major place in the cultural lives of Americans for whom the oral was becoming the "new normal." It is telling that the first major wave of US horror films (including lesser-known part-talkies and full-talkies such as *Darkened Rooms* [1929], *Seven Footprints to Satan* [1929], *The Thirteenth Chair* [1929], and *Midnight Mystery* [1930], all preceding *Dracula* and *Frankenstein* by several months), emerged immediately after the shift to synchronized sound, which brought not only dialogue but also several of the noises that are still associated with the genre (its gasps, groans, moans, and screams) to the receptive ears of audiences. As I endeavor to show in this and the following chapter, those noises, if not exactly genre-defining, are woven so deeply into the fabric of horror that it should come as no surprise that they feature prominently in today's SDH renderings of cinematic sounds (though certain noises, such as gurgles, splutters, squishes, and other indicators of the genre's "wetness," are frequently downplayed). Before exploring the role that SDH and other assistive technologies play in bringing the genre's status as a corporeal category of cultural production to light, let us reflect on the representational aspects of horror that reveal it to be well-suited for explorations of disability as a socially constructed way of framing "abnormal" bodies.

## Hard-of-Hearing Horror: Turning Up the Sounds for a "People of the Eye"

Talk louder! I can't hear you!

—Five-year-old Carol Anne (Heather O'Rourke), speaking to the voices coming from her parents' static-filled TV screen, in *Poltergeist* (1982)

Although the general topic of disability has figured prominently in horror films since the days of studio-era classics such as Tod Browning's *Freaks* (1932) and Michael Curtiz's *Mystery of the Wax Museum* (1933), and has long attracted the attention of scholars with a vested interest in the cinematic framing of physical difference as a kind of monstrous alterity or abnormality, relatively few deaf or hard-of-hearing characters have assumed prominent positions in those texts as either antagonists or protagonists. To be sure, minor characters, such as the movie theater ticket-seller Martha (Judith Evelyn) in director William Castle's *The Tingler* (1959), the deaf child Jane (Janina Faye) in Terence Fisher's *The Two Faces of Dr. Jekyll* (1960), and the murder suspect Thomas (Emmerich Schrenk) in the West German–Yugoslavian coproduction *Cave of the Living Dead* (a.k.a. *The Curse of the Green Eyes*, *Der Fluch der grünen Augen*, 1964), appear from time to time throughout the medium's history, only to quickly disappear from their respective narratives once their fates have been sealed by those whose ability to hear establishes a clear power differential between the able-bodied "self" and the disabled "other."[31] This near-absence of deaf or hard-of-hearing characters throughout much of the twentieth century is perhaps not surprising given filmmakers' and audiences' presumed predilection for onscreen chills and thrills delivered via the medium's full arsenal of *audio*visual signifiers, which—if one is to hold up horror films about able-bodied or aurally capable heroes and villains as the standard against which exceptions to the "norm" are evaluated—might seem of little significance in stories revolving around the absence or reduction of sound as an expressive form. To borrow the words of one online critic (no doubt speaking on behalf of many others), "hearing stuff" is often thought to be scarier than "seeing stuff."[32] Hence the implicit suggestion that, by foregrounding a hearing-impaired character and thereby diminishing a soundtrack's centrality to the evocation of dread and disgust, filmmakers undermine horror's built-in capacity to frighten or gross out audiences through a sonic activation of their own already-active imagination.

Of course, the presence of people with hearing impairments in a film, even as protagonists whose sensorial access to the world around them provides the often-silent "lens" through which spectators gain fluency in the visual language of peril posed therein, does not mean that sound ceases to be important as a signifying element. Anyone who has watched *Hear No Evil* (1993), starring the Academy Award–winning deaf performer Marlee Matlin as a physical trainer who is hounded by a corrupt cop after she unwittingly comes into possession of a priceless coin, will recognize the often-unsubtle musical flourishes and sound effects that flare up in otherwise hushed depictions of a hearing-impaired character's inner life. In his review of this "yuppie-in-peril" thriller, *Los Angeles Times* film critic Michael Wilmington laments director Robert Greenwald's ham-fisted manipulation of the soundtrack, which "he jacks up . . . so wildly that footsteps hammer out like a Wagnerian kettledrum." Although the soundtrack's volume does occasionally decrease from time to time, especially in those moments when Matlin's character, Jillian, becomes a kind of perspectival surrogate for the spectator (who is invited to see and hear—or rather, *not hear*—the world as she does), too often "the faintest noise" is suddenly magnified, becoming "her incessantly repeated death knell."[33] Like *The Tingler* and *Cave of the Living Dead* before it, Greenwald's film proves that a deaf character's precarious position vis-à-vis aurally proficient individuals who might wish to harm her or him often hinges on a dialectical relationship between enveloping silence and cacophonous noise, with the latter typically being the vehicle through which shock and suspense are carried from the diegetic world of the narrative to the extradiegetic world of the audience. Conversely, absolute silence is actually quite rare in horror films and in motion pictures more generally (regardless of their generic affiliation). Even the earliest examples of feature-length cinematic fright—dating back to silent classics like Robert Wiene's *The Cabinet of Dr. Caligari* (*Das Cabinet des Dr. Caligari*, 1920) and F. W. Murnau's *Nosferatu* (1922)—are typically viewed in contexts where the auditory dimensions of spectatorship are accentuated thanks to orchestral scores, organ music, and other types of sonic accompaniment.

Obviously, those cultural productions from the silent era are thought to be more visually audacious than aurally terrifying—a longstanding idea in horror film historiography that is colloquially summed up by a contributor to IndieWire, who notes, "Back in the day, scary movies made frightened viewers cover their eyes," whereas today's audiences are more likely to "cover their ears" for fear of what they might hear when watching—and listening to—films like *It* (2017).[34] Based on Stephen King's 1986 novel of the same title, which tells the story of a group of kids who are terrorized by a transdimensional being in the earthly form of a clown named Pennywise, *It* is similar to other contemporary horror films in that it does not shy away from "disgusting hard-to-look-at gore" (a combination of practical special effects and CGI work). Nor does it hold back on the more appealing visual features (e.g., "bold production design" and polished cinematography) that one might associate with costly studio productions. But its scariest moments, according to this IndieWire reviewer, can be chalked up to musical and other aural elements supplied by composer Benjamin Wallfisch and sound designer Paul Hackner, which not only cue us to the fact that the film's young protagonists are going up against an apparently unassailable supernatural threat but also become "louder and increasingly shrill" until Pennywise (Bill Skarsgård) fully emerges in all of his cacophonous malevolence during the narrative's third act, when those elements finally "combust." Ultimately, the online commentator claims, *It* reveals something that he and presumably other critics have felt to be true for many years—namely, that in horror film, "perhaps more than any genre," sound design and musical scores are "key tools to guide the audience's experience of a scene."[35]

In contrast to the history of representations alluded to above, over the past two decades a number of commercially successful motion pictures have brought deaf or hard-of-hearing characters to the fore, a trend that runs parallel to an increased interest—within academia and the culture at large—in the relationship between cinematic horror, deafness, and disability as a social construct. Examples of that emerging cultural phenomenon include: director Jaume Collet-Serra's international coproduction *Orphan* (2009), in which a nine-year-old "bad seed" brings chaos to her adoptive family, including a deaf girl four years her junior (played by Aryana Engineer) whose hearing aid is hidden by the demonic interloper before considerably worse things happen; Michael Ojeda's independently produced rape-revenge film *Avenged* (2013), in which the female protagonist Zoe (Amanda Adrienne), after being attacked and killed by racist rednecks, is brought back to life by an older Apache man who fills the zombified woman with the spirit of a deceased war chief (but who leaves her hearing condition intact); John Krasinski's sci-fi-horror hybrid *A Quiet Place* (2018), in which a tightly knit family begins to fray, emotionally and physically, after a deaf girl (played by Millicent Simmonds) fails to protect her younger brother from an extraterrestrial attack (though she eventually uses her cochlear implants as a means of surviving this postapocalyptic nightmare); David Allensworth and Monière's low-budget devil-possession film *Soul to Keep* (2018), in which a small group of college students, including a young deaf woman (played by Sandra Mae Frank) who communicates with her friends through American Sign Language (ASL), descend on a secluded country home and engage in a series of *Evil Dead*–like summoning rituals; and the Netflix streamer *The Silence* (2019), in which prehistoric "vesps" (a CGI'ed blend of blind bat and hungry buzzard) locate their next meals through enhanced hearing, forcing teenaged protagonist Ally (Kiernan Shipka), who lost that sense ability following a near-fatal car accident, to use ASL more out of desperation than out of convenience. To varying degrees, each of these films asks viewers to cast their gazes at a world of natural and supernatural threats as seen through the eyes of people who speak to one another nonverbally, through hand-signing and the silent mouthing of words. That they also foreground deaf female characters, usually below the age of thirty, bears considering given the all-too-common conflation of nonagency (or "lack") and femininity in film.

Among these contemporary works, director Mike Flanagan's *Hush* (2016) stands out for its ability to wrap conventional tropes associated with horror's home-invasion and slasher subgenres around an unconventional main character who, as a novelist with deafness forced to defensively fend for herself when a nameless (and, for a time, faceless) serial killer darkens her doorstep, embodies the sense of isolation that Martin F. Norden, Travis Sutton, and other critics detect in many disability narratives. Trapped inside a solitary writer's retreat—the proverbial "cabin in the woods"—far removed from her nearest neighbors, Maddie Young (Kate Siegel) becomes boxed-in prey to the initially masked man (John

Gallagher Jr.) who, for no apparent reason other than his own perverse pleasure in seeing others suffer, predatorially menaces her from outside the house, threatening her with the same deadly violence that he has dealt to her ill-fated friend Sarah (Samantha Sloyan). The literal containment of the female protagonist, who can *see* but not *hear* the killer through the glass partitions that temporarily keep him at bay (e.g., windows, porch doors), suggests the metaphorical but very real institutional limitations placed on people with so-called disabilities in a society that has been slow to accommodate or at the very least acknowledge their needs: obstacles to accessibility and inclusion that horror films might solidify or shatter by either adhering to or breaking from genre conventions. Similar to other cinematic slashers featuring a "final girl"—for example, *Black Christmas* (1974), *Halloween* (1978), *A Nightmare on Elm Street* (1984), and *Scream* (1996)—Maddie is both a victimized plaything of the sadistic, crossbow-wielding prowler and an eventual victor who is not above resorting to violence herself, ultimately defeating this all-too-human monster by narrative's end but bearing the emotional and physical scars (including a bloody leg wound and a crushed hand) that will likely result in unending trauma and perhaps even impact her professional career as a novelist. Notably, as someone beset by writer's block, Maddie ultimately derives artistic inspiration from the cat-and-mouse game into which she has been thrust and manages to craft a more compelling conclusion to her own work in progress after having suffered through a real-life scenario that seems more like the stuff of fiction.

Besides gesturing toward the idea that tragedy begets art, or at the very least an authorial productivity otherwise stymied by the writer's uneventful life or relative inaction prior to her stalker's arrival, the scenes of Maddie typing on her laptop (which contains her in-progress literary manuscript) and texting on her iPhone (which gives her a creative outlet whenever she is stuck for an ending to her story) provide visual inscriptions of written words that are not unlike the use of closed captioning and subtitling options available on home video formats such as DVD and Blu-ray and online platforms such as Hulu and Netflix (fig. 5.2). Notably, the latter streaming service, which purchased the worldwide distribution rights to Flanagan's film before it premiered at South by Southwest in March 2016 (and was given a limited theatrical release in the months that followed), has come under scrutiny for its notoriously

**Figure 5.2:** In *Hush*, Maddie, a novelist who lives alone in a cabin in the woods, is frequently shown typing messages on her laptop and texting on her cellphone, serving as a diegetic subtitler for spectators who, like her, are deaf.

"low standards" of closed captions, which, as one cultural commentator notes, "continue to alienate subscribers who are deaf, hard of hearing, or simply have difficulty understanding dialogue."[36]

Of course, dialogue is only one of the many aural elements comprising a horror film's soundtrack, which might also include sound effects like creaking doors and howling wind, musical cues like screeching violins and trembling theremins, and paralinguistic vocalics like gasps, grunts, and screams. And many other entertainment providers besides Netflix have angered or disappointed advocacy groups for failing to provide captioned viewing options free from typographical, grammatical, or syntactic errors. But few companies have had as rocky or troubled a relationship with deaf or hard-of-hearing viewers. Those troubles can be traced back to 2011, when "the National Association of the Deaf sued Netflix for what at the time was a sparsely captioned streaming collection, which the advocacy organization's representatives said violated the Americans with Disabilities Act."[37] The two parties eventually worked together to ensure that, by an agreed-upon deadline, all of the site's streaming content would be captioned for deaf and hard-of-hearing subscribers. On the surface, Netflix appears to have held up its end of the bargain, and now promotes its ongoing efforts to make subtitles and closed captions "primary assets" for the millions of people around the world who increasingly rely upon "timed text files" owing to how movies and TV shows are often viewed (on the go, in crowded and noisy environments, "in a world without the living room as the primary center of entertainment," according to the streamer's own ad copy). However, as Jon Christian reported in 2015, the streaming service's captions are plagued with "nonsense characters, transcription errors, and dialogue so implausible that it's hard to believe they're actually transcription errors. Many obscure the opening credits, line up poorly with spoken lines, or linger into uncomfortable stretches of silence."[38]

Deaf and hard-of-hearing viewers are familiar with the kind of mistakes that Christian refers to, and which are not just found on Netflix but on every platform or media artifact where cinematic and televisual works are commercially packaged or presented as "content" to be consumed by a public presumably indifferent to or oblivious of lapses in quality standards. In a previous chapter, I alluded to a translation error that occurs on Synapse Film's 2017 home-video release of the 1991 slasher-comedy *Popcorn*, in which a character yells, "Bring on the bugs!" in advance of a giant insect movie, though his words are captioned as "Bring on the *boos*!" A similar subtitling gaffe occurs on Kanopy's streaming version of James Whale's 1932 film, *The Old Dark House*, in which the titular dwelling's old proprietress repeats the exhortation "No beds!" to the group of strangers who have taken shelter in her crumbing house, yet her words are transcribed as "No *bags*!" In both instances, the mistake is forgivable and not terribly consequential to a viewer's moment-to-moment comprehension of what is happening in a given narrative. Not surprisingly, more egregious and worrying examples can be found on YouTube, where viewers can activate the online video sharing platform's autogenerated captions while watching films that take on entirely new meanings with only a few slight textual alterations (e.g., misidentifying the moaning that can be heard in the first scene of *Witchfinder General* as "laughter").[39] The frequently low quality and inaccuracy of sound-to-text transcription have prompted some disability rights and deaf awareness activists to, in the words of one commentator, "call out crappy captions," or what the popular YouTuber Rikki Poynter humorously labels "craptions," as part of an online movement to encourage content creators to subtitle their own work.[40] Among the things that Poynter and other supporters of #NoMoreCraptions would like to see is greater attention paid to proper grammar use as well as the captioning of "*all* words and background noises to the *fullest extent possible*," a goal that has yet to be achieved by the media organizations and independent contractors responsible for SDH options on streaming and home-video releases.[41]

## Head in the Clouds, Hand in the Cuffs, Skin in the Game: Textual Transcriptions

Hello, Fred. Listen, Fred. I want a word with you, and it's kind of hush-hush.

—The Chief of Police (Lucio Fulci) to Lt. Fred Williams (Jack Hedley) after the latter has informed the press about a potential serial killer on the loose, in *The New York Ripper* (*Lo squartatore di New York*, 1982)

We just wanted to hear every little squish and pop and stretch. It's gnarly stuff.

—Mike Flanagan, writer-director of *Gerald's Game* (2017), discussing his production crew's handling of a scene in which the female protagonist, Jessie (Carla Gugino), is shown and heard slicing her wrist in order to peel off the skin of her hand (to free herself from handcuffs)

In her essay "Power in Silence: Captions, Deafness, and the Final Girl," Gwyneth Peaty draws attention to the centrality of writing in *Hush*, not only as the main character's "primary mode of creative expression" but also as a "key source of information for the audience." Instant messages and video chats between Maddie and her offscreen friends, visible in close-up shots of her cellphone that provide expositional glimpses into her personal life, are like the fleeting views that we are given of her computer screen as well as the author's bio that appears on her previous novel's dust jacket (which indicates that she "suffered hearing loss and vocal paralysis after contracting bacterial meningitis" at the age of thirteen).[42] All of these seemingly mundane visual elements, Peaty argues, function as "an alternate form of captioning from within the diegesis," an unusual feature of this film that stands in marked contrast to the pre-attack scene in which Maddie signs to her friend Sarah without the accompaniment of onscreen text.[43] That scene, occurring only a few minutes before the latter woman is slain outside the glass door of Maddie's kitchen (where the protagonist is preparing a meal with her back turned toward her dying friend), throws non-ASL-speaking audiences into a momentary state of confusion that is not unlike the disorientation that she experiences during the initial stages of the attack that follows, when she finally confronts the killer face-to-face.

Moreover, disorientation bleeds into technological unreliability during the second half of the film, when Maddie's attacker—upon discovering her disability—cuts the electricity to her house as well as her internet access to the outside world. That breakdown in communication and assistive technologies, Peaty emphasizes, forces the deaf character to turn toward other survival tactics and senses, including her "enhanced sense of touch," which enables her "to detect the killer when he sneaks up behind her" (after entering the house and breathing on her neck).[44] But it also suggests the need to view online and home-video affordances, including accessibility options like SDH that have only recently been made available on such a large scale, with a mixture of optimism and skepticism, since any practical assistance that they offer to deaf and hard-of-hearing audiences (and hearing audiences, for that matter) is offset by an alarming tendency to shortchange that community with a narrow range of simplified signifiers (including stock phrases that do not meet the "fullest extent possible" goal that Rikki Poynter and other advocates call for). And yet, for all the problems with current standards of captioning, which might seem to be a shallow presentation of horror's sonic complexities, SDH presents us—at least those of us who might be inclined to look at and/or listen to motion pictures differently—with a heretofore untapped reservoir of hermeneutical possibilities. This was how I came to gradually hold a different opinion about *Hush*, a film I viewed several times on my laptop's small screen (and my cellphone's even smaller screen) once Netflix acquired distribution rights, before eventually watching it with the sound lowered and then removed altogether as part of an assignment in a graduate course that I taught in the fall of 2019 (Media Sensorium: Textual Perception of/through the Body).

Four years later, in the spring of 2023, Netflix's acquisition license for *Hush* expired. Thankfully, several semesters before it was removed from the streaming service's lineup of cinematic offerings, I along with two graduate research assistants had compiled and cross-checked lists of every subtitled caption that appeared onscreen during the film's projection, a practice that we continued to undertake while watching other Netflix-distributed movies in controlled settings throughout the period it took me to conduct primary research for this and the following chapter (from 2018 to 2023). Viewing *Hush* individually, we each typed out the captions for all the audio elements that were presented as bracketed parentheticals, hitting pause frequently to transcribe those occurrences. Because I sought to accurately capture the sound effects and musical elements of the film, its nonbracketed dialogue was excluded from our transcriptions, although many examples of paralinguistic respiration that typify horror as a body genre (e.g., gasps, groans, moans, sighs) were accounted for in those long spreadsheets, as were any instances in which a character's name or some other nominal designation popped up within the brackets (e.g., "Maddie," "John," "Man," "Intruder"). Besides indicating the timecode of each captioned text, I observed several moments in which the subtitling did not correspond with the onscreen imagery—mistakes or omissions that were duly noted. With this information at the ready, I would now like to bring forth some of the details of that time-consuming yet eye-opening procedure, which I have since performed several more times with other horror films as my focus. Besides preparing the reader for a more involved consideration of the academic and pedagogical value of SDH in the next chapter, this brief look at transcribed material highlights how horror films can be distinguished from one another and individually appreciated, as singular works distinguished by written words as much as by sounds and visual images, whenever captioning options are provided on home-video formats. The fact that *Hush* is set almost entirely within a person's home that is invaded by someone else—a methodical killer who gains access to the protagonist's private life through technological means—adds another layer of relevance to SDH transcription, which is only possible if the researcher is privileged enough to have access to such features via the kind of home-viewing devices Maddie uses throughout the film.

Let us begin this chapter's ending, then, with a few numbers. During the film's 81-minute running time, a total of 175 bracketed captions appear onscreen. Inside those brackets are 335 words (an average of 1.91 words per caption), none of which describe any of the film's musical elements. That alone was surprising, given how strongly other SDH-enhanced horror films place emphasis on music—as, for instance, in *The Slayer* (1982), which constantly reminds deaf and hard-of-hearing audiences of composer Robert Folk's orchestral score, which goes from being "[dramatic]" to being "[suspenseful]" and "[discordant]" before becoming "[gentle]" near the narrative's end.[45] Like those of many other horror films, most of *Hush*'s captions are short (1 or 2 words each), and the 2 longest ones contain 5 words each, although they combine two events each separated by a comma: "[sound fades in, alarm blares]" and "[sound fades out, thudding heartbeat]." Interestingly, sounds fade *out* more than they fade *in* over the course of *Hush*'s narrative (eight times compared to three times, according to the film's SDH). On the surface, this might suggest that hearing *loss* is a more pronounced part of Maddie's terrifying experience than deaf *gain* is. However, one could interpret that transcribed asymmetry as a sign of how persistently writer-director Flanagan brings the protagonist's impairment to bear on our spectatorial alignment with her, a focalizing agent living apart from society and whose relationship to a world with little-to-no sound ensures that we share that experience, if only momentarily. Notably, the SDH-transcribed film culminates with "[sound fades out]"—the final caption to flash onscreen during the closing seconds, after the murderous intruder has been violently dispatched with a corkscrew to his neck (which houses the upper parts of the respiratory and digestive tracts in addition to the cervical vertebrae).

Somewhat unexpectedly, if one does not count the word "out" (which is part of the expressions "sound fades out," "voice fades out," "man cries out," "cries out"), the word that occurs most frequently among those 175 captions is "panting." This is a type of external respiration widely associated with dogs (as opposed to the cat that Maddie has as a pet), though in this case the term refers to an exaggerated form of labored breathing that comes from the sort of high anxiety she experiences throughout the second half of the film. In fact, "[panting]" is an oft-occurring caption in SDH-enhanced slasher films from the 1980s, visually audible in everything from *Friday the 13th: The Final Chapter* (1984) to *Intruder* (1989), which both feature scenes in which a masked killer or intruder performs that respiratory action while also "[grunting]" and letting his feet fall menacingly with a heavy "[thudding]" sound.

Occurring nineteen times in the captioned version of *Hush* (primarily during the final forty minutes), "panting" is followed by "cries out" and "gasps" as the most repeatedly subtitled sounds in *Hush* (each appearing at the bottom of the screen thirteen times). Other bracketed terms or expressions that appear more than three times include: "[sound fades out]" (eight times); "[message tone]" (seven times); "[alarm blares]" (six times); "[banging]" (six times); "[grunts]" or "[grunting]" (six times); "[ringing]" (six times); "[sighs]" (six times); "[groans]" (five times); "[lock turns]" (five times); and "[wheezes]" (four times).

If one were to input all the film's captions into a word cloud application, creating a visual representation of its subtitled sounds (shown in a tightly packed configuration and in relative sizes according to the frequency of their appearance), certain aspects of the film would leap out. When seen in this way, the most prominent sonic events of *Hush*—at least those that the subtitler felt were most relevant to the film's deaf reception—distinguish it as a home-invasion thriller filled with respiratory activity, especially the exhalation of air. Such an infographic would furthermore make it clear that *Hush* is a very *sound*-oriented film in which door locks are habitually opened and alarm systems as well as other technological devices go off whenever the person responsible for all that heavy breathing and loud banging breaches the physical barriers separating the outside world from the inside spaces of the main setting. Nevertheless, in putting so much emphasis on the "out-ness" of the many cries, gasps, grunts, and sighs that pepper this text, the SDH as transcribed and ranked according to frequency obscures the many instances of *insertion* that likewise occur in the narrative, but which are not referenced in any of the captioned material. Although the expression "forced penetration" might bring to mind a violent sexual act committed by a man against another man or against a woman, the killer's unwelcome movement into Maddie's home is merely one of several nonsexual (or not overtly sexual) penetrative acts on his part, each of which comes with its own distinctive sound.

For instance, when he repeatedly plunges a knife into Sarah's abdomen as she screams for help outside Maddie's cabin, an uncaptioned squelching noise floods the soundtrack for a few seconds, indicating that the young woman's internal organs have been punctured and a significant amount of her blood is pouring out onto the patio floor. A similar sound of exsanguination comes later, when the killer repeats his earlier action and attacks Maddie with a sharp instrument (this time a crossbow arrow, which pierces her leg). Importantly, she manages to finally get the upper hand against the stalker after she drags herself into the wettest, most private space of her house (the bathroom): On the brink of losing consciousness, she plunges a knife into his own leg—yet another splashy sound for which there is no subtitle. Seeing that he is not dead, Maddie blasts his maskless face with insecticide, and then, as he nearly strangles her to death, she deals the final blow with the previously mentioned corkscrew. Piercing his neck, it too produces a moist, gurgling sound, yet no textual description of that noise appears at the bottom of the screen. This is in keeping with the general tendency among SDH providers to omit the slimy, sloshy, soggy audio elements so pronounced on horror film soundtracks, leaving one of the genre's most significant features to the imagination of hearing-impaired viewers. Indeed, horror, to quote Gloria Stuart's character Margaret Waverton in *The Old Dark House* (who steps into the titular abode from a rainstorm outside), is "dreadfully wet," though one would hardly know it if one were reliant upon captioning services to visually hear what other audiences can detect through their ears. As such, from a sonic standpoint, the many slittings and stabbings that occur in modern and postmodern examples of the genre, from Rob Zombie's *Halloween II* (2009) to Matt Bettinelli-Olpin and Tyler Gillett's *Scream VI* (2023), put a decidedly lethal spin on something that has been present since horror's earliest sound-era stirrings in the 1930s, when literally atmospheric gothic chillers devoid of such graphic imagery depended on thunder-cracked rainstorms, dense fog, and other types of wet weather to establish a spooky mood and to exploit the medium's newfound capacity to evoke fright through means other than sight. Tellingly, the SDH viewing option that comes with Sony Pictures' DVD and Blu-ray releases of Rob Zombie's contemporary updating of John Carpenter's franchise of the same title foregrounds the animalistic "grunting" of its own masked killer, Michael Myers (Tyler Mane), whenever he violently stabs the bodies or bashes the heads of his female victims—for example, Nurse Daniels (Octavia Spencer), Jazlean (Betsy Rue), Misty (Sylvia Jefferies), and Mya (Brea Grant)—whose wet deaths, in contrast, receive no captioning.

Significantly, in *Hush* the missing captions that might supply deaf and hard-of-hearing viewers with a stronger sense of that mortal moistness—that "wet death" that Isabel Cristina Pinedo and other scholars identify as a distinguishing feature of the postmodern horror film (a cultural form "intent on imaging the mutilation and destruction of the body")—are diegetically accounted for during a curious passage of dialogue in which the killer refers to Maddie by her nickname: "Squish."[46] Having gone through her cellphone and located that strange bit of personal information, he says the word "Squish" in a creepingly convivial manner, disarming her with yet another instance of invasion of privacy but also readying her for the wetness of the leg wound that awaits her. But the fact that it is *his* blood that noisily spatters from the squishy neck laceration onto the kitchen floor near the end of the film, producing liquidic sounds that are nowhere to be found in the captioning, speaks to what so frequently goes unspoken (or unwritten) in SDH presentations. Indeed, even if one were to revisit the kill scene that seems to have inspired this corkscrew-induced death in *Hush*—a memorable moment in *Friday the 13th: The Final Chapter* (1984) when the same household tool is used by Jason Voorhees (Ted White) to pin the hand of his latest victim Jimmy (Crispin Glover), without any captioned text to describe that sound—one would see that the squishy mess of that kitchen attack is representative of a larger problem with accessibility technologies. This will be elaborated with reference to *Friday the 13th: The Final Chapter* and other films in the next chapter, but SDH sometimes denies viewers access to the very physical and visceral components that make horror such a familiarly *human*, palpably *real* (and, yes, *wet*) body genre, despite the latter's high mortality rates, far-fetched scenarios, and penchant for stylistic excess as well as metatextual structures that call attention to the genre's artifice.

What makes the missing "squishes" of *Hush* so fascinating is that Mike Flanagan, its writer-director, would soon go to great lengths to ensure that his 2017 follow-up, *Gerald's Game*, foregrounded that sound in what is possibly the most stomach-churning scene in his oeuvre (and, according to the editors of *Screen Rant*, the "goriest scene of the 2010s").[47] The scene in question, which is set in yet another cabin in the woods (although its real setting is inside the mind of its main character), involves the skin around a woman's hand being slipped off like a wet latex glove so that she can wriggle free from a pair of handcuffs (fig. 5.3). When he was interviewed about that moment, which reportedly made

**Figure 5.3:** Compensating for the missing "squishes" in *Hush*'s subtitles for deaf and hard-of-hearing audiences, director Mike Flanagan's adaptation of *Gerald's Game* foregrounds that sound during a notoriously gory scene in which Jessie (Carla Gugino) "degloves" her hand to slip free from her captor.

at least one audience member pass out during its premiere screening at L.A.'s Fantastic Fest, Flanagan maintained that his source material (Stephen King's 1992 novel of the same title) went even further in describing the tortuous ordeal that the female protagonist, Jessie (Carla Gugino), undergoes when forced to slit her own wrist with a makeshift scalpel fashioned from a shard of glass. However, for the filmmaker, "the principal difference [between his and King's version] is the sound"—the "squish and pop and stretch" of the skin that made the scene considerably more cringe-inducing compared to what its author had described on the page. "Even when I would look away while we were shooting it, and when we were editing," Flanagan added, he and his creative team could not "get away from the sound." Significantly, King himself listed "squishiness" as one of the "ten key fears that underpin most horror" in its literary form (along with "fear of the dark . . . deformity, snakes, rats, closed-in spaces, insects, death itself, other people, and fear for someone else").[48] More so than literature, however, horror in its cinematic form brings that combined texture and sound to the front as a signifier of disgust. This is why the silencing of that signifier via SDH matters if we are to continue supporting and seeking out accessibility options in the coming years.

Future studies of cinematic horror might benefit from looking at SDH by using something as simple as an app-generated word cloud to lend visual expression to audio elements. Taking a few of the films alluded to earlier in this book as a starting point, one would see how a Depression-era classic of atmospheric dread like James Whale's *The Old Dark House*, with its heavy reliance on "cracking thunder" and "whistling wind," sits apart from a midcentury release like William Castle's *House on Haunted Hill* (1959), with its favoring of interior generators of suspense—including "footsteps" detectable through open and closed doors—over those that would be sourced from outside the titular abode. Despite their differences, these motion pictures, which I viewed with captioned text on the streaming platform Kanopy in the fall of 2020, both bring forth as many "chuckles" as "screams" (diegetically as well as extradiegetically). Even more laughter can be heard and seen in 1980s giallo films and slasher films such as Lucio Fulci's *The New York Ripper* (1982) and John Grissmer's *Blood Rage* (1987). The captions of those two films (available as SDH viewing options on their special-edition DVD and Blu-ray releases, from Blue Underground and Arrow Video, respectively) bring an uneasy mixture of emotions to the fore thanks to the cackling and even "quacking" presence of psychotic serial killers who, like the stalker in *Hush*, derive audibly sadistic pleasure from maiming and torturing innocent victims. Home video releases of more recent motion pictures, including those that have been labeled "elevated horror," such as John Krasinski's *A Quiet Place* and Ari Aster's *Hereditary* (2018), reveal a very different set of spectatorial appeals, catering to fans of films in which "crying" and "whining" (rather than "laughing" and "screaming"—the two most heavily captioned words in *Blood Rage*) are vocalized by characters who experience the trauma of family members' horrible deaths.

Significantly, Netflix not only offers viewers the option of watching *Hush* with onscreen captions, which communicate some—certainly not all—of the film's sonic signifiers, but also allows auditors who have low-to-no vision to listen to spoken transcriptions of the action, thanks to the company's AD service. Written and performed by Roland Bearne, a British voice actor for VSI (a dubbing and subtitling company headquartered in London but global in its reach as a multilanguage content and service provider), the AD that accompanies Netflix's release of *Hush* is similar to those attached to other films, insofar as it creates temporal gaps whenever the spoken narration comes several seconds before or well after the described action takes place. This occurs near the end of the film, when the words "Maddie sprays wasp and hornet killer in his eyes" are spoken a few moments after the killer has already screamed in agony upon receiving that aerosol blast. Likewise, the audible yet uncaptioned "squish" sound produced by the corkscrew plunging into the man's neck comes a few beats before the narrator explains what has happened, leaving a brief but pregnant window of time when visually impaired audiences are left to their own devices and forced to speculate on what or who made that sound. Indeed, descriptive tracks can sometimes create ambiguities of meaning through generalized language or a lack of specificity with regards to details in the mise-en-scène that beg to be seen in order for audiences to understand their meaning. For instance, against the sound of a decelerated heartbeat, Bearne speaks the words "As Maddie's heart slows, images flash of her family and childhood," giving visually impaired listeners of his description no indication that those images are Polaroid-like photos of people posing for a camera in close-up. In translating visual information into a spoken summary, the AD track thus "misses" or fails to convey much of what makes the cinematic image such a semantically rich repository of hermeneutic possibility. But, like other films' audio descriptions, it also "fills in" the image with connotative meanings not readily apparent or available to sighted audiences who listen to the soundtrack without such visual-to-verbal accompaniment. This is a paradoxical aspect of the accessibility option that I will return to in a later chapter, which explores the role that descriptive services available on streaming platforms and home video releases play in either intensifying or undermining the corporeal-sensorial impact of cinematic horror. Before getting to that, though, let us delve more deeply into the hermeneutics of captioned/subtitled horror, with the goal of discovering just what makes it such a paradoxically productive yet destructive way of looking at—or listening to—the world in its own right.

# 6

# THE UNHOLY SIGHT OF UNSIGHTLY SOUNDS

## Horror Film Subtitles for the Deaf and Hard of Hearing

(Hissing machinery). (Speaking in foreign language). (Dramatic music). (Dark chanting voices). (Clicking). (Zapping). (Gasp). (Pounding footsteps). (Winding machinery). (Dark circus music). (Swishing chains). (Cries of pain). (Whooshing). (Grunts and groans of pain). (Squishing flesh). (Tinging metal). (Cries of pain). "The suffering. The sweet suffering."

This series of disturbing, seemingly unrelated words, printed out as subtitled text atop a run of equally unsettling images, describes some of the aural elements at play in the opening minutes of *Hellbound: Hellraiser II* (1988). As parenthetically bracketed bursts of captioning, these onscreen signifiers give deaf and hard-of-hearing viewers a visually rendered entryway into the hellish landscape—or *soundscape*—of a horror film that, not insignificantly, pivots on scenes of bodily disintegration, the cleaving into parts of a formerly unified self for whom "gasps," "grunts," and "groans" are the final guttural utterances before the onset of a particularly bad death. Following on the heels of the original *Hellraiser* (1987), a big-screen adaptation of Clive Barker's 1986 novella *The Hellbound Heart* that the British author wrote and directed himself, this sequel (overseen by American filmmaker Tony Randel) assumes a certain spectatorial familiarity with that earlier film's puzzle-box narrative, which concerns a phalanx of grotesque creatures known as Cenobites who, led by the iconic Pinhead, subject recently harvested human souls to unimaginable physical and psychological torture. However, it is not necessary to have seen this film's predecessor to recognize the genre with which it is affiliated; and indeed *Hellbound: Hellraiser II*'s classificatory status as a supernatural horror film can be intuited through those subtitles alone, without the accompanying images of a British army captain, Elliot Spencer (Doug Bradley), being torn apart by metal hooks sprung from a strangely glowing box and transformed—one hammer-struck nail at a time—into the aforementioned Pinhead. The onscreen text appearing at the bottom of the screen thus fulfills at least two functions, isolating and summarizing (if also simplifying) the complex array of "local" sounds woven into *Hellbound: Hellraiser II*'s representational system while silently announcing the film's generic affiliation, its "fit" within a larger, global corpus of movies that are likewise filled with "dramatic music," "pounding footsteps," and "cries of pain."

With the exception of the phrase "The suffering. The sweet suffering," which is spoken by the now hideously transformed military officer at the tail end of this first sequence, the captioned text quoted above represents the sound effects and musical flourishes that would otherwise be heard by a majority of the film's auditors. Or, rather, those encoded words indicate *some*, but not all, of *Hellbound: Hellraiser II*'s sonic ingredients. There are, for instance, several auditory elements that are *not* included in this parade of parenthetical sounds, including: the accented voice of a shortwave radio announcer bathed in static and issuing from an antique receiver next to Captain Spencer's bed; the clangorous ringing of an offscreen bell; the faint stir of wind outside the cavernous yet prison-like army barracks where he is first shown; and the subtle brushing of his military uniform across the wooden floor as the nervously perspiring man crawls toward that mysterious box (audiences familiar with the original *Hellraiser* will know it as the "Lament Configuration"). Nor does the transcription do more than hint at the paralinguistic shadings of the voices producing some of these subtitled sounds—the chants, gasps, and foreign words that lack specific indicators of pitch, volume, and intonation. Such vocalic absence, however, is partially compensated for by Doug Bradley's performance as Captain Spencer, who opens his mouth in such a way as to indicate a breathiness and loudness befitting his dire situation. Additionally, visual elements within the film's mise-en-scène, including the metal walls of the military barracks, contribute to this compensatory effect, turning the opening scene's eerily lit, sparsely furnished setting into a kind of O-shaped echo chamber that elongates spoken words into ghostly reverberations.

In this way, *Hellbound: Hellraiser II*—or, rather, the captioning service provided by Amazon Prime for the online viewing of this film—is representative of both the affordances and constraints of digital communication interfaces, content-delivery systems, and other assistive technologies that enable deaf and hard-of-hearing viewers to become virtual listeners; that is, to figuratively and literally *see* a horror film's sounds, if incompletely. Subtitles for the latter group, acronymically abbreviated as SDH, have been a staple of the home-video market for years, dating back to the introduction of DVDs in the mid-to-late 1990s and the industry-wide recognition that this "value-added" feature, apart from complying with the recently enacted Americans with Disabilities Act (1990), could be packaged as a selling point along with other supplemental features on commercially released discs (e.g., filmmakers' audio commentary tracks, behind-the-scenes clips, making-of documentaries, outtakes). In contrast to the onscreen text of foreign-language films (i.e., subtitles), which *translates* spoken words for an audience assumed to be lacking in linguistic comprehension, SDH services *transcribe* dialogue as well as non-speech elements for individuals whose access to the sonic dimensions of a motion picture would otherwise be impeded, regardless of the spoken language. SDH thus serves to remove said impediments, making accessibility an option in much the same way that closed captioning did for US network television audiences beginning in the early 1980s (following a decade of field tests and negotiations on the part of broadcasters and federal regulators). However, as Sean Zdenek argues in his book *Reading Sounds*, closed captions and SDH are not transparent "windowpanes" through which a viewer is able to look out onto a cultural production's entire sonic field, but rather a mediating veil, obscuring as much as they reveal "in the course of providing access to it."[1] Fittingly, the "terrible place" in which Elliot finds himself at the beginning of *Hellbound: Hellraiser II* contains several windows that close automatically once his fate has been sealed, plunging him into darkness and suggesting the paradoxical concealment that occurs whenever subtitling appears on screen.

To extend Zdenek's fenestration metaphor even further, one might say that closed captions and SDH are like venetian blinds whose parted slats both facilitate and frustrate one's view of the sounds outside. In this light, subtitles for deaf and hard-of-hearing viewers can be seen as an intermediary layer of information, and what they provide access to is less a comprehensive accounting of the various elements comprising a film's soundtrack than a highly idiosyncratic and selective *interpretation* of those elements. That interpretation, often put forth by independent contractors who are paid by companies like Amazon to distill a complex array of aural signifiers into a few simple words, unfolds moment to moment during a film's viewing, mimicking the linear movement of a story's unfolding. Moreover, it reflects an increasingly standardized approach to subtitling in which industry guidelines and authoring conventions ensure that idiosyncrasies in content are minimized or absorbed into a more uniform language, one that adheres to certain technical specifications (e.g., character limitations, font size) that can be spotted across multiple texts. And yet, for all of this standardization in US and other national contexts, and despite the simplification and actual *subtracting* of sounds that contracted subtitlers are asked to do, Zdenek's notion that captioning constitutes a "complex rhetorical and interpretative practice" gains validity by the sheer number of multiple SDH versions of individual films currently available in the home video and streaming markets.[2] Indeed, *Hellbound: Hellraiser II*, like many other horror films, can today be viewed across different platforms and via different content providers, from DVD and Blu-ray editions published by the US-based Image Entertainment and the UK-based Arrow Video to the online rentals offered by Vudu, iTunes, and Amazon Prime. In fact, the latter subscription service, part of the multinational company's ongoing efforts to extend its brand identity into the realm of e-commerce, has replaced the version of *Hellbound: Hellraiser II* from which the above captions derive (and which I viewed in the spring of 2019) with *another* version, one that (beginning in the fall of 2019) could likewise be rented or purchased on Amazon's website.

Anyone who watches that subsequent version on the streaming service would encounter an even more condensed representation of the film's sounds, with fewer parenthetical captions—or, in this case, bracketed text in all caps—carrying a heavier burden of delivering information to deaf and hard-of-hearing viewers. Although the first image immediately following the opening credits—an extreme close-up of Captain Spencer's radio—is accompanied by a "[BEEPING]" sound as well as the voice of a "[MAN ON SHORTWAVE RADIO SPEAKING HINDI]," gone are any subtitled references to the chains and hooks that shoot up from the Lament Configuration, which "swished" and "whooshed" in the earlier version. The "pounding footsteps" of that previously captioned version of the film have also gone silent, as has any music during this opening sequence that is not sourced in the diegetic world (i.e., that which was generically described as "dramatic" and is distinct from the "dark circus music" coming from the puzzle box). All told, only eight sound effects are transcribed in this opening sequence of the latest version of *Hellbound: Hellraiser II*, including two that were captioned in the earlier version: the "[ZAPPING]" of the mystery box as its springs to life plus the "[GASP]" that it elicits from Captain Spencer. Of those eight, three are the same word, "[SCREAMING]," which appears in quick succession as an unseen demon drives the nails into Elliot's head. Compare this to the seventeen captions that make up the previous SDH rendering of the same sequence, which fleshes out *Hellbound: Hellraiser II*'s sounds in a more atmospherically evocative and affectively visceral way, and one begins to understand just how mutable something like textual transcription is as an object of study.

The "best" presentation of *Hellbound* currently available in North America, in terms of audiovisual restoration, is the 2K resolution scan of the film undertaken by Lakeshore Entertainment and made commercially available as a Collector's Edition Blu-ray by Arrow Video, which notably features a different set of subtitles for deaf and hard-of-hearing viewers. Like the latest Amazon Prime version, the Arrow presentation, which has "cleaned up" the image by digitally removing much of the dirt, debris, and scratches that plagued 35 mm film prints of *Hellbound*, also scrubs away some of the subtitled sounds that were found in the version quoted above. Following fleeting references to the shortwave receiver and to the Lament Configuration—"(Indian man on radio)," "(Continues, indistinct)," "(Distant beeping, whirring)," and "(Music box plays)"—the SDH here does away with the "clicking," "zapping," "pounding," "winding," "swishing," "whooshing," "squishing," and "tinging" noises that contribute to this film's affective power as "body horror." Instead, the Arrow Blu-ray emphasizes Captain Spencer's audible response to the physical threat posed by the box, through captions such as "(Screams)," "(Screaming)," "(Man, shouting)," "(Yelling)," and "(Shouting, grunting)" (fig. 6.1).

Although I could have gestured toward any number of other SDH-enabled horror films that, in their downloadable/streamable or home-video incarnations, provide compelling evidence of selective transcription's instrumentality as a hermeneutic tool, I have opted to begin this chapter with a reference to *Hellbound: Hellraiser II*'s own introductory passages because it so nakedly foregrounds that variability while hinting at the frustrations involved in carrying out such a study. Moreover, that opening sequence is bookended by images that usefully highlight the longstanding emphasis given to two sense modalities—namely, those of hearing and seeing—within a discipline that has largely ignored the phenomenology of smelling, tasting, and touching. Although I emphasized the importance of these latter three affective experiences in chapters 3 and 4 of this book (building upon my previous book, *Body Genre: Anatomy of the Horror Film*), the present discussion sticks to the ears and the eyes as reception organs that are often treated as the first and final word in cinema studies' theoretical framing of embodied spectatorship. Beginning with an extreme close-up of the shortwave radio receiver (a piece of equipment that,

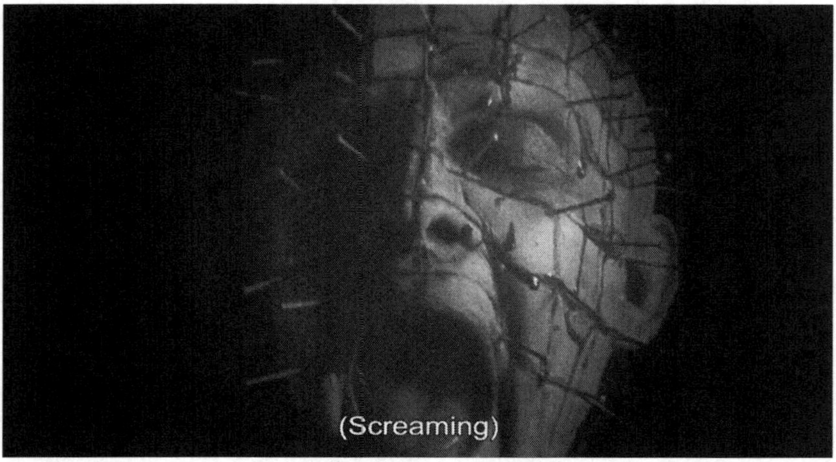


**Figure 6.1:** The SDH provided on Arrow Video's Blu-ray release of *Hellbound: Hellraiser II* does away with several contextualizing subtitles provided on previous releases while accentuating the physical pain experienced by the man who will become Pinhead.

though material, has the effect of dematerializing those oral communicators on the other end), and culminating with an extreme close-up of an eyeball (which coincides with the sound of a disembodied voice musing, "The suffering. The sweet suffering"), this opening sequence encourages the audience to see and hear *Hellbound: Hellraiser II* as a strictly *audiovisual* text, one requiring the use of eyes and ears to pry open its mysteries.

Not surprisingly, the critical discourse surrounding this horror film and many others like it is suffused with ocularcentric and audiocentric language, which has the additional effect of sealing off other sensory pathways (e.g., olfactory, gustatory, tactile) that might render the fleshy "mess" of the text more fully. For example, in his glibly dismissive review of *Hellbound: Hellraiser II*, Roger Ebert lists some of the "gruesome images" that await viewers of the film (and which, he argues, "can be watched in any order" due to its lack of a traditional "beginning," "middle," and "end"): "We *see* lots of bodies that have been skinned alive, so that the blood still glistens on the exposed muscles. We *see* creatures who have been burned and mutilated and twisted into grotesque shapes, and condemned for eternity to unspeakable and hopeless tortures."[3] Like so many other reviewers, Ebert slides "naturally" from a discussion of images to one of sounds in the next sentence, calling on his readers' assumed access to the film's auditory components when he writes, "We *hear* deep, rasping laughter, as the denizens of hell chortle over the plight of the terrified girls. And we *hear* their desperate voices calling to each other."[4] To illustrate what the latter calls for help might sound like, and as evidence of why the film is likely to engender "sarcastic laughter" rather than outright fear or screams from its audience, the critic transcribes a portion of its dialogue, drawing out the vowels so as to approximate how actors Ashley Laurence and Imogen Boorman perform their scripted lines as the film's two main female characters: "*Kirstieeeeeee!!!!!!*" and "*Tiffanyyyyyyy!!!!!*"[5]

As one of several horror films panned by Ebert in his collection of one-star (or lower) reviews, *I Hated, Hated, Hated This Movie* (2000), this critically reviled sequel to *Hellraiser* would seem to be of questionable value to anyone seeking a better understanding of how persons with disabilities might engage the genre in ways that are not often accounted for within the texts themselves or within the scholarship surrounding the subject. Although I do not share his negative feelings toward *Hellbound: Hellraiser II* (which he calls "an ideal movie for audiences with little taste and atrophied attention spans, who want to glance at the screen occasionally and ascertain that something is still happening up there"), I must admit to my own qualms about its usefulness (if not its "worth") given the lengths to which Clive Barker and his creative cohort go to make physical disfigurement or deformity the main, if not sole, source of the Cenobites' monstrosity.[6]

Of course, throughout the history of cinematic horror, (in)human anomalies have frequently been associated with social exclusion and the perceived need to keep monsters at bay lest the somatic or sensorial difference to which their hideous bodies attest bleed over into the realm of the able-bodied. Indeed, long before the motion picture medium was cobbled together, Frankenstein-style, from previous cultural forms, scientific breakthroughs, and technological marvels beginning in the 1890s, anomalous bodies had been stigmatized "as omens or prodigies, visitations of sin, [or] freaks and curiosities."[7] In fact, they were pathologized to the point that the rhetorical move from "disability" to "monstrosity" seemed logical to consumers of gothic fiction, including Mary Shelley's *Frankenstein* (1818). As David M. Turner notes in the introductory chapter of his coedited volume *Social Histories of Disability and Deformity*, monster literature of centuries past harnessed those afflictions as "social metaphors," something that his coeditor, Kevin Stagg, explains further in his own study of sixteenth- and seventeenth-century English ballads, broadsides, and pamphlets that equated bodily abnormality with sin.[8] During the eighteenth century, discourses of sinful "deformity" circulated throughout England, the United States, and other national contexts as rhetorical means of delineating between the morally upright and the debased individual whose presumed predilection for vice could be detected in his or her ugliness.[9] This tendency was addressed over 250 years ago by William Hay, a member of British Parliament whose 1754 book, *Deformity: An Essay*, sought to humanize those individuals—himself included—who had been afflicted as much by social stigmatization as by physical "irregularities" that were mistakenly interpreted as outward evidence of some inner "monstrosity."[10] In perhaps his most quoted passage, Hay writes that deformity "is visible to every Eye," a statement that conveniently sidesteps the lived reality of those who were born with blindness or who have experienced vision loss (an experience that itself might be "invisible" to the eyes of others). In seeking to have his able-bodied readers consider the unseen or unknowable effects of "deformity" as they are felt by people who, like himself, live day to day with disabilities, Hay resorts to the same kind of rhetorical maneuvers that Ebert adopts in his descriptions of what "we" see and hear as consumers of *Hellbound: Hellraiser II*.

The ableist assumption that *everyone* can see and hear the same things when seated before a movie screen and a set of loudspeakers is not Ebert's alone, for it creeps into even the most well-intentioned studies of cinematic accessibility and differentiated spectatorship. Nevertheless, his need to emphasize the imagistic and aural dimensions of *Hellbound*'s hideousness as a text that, like the Cenobites themselves, should be avoided at all costs, makes this horror film—and the discourses surrounding it—all the more relevant to the present discussion. Moreover, the captions that Amazon Prime members and other online consumers might access while watching its opening sequence highlight many of the things that make SDH such a complex rhetorical object or, in the words of Sean Zdenek, a "significant variable in [the] multimodal analysis" of film.[11]

Take, for instance, this opening sequence's parenthetical reference to "(Dramatic music)." Few aural elements of a motion picture are as difficult to transcribe—to make accessible in the form of captioned text—as its musical score or soundtrack, which might be comprised of both diegetic and nondiegetic tunes. Although music has long been theorized as a language through which to communicate feelings, ideas, and meanings, its specific features often mitigate against the very things that language is structured to do, including narrowing down "the range of its possible referents" for the sake of communicative clarity or sense-making.[12] Music's efficacy, on the other hand, lies in its "inherent ambiguity," which puts it at the opposite pole of the "communicative continuum" relative to language, which can "refer unambiguously to complex states of affairs in the world." In Ian Cross's words, "Music's attributes of embodying, entraining, and transposably intentionalizing time in sound and action enable it to be efficacious in contexts where language may be unproductive or impotent precisely because of its capacity to be interpreted unambiguously."[13] SDH's habitual reliance on overly generalized adjectives like "dramatic" keeps the musical ambiguity of motion pictures intact while failing to provide deaf and hard-of-hearing viewers with any information about the specific features of music (related to its form, dynamics, harmony, melody, rhythm, tempo, and timbre) that make it distinctive in the first place.

Some of the countless SDH-enhanced horror films to feature the parenthetical sound effect "(dramatic music)" include the early studio-era talkie *White Zombie* (1932), the Poverty Row production *Devil Bat* (1940), Herschell Gordon Lewis's splatter-fest *Blood Feast* (1963), the British-Spanish sci-fi-horror coproduction *Horror Express* (1972), Dario Argento's supernatural classic *Suspiria* (1977), the disability-themed rape-revenge film *Avenged* (2013), and the psychological thriller *The Blackcoat's Daughter* (2015). Throughout the fall of 2019, these seven horror films, along with dozens more, were available for viewing in digitized form through Kanopy, an on-demand streaming platform that makes captioned videos accessible to millions of public library patrons and US college students. Although undoubtedly valuable as a cultural and educational resource, this along with other online services do a *disservice* to the musical compositions that pepper horror films, ranging from popular songs, jazz numbers, and tribal drumbeats to traditional orchestral arrangements, modern electronic scores, and sonic "stingers" (e.g., synth blasts, screeching violins) accentuating so many of the genre's jump scares. Such elements—admittedly difficult to transcribe as onscreen text—tend to be lumped together under the "(dramatic music)" banner, or under similarly nonspecific captions such as "(suspenseful music)," "(ominous music)," and "(eerie music)."

One of the many examples of this occurs in the psychological horror film *When a Stranger Calls* (1979), when an escaped psychiatric patient, Curt Duncan (Tony Beckley), stalks a woman after she leaves a bar and walks alone to her apartment at night (fig. 6.2). Having earlier killed two preschool-aged children of a suburban family before being institutionalized for criminal insanity, the titular figure now appears ready to resume his murderous exploits, waiting in a darkened alleyway like a predator does while scoping out its prey. As Curt watches the unsuspecting woman from the shadows, the volume of the nondiegetic music—written for strings by composer Dana Kaproff—rises on

**Figure 6.2:** As seen in this moment from *When a Stranger Calls*, one of the most frequently subtitled sounds on home-video releases of horror films is "(DRAMATIC MUSIC)."

the soundtrack, recalling an earlier scene in which the same ascending scale announces a similarly scary moment. That "(DRAMATIC MUSIC)" is likely to prompt a feeling of recognition among contemporary audiences who have heard the distinctive THX "Deep Note." Attributed to Lucasfilm sound engineer Dr. James "Andy" Moorer and first included at the start of a motion picture in 1983 (as a sonic prelude to that year's *Star Wars: Episode VI—Return of the Jedi*), the THX "Deep Note" is a "synthesized crescendo that glissandos from a relatively narrow frequency spread (about 200–400 Hz) to a broader frequency spread (of about three octaves)."[14] Though the section of Kaproff's score that accompanies the nighttime stalking scene in *When a Stranger Calls* is not *exactly* the same as Moorer's deeply resonant chord, it is similar enough and unusual enough in its sudden scale ascension to demand a more specific descriptor than "dramatic," which, musically speaking, could be taken to mean *anything* in the context of the horror genre. Even when horror films' home-video transcriptions incorporate more descriptive terms, SDH sometimes misrepresents the actual instrumentation and harmonics of musical numbers. This happens, for instance, on Shout Factory's Collector's Edition Blu-ray of *April Fool's Day* (1986), whenever the electronic portions of composer Charles Bernstein's minimalist score, reminiscent of his synth-heavy tunes for *A Nightmare on Elm Street*

**Figure 6.3:** This subtitled reference to "(ominous orchestral music)" on Shout Factory's Blu-ray release of *April Fool's Day* (1986) hardly conveys the sonic properties of composer Charles Bernstein's minimalist electronic score.

(1984), are labeled as "(ominous orchestral music)" (fig. 6.3). The latter subtitle—appropriate to something like the 1982 horror film *The Slayer* (1982), which opens with the lushly "(dramatic orchestral music)" of composer Robert Folk as performed by the London Philharmonic—does not accurately reflect the scale or style of Bernstein's arrangements for a film that pivots on winking acts of April Fool's Day subterfuge and narrative misdirection.

As a point of comparison, despite sharing the SDH description "(dramatic music)," the various musical compositions sprinkled throughout *White Zombie*, director Victor Halperin's independently produced film about Haitian voodoo practices, bear little-to-no resemblance to the original score for Dario Argento's *Suspiria* composed by the Italian prog-rock group Goblin. The former soundtrack consists mainly of symphonically orchestrated passages from Liszt's piano work *Liebesträume*, Wagner's romantic opera *Lohengrin*, and Mussorgsky's ten-part suite *Pictures at an Exhibition*, in addition to less-recognizable extracts from Gaston Borch's *Incidental Symphonies* and Hugo Riesenfeld's *Death of the Great Chief*, among other newly recorded pieces.[15] This "curious collection" of music, or what Gary Rhodes refers to as a "bizarre pastiche . . . assembled in large part from silent picture cue sheets," was supervised by Abe Meyer, whose decision to record new versions of these and other compositions lend several scenes in *White Zombie* an air of both familiarity and strangeness—especially so during an eventful moment when a wordless version of R. Nathaniel Dett's 1914 hymn "Listen to the Lambs" is inserted into the audio mix. Like all the other musical passages in the film, this wordless vocal piece with "alternating male and female choruses" (a unique take on the twentieth-century American spiritual, which seems "out of place on the lips of Haitian natives," according to Rhodes) is reduced to the catchall signifier "dramatic music" when transcribed for deaf and hard-of-hearing viewers. That same parenthetical caption occurs whenever the propulsive drumming and Moog synthesizer stylings of Goblin's music blast onto the *Suspiria* soundtrack. Although in both cases "the sounds are not merely accompaniments to on-screen visuals, but an integral aspect of the constructed mood," the vast differences between *White Zombie*'s soundtrack (which was produced at a time when cinematic horror was beginning "to depend heavily on music to generate affect") and *Suspiria*'s "Tubular Bells"-inspired score (which helped to inaugurate a new era in rock-fueled horror cinema) are ironed out for the sake of simplicity in subtitling.[16]

As simple as these two SDH-enhanced films are in terms of their rendering of musical components as onscreen text, other examples of cinematic horror, drawn from different periods and subgenres across the history of the genre, go even further in stripping away any distinguishing characteristics that might give audiences a better understanding of a given composition's formal and tonal properties. An extreme instance of this occurs whenever the captions show a musical symbol (such as an eighth note or a single-bar note) in lieu of descriptive wording, something that occurs at various points in another voodoo-themed zombie film, *The Four Skulls of Jonathan Drake* (1959). In the absence of other musical notations (such as staff lines, clefs, breaks, and rest marks), these free-floating notes give no indication of the meter, pitch, or tempo of composer Paul Dunlap's dynamic score (fig. 6.4). The same goes for the opening seconds of *Silent Night, Deadly Night 3: Better Watch Out!* (1989), released on Blu-ray by Lionsgate (as part of its Vestron Video Collector's Series): Against a black background, two single bar notes in white appear at the bottom of the screen—an interesting subtitle given the name of the film's production company, Quiet Films, which appears as soon as those notes disappear. In both instances, deaf and hard-of-hearing viewers are greeted with an onscreen signifier that

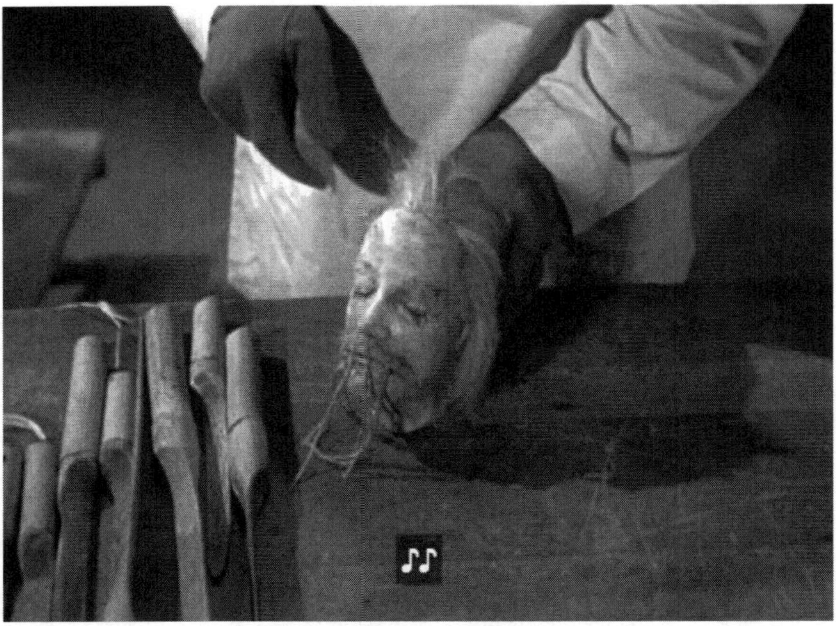

**Figure 6.4:** While indicating that music is playing during a scene, notations such as this, in *The Four Skulls of Jonathan Drake*, provide no information about that music's dynamics, pitch, or timbre.

fails to signify anything beyond the generalized acknowledgment that "music" is playing. Nearly as stripped down is the SDH text for Amazon Prime's version of *Friday the 13th: A New Beginning* (1985). This fifth installment in the famous slasher film franchise begins, rather inauspiciously, with the bracketed caption "[MUSIC]," which does little more than the musical notes of *The Four Skulls of Jonathan Drake* do in terms of hinting at the distinguishing characteristics of a score that, by design, is supposed to make the audience feel uneasy about what will transpire during the opening scene.[17] That intended nervousness is not likely to be experienced by spectators who rely on SDH to hear otherwise inaudible sounds, including musical elements that lack even the most basic descriptors like those cited above (e.g., "dramatic," "eerie," "ominous," "suspenseful").[18]

## Chang(el)ing the Score

I'm sure there are many of you who may recognize this.

—Composer John Russell (George C. Scott), the main character in *The Changeling* (1980), speaking to a classroom full of music students as he sits at a piano and launches into a piece that is simply captioned "[fast piano music]"

As a dramatic, eerie, ominous, and suspenseful horror film about a composer coping with the tragic loss of his wife and young daughter (who died in a roadside car accident that he witnessed before moving to Seattle), *The Changeling* (1980) lends itself well to the present discussion, due to director Peter Medak's prodigious use of musical accompaniment in scenes that furthermore foreground the communicative function of initially unsourced sounds echoing throughout the main setting. The central location of the film is a large Victorian mansion where the protagonist seeks to start a new life but is haunted by more than just the memories of his dearly departed. Not long after John Russell (George C. Scott), the grieving widower, settles into his spacious rented home away from home and adopts the life of a relative recluse (so that he might "pound away on the piano" whenever he is not busy teaching a music composition class at his alma mater), he begins hearing several unusual noises issuing from somewhere inside the house, including a loud metallic banging that startles him awake at the break of dawn. Besides that unnerving sound—captioned on Amazon Prime as "[deep rhythmic pounding]"—he hears "[metal clanking]," "[thudding]," "[clinking]," "[metal squeaking]," "[water trickling]," "[shower spraying]," and "[faucet stopping]," as well as the ghostly utterances of one or more souls in the form of laughter and moaning. The captions come fast and furious when John, snooping around the house in search of their source, discovers a boarded-up door in a closet that leads to a hidden bedroom upstairs. This is the place where, decades earlier, a sickly, physically disabled six-year-old boy was drowned in a bathtub by his father. Though he is forced to cover his ears because of the loudness of those noises, John comes to understand that they are a means for the dead boy's restless spirit to communicate with the living—as if the house and its associated "creaks," "bangs," and "rattles" were a medium through which to deliver a haunting message from the past, not unlike the way that SDH speaks to audiences who are ocularly attuned to a horror film's sounds.

Importantly, the protagonist's gradual comprehension of what took place in the attic is aided by a medium, Mrs. Harmon (Helen Burns), who, accompanied by her husband, performs a séance inside the house and "blindly" transcribes what she hears. As the blank-faced psychic woman stares straight ahead and scribbles doodle-like words onto large sheets of paper provided by her husband, trying to keep pace with the otherworldly words coming to her (including the boy's name, "Joseph"), a reel-to-reel tape recorder captures otherwise inaudible sounds, which John will later listen to with the intent of hearing what she has heard. Throughout the séance scene, composer Rick Wilkins's score—a slow plonking assortment of piano notes in a minor key layered atop a simmering, skittering foundation of violins and other string instruments—is subtitled as "[ominous music]" and "[eerie music]," a pair of vacillating captions that appear onscreen as frequently as Mrs. Harmon's quickly transcribed interdimensional dialogue does. In his discussion of *The Changeling*, Matt Glasby refers to this as the film's "most chilling sequence," an effect that results not only from seeing "the automatic writing of a medium who scrawls, 'Help, help, help!,'" but also from hearing the musical score moving "from melancholy piano to spooky children's choir" as the camera "becomes a spectral presence, floating through the empty rooms, like a lonely ghost."[19]

Additional textual descriptors of *The Changeling*'s score, including "[exciting music]," "[foreboding music]," "[intense music]," "[menacing music]," "[somber music]," "[suspenseful music]," and "[unsettling music]," as well as more instrumentally specific signifiers such as "[dramatic piano music]," "[fast piano music]," and "[pleasant piano music]," which are usually reserved for John's own diegetic performances, pop up at such a fast rate throughout the entirety of the film that viewers who are reliant on SDH might feel as accosted as he does by the omnipresent yet evasive sounds of the house. This quick series of captions is reminiscent of the ever-shifting parenthetic descriptors provided for streaming and home-video releases of *Intruder* (1989), writer-director Scott Spiegel's unique take on the slasher subgenre, one that is set almost entirely inside a grocery store where Muzak plays on the speakers. Within seconds, the SDH for *Intruder* moves from "(ominous music)" to "(suspenseful music)" to "(eerie music)" to "(dark tense music)" to "(mysterious music)" to "(upbeat music)" to "(melancholy music)" and so on, despite there being relatively few significant chord changes, time changes, or alterations in composers Dick Walter and Graham De Wilde musical score. Given how unrelentingly and intrusively these and other captions pop up on the screen (similar to the sudden intrusion of multiple shock cuts over the course of its eighty-eight-minute running time), the title of this horror film is fitting, though much the same could be said about *The Changeling*, the SDH of which shifts or mutates moment to moment but in such an persistent way that it could be likened to John's trauma of familial loss and the manner in which his emotional state keeps changing. What, in theory, should be a positive attribute of an assistive technology—the frequency of the captions in this streaming version of the film—creates a claustrophobic, pressurized atmosphere of fear.

Murray Leeder believes that *The Changeling* "loses its unnerving power at the point" where the house's mysterious sounds are "pinned down to the level of image" (specifically, to flashback shots of the "disabled child, drowned in a bathtub . . . his struggling feet clanging against the side of the tub").[20] I maintain, however, that the layering of SDH atop those and other shots increases spectatorial unease and gives audiences insight into what the protagonist is experiencing, as someone beset on all sides by extrasensory phenomena that are at once within and beyond his grasp. It is as if each bracketed set of words were *assaultive* rather than assistive, and their ever-changing descriptors (shifting from "[somber]" to "[eerie]" to "[foreboding]" to "[dramatic]" even within a single scene, and often without any key changes or chord alterations) make *The Changeling*'s music as difficult to pin down as are Joseph's own posthumously perceived sounds—his cries for help that echo throughout the Victorian dwelling and reverberate through the decades. Those cries for help, which John eventually hears after listening intently and repeatedly to the audio recording of the séance, eventually take him to the seaside property where the dead boy's body had been dumped into a well. Notably, when the protagonist arrives at that other haunted house, owned by the mother of a young girl who claims to have seen a ghostly boy inside her bedroom, the subtitles hint at the manner in which Joseph was killed, with "[water sloshing]" flashing onscreen just as those words had appeared earlier amid a cacophony of other transcribed sounds in the rented mansion.

A deeper interrogation of *The Changeling* might look at how character interactions and the emotional cadences of various scenes, rather than any musical modulations or alterations of the soundtrack, seem to dictate several of the adjectival shifts that occur in Amazon Prime's captioning of this film. For instance, during an early scene, the lullaby that John has recently composed and recorded transforms from a soothing tune into "[somber piano music]," according to the subtitle that appears onscreen when a local historic society agent named Claire (Trish Van Devere) inquiringly picks up the red ball that once belonged to his daughter. Without changing the melody that plays diegetically on his reel-to-reel recorder, the film, through its captions, suggests that the music's tonal properties have altered to reflect the protagonist's melancholic remembrance of his child before her tragic death. Almost as soon as the caption informs deaf and hard-of-hearing viewers of the kind of music playing during this scene, another one takes its place upon Claire's question to John: "Do you ride?" Rendered as "[pleasant music]," that descriptor seems less indicative of the actual music playing over the scene (which has the same uneasiness of the earlier "[eerie music]," violins tense with anticipation) and is more likely a product of her outwardly pleasant demeanor, with a smile flickering across her face when asking her new friend if he has any horse-riding experience. Other instances of this adjectival variance—this fluid movement between signifiers across a single musical composition, segment, or scene—could be marshaled forth as evidence of SDH's potential as a hermeneutic tool whose usefulness lies in its ability to foreground another person's interpretation of the text (that of the captioner, someone who is presumably more attuned to the nuances of cinematic sounds than the average spectator).

Of course, film scholars also benefit from drawing upon the insights of musicologists, music theorists, and music practitioners such as James Buhler, Mervyn Cooke, Kathryn Kalinak, David Neumeyer, and Gregg Redner, whose published works have contributed to a greater comprehension of soundtrack elements than what average listeners (i.e., anyone not trained in music composition) might appreciate even when viewing a film through assistive technologies. A good illustration of why such scholarship matters within the sphere of horror film hermeneutics can be found in Buhler's contribution to Neil Lerner's edited volume

*Music in the Horror Film: Listening to Fear.*[21] Titled "Music and the Adult Ideal in *A Nightmare on Elm Street*," his essay provides a far more detailed account of the sonic dimensions of cinematic signification than what SDH can deliver. Focusing on the first of the many entries in the franchise for which writer-director Wes Craven remains best known, Buhler notes that, in addition to foregrounding the "labored breathing and sound effects" that accompany images of Freddy Krueger (Robert Englund) fashioning finger blades from sheet metal, pipes, fishing knives, and an old leather work glove, the four-minute prologue leans heavily upon the electronic score of composer Charles Bernstein to establish one of the film's main themes. In addition to hearing Freddy pounding on steel and copper to create his signature instrument of torture, the sound of another instrument—that of a synthesizer—emerges from the dense audio mix to convey the "terrible place of the nightmare" that will soon envelope Tina (Amanda Wyss), the teenager who is shown running either toward or away from the source of those sounds. In Buhler's words,

> We hear an atmospheric synthesizer pad, modeled to some extent on vocal sounds and string harmonics, interspersed with hits on synthesized drums. This music is interrupted by a more specifically synthesized sound that sweeps from high to low as the film title appears . . . before settling into an oscillating repeated two-tone pattern behind a disembodied scream. The music at this point shifts to a more string-like tone but it is overlaid with a wind sound and some low-level unidentifiable sounds (laughter, farm animals?) before a prototype of the *Nightmare* theme appears in bell-like tones.[22]

Notably, the critic's description is richly detailed yet nebulous when it needs to be, and does not foreclose the possibility of other interpretations of those sonic events, some of which (e.g., the "unidentifiable sounds") remain confusing or disorientating even to him. Ultimately, the "surreal timbres" of Bernstein's synthesizer, itself a kind of "shapeshifter" (like Freddy) that can emulate the sounds of other instruments, literally sets the tone for the rest of *A Nightmare on Elm Street* as well as for the other films that are part of the franchise, an increasingly "synthetic" assortment of thrills and chills in which the calculated emulation of an "original" would be a conspicuous part of the remaking process (leading up to the tellingly titled 1994 metaslasher *Wes Craven's New Nightmare*).

Importantly, Buhler draws a sonic line between the world of teenagers and the world of adults, the latter being primarily "represented by talk (lecturing as much as dialogue) and noise (ambient sound)," whereas music—specifically synthesized tunes and pop songs (rather than a traditional orchestral score)—functions as "an explicit sign of regression" across the *Nightmare* franchise, beginning with the 1984 original.[23] He elaborates this point by noting how appropriate it is that *natural*, rather than synthetic, sounds wash over those scenes in which adults rather than teens dominate—scenes set inside the police station and the hospital as well as seemingly idyllic spots (including the false or fleeting comfort of one's own home) where the songs of birds and the chirps of crickets can be heard through open windows and open doors. For, in Buhler's words, adults are "agents and creatures of reality" in *A Nightmare on Elm Street*, using spoken language to verbally discipline kids within easily breached institutional and domestic settings where those impressionable teens are to be taught how to properly adjust to the mind-warping changes happening all around them.[24] Speech acts also occur within the film's prologue, specifically those of a maniacally cackling monster whose distinctive voice is layered atop the modulating "mood" music that Buhler describes above. Atop an image of his first female victim, dressed only in a nightgown and running down a concrete corridor in silhouette, Freddy calls out, "Tina! Psst, Tina! Tina!" before bursting into a growly laughter that sends her scurrying toward an exit that does not exist.

Also nonexistent is any subtitled reference to the music that is such an indelible part of *A Nightmare on Elm Street*. Indeed, the two different sets of captions accompanying the film's prologue that I have accessed (available for viewing on the streaming service HBO Max and on the Warner Bros. Home Entertainment Blu-ray release) communicate nothing about Bernstein's evocative contribution to its themes. Instead, the captioned text privileges sound effects over musical elements in its (ultimately failed) attempt to make what Buhler describes above *meaningful* to audiences with deafness or hearing impairments. The bracketed words that flashed up at the bottom of the screen during my viewing of the prologue online (via HBO Max), like so many sudden screams or boogey-man-like "boos," were, in order of their appearance: "[RASPY BREATHING]" "[THUNDER]" "[SQUEAKING]" "[CLANK]" "[GASPS]" "[CLATTERING]" "[SQUEAKING]" "[GASPS]" "[STEAM HISSING]" "[METAL SQUEALING]" "[GASPS]" "[SOBBING]" "[WHIMPERS]" "[MAN PANTING]" and "[SHEEP BLEATING]"—all of which are sourced from within the boiler room where Freddy invisibly preys on Tina. Nothing from outside world of the story (such as music) creeps into the subtitled proceedings. The same goes for the Blu-ray version of the film, in which the prologue's SDH captioning includes the following text over the same scene: "[MAN BREATHING HEAVILY]" "[MAN SCREAMS]" "[MAN CHUCKLING]" "[BLEATS]" "[MAN LAUGHING]" "[CLANKING]" "[METAL SQUEAKS]" "[MAN LAUGHING]" "[GASPS]" "[MAN YELLS]" "[MAN BREATHING HEAVILY]" "[SCREAMS]" "[SHEEP BLEATING AND BABY CRYING]" "[MAN YELLS]" "[KNOCKING ON DOOR]." Notably, the subtitles on this home-video release put greater emphasis on the monstrous "man" producing many of the prologue's sounds (e.g., chuckling, screaming, yelling) than it does on the young recipient of his unwelcome advances. Indeed, the two audible noises that Tina makes—the "gasps" and the "screams"—lack nouns through which to designate a subject of those actions, though her visible presence onscreen establishes that vital information (as opposed to the nonvisible presence of Freddy offscreen).

Also absent are any references to the wet footsteps and dripping water that are an even more conspicuous part of the soundtrack than the gasps and whimpers issuing from the ill-fated character, who can be seen (but not visibly "heard") splashing through puddles on the concrete floor before being roused from her nightmare by a "[KNOCK ON DOOR]." Significantly, those moist atmospheric sounds are not even found in Buhler's comparatively "thick" description of the scene, which puts greater emphasis on musical elements than on noises that, frankly speaking, most film scholars tend to ignore. With that in mind, I would like to dwell momentarily on the actual fluidic stuff that seems to fall by the wayside whenever SDH are produced by content creators or third parties who—like many of us who study the genre—seem strangely inattentive to the terrifying *wetness* of horror.

## "Dreadfully Wet": Thick/Slick Description

They made a horrible sound!

—Nancy Thompson (Heather Langenkamp), describing the finger knives of Freddy Krueger (Robert Englund) to her friend Tina (Amanda Wyss), in *A Nightmare on Elm Street* (1984)

Is it wet? It's *wet*!

—Vanita "Stretch" Brock (Caroline Williams) to Leatherface (Bill Johnson), who is about to put the shaved-off skin of her radio show coworker L. G. (Lou Perryman) onto her own face, in *The Texas Chainsaw Massacre 2* (1986)

The monstrous surfaces of cinematic horror, be they the actual physical bodies of monsters or those prosthetic extensions of the latter's radical alterity that reflect our own abjection, are often "slimy, dripping, [and] glistening" in their "wetness."[25] According to Steffen Hantke, these and other haptically felt attributes of the genre suggest an exteriorizing of the body's interiors, "the excretion of unspeakable bodily fluids that breach the boundary between inside and outside" as surely as Freddy does to households and dreamworlds in *A Nightmare on Elm Street*.[26] Importantly, as Larrie Dudenhoeffer notes in *Embodiment and Horror Cinema*, "the 'body' in 'horror' . . . does not simply reside in the film's antagonists, in the monsters, aliens, mutants, murderers, or victims of some virus, experiment, or curse; nor does it simply reside in the imagination of its viewers, as certain images make their skin crawl, their muscles tense up, their stomachs churl, their senses falter, or their synapses fire."[27] For Dudenhoeffer, the "search for the 'ungraspable bio-logic' of the functions, dynamics, and components of embodiment" in a given horror film starts by first acknowledging "the nearly 'ungraspable' or self-erasing details of the film's construction." The latter include individual images, dialogue fragments, and other audiovisual elements that might give "the viewer a 'clue' as to which aspects of the flesh will come to overcode much of the film's narrative structure, editing rhythm, mise-en-scène, and other representational strategies."[28] Among the four tissue types that Dudenhoeffer draws upon in his anatomo-hermeneutic exploration of cinematic embodiment and the "organicity" of the medium's audiovisual codes, the epithelium (more so than the connective, muscular, and nervous tissues) leaps out as an apt means of theorizing the "overcoding" function of SDH or captioning more generally vis-à-vis the film on which it is placed.

A virtual skin upon the skin of the text, SDH as a doubly epidermal set of signifiers is not unlike the bloody facemask fashioned by Leatherface in Tobe Hooper's *The Texas Chainsaw Massacre 2* (1986). Removed from the face of one nearly dead victim (a radio show producer named L.G. [Lou Perryman]) only to be placed atop the face of another terrified individual (the film's female protagonist Vanita "Stretch" Brock [Caroline Williams]), the shaved-off skin is disgusting in its wetness. Disgust is magnified by virtue of the scene's setting, a "labyrinthine underground structure" that, in the words of Jack Halberstam (author of *Skin Shows: Gothic Horror and the Technology of Monsters*), "resembles nothing so much as an intestinal cavern."[29] What is most disturbing, though, is the way that the "dark vitality" of that sliminess, which is paradoxically emphasized when the monster *stretches* the tissue out into a thin membrane in front of a light source that registers its semi-transparency, soon covers up the once-animated facial features of the main character, who now appears divested of life. Fittingly, Vanita's nickname, "Stretch," hints at how Leatherface (whose own visage is overlayed with the skins of others) went about fashioning that epithelial surface into something resembling a death mask. Although she recoils in horror and exclaims, "It's *wet*!" seconds before her besotted assailant slips the slimy thing atop her face, no reference is made to the squishy, squelching sound that this second skin makes when it touches her own skin in the optional subtitles included on Arrow Video's Blu-ray release of *The Texas Chainsaw Massacre 2*. Though the visual hapticity of the scene remains intact, the aural suggestiveness of that wetness is not translated for deaf and hard-of-hearing audiences.

Similarly, gloopy, wet sounds abound in all four of the individual episodes (along with the wraparound narrative) of the multidirector film *V/H/S 94* (2021), though viewers reliant on the captioning services made available through Amazon Prime's online presentation of this more recent comedy-horror mashup would hardly know it. Besides featuring an episode set almost entirely inside a sewer system (writer-director Chloe Okuno's "Storm Drain"), which is effectively "dried out" through SDH, *V/H/S 94* shows a rainstorm brewing outside a funeral home during writer-director Simon Barrett's "Empty Wake." As the film's centerpiece, "Empty Wake" builds toward the moment when the reanimated corpse of a horribly disfigured man—guts spilling from its rib cage—rises from its coffin to attack a woman who has been locked inside the funeral home with it. When the undead man's innards splash out, no captions appear, in contrast to the subtitled sounds "[thunder cracks]," "[tornado siren wails]," and "[wind whistles]," which are sharper, more percussive, sonorous (high-pitched) noises that call attention to the contrasting silence of the goo dripping from the open casket to the funeral home floor. Although the haptically felt sensation of wetness is something that ties together the four episodes and wraparound frame narrative of *V/H/S 94*, Amazon Prime's subtitling of the film notably turns composer Greg Anderson's "[ominous music]," which appears throughout the film (and is captioned as such in each of the segments), into a stronger sort of connective tissue—a sonic through-line that furthermore connects it to countless other productions bearing that overly generalized SDH description.

From Clive Barker's *Hellraiser*, in which a character named Clare Higgins (Julia Cotton) first steps into the hellish northwest London house at 55 Ludovico Place and casually remarks, "Smells damp," to Peter Jackson's *Braindead* (1992), which James Marriott and Kim Newman refer to as "perhaps the soggiest gore film ever made," the grisliest horror movies tend to be the wettest.[30] Less gruesome, more psychological examples of the genre (such as Rose Glass's *Saint Maud* [2019], which begins with the sound of dripping blood and shows close-up shots of bubbling red liquid soon thereafter) also bring that distinguishing characteristic—the atmospheric flipside to the Western genre's arid dryness—to the fore. The relative dearth of wet, squishy sounds in SDH captions contrasts subtitlers' tendency to overemphasize the musical accompaniment of horror films, though in certain cases that stressing of the score's significance is warranted, and the effort to lend specificity to what plays on the soundtrack should be applauded. For instance, the musical score that plays during the opening credits of the 1960 British film *Circus of Horrors*, composed by Franz Reizenstein and Muir Mathieson, is rendered in a way that suggests moment-to-moment tonal and timbral changes, at least when viewed via Amazon Prime. In just a few seconds of screen time, the parenthetically captioned text reads, "(slow-building, dramatic orchestral music)," which then "(moves into proud, energetic circus music)," which then "(moves into uncertain, despondent orchestral music)," which finally "(moves into elegant orchestral music)." This conveyance of information, which is notably reliant on a conveyor-like verb ("moves"), is "thicker" than what typically accompanies horror films' title sequences.

Consider *Friday the 13th: A New Beginning*, the first five minutes of which present audiences who are not deaf or hard of hearing with a sonically dense mix of aural signifiers on top of composer Harry Manfredini's multilayered score. Framed as a dream sequence in which Tommy Jarvis (Corey Feldman), the twelve-year-old survivor from the previous film in the franchise (*Friday the 13th: The Final Chapter* [1984]), witnesses two grave robbers getting stabbed to death by a newly exhumed Jason Voorhees, this subtly metatextual beginning to the "New Beginning" foregrounds an embedded form of spectatorship—that of the young protagonist five years prior to the present day—while planting seeds of fear in the listener's ear. The "grunts," "groans," and "gasps" of the grave robbers, which are captioned as such on the Amazon Prime edition of *Friday the 13th: A New Beginning* as well as on the Warner Bros./ Paramount Blu-ray release, are nearly drowned out by the thunder in this storm-swept scene, which either "roars" or "rumbles," depending on the version being watched. Because his glasses are dotted with raindrops, Tommy's vision is initially obscured, forcing him to first rely on his ears before taking his spectacles off to see the other spectacle of the two men's grisly demise more clearly (fig. 6.5). Like the eyeglasses that can be glimpsed sitting atop a workbench full of metal objects (including razor blades) that Freddy Krueger uses during the opening prologue of *A Nightmare on Elm Street*, the eyewear adorning Tommy's face promises clarity and access to images that would otherwise be blurry. But what these water-dotted objects do is quite the opposite, materializing the boy's inability to clearly make out—or, more to the point, to make *sense* of—anything so unbelievable or outside the realm of everyday experience as a revivified corpse, especially if reliant on a single sensing organ (like the eyes).

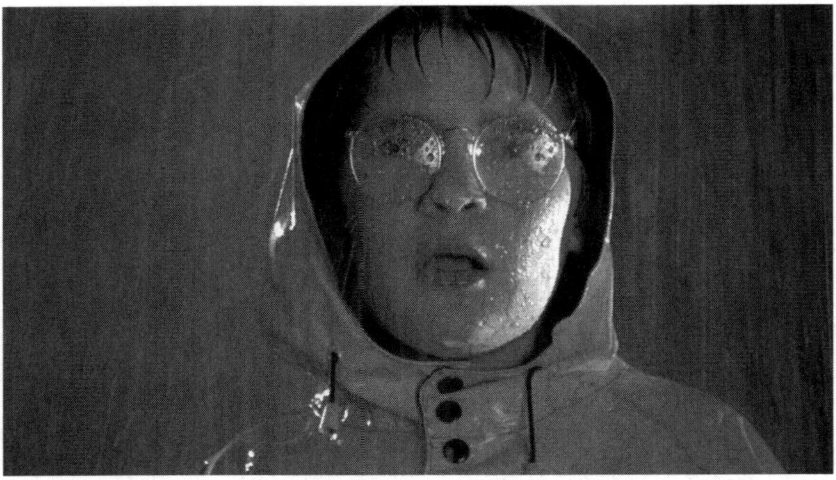

**Figure 6.5:** Waterdrop-speckled eyeglasses in the opening scene of *Friday the 13th: A New Beginning* recall the similarly wet eyeglasses glimpsed briefly at the beginning of *A Nightmare on Elm Street*. Moreover, throughout that opening scene, parenthetically bracketed SDH is employed to refer to noises emanating from onscreen sources (e.g., a stalker's victim groaning in pain) as well as to offscreen environmental, atmospheric, and meteorological events that frequently punctuate the actions occurring within the frame.

During this prologue of *Friday the 13th: A New Beginning*, water glistens on the boy's yellow rain slicker as well as Jason's worm-ridden hockey mask in the seconds before he bolts up from his muddy grave, thrusting a machete into one man's stomach and then into the other victim's neck. Unlike the "squishing" of flesh that was once (but no longer) included in the opening scene of Amazon Prime's SDH-enhanced version of *Hellbound: Hellraiser II*, neither of these two phallic stabbings are transcribed as captioned sound effects, just as the sloshing of feet along the rain-soaked forest floor—so prominent within this scene's sound mix—is left to deaf and hard-of-hearing viewers' imaginations. As Jason walks slowly toward the camera, planting footsteps in the mud that lack their own subtitled "squishes," Tommy whimpers quietly behind a bush in the forest clearing. Stopping only a few feet away from the boy, who—temporarily "paralyzed" and apparently "mute" with fear—is unable to call for help, Jason raises his bloodied weapon above his head. Then, intercut with a sudden downward movement of the killer's arm is a slow-motion shot of Tommy screaming a long, drawn-out "No!," the word subtitled for the sake of anyone who cannot read lips.

Besides demonstrating how SDH often fails to connote the sonic complexities of motion pictures, this opening scene in *Friday the 13th: A New Beginning* should remind audiences who are able to see its water-logged images that horror is a very wet genre. In countless other examples of cinematic horror, that wetness comes not from the kind of outdoor precipitation on view in this film, but instead from the splatter of blood and other viscous liquids that originate in the body, the insides of which are sometimes shown glistening, much like the watery drizzle on Tommy's rain slicker. Across subgenres (from the slasher film to the supernatural ghost story), soundtracks are saturated with the moist music of wet death—the fleshy, mushy, pulpy exsanguination or physical penetration that, despite the frequency of its occurrence, rarely gets captioned on SDH-enhanced DVDs and Blu-rays or streaming services such as Amazon Prime and Netflix. A good, gross example of this can be found on the 20th Century-Fox home-video release of *The Lazarus Effect* (2015). This supernatural horror film from Blumhouse Productions features a scene in which a medical researcher named Zoe spits up a milky substance after ingesting an unusually powerful serum. Her "groaning" is subtitled, just as the same sound emitted by the two graverobbers in *Friday the 13th: A New Beginning* is. But the disgusting splash of Zoe's vomit hitting the laboratory floor receives no captioned notice. Tellingly, seconds before that white liquid spills from her mouth, Zoe tells fellow scientist (and fiancé) Frank, who has used the "Lazarus" serum to bring her back to life following a fatal electrocution, that she can "see things" and "hear things" that would have been invisible or silent to her prior to that scientific miracle. One thing that deaf and hard-of-hearing viewers will *not* see, however, is any onscreen text that might indicate what this and other horror films' "wetness" sounds like to many hearing audiences. Indeed, SDH tends to "dry out" the genre while leaving intact—and literally spelling out—the brittle, cracking, shattering sounds that likewise characterize cinematic horror.

Such cauterizing of the text has hermeneutic implications, for the foreclosing of fluidic captioning can hinder one's comprehension of certain narrative events and character actions, if only temporarily. Take, for example, a brief scene that occurs midway through director Teruo Ishii's yakuza-themed *Blind Woman's Curse* (*Kaidan nobori ryū*, 1970). A female operative working for a rival gang has been spotted hiding opium packets inside stalls at an open-air market. When she is taken into custody by a local do-gooder, who escorts her past the stalls on the way to see Dobashi (Toru Abe), the gang leader whose bidding she has been hired to do, the woman suddenly lurches forward with a yelp. Many audiences would have heard a "splurt" sound two seconds before she took that fall and could have intuited the reason for this unexpected movement prior to seeing a shot of a knife lodged in her bloody back. The knife was planted there by another of her boss's operatives, who speeds past her when she cries out in pain. Without the aid of that sound, deaf and hard-of-hearing viewers might be momentarily confused about her physical state. Thus, a gap opens up between groups of spectators whose cognitive piecing-together of a narrative puzzle or ability to perceive moment-to-moment behavioral shifts in characters is at least partially contingent upon access to an audio track that, on Amazon Prime, has been doubly (but redundantly) subtitled: once for non-Japanese speakers (translating the characters' dialogue into English) and again for deaf and hard-of-hearing viewers (doing exactly the same thing but leaving out the many sound effects and musical elements that assist in hermeneutical sense-making). Although that gap is not permanent—it closes almost as soon as it opens (thanks to the knife-in-the-back reveal)—it is indicative of the general disregard with which media companies and their contracted captioners look upon those who cannot hear cinematic texts in quite the same way that other audiences do.

Such discrepancies accumulate over the course of this supernatural narrative, which concerns female protagonist Akemi (Meiko Kaji)'s need to keep her eyes and ears open as ever more threats to her life and livelihood present themselves, all of which can be traced back to her initial encounter with another swordswoman, whom she blinded in gang-related combat. That slow-motion battle features a cacophony of sounds, including shattering glass, swishing swords, shuffling feet, ringing gongs, musical trills, and the desperate yelps of men being slashed along their midsections, culminating with perhaps the most disturbing aural and visual moment in the entire film: a black cat lapping up the blood from the sliced eyes of the unfortunate bystander, who will thereafter seek revenge against the protagonist. Tellingly, this first extended scene of the film takes place in a heavy thunderstorm and—like the opening of *Friday the 13th: A New Beginning*—lacks the captioned language of "wetness" that might give deaf and hard-of-hearing viewers a more accurate representation of the horror genre's affective appeals. The spectatorial hindrances that occasionally manifest, even in subtitled films providing more richly evocative descriptions of onscreen and offscreen sounds, are compounded by the fact that *Blind Woman's Curse* is, as its title suggests, about the very disability-related ordeals that assistive technologies are designed to address. In the next chapter, I turn toward disability as a social and cultural construct and to "blindness" more specifically as a frequently mobilized metaphor in early motion picture history—a period during the 1910s and 1920s when the first efforts to audibly describe moving images were part of cinema's intersensorial appeals.

# 7

# "HEARTS THAT SEE"

## Blind Spectatorship, the Horrors of War, and the Historical Roots of Audio Description

One little girl in California writes me that she is blind and has never seen me on the screen, but that her sister has told her all about my pictures until she feels that she can really see me. She *does* see me—thru the eyes of the heart—and I only hope I have pleased the rest as well as I have that little, blind girl.[1]

—Actor Crane Wilbur, famous for his performance in the 1914 serial *The Perils of Pauline*, recounting a personal anecdote in the pages of *Motion Picture Magazine* (October 1915)

On May 22, 1915, Kenneth C. Crain, a Cincinnati-based correspondent for *The Moving Picture World*, reported a curious event; or, rather a very normal, natural occurrence in the all-too-short lives of people that was made strange by virtue of the very unusual, "unnatural" mode of spectatorship that had preceded it. Topped with the title "BLIND 'SPECTATOR' DIES," Crain's article noted that "a figure which had become familiar in several suburban moving picture houses" near his hometown—a person by the name of Nick McCarthy—had passed away recently.[2] Although news of other people's deaths had been reported in the pages of this trade journal for years (ever since its launch in 1907), typically those individuals would have been well known among the nascent bicoastal community of film producers and technical staff, if not the wider moviegoing public across the country's heartland. In this case, however, an otherwise nameless audience member from the suburbs of Cincinnati rather than an actor, camera operator, distributor, or executive from either New York City or the industry's new base of operations, Los Angeles, was the subject of this short piece. As explained by Crain, before passing away Mr. McCarthy was always admitted into film screenings free of charge by proprietors of local theaters, who had taken pity on the man. And why had those bottom-line-minded exhibitors so generously made an exception to their standard business practices? Because, in the words of Crain, the recently deceased moviegoer had been "stone blind." The reporter adds: "In spite of this," Mr. McCarthy frequently "seemed to enjoy attending the exhibitions" and would sit "quietly for hours . . . listening to the music and the comments of those" who sat near him.[3] Revealingly, Crain concludes his piece by musing, "When blind people can enjoy pictures, it seems that the one class to whom they were supposed to be barred is thus brought within their influence, the totally deaf having always been on an equality with the unafflicted in the enjoyment of film drama."[4]

As historical events in May 1915 go, the passing of an individual moviegoer—even a local legend known to many in the city of Cincinnati—is hardly newsworthy compared to the seismic occurrence that took place a couple of weeks before his death. On May 7, a German U-boat torpedoed and sank the RMS *Lusitania*, a British ocean liner that had been making its return voyage from New York to Liverpool. Aboard the cruise ship were nearly two thousand people, including civilian passengers from the United States. The vast majority of those on board died. To say that American sentiment toward Germany soured would be an understatement. Several commentators, speaking for a saddened and stunned citizenry, expressed outrage in the pages of the nation's dailies. Some of them even called for a swift retaliation, a move that President Woodrow Wilson and a large cross-section of the American public (who had generally supported his administration's neutrality policy throughout the previous year, as war raged in Europe) were now cautiously considering or openly discussing as an option. Notably, one such writer penned an editorial for *The New York Times* that equated ignorance—that of the German government with regard to US public opinion of that attack—with blindness.[5] Titled "The Blindness of Not Seeing," that article begins by noting that transatlantic cable communications between the two soon-to-be-warring nations had been hampered by adverse meteorological conditions as well as by British censors who likely edited the wireless messages, thus contributing to the Germans' dangerously "distorted" perception of American grievance on the matter of the *Lusitania*'s sinking. More pertinent to the present chapter, that newspaper article reflects the rhetorical tendencies of other published pieces from that period, insofar as a physical condition associated with a certain type of "lack"—that of light perception—was used as a metaphor for the "darkness of mind" that gave rise to delusional beliefs like those of government officials who seemed incapable of seeing "anything they wished not to see." The German mind, scowled the writer, was so "hermetically sealed against light," so deluded by its presumed superiority over "the rest of mankind," that it was *blind* not only to American feelings but also to the strength of global opinion on the threats posed to the world's "great democracies" by a sudden, unchecked rise in militarism.[6]

Just as torpedo-equipped submarines at that time, prior to the use of sonic navigation and ranging (or sonar), were said to operate "blindly," so too have other ableist or, rather, *disabling* terms been applied to actions that are made to appear deficient or defective in relation to how things ought to work. People, too, have been objectified through such language, which further infantilizes them by making it seem as if something like "blind rage" or "blind confusion" were beyond their bodily control or intellectual capacity. Relatedly, persons with disabilities have long been turned into objects of paternalistic pity by societies that perceive a physical condition like visual acuity loss as something abnormal (when, in fact, it is quite common, especially among adults over the age of fifty). This is as true today as it was more than a century ago. What is fascinating about the historical context in which the two events from May 1915 were reported is that blindness as both a lived reality for millions of Americans and an all-purpose metaphor for describing a host of social ills or personal failings was prominently featured in that era's cinematic offerings. Indeed, if the presence of a vision-impaired audience member like Nick McCarthy seemed novel or newsworthy to other moviegoers at that time, those same patrons had nevertheless been encouraged to look sympathetically upon an endless parade of blind characters on the silver screen, in motion pictures that habitually exploited the melodramatic, comical, and sometimes *horrific* predicaments that those characters might get into as a result of their visual impairment.

A sample of the many fictional shorts and multireelers from that period centering on characters with low-to-no vision (nearly always played by sighted actors) includes: *A Blind Deception* (1911), *The Blind Princess and the Poet* (1911), *The Better Part* (1912), *Blind* (1912), *The Blind Cattle King* (1912), *The Blind Man's Sacrifice* (*Angoscia segreta*, 1912), *The Blind Musician* (1912), *The Glory of Light* (1912), *Man's Best Friend* (1912), *The Melody of Love* (1912), *The Penitent* (1912), *The Serpent* (1912), *So Speaks the Heart* (1912), *Tricked into Happiness* (1912), *The American Niece* (*La nièce d'Amérique*, 1913), *The Blind Basket Weaver* (1913), *The Blind Composer's Dilemma* (1913), *The Blind Shall See* (1913), *Brother Love* (1913), *Deedee's Blind Master* (1913), *The Doctor's Blind Child* (1913), *The Gallop of Death* (1913), *The Guiding Light* (1913), *The Highgraders* (1913), *The Lost Note* (1913), *Love Is Blind* (1913), *The Risen Soul of Jim Grant* (1913), *Seeing Is Believing* (1913), *A Wife's Battle* (1913), *With the Eyes of the Blind* (1913; fig. 7.1), *The Wrong Bottle* (1913), *Blind Fate* (1914), *The Blind Fiddler* (1914), *Called Back* (1914), *A Good Little Devil* (1914), *Her Escape* (1914), *When the Blind See* (1914), *Greater Than Art* (1915), *Her Triumph* (1915), *The Lady of the Lighthouse* (1915), and *The Tides of Retribution* (1915). As "silent" films, albeit ones that usually would have been accompanied by small-scale musical performances, several of the productions cited above placed visual emphasis on the differences between those who can see and those who cannot, often by dwelling on eye coverings (e.g., wraps, bandages) and by literally spelling out those differences as printed intertitles, including those which suggest that a condition like blindness might actually be a positive attribute or superhuman ability under certain conditions. For instance, the title character in Vitagraph's *The Blind Miner* (1912), a sightless man by the name of Old Tom who has ostensibly "passed the age of usefulness," stands at the entrance of a mine shaft and implores the foreman to let him descend in search of those who have been trapped underground by an explosion, insisting that "the blind can hear what the eye cannot see" (words that appear as an intertitle on the screen). Allowed to enter the mine shaft, Old Tom makes his way into that dark labyrinth in search of the suffocating miners, whom he eventually locates through his intuitive, preternatural grasp of his surroundings, which would have confused many of the sighted people waiting nervously outside the mine.[7]

Though not a horror film in any traditional sense, *The Blind Miner* was praised by critics at the time of its release for the way that it portrayed the

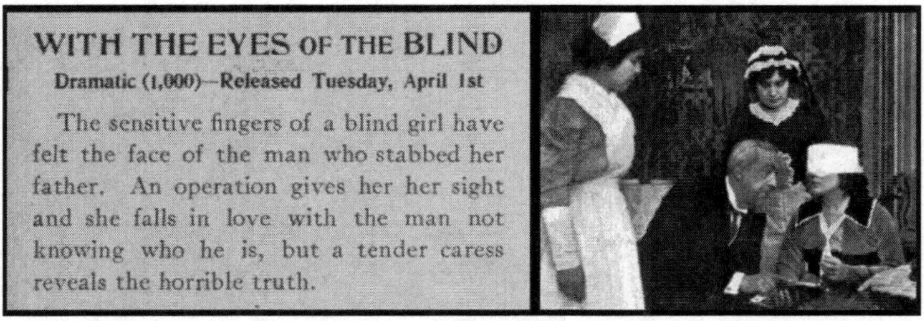


**Figure 7.1:** Touch and tactility are emphasized in this publicity synopsis for the Edison Company's 1913 short *With the Eyes of the Blind*, *Moving Picture World* 15, no. 13 (March 29, 1913).

"panic and horror of the crowd" gathered outside the pithead when the explosion occurs. Similarly, Universal's *Called Back*, a 1914 adaptation of Hugh Conway's 1883 novel of the same title, was looked upon favorably by reviewers who remarked that the film's blindness-themed mystery plot succeeded in visually communicating to audiences the "horror and despair" experienced by Gilbert Vaughan (Herbert Rawlinson), a wealthy man "suddenly stricken blind" during an early scene only to later find himself in the presence of two murderers. In a sense, he unwittingly becomes a *non*seeing "eyewitness" to the deadly actions of these Italian assassins, but he is also an *ear*witness to the gasp and groan of a woman who passes out due to the shock of beholding the sight of a man in her apartment building being killed. A sound rendered as text on the screen (which audiences of the silent era could only imagine hearing), her "piercing cry of horror" continues to haunt Gilbert well after his sight has been restored through an expensive medical procedure. That operation puts him on the "reenabled" path to finding the men responsible for that death but requires that he go back to his "enhanced" senses of hearing and touch before he can become the hero he was set up to be (by narrative design). Trumpeting the film's "startling mystery," driven by questions that would not be unusual in a more terrifying cinematic context ("What happened to Gilbert Vaughn on his way to the eye specialist for treatment? What kind of house did the sightless man enter? Why did the occupants spare Vaughn's life? What was Pauline doing there? What did the murderers force the blind man to drink? Where did he find himself the next morning? Why was Pauline's mind a blank?"), the language of the promotional ad copy is not unlike the rhetorical mode that would be adopted years later by publicists reaching out to horror enthusiasts who would presumably find such creepy content appealing (fig. 7.2). As indicated in some of the film's other publicity materials, that creepiness was partially achieved through some fairly advanced special effects for its time, including spectral superimpositions and other types of "trick photography."[8]

While a few films from that period, including those helmed by some of the world's greatest directors, only make titular reference to blindness or feature vision-impaired characters fleetingly—for example, Allan Dwan's *The Hopes of Blind Alley* (1914), Ernst Lubitsch's *Blind Man's Bluff* (*Blindekuh*, 1915), and Benjamin Christensen's *Blind Justice* (1916)—many noteworthy releases, such as D. W. Griffith's *Through Darkened Vales* (1911), delve more deeply into the phenomenon, dramatizing the feelings of social isolation, familial hardships, and financial strain experienced by individuals who are certainly deserving of the audience's sympathy (and for reasons other than their physical conditions). And yet, as a writer for *The Moving Picture World* notes in his contemporaneous review of Griffith's film, blindness—one of the most pronounced themes of US motion pictures in the years leading up to and immediately following the outbreak of war in Europe—frequently comes across as an "unnecessary complication of the plot."[9] As a convenient narrative device, or what that writer sarcastically refers to as a "curious coincidence," vision loss turns unfortunate characters like the "poor clerk" in *Through Darkened Vales* (who, having given up his life's savings "to pay for the [eye] operation on

**Figure 7.2:** Promotional ad for the blindness-themed film *Called Back*.

the girl who scorned him," is not able to afford his own sight-restoring surgery) into individuals defined by more than one type of "lack" who, in the end, are themselves in need of assistance or "treatment."

Martin F. Norden explains that several blindness-themed films from the first two decades of the twentieth century perpetuated the "dominant mainstream belief that people with physical disabilities are helpless and must depend on others."[10] Motion pictures such as Pathé's *A Blind Woman's Story* (*Pauvre aveugle*, 1908), which concerns the miserable life of an indigent woman who nearly dies from a tumble down a cliff after her guide dog is taken from her by an abusive son, were designed to make able-bodied audiences feel initially sad but ultimately as "comfortable" as she eventually is made to feel, once a compassionate painter and his wife step in to care for her. In other words, such releases were "feel-good" movies that "appealed to a cinema-going public that wanted to think something was being done to ease the plight of destitute people with physical disabilities, if only on a grassroots level."[11] "These films," Norden goes on to state, "almost always portrayed aid-givers as concerned relatives, acquaintances, or passers-by (people with whom able-bodied audience members could readily identify, of course), an approach that reflected an exceedingly old-fashioned way of thinking." If the narrative films cited above failed to advocate or even acknowledge "the emerging concept of governmental assistance to people with physical disabilities" as well as the "important work conducted on behalf" of those individuals by charitable organizations, they were nevertheless instrumental in shoring up a sense of the institutional obstacles laid before visually impaired individuals by a society that was at once drawn to and repelled by the sight of sightlessness. If, in the words of James Bordley (a US medical corps officer during World War I), people with blindness were "the Ishmaelites of [that] century . . . driven out of community life, out of industry, prevented from owning their own homes and maintaining them," they were also—for a short period, at least—paradoxically privileged as protagonists in stories designed to pull the heartstrings of anyone with a "heart to see."[12]

Furthermore, several nonfiction films and documentary shorts (or actualities) from that same time, including *Wolcott Coombs: The Phenomenal Deaf and Blind Boy* (1912) and *Hearts That See* (1916), depicted benevolent acts on the part of medical specialists and child psychologists (rather than family members and other loved ones) to bring visually impaired people more fully into a sighted society. The former film, produced by motion picture pioneer William Nicholas Selig and described by a critic at the journal *Motography* as a "scientific picture" that would be of interest primarily "to the thinking class of people," is noteworthy for the way that the titular recipient of that benevolence—a seventeen-year-old boy who could neither hear nor see—is revealed to have gained proficiency in hammock-weaving and typewriting under the instruction of Harry L. Virden. As the principal of the Oklahoma School for the Blind, Virden had taken an interest in Coombs three years earlier, seeing in him the potential for greatness. More than the deaf-blind boy's significant accomplishments, Virden's charitable act, performed "without hope of remuneration," became the centerpiece of a lengthy article published in April 1912 by *Motography*, the author of which dwells on the "broad humanitarianism" and heroic feats of the good professor to teach Coombs how to communicate (with Virden using his fingers to draw letters on the youth's palms) and how to use his vocal cords properly (by having Coombs place his own fingertips to the lips of his instructor).[13] Three months earlier, the same film journal had published an article about the "deaf-blind boy from Oklahoma," who was reported to have traveled to Chicago in the company of his professor to visit the set of another Selig-produced picture, *Cinderella* (1912). In the words of Selig's biographer, Andrew A. Erish, "*Cinderella* seems an especially appropriate subject to introduce Coombs to the world of motion pictures, for like the exploited title character, he had known little of the outside world."[14]

Significantly, Coombs's own impressions of the film's production, written by him, were published in the January 1912 issue of *Motography*.[15] His chronicle of that event begins by comparing the fairyland of the film's source material (home to fictional kings and queens) to that of the "big glass studio at the Selig plant," where he was introduced to the film's star, Mabel Taliaferro ("a little fairy princess in spite of the rough burlap dress she wore"). Besides alluding to other tactile elements of *Cinderella*'s costumes and set dressings, Coombs, who apparently "was at the studio nearly every day while this film was being taken," used a number of unexpectedly ocularcentric terms to indicate what he "saw," including properties "representing different periods [that] added to [his] knowledge and interest in history." He writes:

> Watching the production of *Cinderella* has also added to my interest in the study of the drama. Now when I attend the theater or read a play it is easy to picture the stage settings and watch the actions of the actors. The scenic artist, and my tutor Mr. Virden, first showed me various small cardboard models of the stage settings used in *Cinderella*, then we visited the bridge where the scenery is painted, and the carpenter shop where they were making different sets. Up in the studio, I studied bit by bit the sets as they were ready for the actors. Then, through my tutor's fingers, I witnessed practically every scene as it was acted in front of the camera. Day after day I understood a little better how much brains and hard work it takes to produce a film like *Cinderella*.[16]

Coombs concludes his written account by expressing great anticipation for the arrival of New Year's Day, the theatrical release date of the picture. In fact, the visually impaired youth believes he will "understand [the film] . . . better than most people" when he finally has the privilege of watching it with his eyes closed.

By 1916 (one year after Nick McCarthy's death and one year before Wolcott Coombs's registration card for the World War I draft listed him "as an insane inmate in Eastern Oklahoma Hospital Asylum"), the presence of visually impaired audiences—like the onscreen appearance of visually impaired characters—had become increasingly common in many of the nation's motion picture houses.[17] Nevertheless, the question remained, at least among some contributors to the major film journals at that time, of why blind spectators might be drawn to a medium that did not appear to have their interests in mind. In one of the most condescending pieces written by a film critic from that period, Ernest A. Dench (a writer for *Motion Picture Classic* magazine) surmised that it would be "much better" for "those folks who have the misfortune" of being "deprived of their sight" to patronize vaudeville houses or show up to legitimate stage plays than to attend theatrical screenings.[18] His reasoning—blind audiences "can follow intelligently the trend of the play or act by the conversations of the actors" but cannot appreciate the silent actions of movie performers "so much as you and I [can]"—seems to be founded on an impressionable and subjective understanding of how visually impaired people engage cultural productions. Still, Dench acknowledges that tremendous strides had been taken (as early as 1916, both in the United States and in Great Britain) to accommodate individuals with disabilities through spoken narration and musical accompaniment. Titled "Enjoying the Movies Tho Blind," Dench's article, which references a series of recent screenings for "pupils of institution for the blind" in Nottingham, England, in which "every little point that occurs in each photoplay . . . is ably brought home to them by the rendering of appropriate music and effects," cites one particular film—the appropriately titled *Hearts That See*, a documentary short about an ophthalmologist who "restores the sight of a blind girl"—that "brought tears to the audience."[19] According to him, the visually impaired students cried not because of the powerful effects of the film but rather because the pianist (who was himself visually impaired) "played a most haunting melody" as musical accompaniment. Most importantly, "Enjoying the Movies Tho Blind" concludes with the author gesturing ahead, to "some distant date [when] the sightless will be watching photoplays especially produced for them," something that the French physician Dr. F. Dussand is reported to have set about accomplishing by way of a mechanical "contrivance which enables the blind to *feel* the films."[20]

*Hearing* and *feeling* as substitutes for seeing were apparently on the minds of many motion picture producers and exhibitors during the 1910s, if contemporaneous accounts by film critics are to be trusted. In one published article after another, mounting evidence is provided that special theatrical presentations of everything from *The Fall of a Nation* (Thomas Dixon Jr.'s 1916 sequel to D. W. Griffith's 1915 blockbuster, *The Birth of a Nation*) to Griffith's own *Intolerance* (a 1916 epic that, on May 10, 1917, was screened for King George and Queen Mary of England to benefit Lady Paget's fund for blinded soldiers) catered to "sightless guests" and their benefactors. In the words of one reviewer of *The Fall of a Nation*, which was screened for the Institution for the Blind in the summer of 1916, "a few explanatory words and music properly synchronized and sufficiently atmospheric as was the score prepared by Victor Herbert" were all that were needed in order for "the blind man . . . [to] visualize by his ear."[21] Such historical background lends support to Katherine Anne Avery's argument that "vision-impaired people have always been participants in cinema spectatorship and media consumption," and that the contemporary practice of audio description (AD)—a subject that I will pursue further in chapter 8—has roots in the earliest motion picture exhibition in the United States, Great Britain, and beyond.[22]

Today's home-video and online viewing technologies present audiences with accessibility options that were not widely available in those formats during previous generations. Such advancements have given people with disabilities the opportunity to engage the audiovisual components of horror films in a more expansive, if not unproblematic, way than what earlier generations of genre enthusiasts were able to enjoy. One such tool, AD, has become increasingly recognized as a "constituent part" of cross-modal translation over the last two decades and is sometimes referred to as a technical solution to some of the problems inherent in communicating visual material to audiences who would otherwise remain "in the dark" were it not for such recent developments. However, as suggested above, the practice of verbally describing or translating onscreen signifiers to an audience made up of blind and/or partially sighted people predated the emergence of DVD, Blu-ray, and other electronic/digital devices distinguished by their multiple audio tracks and other supplemental materials. Indeed, one could go back to the early history of feature-film projection and theatrical presentation during the "silent" era (1910s–1920s) to find precedents for the kind of assisted or enhanced spectatorship that I will be discussing in the following pages.

A further consideration of that history is therefore necessary if we are to uncover some of the elements that distinguish AD from other assistive tools. In the process of digging up the largely hidden historical roots of today's AD services, including those that seem to have no connection to the genre with which this book is chiefly concerned, we might also learn why this tool plays an important role in unleashing new interpretive and intersensorial opportunities for anyone who believes they have seen—or heard—it all, including those of us who might be unaware just how old this mode of assisted viewing-by-listening really is. Let us turn, then, to a case study predating by several decades the ones that will be taken up in the chapter that follows, and which, at first blush, is as thematically remote from them as it is temporally distant from the present day. I hope to reveal that the very notion of horror as a repository of images and ideas "beyond description" (to borrow the words John Carpenter used when enumerating the challenges involved in visually translating the most terrifying elements of H. P. Lovecraft's written work into something resembling cinema) should remind us of the need to continually test the limits of what is theoretically possible or even "permissible" within the discipline of film studies and to seek out precise yet expansive definitions of what counts as "horror" as the field becomes more inclusive or accommodating of neurodiverse and differently abled perspectives.[23] The fact that the first audio-described motion picture in the United States, *The Battle Cry of Peace* (1915), was not officially categorized as horror, but is nevertheless one of the most fear-inducing examples of wartime propaganda ever produced, underscores the need to expand those categorical markers and to remove the proverbial "blinders" that have prevented historians from acknowledging the genre's tentacle-like peripheral reach: its preclassical origins within adjacent categories of cultural production that were anything but "primitive" (and which, in many cases, anticipate many of today's most socially and politically relevant horror films). Compounding its relevance to the matter at hand, no prints of that silent-era war film exist today—a fate that also limits our access to many of the blindness-themed shorts alluded to earlier (which have likewise been "lost to history"). Importantly, the material absence of *The Battle Cry of Peace* makes *description itself* the primary medium through which contemporary audiences—blind or otherwise—are able to gain access to it.

## Lecturing the Masses: Early Audio Description and the Unspoken Horrors of War

> Mother, I heard a most wonderful lecture this afternoon. It was both truthful and terrible.
>
> —John Harrison, the protagonist of *The Battle Cry of Peace* (1915), in a passage from the film's novelization of the same title (written by its producer, J. Stuart Blackton)

As early as December 1915, when representatives from the Vitagraph Company hosted a special screening of Wilfrid North and J. Stuart Blackton's patriotic epic *The Battle Cry of Peace* for several hundred charges of the Massachusetts Commission for the Blind and the Perkins Institute in Boston, industry insiders and exhibitors seemed at least mildly sympathetic to the needs of those who were, in the language of the day, "stricken," "crippled," or "beset" by blindness. Such language indicates that blindness was frequently spoken of as an affliction deserving of pity if not any major overhaul of existing social institutions outside movie theaters or beyond the occasional "special screening."[24] Significantly, that event, held at Boston's Majestic Theatre during a holiday season associated with charitable gift-giving, was referred to by a contributor to *The New York Clipper* as "one of the most remarkable instances of progress" in the nascent history of the medium that he and the other few sighted spectators in attendance had ever witnessed.[25] Interviewing one such onlooker, the newspaper critic conveys the combined compassion and condescension that characterized much of the popular discourse surrounding disability at that time, when "one thousand unfortunates" could collectively experience the thrill of this new, democratizing art form just as any able-bodied person could do. "I never saw a more pathetic sight in my life," the interviewee is quoted as saying, before painting a descriptive picture of an event that, fittingly, was among the first instances to harness *actual spoken description* for the benefit of blind audience members: "These poor people felt their way down the aisles and were shown to their seats, settling themselves and turning their sightless eyes toward the screen they would never see. Their interest was great, and if their eyes were useless all their other senses were on the alert."[26]

Those other senses include, of course, that of touch, which was put to use while holding the raised-letter "point system" programs that had been printed at the Perkins Institute and that—distributed to the gathered guests inside the auditorium—"could be read with the finger tips."[27] Katherine Avery notes that the inclusion of printed materials dotted with New York Point or Braille, which had been "a common component of earlier AD theatre performance" (on the nation's vaudeville circuit and legitimate stages prior to the advent of cinema), "not only gestures to an existing tradition of efforts to make public entertainment accessible, but also highlights the work of one of the organizations key in bringing about such events," specifically the oldest school for the blind in the United States: the Perkins Institute.[28] "Issued to this audience in a format that quite literally speaks to them on their own terms," the programs and invitations, Avery goes on to state, "highlight the multidimensionality—the need for multiple points of entry and multiple forms of legibility—required of true accessibility."[29]

According to the account published in *The New York Clipper* on Christmas Day (and substantiated by an earlier report in *The Boston Daily Globe*), a lecturer by the name of Geoffrey O. Whalen was on hand that evening to extemporaneously narrate the action of the eight-reeler "exactly as the screen portrayed it."[30] The onlooker's use of the word "exactly" reminds us of the widely perceived *incommensurability* between two modes of communication—one verbal, the other visual—that screen narrators or oral interpreters outside the United States (including *benshi* in Japan and *pyeonsa* in Korea, where "cinema was never truly silent" and local audiences sometimes needed assistance understanding imported American and European releases) had set about trying to blend throughout that same period.[31] Besides reading aloud the intertitles and rapidly narrating the flickering images, the lecturer who translated *The Battle Cry of Peace* to his blind listeners "went so far as to describe the theatre and himself," creating a full picture for their "mental vision." Even the orchestral music that accompanied the film's projection was (to use the critic's own adjective) "descriptive."[32] In other words, it was a means for the "sightless spectators" to form a combined cognitive-corporeal impression of the proceedings, starting with the diegetic universe of the movie and encompassing the extradiegetic elements of the live theatrical presentation itself.

Ultimately, that night's exercise in cinematic accommodation gave the blind members of the audience "so much evident pleasure and instruction that it was well worthwhile to be present and watch their countenance during the showing."[33] This comment suggests how, in the eyes of sighted patrons, the spectacle of blindness could sometimes overshadow the drama playing out on the screen; as if the "pathos" visible on spectators' "upturned faces" made such a lasting impression on sighted viewers that the movie itself was almost an afterthought (merely window dressing for the night's main attraction, which was the group of invited guests from the Massachusetts Commission for the Blind). This suggests another correlative to what was taking place halfway around the world, in East Asian contexts in which the oral interpreters of motion pictures—usually standing in a spotlight next to the screen, separate from the crowd of seated (and sighted) moviegoers—would sometimes steal focus away from the very medium they were hired to support.

Just as a Japanese film from the 1910s or 1920s might be seen as a supplemental sideshow or backdrop to a skilled benshi, who not only made that movie legible in his or her role as a "photo-interpreter" but also added artistic flair to its presentation through verbal flourishes and invented dialogue (and was often the very reason why audiences attended such screenings in the first place), so too does North and Blackton's codirected movie recede to the background in this anonymous critic's account of its AD-assisted screening in Boston.[34] Nevertheless, as a propaganda picture that advocated the use of US military power and therefore served the needs of the federal government's preparedness campaign (in the lead-up to the country's entry into World War I), *The Battle Cry of Peace* is worth dwelling upon, if only to reflect on how the "battle for meaning" that came to define its international reception (in places where it was exported, such as Switzerland and the Netherlands) can be extended into the overlapping arenas of disability studies, horror studies, and reception studies.[35]

Now considered lost, the 1915 film is not as well remembered today as other motion pictures with which it was favorably compared by many reviewers, including *Quo Vadis?* (1913), *Cabiria* (1914), and *The Birth of a Nation* (1915). This itself is noteworthy, given how monumental an undertaking *The Battle Cry of Peace* apparently was, and how passionately critics had predicted that it would "out-Griffith anything that has yet been done on the screen" in the lead-up to its general release (after it had been screened for US government officials and officers of the Army, Navy, and Marine Corps as well as Washington newspaper correspondents who gathered at the National Press Club in August of that year).[36] Contributing to its notoriety, an unprecedented amount of technical and material resources was laid at the feet of Commodore Blackton, a filmmaker who had pioneered stop-motion animation a decade earlier and dabbled in cinematic "horror" before it was named as such (making *The Haunted Hotel* in 1907). Blackton's connections to Washington insiders and the nation's top military brass made it possible for him to mount a production of truly epic proportions (far bigger than any of his previous shorts). Calling on the support of newly installed Secretary of State Robert Lansing, Secretary of War Lindley Miller Garrison, Assistant Secretary of the Navy Franklin D. Roosevelt, and other government officials who not only vocally backed the film throughout the autumn of 1915 but also appeared in it, Blackton was able to mobilize "16,000 National guardsmen, 800 G.A.R. (Grand Army of the Republic) members, 5,000 horses, 17 aeroplanes, seaplanes, dreadnaughts, torpedo boats and armored motor cars" in an attempt to realistically portray, in his own words, "what would happen to New York City if an invading force should be landed, as well as how the interior of the country would be affected by such an invasion."[37] No expense was spared in rendering the fictional bombardment of the Big Apple, with images of Wall Street in flames and architectural landmarks in ruins contributing to an effect that was as horrifically disturbing as it was thrilling to witness.

In one interview after another leading up to the film's nationwide release, Blackton emphasized the need to shock audiences out of their complacency, to force them to confront the "horrors" (his word) of that hypothetical scenario so that they might be convinced of the urgency with which preparation for real-world armed conflict should be undertaken.[38] Nevertheless, as someone well versed in the narrative pleasures of commercial filmmaking, he understood the need to entertain audiences through sheer visual spectacle—the very thing that, even at that early stage in the medium's history, distinguished cinema as a popular, democratizing form of mass culture. As such, Blackton worked to ensure that the theatrical experience would be as memorable and inspiring as the story he had written.

On the exhibition end, he and Vitagraph Studios cofounder Albert E. Smith worked with local organizations around the country to have brass bands at the ready and cannons, machine guns, and other war munitions put on carefully guarded display in theater lobbies. Vitagraph executives also hired the theatrical impresario Samuel Lionel Rothafel to incorporate twenty-five-piece orchestras and other large-scale musical accompaniment into screenings.[39] Rothafel was even tasked with creating several unusual stage effects for the film's theatrical presentation, including those that anticipate the flamboyant showmanship of producer William Castle, who, decades later, would inject a circus-like atmosphere into screenings of *The Tingler* (1959), *13 Ghosts* (1960), *Homicidal* (1961), and other horror films promoted through ballyhoo-style publicity stunts and big-screen gimmickry. As detailed in a September 25, 1915, article in *The Moving Picture World*, the man popularly known as "Roxy" (who would open up his own eponymous theater near

Times Square twelve years later) arranged to have large groups of men and women located behind the screen so that their loud roars could be timed to coincide with scenes of a mob fleeing the terror-stricken city. A woman was hired to scream at one point in the film's presentation, an effect that audibly "intensified the horror of a situation already close to the straining point."[40] The bloody action scenes that occur throughout the first half of *The Battle Cry of Peace* were made even more visceral through the deep, punctuating drones of an organ, which is reported to have sparked spontaneous applause among the audience, who (by this and other accounts) had never seen or heard anything quite so exciting if also harrowing in its visual and, yes, *aural* depiction of American civilians being bayonetted, blown up, and gunned down in cold blood by a foreign army on their own soil.

As discussed in Klaas de Zwaana and Adrian Gerber's essay about its international reception, the film—remarkable for the graphic brutality of its onscreen violence—was marketed to the war-weary Dutch public as a "spectacular attraction," an entertaining story of heroism rather than a "topical" release carrying an overtly political message.[41] In advance of its showing in Switzerland one year earlier, the pro-armament politics and anti-German sentiments of *The Battle Cry of Peace* were more nakedly apparent, though Blackton—aware of the diplomatic fallout that might result from the film's international release—insisted that "every possible means to prevent arousing enmity against any other country has been used."[42] Nevertheless, Germans living abroad in Zürich, Geneva, Lucerne, Bern, and other cities saw through that promotional charade and were "horrified" in a very different way. Not only were they *not* fooled by the generic-looking uniforms worn by the invading soldiers, but they also recoiled at the thought that atrocities committed by their own nation's military (which many were hesitant to even acknowledge) should be exploited or blown out of proportion by American filmmakers for narrative purposes. Undergirding this localized reading of the film is what the authors call a *mode de lecture*, a combined diegetic and nondiegetic framework that made it possible for other Swiss audiences—including French-speaking citizens—to see it through two lenses simultaneously. That is, they were able to acknowledge but also *look past* its propagandistic content and derive pleasure from its exciting if unusually gory scenes of bloodletting.[43] That French expression is doubly indicative of how a motion picture described by one clearly offended American reviewer as an oddly plotless yet dramatically overcooked "preparedness picture" could be conceived of as a "lecture" on the strangely peace-loving merits of going to war.[44]

Indeed, *mode de lecture* also reflects the manner in which the film's protagonist John Harrison (Charles Richman) sets about warning others about the dangers of pacificism after attending an impassioned lecture on the subject by armament manufacturer Hudson Maxim (who plays himself in an early scene). As the author of the 1912 book *Defenseless America*, upon which this film is based, Maxim lends his presence not only to the film (as a silver-haired orator inspiring a change of heart and mind in the main character) but also to the novelization of *The Battle Cry of Peace* that Blackton wrote after completing his photoplay. As described in that novelization, which was published piecemeal in the pages of *Motion Picture Magazine*, the "succession of inconceivable statements" spoken by Maxim from the main platform at Carnegie Hall (e.g., "Aeroplanes . . . are the eyes of the Army and Navy—without them an Army and Navy are blind") came like "a stream of shrapnel . . . shattering with their explosive force all John's preconceived ideas about America's strength and impregnability."[45] But de Zwaana and Gerber's chosen term also suggests how a motion picture designed to prepare audiences for war—specifically, one whose aftermath, Avery reminds us, "would bring about a new awareness of the disabled, particularly the disabled soldier"—could itself be likened to a mode of discourse in which verbal *instructions* or recommendations on proper ideological comportment are relayed to an audience as if they were issuing from a speaker at a lectern.[46] This seems to be the main reason why the aforementioned reviewer for the New York–based magazine *The Independent*, who wrote one of the few naysaying articles of dissent published at the time of the film's release, detested *The Battle Cry of Peace*, which he derided as "nothing but a Security League lecture set to the movies with an accompaniment of horrendous stage thunder, bugle calls and waving of 'Old Glory.'"[47]

Judging from the copious commentary attending this film's general release (which extended into the early spring of 1916, when at-capacity theaters were still turning people away from full houses and charging up to two dollars per ticket in certain markets), that reviewer for *The Independent* represented a minority opinion on the matter. A great many more genuflective reviews filled the pages of the nation's film periodicals, singing the praises of its creators' lofty ambitions and applauding the performances of Richman and his costars Norma Talmadge, Charles Kent, and L. Rogers Lytton. A representative extolment was penned by W. R. Andrews of the *Motion Picture News*: "It is like a huge painting filled with minute incidents and character groupings—all swept along, however, in the epic surge of the ensemble, gripping the imagination with unforgettable power."[48] Importantly, Andrews—like many other commentators at the time—speaks positively about the *negative* emotional effects of watching *The Battle Cry of Peace*, a film that presents a "swift panorama" of "all the horrors of war descending upon the resistless heads of an unprepared people," and was sure to generate as many sobs and screams as it would cheers from its audience. The peak moment of "Dantesque horror," according to the critic, occurs when a mother shoots her two young daughters to "prevent them from becoming victims of the invaders"—a plot point that anticipates countless scenes of mercy killing in contemporary war films as well as horror films set far away from the fields of battle (e.g., *The Descent* [2005], *Land of the Dead* [2005], *The Ruins* [2008], *Midsommar* [2019], *Wrong Turn* [2021]).

In fact, one emotion more than any other—*horror*—was consistently referenced not only in the critical commentary but also in the film's promotional materials (fig. 7.3). Ringing an alarmist bell, one newspaper ad proclaimed that *The Battle Cry of Peace* "actually shows in all its horror what would really happen if an invading army landed on our shores," while Lynde Denig, writing for *The Moving Picture World*, emphasized that the "appalling horror of it all stupefies the imagination."[49] A journalist for the same magazine, W. Stephen Bush, shared the producers' belief that Americans, at present, "are utterly without means of defense" and would be unable to protect their homes "against the horrors of a foreign invasion" lest they heed the film's warning and ramp up defensive measures in advance of an imminent stateside attack.[50] Even the nation's top government officials, including members of the Supreme Court and President Woodrow Wilson's cabinet along with Navy and Army officers who attended a private screening at Washington's Memorial Continental Hall (on December 18, 1915), were reported to have burst out not only in rapturous applause but also "audible exclamations of horror."[51] This is something that one can imagine happening during a screening of *Psycho*

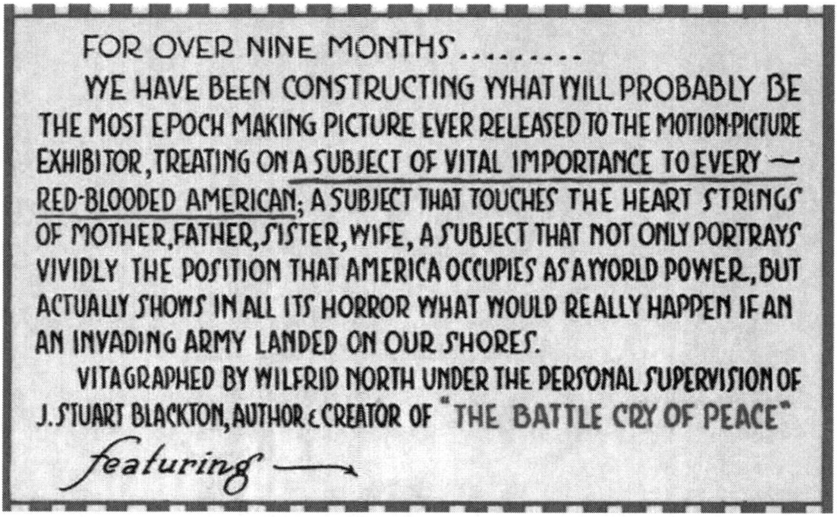


**Figure 7.3:** Real-world "horror" is evoked in this newspaper ad for *The Battle Cry of Peace*.

(1960) or some other example of the horror genre rather than a wartime propaganda picture.

One can only speculate as to whether any of that shudder-inducing content had been described in detail to the vision-impaired audiences in attendance at Boston's Majestic Theatre two weeks earlier; or, for that matter, whether Whalen had made the subtly Germanic outfits of the invading army audibly apparent to his listeners. Regardless, the aforementioned articles suggest that his orchestrally accompanied "lecture"—similar to the one that Hudson Maxim performs in an early scene of the film—left a deep impression and likely won over at least a few of the gathered guests to the "preparedness" side of the armament argument. With no existing footage of *The Battle Cry of Peace* to consult (apart from a few production photos), historians are forced to rely on the copious written descriptions of that critical and commercial hit to sketch their own mental pictures of what it might have *looked* like, and to conjecture why it might have been so "horrifying" in its visual treatment of a subject that weighed heavily on the hearts and minds of millions of people. One thing is certain, though: World War I (July 28, 1914–November 11, 1918), colloquially known as the Great War, was unprecedented in its global scale and the degree to which machines played a role in cataclysmic destruction and human carnage. And, judging from written descriptions, North and Blackton's film was unparalleled in its day as a nightmarish rendering of the bodily horrors of that war.

With a total number of civilian and military casualties approaching 40 million, the "war to end all war" remains one of the deadliest conflicts in history, and the lingering effects that it had on military personnel and noncombatants alike would assume sundry forms in its aftermath. Among the roughly 4.6 million soldiers, sailors, and airmen who returned home to the United States alone, 224,000 of them were left with permanent physical or mental disabilities.[52] As a response, on June 2, 1920, President Wilson signed into law the first civilian rehabilitation act, the Smith-Fess Act, so that World War I veterans might transition more easily to the life they had left behind two or three years earlier, though, from a funding standpoint, rehabilitation services were limited to vocational support, prostheses, and job placement assistance (thus excluding socio-psychological services).[53] Over 4,000 US veterans of World War I were amputees, and nearly 100,000 more suffered psychological injuries, or what in the parlance of the day was colloquially known as "shell shock." Of course, those numbers were far larger in European countries, where the sometimes-undiagnosed neurotic symptoms of the trauma induced by trench warfare or prolonged exposure to mass death, on top of the many missing or artificial limbs and noticeable limps that marked former servicemen as disabled "others" in the eyes of their countrymen, laid the existential groundwork for what would become the world's first significant wave of horror films. Those productions initially came from Germany, where *The Cabinet of Dr. Caligari* (*Das Cabinet des Dr. Caligari*, 1920), *The Golem* (*Der Golem*, 1920), and *Nosferatu* (*Nosferatu—Eine Symphonie des Grauens*, 1922) were made, before American studios threw their hat into the ring, making *The Phantom of the Opera* (1925), *Dracula* (1931), *Frankenstein* (1931), and a host of other films that are today recognized as "classics." Significantly, several noteworthy contributions to golden age horror films sprang from the imaginations of men who had witnessed fighting on the Western Front, including James Whale, director of *Frankenstein* and its 1935 sequel *The Bride of Frankenstein*, and R.C. Sherriff, screenwriter of *The Invisible Man* (1933), also directed by Whale.[54]

In *Wasteland: The Great War and the Origins of Modern Horror*, W. Scott Poole makes a convincing case for the consanguinity between the war film and the horror film throughout the third decade of the twentieth century, prior to the formal recognition of horror as a distinct type of cinematic output within the national industries that would serve as its official "birthplace" during the 1920s and 1930s.[55] Although cultural historians have traced the origins of the genre to the tradition of gothic literature epitomized by Horace Walpole's *The Castle of Otranto* (1764) and Mary Shelley's *Frankenstein* (1818), and then to the fantastical "trick films" made by Georges Méliès, George Albert Smith, J. Stuart Blackton, and other big-screen magicians who experimented with the medium's formal properties around the turn of the twentieth century—pioneering supernatural special effects in such humorously spooky shorts as *Le manoir du diable* (1896) and *The X-Ray Fiend* (1897)—horror in fiction and film did not truly begin its "danse macabre," according to Poole, until the wake of the Great War.[56] Indeed, war films from that period, including silent newsreels shot by British agents working on behalf of their government, bear a remarkable affinity for the kinds of "body horror" that would emerge decades later, in the aftermath of yet another global conflict (the Vietnam War) that would leave tens of millions of people dead or disfigured. Sight unseen (based on description alone), it is easier for me to figuratively see a connection between a motion picture like *The Battle Cry of Peace* and gore-filled shockers like David Cronenberg's *Rabid* (1977), *The Brood* (1979), and *The Fly* (1986) than it is to draw a direct line from Blackton's *The Haunted Hotel* to the latest batch of CGI-enhanced ghost stories. Frequently dealing with the destruction and degeneration of the human body, today's most gripping examples of body horror owe something of their existence to the manner in which silent-era war films documented and dramatically imagined the corpse-littered battlefields of Europe (from the dunes of the West Flanders Belgian coast to the frontier of the Swiss-German border). At the very least, the massive uptick in the number of times the word "horror" (or some language-based variant thereof) appeared in accounts of World War I "written by English, German, Austrian, French, Russian, and American veterans" (and in the promotional materials accompanying the release of never-truly-"silent" war films) should alert us to the fact that the historical context of the 1910s was a necessary *pretext* for subsequent examples of the genre.[57]

## "Poets of Darkness" and the Protocols of Description

Description should aim to get to the heart of a work of art and to recreate an experience of that work by bringing it to life. It should not be content with telling someone the physical details of what they cannot see.

—Andrew Holland, "Audio Description in the Theatre and the Visual Arts: Images into Words"

In the years following *The Battle Cry of Peace*'s theatrical release, a few other US productions were screened for blind audiences through audibly described efforts to reach as wide and diverse a moviegoing demographic as possible. These include Metro Pictures' *Forget Me Not* (1922), a W. S. Van Dyke–directed melodrama that was presented to six hundred blind people at the New York Theatre Roof (with hostess Hope Hampton on hand to narrate each scene and read the intertitles), and Warner Bros.' *The Lighthouse by the Sea* (1924), a Malcolm St. Clair-directed adventure film starring "canine sensation" Rin Tin Tin, whose heroic exploits were described to more than one thousand blind guests of New York's Piccadilly Theatre (an event organized by the *Matilda Ziegler Magazine for the Blind*).[58] It should be noted that the latter film was one of several productions from the late silent period to feature a visually impaired character, building on the previous decade's copious representations. In *The Lighthouse by the Sea*, Caleb Gale (Charles Hill Mailes), the aging keeper of the Seville lighthouse, has begun to experience vision loss, which puts his livelihood at risk and attracts the attention of bootleggers who seek to exploit his condition (by extinguishing the light so that they might discharge their illegal cargo undetected). The old man's presence turns the German shepherd star of the film—one of Warners' top money-earners of the 1920s—into a creature resembling a service animal, one that aids and supports his "master" as surely as Mailes was asked to play a supporting role opposite Rin Tin Tin.

Additional instances of descriptive narration occurred in US theaters once synchronized sound technologies were adopted by the major studios and became an industrial norm at exhibition sites beginning in the late 1920s. For example, a screening of director Alan Crosland's *The Jazz Singer* (1927), starring Al Jolson—Warner Bros.' biggest box-office draw after Rin Tin Tin—as a young Jewish American man torn between his longing for a successful career as a musical entertainer on stage and his familial commitments at home, was presented to a group of vision-impaired patrons at the Tudor Theatre in New Orleans in September 1928 (nearly a full year after its New York City premiere). As reported in a *Times-Picayune* article, the venue's manager, Ray V. Powell, served as the evening's audio describer, speaking during several parts of this largely silent "sound" film (which features only a few instances of synchronized recorded music and lip-synchronous singing).[59] As Katherine Avery notes, in the absence of any details about the content or vocal delivery of Powell's live/nonrecorded performance, "scholars can only guess at how Jolson's conspicuous use of blackface might have been described to this Southern, presumably white audience of Blind and low-vision people."[60] But what is certain is that "the incorporation of sound into cinema," which *The Jazz Singer* is famous for inaugurating, "did not necessarily render the medium accessible to blind audiences."[61]

In fact, the introduction of synchronized sound might have been a hindrance to some audiences' comprehension, and most certainly made it more difficult for interlocutors to describe or narrate onscreen events, since lines of spoken dialogue and other auditory elements provided fewer opportunities to do so (relative to a silent film accompanied by musical pieces). Katie Ellis, one of the foremost authorities on disability and the media, singles out a special screening of the early "talkie" *Bulldog Drummond* (1929), a crime film produced by Samuel Goldwyn, directed by F. Richard Jones, and distributed by United Artists. That film played to "100 members of both the New York Association for the Blind and the New York League for the Hard of Hearing," though no accommodations were provided to deaf audiences during the interlocutor's description of the action.[62] Interestingly, the film begins with a long wordless opening passage, set inside a Senior Conservative Club whose humorless members have insisted upon a strict no-speaking policy (indicated by a sign that hangs on the door to the club's entrance and reads "Silence!") and become visibly upset by something as innocuous as the "plink" of a dropped spoon on the tiled floor.

In her book *Disability and Digital Television Cultures: Representation, Access, and Reception*, Ellis also notes the "paucity of literature regarding any form of formal audio description for a number of decades," which has hampered historians' access to the very topic of accessibility that a few studio representatives, conscientious filmmakers, and arts organizations in large metropolitan areas occasionally brought to the fore whenever they supported efforts by the American Foundation for the Blind to translate motion pictures like Walt Disney's *Snow White and the Seven Dwarfs* (1937) into "talking books" (on long-playing discs), and through audio-described events like the one hosted by the Brooklyn Academy of Music in December of 1943.[63] As reported in an article for *The Exhibitor*, that was when director Robert Florey's swashbuckling musical *The Desert Song* was verbally "shown" to a blind audience through a "seeing eye" commentator, Tom Slater, who had been hired by Warner Bros. publicists and whose words were accompanied not by musical orchestration but by a printed Braille description of the film.[64]

Ultimately, it would take several years—decades, in fact—before a robust institutional framework for AD began to solidify in the US national context, an initiative that was spearheaded in the early 1970s by academics such as Gregory Frazier. As a San Francisco State University graduate student, Frazier wrote a master's thesis concerning "television for the blind" and eventually founded the AudioVision Institute, a nonprofit organization that would provide AD services to local theaters and tourist attractions in the Bay Area for years to come.[65] He was among the first group of scholars to contend that the process of describing both the content and form of media for people with low or no vision was not merely a craft but an *art*. To Frazier's way of thinking, creating an AD track was indeed an inspired act of *creation*, one that required deep sensitivity and empathy on the describer's part in addition to a good speaking voice and a strong vocabulary (which was useful in poetically rendering the subtleties of performance and cinematography that many sighted audiences overlook).[66] Although revolutionary in some respects, his notions of the describer's role in soulfully evoking the world of the story recall earlier conceptions of Japan's silent-era benshi being "poets of darkness" who frequently let personal feelings or subjective interpretations color their play-by-play recounting of events and who were skilled in modulating the pitch, timbre, and volume of their voices for dramatic effect.[67]

Modern-day variations on that style of narrational drama can be heard in the descriptive tracks provided for *The Thing* (2011), *Umma* (2022), and several other horror films from the twenty-first century. The Netflix presentation of the former film showcases the vocal talents of Miles Neff (of the Media Access Group of WGBH), who reads—or, rather, *performs* with considerable gusto—such lines as, "The creature *bursts* through the ice *then* through the ceiling!," "Juliet's shirt falls away as an alien shape *bulges* beneath her *chest!*," and "Juliet's head tilts back as sprouting tentacles *rip* away at her *flesh* and uncover rows of fang-like teeth in her *torso!*" Indeed, as Neff says these lines, he raises the volume and pitch of his voice as steadily as do the isolated scientists in this prequel to the 1982 film of the same title. *Umma*'s AD track, also currently available as a listening option on Netflix, similarly features an excitable voicer of the film's mounting terrors. In this case, British actor Roland Bearne (a.k.a. Roland Stone) switches back and forth between dulcet-toned describer of the action and shrieking imitator of a dead and cremated Korean woman. Indeed, he seems to channel the latter's spirit whenever he is required to translate Umma's words into English, and he does so as dramatically (and uncannily) as does her daughter Amanda (Sandra Oh), whom she possesses and speaks through for much of the film's second half.

Author Joel Snyder echoes Frazier's belief in the artistry of AD, which he likens to haiku, a literary-poetic form that is equally "succinct, vivid, and imaginative" in its precise use of words to conjure a broad spectrum of visual images (including those that are "not fully realized by the rest of us . . . sighted folks who see but who may not observe").[68] Like his predecessor, Snyder put his own words into practice several years ago, becoming a highly sought out describer of theatrical events beginning in 1981, after having spent the previous decade recording "talking books" for the Library of Congress. He has since lent his voice and expertise to the American Council of the Blind's Audio Description Project, for which he was the founder over two decades ago and currently is a senior consultant. One of the Audio Description Project's ongoing goals since its launch in 2010 (or, rather, its continuation of the work started years earlier by Barry Levine, president of the now-defunct Audio Description International) is to "sponsor a broad range of activities designed to build awareness" of AD, not only among its principal users but also among the general public.[69] Snyder and other leaders in the field have also been instrumental in establishing certain guidelines, protocols, and quality standards to help newcomers to AD production achieve some degree of consistency across their own recordings and, on the reception end, to acclimate first-time listeners to audio texts that are as immersive, engaging, and carefully conceived as the films being described.

Not coincidentally, Frazier, Snyder, and other early proponents of good-practice guidelines were doing that foundational work around the same time that blindness rose to prominence as a plot device in several horror films and psychological thrillers, including *Wait Until Dark* (1967), *See No Evil* (1971), *Young Frankenstein* (1974), and *The Sentinel* (1977), as well as segments of the anthology films *Night Gallery* (1969) and *Tales from the Crypt* (1972). Those films occasionally thrust audiences into a discombobulating state of sensory deprivation. More problematically, they also feature lead and supporting performances by actors without any visual impairments "playing blind." Such representations are perhaps to be expected in horror, since it is a genre that is typically thought to revolve around a fear of the unknown. What better way to stoke that fear than to keep audiences and characters in the dark for as long as possible, or under conditions of intense duress that play on "humankind's strongest and [most] primal emotions"? Jeffrey Bullins argues that darkness and the unseen are "instinctually frightening, and some horror films have attempted to tap into this ancient fear through the inclusion of blind characters. At times, the audience experiences the story as they do, but in other instances the perspective of the audience is more objective, resulting in sympathy or concern more than identification."[70] While I share Bullin's commonsense approach to the genre's cognitive appeals and representational tendencies, it is harder for me to embrace his notion that "when we can see something, we can know or understand it." In earlier chapters, I gestured toward the genre's capacity for activating one's sense of seeing through organs other than eyes (e.g., the skin, the ears, the nose)—an intersensorial play that is expedited through the incorporation of AD. Nevertheless, the aforementioned films from the 1960s and 1970s are partly responsible for solidifying the taken-for-granted supposition that "understanding is seeing."[71] Importantly, the first term in that expression (which is generally defined as "perceiving the meaning of something") is often conflated with "believing" (which is generally defined as "accepting something as true"), a concept that sits more comfortably with horror's ocularcentric tendency to favor eye- and sight-based terrors.

Together, the scholarly and cultural activity taking place in North America during the 1960s, 1970s, and 1980s formed the backdrop to a range of important developments in the years that followed, including the creation of blind novelist James Stovall's Narrative Television Network (NTN) in 1989, WGBH-TV's launch of AD services via thirty-two participating PBS member stations the following year, and the Federal Communications Commission (FCC)'s subsequent announcement that fifty hours of audio-described content should be produced and broadcast by the networks each quarter. The US Supreme Court would soon overturn that policy before it was reinstated with slight revisions through the signing into law of the Twenty-First Century Communications and Video Accessibility Act (CVAA) of 2010.[72] In the years since that time, all of the major theater chains in the United States, including AMC, Cinemark, and Regal, have begun offering blind and low-vision customers access to assistive equipment (e.g., amplified headsets, earphones, wireless receivers) in addition to providing personal closed-captioning devices to deaf and low-hearing patrons. The switch from film projection to the digital cinema package (DCP) format, in which multiple soundtracks (including descriptive tracks) and subtitling options can be stored on a small hard drive along with a digital file of the movie itself, has only further optimized listening and viewing experiences over the past decade and a half. Ontological purists might blanch at the idea that digital *files* rather than celluloid *films* are now being screened at multiplexes that cater to *mainstream* rather than cinephile audiences. For the most part, such developments have been welcomed by members of the National Federation of the Blind and other disability activists who feel that additional resources and funding should be directed toward technological enhancements that might improve listener comprehension. They also believe that a large number of newly created jobs within the entertainment industry could be done *better*—and more sensitively—by people across a spectrum of newly understood, previously untapped *abilities* (including those strengthened by full or partial blindness).

The same year that President Barack Obama signed the CVAA into law, ensuring greater accessibility of telecommunications (including over-the-air programming and streaming video) to people with disabilities, Snyder's Audio Description Project (ADP) took flight. Since that time, the website for this member-driven advocacy organization has served as an invaluable archive for scholars. It brings together multiple lists and documents that have been instrumental to my own thinking about AD's growth in recent years, including a living directory of AD companies and consultants (many of whom are blind or visually impaired) and a continually updated compendium of commercially available films and television programs that have been supplemented with descriptive tracks as part of their streaming or home-video presentations (nearly ten thousand at the time of this writing). Among the clickable resources on the ADP's website are several "guidelines for description," including those that begin by emphasizing the need for self-effacement on the voicer's part ("You're not providing descriptions to show off your vocabulary or to highlight your beautiful voice") and the importance of communicating something specific about the individuals who appear onscreen by using their "most significant physical characteristics" (including hair color and skin color) as a starting point. The natural pauses of conversation and breaks in the soundtrack are where most of the voicer's words should be inserted, so as to avoid "stepping on" any dialogue or musical cues that can be just as important to listener comprehension. Jargon and slang are also to be avoided, as is the temptation to editorialize or censor any material that might upset some segments of the moviegoing public (including nudity, sexual acts, and violence). The "first rule of description," according to one set of guidelines, is "What You See Is What You Say." This means that clarity and concision rather than colorful imagery and elegant turns of phrase should come through in the spoken narration, which benefits the listener by providing access to only the most essential ("nondecorative") visual elements while leaving aside any subjective feelings or qualitative judgments—including those about a character's mental or emotional state—that might obscure that listener's audible "view" of the events.

The objectivity vs. subjectivity issue has been a point of contention among some experts in audio-visual translation (AVT), with a growing minority of authors and scholars in that field asserting the need to balance description with *interpretation*. While some theorists and practitioners with a long-standing commitment to accurately translating what is visually depicted in a film have strongly advocated for *neutrality* (with regard to the AD writer's and voicer's personal feelings, which they believe should go unspoken), Jan-Louis Kruger offers a slightly different take. Like other scholars in AVT, Kruger has dedicated much of his research to the theoretical yet practical problem of what happens "when the picture or the sound, the visual or the auditory, is unavailable to an audience." But, unlike many of his academic forebearers from decades past, he believes that "the absence of codes from one of these semiotic systems means that the original narrative no longer operates in the same way and has to be *re-narrativised* in order for the audience to get the benefit of a coherent narrative."[73] *Narrativity*, rather than neutrality, is thus stressed in his and others' assessments of how best to go about not only translating semiotic codes to blind or low-vision audiences but also *transporting* those audiences into a fictional world that is made tangibly "real." Rather than hew to absolute fidelity to the original text, and instead of cleaving to a "clinically objective" commitment to reporting narrative events as they occur (by simply substituting aural signifiers for visual signifiers), the audio narrator should strive for greater intradiegetic coherence—across diegetic and extradiegetic voicings—while giving the decidedly *non*-passive recipients of that assistance opportunities to become narrative agents themselves (taking up their own active positions or "imaginary vantage points" within the text).[74]

According to this line of reasoning, providers of AD services would thus serve their visually impaired audiences best by carefully considering not only *what* is being shown in a film at any given moment (in accordance with the paradigmatic code) but also *how* it is being shown moment to moment (in accordance with the syntagmatic code). That would seem to suggest that an emphasis on the formal properties and cinematographic style of a given film with regard to shot angles, shot distances, shot duration, and so forth is in order before someone is able to aurally envision what sighted spectators can see. But "seeing," Kruger suggests, is not really what blind or low-vision audiences seek when they sit down to experience a motion picture (with or without AD support). Instead, some degree of narrative *immersion* is sought out. Thankfully, immersion can be facilitated through subtle means of focalization and by allowing the writers of AD to interpret what *they* experienced when watching the film.[75] Rather than being a *mirror*-like reflection (in the visual sense) of the images that appear onscreen, AD can therefore be conceived of as a *mind*-like reflection (in the cognitive sense) of what the describer *thinks* about those images, having earlier *reflected* on their narrational relationship to one another as well as the mindset or intentions of characters that might be only partially communicated through their physical actions. As such, it is less important that close-up shots, long shots, over-the-shoulder-shots, and the like be described in exacting detail than to position the audience within the fictional world by means of verbal markers and literary techniques such as deixis, modal adverbs, possessive adjectives, and locative expressions (often tethered to the personal pronouns "we" and "us"). Of course, some attention to how static or dynamic a given shot is, how it is composed (as in *Umma*'s audio-described "Close-up on Amanda screaming"), and how long it lasts on screen before being replaced by another shot is expected if we are ever to arrive at a fully immersive experience for blind and low-vision audiences. But Kruger asks that AD providers also consider the additional question of *why* something is being shown at any given time. It is another potentially contentious point that could further divide the "objective" and "subjective" camps of AVT studies or at the very least swap out the aesthetic concerns touched on earlier with a series of even more divisive *ethical* concerns.[76]

Notably, Kruger's essay was published in 2010, around the same time that the ADP website launched. Another, more seismic event occurred that year, bringing a sea change to the entertainment industry that few commentators could have predicted only a decade earlier (but which, in hindsight, seems inevitable). Occurring at the intersection of motion picture distribution and home-video exhibition, it has had a ripple effect across media platforms that are increasingly tailoring their content around issues of accessibility, algorithmic personalization, and consumer choice. That year was when Blockbuster Video declared bankruptcy and the online subscription service Netflix—the company largely responsible for that video chain's demise—shifted its business model from that of a mail-based delivery service to that of an online streaming service. That decision on the part of the company's leadership, including cofounder and executive chairman Reed Hastings and chief content officer and co-CEO Ted Sarandos, set the stage for the gradual phasing out of mailable DVDs and Blu-rays in favor of instantly delivering digital "content" to a global audience that now surpasses 300 million subscribers. Today, most Netflix customers "tune in"—to use a now-outdated expression—on Android and Apple iOS devices (personal tablets and cellphones) by tapping the company's app, which currently makes drop-down menus for multiple languages and soundtrack options, including those for English,

French, Korean, Polish, Portuguese, and Spanish descriptions, available at the touch of a screen.[77] That alone has prompted Carl Augusto, President and CEO of the American Foundation for the Blind (a nonprofit organization formed in 1921 as a national clearing house to support the large number of veterans blinded in World War I) to give the streaming service a "standing ovation" in 2015.[78]

Despite Augusto's claim that "Americans with vision loss can more easily and fully enjoy their favorite Netflix shows alongside their sighted peers," as a globally recognized "content-provider" with an international reach approaching two hundred countries Netflix has been at the center of several accessibility debates in recent years. In fact, Hastings, Sarandos, and other Netflix executives have sometimes gone on the defensive whenever they are questioned about their ability to make good on the promise of inclusivity that has partially characterized the changes occurring within global entertainment industries since the turn of the twenty-first century. Just as Netflix has continued to tout its record on accessibility by highlighting (on the website's landing page devoted to the topic) how adjustable font sizes, assistive listening systems, closed-captioning, playback speed controls, screen readers, and voice-command options put power in the hands of audiences marked by a presumed "powerlessness" located in other parts of the body, so too has the company's spokespeople felt the need to emphasize the success of its inclusion strategy. Vernā Myers, the vice president of inclusion at Netflix, emphasizes that the streaming service has adopted what she calls an "inclusion lens," which—despite that ocularcentric expression's privileging of one sense (that of sight) over others—has spurred the company's leadership to ask, "Whose *voice* is missing?" and to therefore *listen* more attentively to those who might otherwise be excluded from decision-making processes (behind the scenes) and representational practices (on the screen).[79]

Adopting Myers's optical term, or, rather, *adapting* it to the matter at hand, in the next chapter I discuss the ways that AD services provide a "hearing lens" onto horror film, filtering image-based fears—for instance, "Lightning flashes and the shadows of several figures appear on the wall," spoken by an offscreen describer during *The Darkness*, and "Ally crouches over a dead body that appears to be moving," spoken by an offscreen describer during *The Silence*—through the ghostly vantage of someone who is simultaneously "inside" and "outside" the text (fig. 7.4). In one example

**Figure 7.4:** During this moment from the tellingly titled film *The Darkness*, the audio description service provides a partial auditory view of mysterious figures' shadows on the wall, leaving those figures' animal shapes in the proverbial dark.

of accessibility-enhanced horror after another, the unseen speaker draws attention to details that might otherwise pass by undetected by audiences who, in the absence of any verbally described audio, would use only their eyes to see. As such, AD nudges us into a new, more receptive relationship to the text in which improved *earsight* rather than eyesight might result from adopting the "inclusivity lens" referred to above. Nevertheless, mistakes occasionally make their way into audio descriptions. As such, we should ask ourselves if cinematic horror—a genre already predisposed to textual aberrations (not to mention narratives premised on potentially deadly blunders on the part of characters either too delusional or, in the case of people like Uncle Ned [Royal Dano] in *Ghoulies II* [1987], too drunk, to "see straight")—is perhaps better suited than other categories of cultural production to an accessibility feature that is at least partially distinguished by all-too-relatable human errors.

# 8

# IT DOESN'T FOLLOW

## Audio Description and Verbal Premonition in Horror's Home-Video and Streaming Presentations

> The film offers a multitude of visual details, more than any viewer could mentally specify; the specification would be in words, and we do not name every detail we see.
>
> —Seymour Chatman, *Coming to Terms: The Rhetoric of Narrative in Fiction and Film* (1990)

> We'll never look at them the same again.
>
> —Paleontologist Kate Lloyd (Mary Elizabeth Winstead), looking up at the stars, in *The Thing* (2011)

In the preceding chapter, I explored the historical roots of audio description (AD), drawing upon published reviews of motion pictures produced not long after the turn of the twentieth century, including those that are ostensibly disconnected from the history of cinematic horror. This was done primarily to demonstrate how audiences with visual impairments were accommodated through "special" theatrical presentations. In singling out *The Battle Cry of Peace* (1915) as an exceptional yet representative "preparedness picture"—one that sought to generate consensus around the prospect of the United States going to war but resorted to gruesome displays of physical violence that were nearly unprecedented for its time—I noted how "horror" as a mode of spectatorial engagement (rather than as a discrete category of cultural production) informed the earliest attempts to translate potentially shocking or controversial ideas and graphic images into something approachable by anyone with a "heart to see." Like D. W. Griffith's 1918 war film, *Hearts of the World*, which was a similarly high-profile attempt to persuade the American public that its government's recent abandonment of neutrality (with regard to military and political events in Europe) was morally justified, but which was promoted by distributor Paramount Pictures as a work of art that would fully reveal the "horror and futility" of armed strife, the patriotic epic Wilfrid North and J. Stuart Blackton made three years earlier anticipated the more conventional "chills and thrills" of 1930s monster movies. Of course, the latter were produced and released after horror had shifted from being strictly a mode of wartime spectatorship to an official genre with its own unique iconography and thematic concerns.

This chapter builds upon that history but goes even farther afield by applying some of the protocols of AD mentioned earlier (i.e., conventions of that technological-translational format that began to firm up in the 1980s and 1990s) to horror films of the past two decades. In the pages that follow, I argue that the scripted, spoken descriptions provided on several DVDs and Blu-rays as well as streaming platforms such as Amazon Prime, Hulu, and Netflix not only function to make the pictorial elements of a given motion picture (e.g., camera movements, character actions, colors, costuming, hair and makeup, lighting design, props, sets, staging) accessible to people with congenital blindness or anyone who has experienced full or partial vision loss, but also enable auditory "views" on visual phenomena that might otherwise pass by unnoticed or go unseen by sighted audiences. Indeed, just as subtitles for the deaf and hard of hearing (SDH) do with regard to auditory elements such as sound effects, musical cues, and spoken dialogue (which, rendered as onscreen descriptive text, are made accessible to individuals who have experienced mild-to-severe hearing loss), AD frequently gives listeners a surplus of signifying information, attuning one's ears to the intricate mise-en-scène of cinematic horror and giving lie to the "lack" that has traditionally been attached to blindness as a socially and discursively constructed "disability." Looking at—or, rather, listening to—Greg McLean's *The Darkness* (2016), John R. Leonetti's *The Silence* (2019), Leigh Whannell's *The Invisible Man* (2020), Oz Rodriguez's *Vampires vs. the Bronx* (2020), Nia DaCosta's *Candyman* (2021), Patrick Brice's *There's*

*Someone Inside Your House* (2021), Shari Springer Berman and Robert Pulcini's *Things Heard & Seen* (2021), Nikyatu Jusu's *Nanny* (2022), and other films, I seek to demonstrate how the gendering and racializing of AD voices, the sometimes-vexing selection of descriptive words, and the pacing of that external narration (which often anticipatorily *precedes*, rather than follows, the onscreen action) introduce new meanings not apparent to all or even most audiences upon first "viewing." Rather than treat AD as merely a supplemental feature of modern-day horror film releases on home video and streaming services, I argue that it can and *should* be used as a paratextual framework for alternative forms of textual interpretation. This chapter therefore extends my exploration of the technological and perceptual affordances of contemporary media to accommodate a more capacious understanding of cinema's visual register, which, I argue, can be sensorially engaged through the *ears* whenever AD services are provided on DVDs, Blu-rays, and websites catering to a diverse, demographically mixed audience.

## We, She, He, It: Point of View, Pronouns, and Meaningful Mistakes in Audio-Described Horror Films

> You are blind. You are blind. I am the exposer. I am a seer.
>
> —"Pop Pop" (Peter McRobbie), an escaped patient from a psychiatric hospital, speaking to Tyler (Ed Oxenbould), a boy who previously believed that the old man was his grandfather (but is now literally frozen in fear in the presence of an imposter), in M. Night Shyamalan's *The Visit* (2015)

What an accessibility option such as AD makes "accessible," beyond the opportunity for tens of millions of audiences with some degree of visual impairment to engage a text on their own corporeal terms, is a set of interpretative tools that enable oscillatory moves between *sense*-making and *meaning*-making. One way to make sense of this particular feature of today's home-video and online releases, aside from relying primarily or exclusively on auditory elements to imaginatively coconstruct the diegetic universe of a given film, is to focus on the rhetorical moves of the offscreen speaker, who at times seems to be "directing" the director of that film (giving *instructions* as much as play-by-play descriptions about the framing of shots, the movements of the actors and camera, and the staging of scenes). Consider, for instance, how the AD narrator for directors Matt Bettinelli-Olpin and Tyler Gillett's 2014 supernatural horror film *Devil's Due* (released on home-video formats by distributor Twentieth Century-Fox) begins her description of the opening flashforward scene: She notes that the character whom we will later learn is Zach McCall (Zach Gilford)—a young murder suspect who has been arrested following the mysterious deaths of his wife, Samantha (Allison Miller), and his sister, Suzie (Vanessa Ray)—initially appears in police interrogation footage as a "traumatized man with chiseled features fidgeting with his wedding ring." "Congealing blood cakes one side of his brow," the narrator states, before noting that more blood "smears his hands." Calling attention to Zach's physical attributes and to particular parts of his body, the speaker creates a series of verbal "zoom shots" throughout this scene, whereas the cinematographer of *Devil's Due*, Justin Martinez, keeps his stationary camera at a slight distance from this "traumatized" subject so as to emulate the look of a police-station video (fig. 8.1).

Pacing back and forth across the foreground of this medium shot is the out-of-focus body of a police detective, whose girthy midsection

**Figure 8.1:** The opening scene of *Devil's Due* emulates the look of a police interrogation video—the camera keeping its distance in a medium shot—while the audio descriptor draws listeners' attention to the subject's blood-caked brow and to the wedding ring on his blood-smeared hands.

spills over his belt and holstered automatic pistol. At this point, the off-screen narrator, who says nothing about this male investigator in the extreme foreground (keeping his conventionally cop-like features "out of focus" aurally as well as visually), halts her description to let him speak: "Let's just take it from the top, Mr. McCall." A short break in the dialogue lets the AD provider interject additional details: "Without looking at the detective, the haunted young man remains fixed on his bloody hands." Viewers who are able to use their eyes might notice that the character's lowered gaze makes it difficult to discern if it is his hands or the ring on his finger that holds his focus. "I told you I didn't do it" are the first words spoken by this man, whose first name has yet to be revealed, but whose subtle movements—a "slight shake of his head" as he "swallows hard"—are verbally highlighted by someone who seems almost detective-like in her own right (meaning that she is attuned to nonverbal clues that would be of interest to the actual cops in this footage, which bears the time stamp "MAR. 30, 2013, 3:28 AM" in the lower left-hand corner of the frame).

The devil is in the details in the appropriately titled *Devil's Due*—or, rather, in the AD track that accompanies the DVD and Blu-ray releases of this film. That track shifts the listener's attention to facial features of the main and supporting characters as frequently as the directors and cinematographer attempt to recreate the look of surveillance tapes and "found footage" videos. Seconds after the opening scene ends, the narrative proper picks up with a much earlier moment in Zach and Samantha's life, showing their decision to document their impending wedding and honeymoon trip to the Dominican Republic with a newly purchased camcorder. Home movie footage from that video camera is what first appears after the police interrogation scene. The shakiness of the nighttime image tells sighted viewers that they are sharing the perspective of the camera's operator, who moves to a tree and, "partially hidden behind its trunk," gazes up at a "charming suburban home, which boasts an upstairs terrace." Actually, the pronoun used by the speaker is "we" (not "he," "she," or "they"), as if the *audience* rather than the character (whose identity has thus far remained hidden) is creeping toward the house, ascending its steps to the front porch, passing by "a couple of quaint wooden rocking chairs," and sidling up to the building to "peek in through a downstairs window."

For a split second, anyone who cannot see what sighted audiences can see might be reminded of the opening scene in John Carpenter's *Halloween* (1978), which likewise begins with a first-person point-of-view shot of someone stalking the occupants of a two-story suburban house at night and peering inside a window during two teenagers' make-out session in the living room. In *Devil's Due*, however, the handheld footage, considerably shakier than the smooth images that kick off Carpenter's film (which was shot with a camera outfitted with a Panaglide stabilizer), shows not a couple of horny adolescents through the window, but instead (as the AD provider tells us) "a few young women relaxing in the living room." At this point, she describes the person who will later be identified as Samantha, sitting among this group of women: "Our view zooms in on a slim brunette with sweet girlish features and a wide smile." As the speaker says these words, the camera does in fact *zoom in*, as if the invisible operator—be it a character in the film or the film's own cinematographer—has been prompted to do in visual terms what the descriptor has already done through locutionary means (in both this and the previous scene inside the police station).

*Halloween* and a host of other slasher films leap to mind as the AD paints an aural picture of what transpires immediately thereafter, once the brown-haired woman is shown—or, rather, described—hugging her friends goodbye and ascending the flight of stairs to the second floor. As she does so, the operator of the camera likewise moves to the second floor, only from outside the house and by scaling its exterior (in true movie-stalker fashion). Here is how the scene is described via the Bluray's AD:

> With our view shaking erratically, we climb the home's exterior to the upper terrace. We face a door and carefully open it. Passing through a small room in the midst of renovations, we step onto a dark upstairs landing. We peak down the staircase to find the coast clear, then proceed into a softly lit master bedroom provided with an adjacent lounge area. Across the bedroom lies a bathroom door left ajar. Moving closer we find a brunette wrapped in a towel as she blow-dries her long soft hair. Unaware of our presence, she keeps her back to us as we inch closer.

Suddenly, the loud barking of a dog interrupts the AD. The sound of the canine startles both the woman (who, turning around quickly, is immediately revealed to be Samantha) and the operator of the camera (who, reflected in the bathroom mirror, is eventually revealed to be Zach). Caught off guard, he nearly drops the camcorder as the dog, a retriever whose name is Maverick, leaps up to be petted. Meanwhile, Samantha, regaining her composure in the bathroom and securing the towel around her body, yells, "You nearly scared the shit out of me!"

As the first of many jump scares in *Devil's Due*, this moment is what Robert Baird, who has written about spectator cognition in film, would call a "false startle."[1] In other words, the implied offscreen threat posed by the operator of the camera is diffused once his identity and intentions—as a loving fiancé trying to pull a prank on his partner—are revealed. According to Baird, for a startle effect to occur, there should be a "disturbing intrusion into the character's immediate space," though in many cases (such as the scene described above) that intrusion is not an actual threat to the person but a benign violation of the space they inhabit.[2] Maverick, whose sudden burst into the frame had not been anticipated by either of the two main characters in this scene or by the audience who has been told that it is *they* (or "we") who were peeking down the staircase and proceeding toward the bathroom, means no harm and poses no threat. Indeed, the verbally described sight of him wagging his tail and trotting merrily out of the bedroom confirms this as a safe space. However, that itself will be proven *false* much later in the film, after other, far less benign intruders make their way into the couple's home.

What is remarkable about this early scene in *Devil's Due*, aside from the skill required to choreograph and manipulate several familiar yet effective scare-provoking components (e.g., the arrangement of the actors and props, the editing of the shots, the staging of the action), is how *we*, the audience, are made to feel like intruders. This is especially true in terms of the way the scene is verbally described by the AD voicer, whose insistence upon using that first-person plural pronoun makes it seem as though the camera as well as the actions of its operator were *ours* alone. Those kinds of rhetorical moves bring ethical considerations to bear on how we look at, and *listen* to, horror films, including those like *Devil's Due* in which characters themselves sometimes narrate the action as camcorder-toting protagonists in their own home movies and travel videos (as Samantha later does when describing the appearance of her sleeping husband on white bedsheets and the architecture of Santa Domingo during their ultimately tragic honeymoon). Are we witnesses to or participants in these and other characters' misfortunes? Can a spectator be made to feel complicit in the visual register of motion pictures that revolve around acts of violence—frequently directed against young women like Samantha—if they are blind or have low vision? And might a service like AD actually do a *disservice* to the spring-loaded fears and other startle effects so intrinsic to cinematic horror if it anticipatorily prepares audiences for what is to come or simply encourages a heightened form of auditory perception in excess of what is required to understand basic elements like plot points and character motivations? These and other AD-inspired questions form the epistemological framework for the remaining parts of this chapter, which seek to expand conventional notions of spectatorship and offer a fuller, sonically resonant "view" of the horror genre through optical as well as nonoptical "lenses."

Theatrically released a few months after *Devil's Due* debuted on home video, writer-director David Robert Mitchell's *It Follows* (2014) is equally instructive as a motion picture that gained additional layers of meaning once it made its way to DVD and Blu-ray formats as well as streaming services equipped with AD. Almost immediately after it was released, the film—a nostalgic throwback to the audiovisual poetics of classic teen slashers from the 1980s—was taken up as an object of study by scholars drawn not only to its intertextual nods to previous productions but also to its subtler depictions of socioeconomic precarity and the structural violence that results from the "organized abandonment of the inner city" in late-capitalist America.[3] Casey Ryan Kelly elaborates that the titular threat posed to the teenaged characters in *It Follows* is less a supernatural manifestation of sexually transmitted diseases (i.e., an "AIDS-as-monster" metaphor indebted to an earlier era of moral panics) than the ambient dread that comes from living in a postindustrial city on the verge of collapse.[4] Diffuse and hard to pin down, that dread spreads beyond the racially codified confines of Detroit's crumbling urban center (the area north of the Eight Mile Wall) into the comparatively safe, seemingly idyllic suburban enclaves where white middle-class residents confront their own increased vulnerability to substandard living conditions, property foreclosures, prolonged unemployment, and other indicators of a stagnant US economy.[5] Indeed, "stagnation" is a doubly operative term, according to Joel Burges, for it conveys not only the "material reality in which contemporary laborers find themselves stalked by class morbidity" but also the sensation of slow creeping menace that distinguishes *It Follows* and a host of other recent films in which financial insecurity is a fact of life for people whose impending deaths mirror that of the dream of abundance and prosperity which once served as a unifying national myth.[6]

Of course, the "dream" of which I write has long been absent from this country's cultural imaginary, having been replaced by the realization that only a limited amount of the wealth and opportunities available to a privileged few will make its way into the hands of the less fortunate, or, better yet, trickle down to those social and educational institutions that serve a greater public good. In fact, the very foundations of modern horror, traceable to the slow-moving ghouls and quick-to-shoot militia in George A. Romero's *Night of the Living Dead* (1968) as well as to the academic study of that and other films undertaken by Robin Wood a decade later (in his appropriately titled collection of essays, *The American Nightmare* [1979]), rest upon an understanding that the most oppressed and dispossessed among us—members of the working class, racial and sexual minorities, homeless people, and others in need of institutional support—might see in horror an eerily familiar or all-too-relatable set of existential dilemmas. In the introduction of their collection *Labors of Fear: The Modern Horror Film Goes to Work*, Aviva Briefel and Jason Middleton allude to the fact that the title of Wood's book was not only an accurate description of the cultural productions that came out of the social unrest and political turmoil of the 1960s and 1970s but also a prescient indicator of how cinematic horror would continue to mine fears related to "deindustrialization, automation, globalized labor, union busting, and rising income inequality" in the decades that followed, leading up to the production and release of post-recession films like *It Follows*.[7]

Although slow in its movements, the shape-shifting entity that relentlessly pursues Jay (Maika Monroe), the female protagonist of *It Follows*, is as inescapable as the prospect of there being no prospects for young adults lacking the professional opportunities of their parents' or grandparents' generations. In that sense, the American nightmare that Wood wrote about in the late 1970s has only magnified in intensity and become more pervasive in the intervening years. As such, the infection-like "curse" that comes for Jay after her initial foray into consensual sex—with her new boyfriend, Hugh (Jack Weary)—and which notably assumes the physical shape of human hosts (including a "frail elderly woman in a hospital nightgown" and a "sickly woman dressed as a sex worker") whose dirty, disheveled appearances suggest a lower-class status, is not hers alone.[8] Nor is it strictly a monstrous malediction brought on by the promiscuous behavior of horny teenagers (as was the case in so many 1980s slasher films). It is shared by anyone who has ever worked a dead-end job, or been laid off from work, or needed medical treatment without the safety net of health insurance. Casey Ryan Kelly emphasizes this in his fleshing out of the titular "It," a monster with "no backstory, motive, affliction, voice, or identity" that nevertheless functions as an abject figuration of unavoidable contamination—a "stand-in for the structural violence that produces poverty" and extends precarity to the previously protected middle classes.[9]

The film's politics of mortality, or what Kelly calls "thanatopolitics," thus reveals something about the "brutal realities of human existence" to which horror as a culturally resonant body genre is well suited. But equally revealing is the way that the AD of *It Follows* does not actually follow the interpretative path taken by the scholars cited above, referencing very few of the visual markers of "systemic, structured vulnerability" that Kelly and others have singled out as signs of the film's social relevance: "unemployment, limited upward mobility, substandard health care, crumbling infrastructure, environmental degradation, and divestment in the public good."[10] While Kelly dwells momentarily on the subtle clues of "disorganization, corrosion, and decay" that are visible in the largely white neighborhood that serves as the film's principal setting, including the "yellowed, cracked" exterior of Jay's midcentury home (which is "stained with dirt and mildew" and in need of basic upkeep) and leaf-filled above-ground backyard pool (which "stands as a cheap imitation of bourgeois luxury"), no such information was made available to vision-impaired listeners of the AD track created by the Sheffield-based media company zoo Digital. That track, written by Noel Urbano and narrated by voice actor Joe Hernandez, was available as a listening option on Netflix before *It Follows* was removed from the streaming platform's catalog of titles in 2023. Before its removal, I accessed the film's AD and found it to be illustrative of both the affordances and limitations of a device that obscures as much as it reveals.

On the surface, that AD paints a fairly accurate picture of the physically manifested threat posed by the monster, in the person of a "young brunette woman with bruised eyes and her bra hanging off" while "urine trickles down the inside of her short skirt and puddles around her feet" (fig. 8.2). But in lavishing greater attention to the individual personifications of monstrosity that doggedly pursue Jay, while having relatively little to say about the spaces and places in which she and her friends seek shelter (including decrepit if not completely dilapidated buildings only a short drive away from their own mildewed homes), the providers of this service steer the listener's ears toward a reading of *It Follows* that does not hew to the film's critical trajectory. In other words, the AD does not communicate very much about the film's blending of urban and suburban geographies across a textual terrain that sees its own "buffer zones" dissolving as surely as have those in Detroit that separate one segment of the population (rich people) from another (low-income people). As such, the audibly described "It" of *It Follows* is presented to the listener as a strictly foreign element: an aberrant, abject incursion of the Real into the falsely comforting environs of a white middle-class neighborhood. Had Urbano and Hernandez written and spoken about the city's crumbling infrastructure and architecture as precisely as David

**Figure 8.2:** The audio description track included in the home-video release of *It Follows* draws greater attention to individual personifications of monstrosity than it does to the interior and exterior locations in suburban Detroit where much of the film's horror emerges.

Robert Mitchell and cinematographer Mike Gioulakis show with their camera, audiences reliant upon AD might have had a clearer sense of the spread of postindustrial dread I referred to earlier, past chain-link fences into sites of human precariousness that are likely to linger in the minds of anyone who has watched the film with their eyes: abandoned buildings, clapboard houses, derelict factories, empty residential lots, polluted brownfields, and overgrown railroad tracks.

To be fair, the temporal restrictions placed on audio describers, who are tasked with verbally summarizing visual information in brief, punctuative segments (so as not to overlap with any spoken dialogue), make it nearly impossible to render such detail in the span of a few seconds. In her essay "Creating Coherence in Audio Description," Sabine Braun mentions this technical aspect, noting that AD is "normally delivered in chunks of no more than a few seconds, fitted into silent moments," thus creating a hierarchical relationship between "essential auditory elements" on the "primary" track and the added narration on the "secondary" track, which should itself remain silent for long stretches of time (whenever dialogue, musical flourishes, and sound effects are occurring).[11] Like other writers and speakers of AD, Urbano and Hernandez should be congratulated for the way that they keep pace with the film's narrative, though their tendency to "sprint ahead" and narrate events several seconds before they transpire—something that likewise occurs in many other AD-supplemented streamers—creates ruptures for anyone who can see those events on screen (or, for that matter, hear the contextualizing sound effects through speakers).[12] Perhaps more egregious are the numerous mistakes that they and other AD providers make when translating images into words. Putting aside some fairly obvious yet debatable points of contention (e.g., Does Jay, who is initially referred to as "the blonde," really smile "faintly" at the five-minute mark of the film? Is she also smiling "softly" while looking in the mirror three minutes later?), there are several instances in which the AD of *It Follows* is not merely misleading but *incorrect*, either misattributing actions to certain characters or confusing their names to the point where listeners might genuinely be *confused* about plot details.

An example of this occurs near the thirty-four-minute mark, just before a dinosaur-like creature from a black-and-white movie that appears on television is described as a "dragon": "Jay nods and walks towards the couch. Nick scoots over, making room. She sits and faces the TV." This would not be a problem if the teenaged boy who makes room for Jay on his sofa (and who is played by Keir Gilchrist) were named "Nick," but a previous scene had established that his name is "Paul" (a fact literally spelled out on his nametag as an ice-cream shop employee). The describer continues to call Paul "Nick" throughout the scene in which he and Jay watch *Voyage to the Planet of Prehistoric Women* (1968) on her small cathode-ray monitor, and further into the film (for a total of forty-three instances), though Hernandez also calls him by his actual name enough times to suggest that Paul might have a split identity, or is putting up a false front (pretending to be someone he is not). To be clear, no one named "Nick" exists in the film's narrative, though his occasional reappearance throughout the run of the secondary audio track suggests the presence of another world or a different set of identities within this diegetic space. Though inaccurate, that unintended mistake on the part of zoo Digital brings the latent theme of displacement to the fore, but in a way that differs considerably from how the already displaced fears of "urban contamination" embodied by the sexually transmitted, transmutable monster manifest racist and classist delineations between insiders and outsiders. And it does so through verbiage that is as "impoverished" (metaphorically speaking) as the locations in Central Michigan that serve as this film's main settings, where infected people are forced to pass "It" along to other unsuspecting victims if they are to escape death if not the stagnation that defines their existence.

Misnaming a character is one thing, but *misgendering* a nonbinary or transgender person presents a more serious problem for audiences who are reliant on AD to accurately represent someone as he, she, or they would like to be identified. Although it does not occur often, a mistake of this kind should be taken seriously. It can unintentionally cause harm to anyone who might "see" themselves in the person or predicaments of a genderqueer character who, besides dealing with homophobia, transphobia, bullying, and outright violence, is sometimes forced to fend off monsters of a more literal kind (in supernatural scenarios that are nevertheless grounded in real-world fears for members of the LGBTQI+ community). At the very least, it is disrespectful to those whose fight for inclusion, rights, and visibility gets more difficult with each misrepresentation or poorly translated description that comes their way.

The increased presence of nonbinary and transgender actors and characters in horror films, including writer-director Brad Michael Elmore's vampire-themed *Bit* (2019) and John Logan's Blumhouse-produced *They/Them* (2022), should at the very least encourage audio describers to take a more mindful approach to pronoun use, applying words like "he," "she," and "they" in accordance with how the characters *identify themselves*, beyond simply noting whether those people are feminine- or masculine-presenting. The title of *They/Them*, a slasher film set at a "conversion camp" where electroshock torture and other types of "aversion therapy" are used against nonbinary and trans kids, is especially significant. It reclaims two words—a subject pronoun and an object pronoun divided by an equally important slash—that, throughout the history of cinematic horror, has typically been used to denote monstrous "others" from whom the heroes (as stand-ins for "us," the audience) are to be shielded if those protagonists are to be spared some horrible, potentially deadly fate. That pronominal tendency, not unlike the use of "It" to denote the mortal dangers faced by small tightly knit families and groups of adolescent characters in *It Follows*, *It Comes at Night* (2017), and *It* (2017), is highlighted by David Moreau and Xavier Palud's home-invasion film *Them* (*Ils*, 2006), in which the titular threat takes the form of hooded assailants—a small group of teenaged delinquents—preying on the older, wealthier occupants of an idyllic country house outside Bucharest.[13]

In director Patrick Brice's *There's Someone Inside Your House* (2021), which screenwriter Henry Gayden adapted from a 2017 novel of the same title by Stephanie Perkins, a transgender student named Darby (Jesse LaTourette) presents himself as male, though some of his classmates at Osborne High persist in calling him by his dead name, "Justine" (thereby assigning him a female identity). In the AD track provided by Descriptive Video Works and attached to the film as an accessibility feature by Netflix, an unidentified voicer (whose name is not provided at the end, but whose youthful voice is in keeping with the themes of this coming-of-age teen slasher film) occasionally labels Darby "her" rather than "him" or "them" (the nonbinary character's preferred pronouns). For instance, early in the film, following an opening scene that shows a masked killer murdering a high-school football player who is revealed to have bullied a gay teammate, Darby discusses that recent event with his classmates. The scene is set up by the audio describer in this way:

"Outside, Darby is with her four friends." Were it made only once, the mistake would be easy to overlook. But the voicer continues to misgender the character in subsequent scenes—for instance, when describing a shot in which "Darby shows off a letter from NASA on her phone," before the same character is said to be pointing "her constellation app at the night sky" while "lying on her back." Ultimately, little thought seems to have been given to Darby's own gender expression (evident to anyone who pays attention to his mannerisms, behaviors, and appearance), making *There's Someone Inside Your House* a noteworthy example of the less-conspicuous but no-less-painful daily horrors that are visited upon people who continue to be viewed through a cisgendered lens. Nevertheless, its AD, like the one provided for *It Follows*, creates productive ruptures in the diegesis, unwittingly alerting listeners to the ideological parameters that limit onscreen representation and reflexively drawing attention to the presence of an offscreen "threat" to the very existence of those whose lives depend on recognition and, yes, *visibility*.

## Eyes Wander, Brows Furrow: Minor Details, Distracting Actions, and Facial Reactions

What the hell are we looking for?

—One of three Norwegian scientists inside a snowcat speeding across a desolate Antarctic tundra, seconds before the vehicle falls nose-first into a steep, dark crevasse, during the opening scene of Matthijs van Heijningen Jr. and Eric Heisserer's *The Thing* (2011)

Wilf blinks. His brow knits.

—Audio description during a scene in the horror film *1922* (2017)

Few of the nearly eighty AD tracks that I have consulted for this chapter are as confounding in their combined truthfulness and deceitfulness about thematic and narrative material as the one provided for *It Follows*. And yet they are all eye-opening—or ear-opening—in their own ways, bringing forth unique perspectives on narrated events and visual material that are worthy of discussion. One of the most valuable contributions that AD makes lies in its ability to draw attention to small, nearly imperceptible or easily missed elements within a film's mise-en-scène, including details about props, costumes, hair and makeup, settings, and lighting setups that would otherwise fall by the wayside, but which are endowed with special salience in the context of cinematic horror. And yet, for each textual Easter egg that the description singles out, several other potentially important specificities—related to characters and locations, for instance—are ignored or left unspoken.

An example of this occurs in the narrational track provided by Descriptive Video Works for director Santiago Menghini's *No One Gets Out Alive* (2021). The film begins with shaky handheld footage of an archeological dig in the jungles of Mexico, presented in the style of a vintage, black-and-white 8 mm recording, circa 1963. This movie-within-the-movie shows local lackeys of a group of white Europeans pulling up a sinister-looking box from a deep, skeleton-lined pit. As the voicer is quick to point out, that hole in the ground is illuminated by a small lantern that "attracts a cloud of moths." Moving on from its opening scene, *No One Gets Out Alive* takes the viewer-listener into the dark, modern-looking interior of a large house, though there is no indication at this point if the setting has shifted from Mexico to some other location. A woman named Simona (Joana Borja) sits alone at night, her gaze shifting from the glitching image on her television screen (which, in addition to a nearby low-wattage lamp, provides the only source of light in an otherwise pitch-black living room) to a couple of dark shapes on the wood floor. Those marks disappear almost as soon as they appear, once the power in the house goes out, thrusting her (and the sighted viewer) into an even inkier darkness. Getting up from the sofa, Simona "takes a few steps then looks down a dark hallway towards a dining room." Anyone watching this scene without the benefit of AD would likely struggle to see very much besides what is illuminated by the moonlight outside a shaded window, which, like a miniature movie screen, shows the flickering shadow of a moth flying by. At least, that is what appears onscreen according to the AD voicer, who draws a connection between the swarm of moths that had been shown during the earlier scene and the same insect that—viewed from a distance and in the span of a single second—would be difficult to make out for anyone with 20/20 vision. Even more telling is the way the voicer describes a strange object that suddenly appears at the end of the hallway: a "box on the floor." As yet another physical link to the preceding scene, that box is "made of ornately carved stone"—a detail that, if unspoken, would otherwise be lost on most sighted viewers.

Here, the dimness of the lighting puts viewers on shaky ground, making it easy for them to be "blindsided" by the sudden appearance of pale white hands reaching up from behind Simona, who is dragged screaming into some undefined place, out of sight, right as the box lurches forward on its own accord. The audience has only a brief moment to catch their breath during the shot that immediately follows. In medium close-up, one of several pinned specimens in a large collection of moths flutters to life. From there the film takes us outside the building, but only fleetingly, granting us a nighttime view of its exterior as "the lights in the second-floor windows flicker back on." "The screen goes dark," continues the AD voicer, right before the title of the film "appears as white lettering on a black background." This, we soon learn, sets up the narrative proper, which begins once another young woman, Ambar (Cristina Rodlo), is introduced as human cargo inside the back of a transport truck. A flashlight's beam scans its interior, revealing "a group of people huddled on the floor" and forcing her to "shield her eyes against the bright light." Although she will later be identified as an undocumented immigrant from Mexico seeking employment in the aftermath of her mother's death, at this point listeners only learn that she is "wearing a leather jacket" as she exits the vehicle, with a "city's skyline in the distance." No other descriptors help us to draw a mental picture of what Ambar or the space in which she is first shown looks like.

For sighted viewers, certain architectural landmarks visible against the night sky, including Cleveland's Key Tower and Terminal Tower, designate the specific city in which this and subsequent scenes take place. But that information is notably withheld from the listener, an absent signifier lent humorous subtext when, during a later scene, the landlord of the ramshackle room that Ambar is renting informs her that she will "have a good view" of the city from her second-floor window, before adding, "not that Cleveland's much to look at." In the seconds before her arrival at her new (old) residence, she is described as walking "down a residential street carrying a full backpack" and approaching "the front steps of a porch." "A view of the large house reveals it to be the same one that Simona was in," the voicer intones, injecting a narrational element that links past and present and cues us to the as-yet-unclear relationship between the two female characters. In doing so, the audio describer reminds any sighted viewers listening to the track that *they too* might need assistance in perceiving things that pass by too quickly for the mind to fully comprehend.

Another example of detail-oriented audio-description-as-narration occurs on the track provided by International Digital Center for director J. J. Perry's *Day Shift* (2022), an action-and-comedy-filled horror film distributed by Netflix. Written by Dakota Green and voiced by Sri Gordon, the AD for this film is given ample room to paint a detailed picture of its opening scene, which is set in the Reseda neighborhood of San Fernando Valley. It shows a Black man with short hair and a goatee, who will later be revealed as the film's down-on-his-luck hero Bud Jablonski (Jamie Foxx), scooping up a dead possum from a swimming pool with a pool skimmer. Then, glancing around to make sure that no one is around to witness what is about to take place, he pulls a pistol out from a secret compartment beneath his crate of cleaning supplies and holsters it on his utility belt. "A pair of dice showing snake eyes marks the grip of the handgun," voicer Gordon says, just as Bud—still silent but now wearing a ski mask—uses a pry bar to open the sliding door of a house where two vampires lie in wait. At first listen, the white dice on the black pistol grip would seem to be of little significance, hardly worth noting given its smallness and the briefness of its appearance onscreen. But that tiny detail not only visually communicates the "name" that Bud has given to his sidearm ("Snakes Eyes"); it also anticipates subsequent shots inside his "beat-up blue pickup truck," where a pair of fuzzy dice hangs from the rearview mirror. In his discussion of the film for the website Looper, contributor Chris Condry states that the kitschy automotive decoration is "symbolic of Jablonski's constant risk-taking, as he gambles with his life against vampires and gambles with his relationship [with his teenage daughter and ex-wife] through his behavior."[14] Fittingly, Condry's comments about *Day Shift*'s dice-rolling-motif, which extends to the film's soundtrack (nondiegetic songs like Nipsey Hussle's "Grinding All My Life" that likewise paint an audible picture of the protagonist's life), are included in one of that website's ongoing series of "Small Details You Missed" articles. It and the other articles in the series are designed to draw readers' eyes to overlooked cinematic elements that, once seen, cannot be unseen and might actually enhance one's appreciation of a motion picture's "deeper meanings."

Besides drawing a listener's attention to details that many viewers overlook, AD sometimes breaks a seemingly mundane scene into several constituent actions or events that, taken together, suggest the presence of something more menacing or life-threatening than what first appears. Indeed, there is "more than meets the eye" in many supernatural horror films, including those like *Ouija* (2014) that hinge on paranormal events and show objects moving on their own accord, or through the prompting of some spiritual presence made visible only in its manipulation of physical things. An early scene of this film, following a precredits sequence showing two preteen girls attempting to commune with the dead through a Ouija board, takes place years later, now that they have matured into college-aged women. One of them, Debbie (Shelley Hennig), has decided—for reasons that are not yet clear—to throw the now-tattered board and old wooden planchet into the fireplace. After watching the bubbling surface of the game go up in flames with a "pensive" gaze, she steps outside her house at night to meet her friend Laine (Olivia Cooke). She explains to Laine that, rather than going to the basketball game, she has decided to stay behind and heat up some leftovers before her parents return home. A hint of trepidation can be detected in Debbie's voice when she tells Laine that Ouija is just a game—a statement spoken with a question-like inflection, as if she were needing confirmation from her friend that her otherwise unstated but discernible anxieties are unfounded. Bidding her friend goodnight, Debbie returns to the interior of her house while "the Ouija board continues to burn in the fireplace." These words, spoken by Christopher Flowers (a voice actor whose description services were provided by the Media Access Group at WGBH), alert us to the enduring threat of something that is still within her grasp but deadly to touch, though the voicer tellingly adopts not only first-person plural pronouns but also ocularcentric language to denote the ensuing camera movement: "*Our view creeps* past a staircase and through a dark foyer. Beyond a dimly lit dining room, *we move* past a doorway and *see* a small kitchen."

What follows is a two-minute-long scene in which nothing much seems to happen, and little else besides the female protagonist's consumption of food and her investigation of unusual noises takes place. However, when narrated by Flowers, the scene contains multitudes—so full is it of microactions whose meanings are made "big" by way of a lengthy description that imbues hermeneutic significance to even the smallest of details and subtlest of gestures:

> Debbie sets a plate down on a small table in the center of the room. She takes a seat, then wraps pasta around a fork. She casually dines on the leftovers and wipes her mouth with a paper towel. She sips from a glass of water. The pretty blonde picks up her fork and continues eating. Behind her, a windowed door creaks open. Debbie turns back and gets up. She steps through the doorway into a small laundry room where she spots an open back door. Debbie glances around the tiny room then closes the door and locks it. Leaving the keys dangling in the lock, she returns to the kitchen. A stove-top burner ignites. She stares at the dancing flames then glances beyond the kitchen into the house. Debbie hesitates then steps to the stove and switches the flame off. She watches the extinguished burner then reaches around the wall and into the laundry room. She clicks off the laundry room light. Debbie crosses the kitchen to a light switch and surveys the room. She lingers by the switch, then dims the lights, leaving her unfinished meal in the dark. She gives the kitchen one final glance, then enters into the dark foyer. Debbie moves to the staircase and creeps up the steps past several framed photos on the wall. Pausing halfway up, she glances over her shoulder then continues to climb. At the top of the stairs, she crosses the landing overlooking the foyer and peers down past a hanging light fixture. She makes her way across the dimly lit hall and enters a room.

By my count, this short scene contains thirty-eight actions on Debbie's part, each conveyed through a present-tense verb: "sets," "takes," "wraps," "dines," "wipes," "sips," "picks up," "continues," "turns," "gets up," "steps," "spots," "glances," "closes," "locks," "returns," "stares," "glances," "hesitates," "steps," "switches," "watches," "reaches," "clicks," "crosses," "surveys," "lingers," "dims," "gives," "enters," "moves," "creeps," "glances," "continues," "crosses," "peers," "makes," and "enters." Hardly a passive victim of the terrible event that is about to come (once she sees what is inside her bedroom), she is an active driver of events, doing more than three dozen things in the span of two minutes. Besides her own actions, there are two additional instances of things appearing to move on their own: the door to the pantry creaking open and the flame of the stovetop burner suddenly igniting. Together, those events—either initiated by Debbie or occurring without any human intervention—create a push-pull tension that is in keeping with the ideomotor phenomenon of Ouija movements, whereby a planchette touched by several hands seems to slide across a board and spell out words on its own, or through the manipulation of a spirit (though, in actuality, it is the unconscious muscular exertions of the operators that cause those movements).

Actually, there are other actions not accounted for by the describer—namely, those of the camera as it glides through the open doorway of the kitchen and, with a cut to a medium close-up, sidles up to the small table where Debbie eats spaghetti. The sighted audience's view of the young woman gets even closer as the door behind her swings open on its own, though Flowers only narrates the latter of the two movements, leaving the creepy "we-ness" of the dolly shot (with its connotation of voyeurism, similar to the early description "Our view creeps") unspoken. This, too, carries implications for how one might interpret the agential behavior and physical actions of someone who, at this early stage of the film, appears to be the main female protagonist, the one person who will presumably survive until the narrative's end (as the proverbial final girl). That presumption, however, is quickly proven to be incorrect. Interestingly, even after she is possessed by the wooden Ouija board (which somehow has made its way from the fireplace to her bed, unburned and completely intact), Debbie—as narrated on the AD track—seems to be in control of her actions, leading up to her death-by-hanging (an apparent suicide that is eventually revealed to be the work of a dead girl's ghost).

Another noteworthy thing occurs in the AD of *Ouija*'s pretitle sequence, right before Debbie drops down from the second-floor ceiling and an image/description of her "stiff lifeless" body dangling from a string of electric lights is followed by a sudden cut to black and the title of the film in white letters. When she sees the game board on her bed, Debbie "furrows her brow and swallows hard," according to Flowers, whose description recalls the AD-voiced reference to Zach swallowing hard during the first scene of *Devil's Due* (fig. 8.3). At first listen, this remark about brow furrowing would appear to be unremarkable—a small gesture that communicates little about the supernatural nature of the threat or the psychological state of the character in the seconds leading up to her demise. However, few expressions are uttered as frequently in AD-supplemented horror films as "a furrowed brow," and the recurrence of that phrase (or slight variations thereof) merits at least passing consideration as we narrow the proverbial lens on one of the most exceptional aspects of this accessibility tool.

Anyone who doubts either the frequency or significance of that phrase within audio-described horror films should listen to the assistive track that was produced for writer-director Leigh Whannell's *The Invisible Man* (2020). In this modern, #MeToo-era updating of the H. G. Wells story of the same title, audiences are asked to share the "unbearably tangible" feeling of trauma endured by the film's protagonist, Cecilia (Elisabeth Moss), as she flees from a toxic relationship only to find herself in the presence of an even deadlier, unseen threat, all while trying yet failing to convince others that her fears are not unfounded. In the words of one critic, the filmmaker turns the long-exploited "crazy-woman-no-one-will-listen-to" cliché on its head, and "we believe Cecilia through and through, when others, perhaps understandably, refuse to do so, questioning her sanity instead."[15] In fact, the repeated acts of *listening* and *questioning* are very much what *The Invisible Man* foregrounds during scenes in which offscreen sounds—including those heard by Cecilia—announce the presence of the titular threat and prompt her

**Figure 8.3:** As with many other contemporary horror films released on home video, the audio description track on *Ouija* draws attention to microevents and easily overlooked behavioral or physiological shifts among characters whose brows furrow frequently.

to furrow her brow in the seconds leading up to some truly terrifying revelations.

She spends much of the narrative being stalked and terrorized by her ostensibly dead ex-boyfriend, a wealthy optics engineer named Adrian (Oliver Jackson-Cohen), who created an invisibility suit before his passing. However, as anyone who has watched and/or listened to this film in its entirety will know, my description is not correct; it is later revealed, through an elaborate twist ending, that someone else has taken the suit and has been following her. Cecilia spends a significant portion of the film hiding out in the home of a childhood friend, an African American detective named James (Aldis Hodge) who lives there with his teenaged daughter Sydney (Storm Reid) and who is described on more than one occasion by the AD provider as an "athletic man." Around the narrative's midpoint, as Cecilia aurally senses the presence of something or someone nearby, the AD accompanying this film's online and home-video releases informs us that, "with an anxious look she glances around the room" and "her brow furrows." Three minutes later, when Cecilia enters the attic and finds Adrian's cellphone, "she swipes through more pictures of her and Sydney slumbering and her brow furrows" (fig. 8.4).

**Figure 8.4:** According to the audio description track on the home-video release of *The Invisible Man*, Cecilia, the main character, furrows her brow frequently in the midst of mounting auditory evidence that she is not alone in the house.

A form of body language etched on the forehead, suggestive of concentration, confusion, or disapproval, the furrowed brow has already made several appearances up to this point, beginning with the film's first scene, which depicts Cecilia breaking out of Adrian's high-security mansion/prison only to be distracted by the laboratory apparatus that, unbeknownst to her, holds his invisibility suit. The fact that our hero continues to furrow her brow at least a dozen more times over the course of the film (according to the AD) suggests that, while she might have successfully fled from the physical space in which she was victimized for so long, Cecilia cannot escape the past and in fact carries it forward *on her body*, communicating it in her otherwise subtle—dare I say "invisible"—facial reactions to traumatizing events inside another man's home.

Besides *The Invisible Man*, a host of other contemporary horror films and psychological thrillers, from Matthijs van Heijningen Jr.'s *The Thing* (2011) to the Spierig Brothers' *Jigsaw* (2017), Oz Rodriguez's *Vampires vs. the Bronx* (2020), Shana Feste's *Run Sweetheart Run* (2020), Shari Springer Berman and Robert Pulcini's *Things Heard & Seen*, and Iris K. Shim's *Umma* (2022), feature AD tracks in which characters are described creasing, furrowing, or knitting their brows several times. It is as if the things they are hearing or seeing so defy logic that only a look of consternation or bewilderment would suffice in summing up their unspoken feelings (fig. 8.5). It is an unusually evocative if subtle sort of nonverbal action that can be seen, or *heard*, a total of fourteen times in Veena Sud's *The Lie* (2018), which revolves around a divorced couple's escalating anxiety as they attempt to shield their teenaged daughter, Kayla (Joey King), from murder charges only to learn, in the film's penultimate scene, that the girl's missing friend, Britney (Devery Jacobs), faked her death as a prank. Their stunned confusion at seeing the girl, whom they had been told was dead but who now stands before them smiling and unharmed, is communicated by way of *two* furrowed brows: that of Kayla's mother, Rebecca (Mireille Enos), and that of her father, Jay (Peter Sarsgaard). By this point in the narrative, audiences have learned that they are the kind of parents who would stop at nothing—not even the murder of Britney's prying father (who had been growing suspicious of their evasiveness and had started hounding Kayla about the whereabouts of his daughter)—to protect their child. While such actions would be beyond the pale for many spectators, our own confusion at seeing, or hearing,

**Figure 8.5:** In several contemporary horror films such as *Things Heard & Seen*, the vertical wrinkles that appear on characters' foreheads whenever they are worried, stressed, or concerned are as central to the physiological makeup of the genre as terrified screams are, according to these films' audio description tracks.

that the entire premise of the film has been a lie makes it possible for us to side with Rebecca and Jay as they struggle to process the horrible truth of the situation. In fact, the dozen instances of audio-described brow-furrowing that preceded this "big reveal," though prompted by the concern they felt for a loved one they feared would go to prison or suffer a worse fate, set the stage for *The Lie*'s concluding scenes, as if Rebecca and Jay had suspected all along that something even more troubling and traumatizing than the death of a daughter's friend awaited them at the narrative's end.

Besides furrowed brows, which I am now convinced are as ubiquitous within cinematic horror as shudders and screams, everything from cocked heads to flared nostrils to slightly opened mouths have been habitually singled out as description-worthy signs of characters' negatively valanced emotions, audibly registered in *Bingo Hell* (2021), *Blood Red Sky* (2021), *Grimcutty* (2022), *M3GAN* (2022), and a host of other contemporary productions. The latter film, directed by Gerard Johnstone, written by Akela Cooper, and starring Amie Donald as a child-sized humanoid robot doll powered by artificial intelligence (a Model 3 Generative Android), is filled with several microexpressions—the actors' and characters' subtle facial tics and small physical gestures—that would hardly make an impression were it not for the work of an especially attentive audio describer. For instance, when a social worker/therapist named Lydia (Amy Usherwood) steps into the house of a robotics engineer named Gemma (Allison Williams) and spots the latter's teenaged niece Cady (Violet McGraw) mindlessly transfixed by a television screen rather than doing something more productive with her time, the woman "flashes Gemma a tight smile." This is Lydia's nonverbal way of communicating her feelings about the other woman's parenting abilities, but so understatedly that those emotions are all but invisible until *literally verbalized* by the AD voicer. Indeed, the tightness of Lydia's smile, while present in the image, is nearly imperceptible owing to the quickness with which she "flashes" it and the subtlety of the actor's performance, which anticipates that of Amie Donald once faint hints of her uncannily human character's mechanical "personhood" begin to bleed through the placid surface of M3GAN's artificial skin during the second half of the film.

## Technological Beasts: Things Heard and Not Seen (or Things Seen and Not Heard)

The title's phosphorescent glow dies out, leaving us in the dark.

—Audio description for Matthijs van Heijningen Jr.'s *The Thing* (2011), at the end of the film's opening sequence

The kind of sharp attentiveness on the part of AD providers that I have mentioned above is commendable. Indeed, it is one reason why this accessibility tool should matter to anyone with a vested interest in horror film hermeneutics. However, there are just as many examples of either intentional or unintentional omission that speak to what goes unspoken in audio tracks, and which must be reckoned with if we are to determine its "usefulness" as an *interpretive tool*. Consider, for example, how one of the most important signs of a young boy's history of self-harm in John Ross's Hulu-released *Grimcutty* goes unremarked by the film's AD voicer: In the opening scene, the voicer, Roy Samuelson, describes the as-yet-unnamed boy's movement toward a bedroom window (from which he climbs onto the roof before sneaking into another second-floor room) but says nothing about the character's heavily bandaged hands and wrists. Those damaged appendages are conspicuously framed by the camera as an early indicator that something is not right either in this house or with his mental and physical health. However, anyone reliant on AD would not be made aware of this visual clue to some past trauma or impending event. The scene that follows, showing the nervous boy suddenly lunging at his mother with a kitchen knife and stabbing her in the stomach after the film's mysterious title creature ("a gangly white-faced figure") has slipped into the house, would certainly clarify that, though, and is described more carefully by the voicer. But one wonders why narrator Samuelson or the company he works for (AD provider Point.360) chose not to mention the boy's bandaged hands, especially since something as small and insignificant as his ill-fated mother swallowing hard before shutting the bedroom door in the minutes leading up to her death is described with an eye to a detail that barely registers in the image.

Samuelson's dispassionate voice, which remains calm as he describes the boy's mother looking "down at her stomach as it spurts blood" at the end of this disturbing precredits sequence, is similar to the way Sam Clark—the AD voicer for the DVD and Blu-ray releases of the found-footage horror film *Paranormal Activity 2* (2010)—barely modulates his intonation even when all the lights go out in the house of Daniel and Kristi Rey (Brian Boland and Sprague Grayden) and a full realization of its long-dormant threats finally dawns on the married couple amid this supernatural, scream-inducing moment of "blind" clarity. Indeed, Samuelson's and Clark's nondiegetic voices could be said to have a *soothing* effect, though their unperturbed delivery might also heighten the feeling of *terror* that comes from being in the virtual presence of someone so detached from, or unaffected by, gruesome acts of domestic violence. Interestingly, Samuelson's voice during the first few minutes of *Grimcutty*, leading up the audible spurting of the mother's blood onto the tiled kitchen floor, anticipates the vocalic performance of actor Sara Wolfkind in the scene that immediately follows—or, rather, that of her character, Asha, who appears in an ASMR (autonomous sensory meridian response) video after the red letters of the film's title come up against a black background.[16] Speaking in a hushed whisper and confiding in her viewer-listeners that something like the sound of a car tire crushing a plastic track-and-field trophy or a pair of "old headphones that don't work anymore" (which is shown in the video and audible on the soundtrack) can help to relieve the "stress and anxiety" of living in a highly competitive, success-driven society, Asha exudes serenity and calmness. However, when shown in a profile shot, biting her thumbnail while watching her own video on YouTube, the girl appears noticeably anxious or unsure of something, perhaps as a result of the low number of "views"—only twelve—that her ASMR performance has amassed. Interestingly, while Samuelson reads aloud the title of Asha's video ("Crushing Your Worries—Crunchy and Soft Crushing"), he does not mention those dozen YouTube views, thus depriving visually impaired audiences of the opportunity to intuit the cause of her nervousness.

Similarly, in director Leo Gabriadzes's horror film *Unfriended* (2014), many of the unique typographical features of online communication are not conveyed by Claudia Dunn, the vocal performer hired by Media Access Group at WGBH to help vision-impaired audiences keep up with its ceaseless stream of printed text. All of the Facebooking, Googling, iMessaging, and Skyping that takes place in the film, and which appears to be contained on a teenaged girl's Macintosh laptop, would be difficult for anyone—blind or otherwise, and regardless of age—to fully comprehend in terms of the frequency and quickness with which words appear on the screen. As such, we should not be surprised that Dunn's AD does not capture that textual density, which includes the keyboard-typing characters' heavy use of abbreviations (e.g., "something's srsly wrong"), ALL CAPS (e.g., "why don't u KILL URSELF lol"), ellipses (e.g., "no . . . why?"), emoticons (e.g., ";)"), elongated vowels (e.g., "heeeeeeellllloooooooooo"), and superfluous punctuation (e.g., "ready to play the game??????"). None of those slang words, linguistic modifiers, and intentional misspellings or grammatical errors are rendered audibly, leaving AD users in the proverbial dark when it comes to accessing the novel ways in which *Unfriended*'s technologically savvy high schoolers communicate their gnawing fears about the secret identity of a killer online in a language all their own.

Another horror film whose narrative is predicated on young people's technical mastery over something that ultimately threatens to control their "always online" lives is director Daniel Goldhaber's *Cam* (2018). Concerning a camgirl named Alice (Madeline Brewer) whose live strip shows are hosted by a website called FreeGirlsLive.com, this production and its accompanying AD (currently available for listening via Netflix) track her gradual realization that someone else—a carbon copy of herself who stages strip shows inside an exact replication of Alice's own home studio—has taken over her livestreams and poses a threat not only to her livelihood but also to her very existence. Relatedly, both the film and the AD track emphasize how the protagonist (whose virtual "stage name" is "Lola_Lola") is one among many young women earning a living in this way, in front of laptop cameras and under pseudonyms or false wigs that tellingly *reveal* rather than mask their true identities. During one of *Cam*'s many montage sequences, a quick succession of shots showing other camgirls of varying ages, body sizes, ethnicities, and skin tones appears on a computer monitor, in short bursts of simulated sexual activity interspersed with "LOADING . . ." screens. As described by the AD voicer, the sequence proceeds in the following way:

> Various webcam shows of women appear. A scantily clad woman spanks another. A naked brunette woman checks her phone. A black-haired woman swings a cat-o-nine tails. A naked woman puts a gag ball in her mouth. A woman in a blue wig reads from a book. A dark-haired woman heats a poker in a fire. Two blonde women dance. A black-haired woman in a leopard print jacket. A naked blonde woman reads a book. A naked woman covered in blue glitter paint. A woman with black braided hair lies on her stomach on a bed.

What stands out about this AD is how hair colors and hairstyles are what distinguish yet connect these strangely depersonalized women. Along with the furrowed brows discussed earlier, this head-topping trait is mentioned repeatedly within *Cam* and other AD-supported horror films. Indeed, it is often how individual characters in horror films are introduced to listeners, who might otherwise be forced to rely on other, potentially problematic distinguishing features in order to form a mental picture of those characters' physical appearance.

For example, Gore Verbinski's *The Ring* (2002), a US remake of Hideo Nakata's 1998 film *Ring*, begins inside a girl's bedroom, where two teenagers discuss an urban legend about a cursed videotape while watching TV. Before Katie (Amber Tamblyn) and Becca (Rachael Bella) say each other's names, the film's AD voicer (Marsha Bartenetti of Pixelogic Media) refers to them as "the blonde" and "the brunette," choosing generic terms for the Caucasian American characters' hair color rather than noting more specific details about their clothing, eye color, physical size, skin tones, or other visual elements to delineate between the two. On the one hand, this points a predictive finger toward the eventual presence of another girl—the long-haired ghost Samara (Daveigh Chase)—who will later manifest as the film's psychically endowed, technologically birthed "monster," one that notably crawls out of another TV set near the end of the narrative. Indeed, that nightmarish figure, like her Japanese predecessor Sadako (Rie Inō), is practically *all hair*—at least, that which grows from her head and obscures most of her pale white face. On the other hand, Bartenetti's repeated use of the descriptors "the blonde" and "the brunette" throughout the opening scene of *The Ring* is in keeping with the AD industry's tendency to single out hair as an easy, effective, and generally nonoffensive way to describe characters. Indeed, it follows a pattern that continues to haunt horror films today, at least those that are supported with AD in which hair is repeatedly foregrounded as one of this body genre's most enduring sites of meaning.[17] If, as an apparent point of contrast, the audio-described online release of Alistair Legrand's *Clinical* (2017) is practically "clinical" in the way the voicer introduces the main character, a psychiatrist named Jane Mathis (Vinessa Shaw) whose "high cheekbones are cast in shadows" and who "wears darks slacks and a loose shirt," it is only because that voicer prefaces these remarks by noting that the protagonist's "blonde hair is pulled back in a ponytail."

In fact, there is much about Dr. Mathis's physical demeanor and facial features during the opening scene of *Clinical* that is *not* mentioned, including what I see as her exhausted and probably bored expression. Partially indicated by a rubbing of the temples, the character's fatigued look communicates the monotony and long hours of her appointment-based professional work. But it also serves to contrast the sudden terror that flashes on her face when—opening a door to a waiting room late at night—she is shocked to see "a brunette with large dark eyes [putting] a shard of glass to her bloody palm." The unidentified AD voicer, whose articulation, pronunciation, and rate of speaking sound eerily similar to that of Shaw's character (so much so that is sometimes difficult to pull those voices apart, making it seem as though the hero is narrating her own dreadful story), accurately if robotically describes the brunette's violent actions: lashing out and slashing at her doctor before putting the "glass shard to her own neck at the jugular." However, the voicer fails to mention that the young patient's entire body—not just her palm—was already covered in blood before she attacked Dr. Mathis, indicating that something more nefarious than mental instability lies at the heart of her ultimately suicidal act.

I have sought to underscore the instrumentality of AD not only as an accessibility feature of today's home-video and streaming releases—one that, as the previous chapter laid out, has roots in silent-era accommodations of visually impaired moviegoers—but also as a technological tool that grants *all audiences* an array of viewing and listening positions outside of their own embodied spectatorship. Although, as an academic subject, AD has primarily been of interest to scholars in audiovisual translation studies, anyone who seeks to get at the cinematic medium's surplus of signifying details would find this service useful and perhaps even insightful as a second set of eyes.[18] One could even say that AD's most significant contribution to the field lies in its *inability* to fully convey the "multitude" of visual signifiers that Seymour Chatman believes is "more than any viewer could mentally specify" or conjure through words.[19] Here, the narratologist's own words evoke Raymond Bellour's notion of "textual volume," which emphasizes "the complexity and the multiplicity of the operations that exist within the film."[20] Textual volume makes something like audiovisual translation from one medium to another a necessarily challenging affair. Bellour went further, claiming that the cinematic text is "unattainable" because it is *unquotable*, meaning that no written or spoken analysis—or, for that matter, description—of a scene or a shot would do justice to the semiotic excess that defines the moving image as a *temporal* if also technological art form.

If, as Roland Barthes remarked nearly fifty years ago (in his 1975 essay "Introduction to the Structural Analysis of Narrative"), "*everything*, in one way or another, is significant," then it would be foolish for contemporary audiences to expect even a modicum of that textual fullness—the abundance of meaningful content with which the cinematic image is associated—to make its way onto an AD track. And yet, because the French poststructuralist stressed that all texts are irreducibly plural, weaving together voices or codes that cannot be tied to a single point of authorial origin, one can also make the case that the addition of *other voices* (those of the audio describers) within a narrative context where characters are prone to question one another's belief (in a higher power or some other supernatural entity) and claim to hear "voices" of their own (from some other dimension or from the darkest recesses of their homes) enhances horror's sense-making appeals. As a sense-making device, AD enables audiences to see horror aurally and, in doing so, brings latent features of the genre to the surface. By sparking heightened spectatorial awareness to certain facial tics and other outward signs of a character's inner feelings (including furrowed brows), AD therefore distinguishes itself as an accessibility tool that is simultaneously shallow and deep, skimming the surface of the diegetic world while providing insights into behaviors for which sight alone would seem to be insufficient as a means of perceiving the underlying meaning of things. Although it would appear to be reductive in the way that it verbally sums up "untranslatable" moving images and takes up a perspective on narrative events as "feebly and one-dimensionally" as the most superficial reader of a text would, this accessibility feature can lead to a more productive set of critical methods than what has thus far been applied to cinematic horror as a body genre.[21] Those methods might look or sound like the one I have advocated throughout this book, an approach that harnesses intersensoriality as a way of reckoning with the genre's centering of irrationality alongside its fixation on broken, fractured, and mangled bodies.

The sorts of mistakes that I have gestured toward in this chapter—those glaring errors or subtle misjudgments on the part of AD providers that are perhaps a result of the "inherent limitations" to which any descriptive technology is bound (since it entails a refusal to "interfere with the semiotic channels the target audience does have access to: the dialogues and relevant sound effects")—hint at a different sort of broken, fractured, and mangled corporeality: that of the film body itself, a technological "beast" marked by all-too-relatable human failings.[22] Moreover, those technical mistakes are rhetorically *meaningful*, prompting listeners to question other audiences' prioritizing of narrative information and to more closely scrutinize their own potentially divergent interpretations of otherwise carefully narrated events. As I have already suggested with regard to its AD, the "Follows" of *It Follows* is just as important as the film's titular "It," and not only because the visual representation of events frequently takes a backseat to their aural recounting, which often precedes them. Through a considered look at, and listen to, that particular film as well as others from the past two decades, one can conclude that AD does not always correspond to what viewers might see on the screen (i.e., it does not "follow"). As a result, listeners who rely on this service might not follow or comprehend a scene as it was meant to be received by its "authors." An instance of this occurs on the AD track of David Robert Mitchell's film when zoo Digital's voicer describes the main character, Jay, peering through "half-drawn blinds," though they are, in fact, curtains. Seemingly innocuous, this fleeting moment is significant insofar as the very act of looking—past a window-covering that is meant to obscure, to keep the light out, and which is correspondingly mistaken for "blinds" (another in a long list of disabling terms)—is what is being described. Furthermore, that diegetic act of looking is what is being *emulated* auditorily, through an extradiegetic voice that visualizes, and through a set of ears that could be said to *see*. Whether one's "heart" or any other organ of the body is also prepared to witness the more distastefully hideous, frequently misogynistic things for which this genre is known is a question that I take up in the coda that follows.

# CODA

## Believing Women and Writing Tomorrow's Histories of the Horror Film

Today, over a half-century after the publication of Carlos Clarens's pioneering book *An Illustrated History of the Horror Film*, one can no longer accurately claim (as he did in 1967) that this once-disreputable genre "has not attracted sufficient critical attention."[1] Indeed, time has been kind to this most unkind category of cultural production, and countless scholarly tomes alongside an equally large number of journalistic and online reviews can now be cited as evidence not only of horror's enduring power to fascinate and frighten audiences around the world, but also of its vaunted status as a widely respected form of cinematic storytelling. For all the changes in public opinion and critical estimation that have occurred during those intervening decades, however, much of Clarens's book—published on the cusp of the following year's genre-redefining theatrical releases *Night of the Living Dead* (1968) and *Rosemary's Baby* (1968)—remains relevant to the current state of horror as a highly fictional yet politically resonant "safe space" in which to work through some fairly treacherous real-world problems. From the darkly satirical takes on social inequality and systemic racism on view in Jordan Peele's *Get Out* (2017) and *Us* (2019) to the lacerating looks at toxic masculinity, casual misogyny, and domestic abuse that make Zach Cregger's *Barbarian* (2022) and Alex Garland's *Men* (2022) such noteworthy releases in light of the #MeToo movement, a number of recently produced motion pictures have *re*-redefined the genre, literalizing the allegorical elements of earlier horror films (often with unflinching directness) and grounding their fantastical scenarios in realistic evocations of a world—one recognizably our own—descending into a truly hellish state where right-wing extremism, police brutality, online harassment, and other nightmarish things are ever-present fixtures of waking life.

Today's terrors—the ones put to practical but potentially triggering use in the aforementioned films—are decidedly gendered. Much of the frisson that audiences experience when watching a movie like Steven Soderbergh's *Unsane* (2018) or John Lee's *False Positive* (2021), according to Kylie Cheung, comes from seeing and hearing deceptively "disbelieving" male characters questioning women's sanity or gaslighting them to the point that they no longer trust themselves (or, rather, their own sensing organs, including their eyes and ears).[2] Of course, disbelief has long been an ingrained feature of cinematic horror—both diegetically in the person of the prototypically rational figure of science who seeks a sensible explanation for seemingly supernatural occurrences, and extradiegetically in terms of our own spectatorial tendency to question the plausibility of narratives in which monsters exist, spirits materialize, and even the most levelheaded or rightminded of people act irrationally, impulsively, or immorally (i.e., abusively, violently, wrongly). But Cheung justly underscores the frequency with which men assign credibility in contemporary stories of female imprisonment, trauma, and victimhood. Few readers would challenge her contention that the palpable fears experienced by Tess (Georgina Campbell) in *Barbarian* and Harper (Jessie Buckley) in *Men*—written off by male characters as the ravings of madwomen—gained layers of significance beyond what these films' male writer-directors had imagined once *Roe v. Wade* (the landmark 1973 US Supreme Court decision protecting women's reproductive rights) was overturned within a few weeks of their theatrical and online releases in the summer of 2022. Indeed, her remarks about the basement-like deeper meanings of *Barbarian* (which suggests, "beneath all the bloodshed and limb-hacking," that "trust and believability are determined based on gender") are well-reasoned responses to the way that *reason itself* has been codified as a masculinist asset in this and other female-focalized films of the past few years.[3]

One wonders what Clarens, who passed away in 1987 at the age of fifty-six, might have said about such developments had he lived long enough to witness this recent, post-Recession renaissance in cinematic horror. As a historian who tended to make value judgments of films based on relative levels of gore and gruesomeness, singling out a handful of studio classics of the 1930s—Universal's *Dracula* (1931), *Frankenstein* (1931), and *The Mummy* (1932)—as the epitome of "good" horror (in contrast to innumerable "bad" films from the 1960s that, according to him, lacked their predecessors' "imagination, taste, and restraint"), Clarens likely would have balked at the extreme levels of carnage and brutality that infuse even the most thoughtful and politically progressive motion pictures from the past decade (and from various corners of the world).[4] From *Prevenge* (2016), British writer-director Alice Lowe's darkly humorous take on the slasher subgenre, to *Revenge* (2017), French writer-director Coralie Fargeat's feminist rape-revenge thriller, contemporary horror films frequently push representations of violence to an extreme level of affective intensity that would surely have tested the genre's most ardent champions only a few decades ago. Trumping them both, *Titane* (2021), writer-director Julia Ducournau's follow-up to her controversial, critically adored coming-of-age film *Raw* (*Grave*, 2016), takes viewers on a harrowing trip into the murderously psychopathic protagonist's twisted subconscious, fleshed out in the form of a car fetishist's desire for something more metallically tangible and polymorphously perverse than what she has thus far found in human relationships.

As one of only a few body-horror films to have been officially selected for competition at the Cannes Film Festival, the Palme d'Or–winning *Titane* was unleashed on a public becoming ever-more-attuned to graphically violent images of anatomical agony. The latter include shots of Alexia (Agathe Rousselle), the main character (whom we first see working as a hood-twerking model at an auto show), plunging a long hairpin into the ear of an overzealous male fan and then using that same weapon in an unsuccessful attempt to abort her unborn baby—the product of her sexual dalliance with a vintage Cadillac. Like Lowe's *Prevenge*, which tells the story of a pregnant widow who, grief-stricken after the death of her husband, is driven to kill innocent bystanders at the behest of her fetus, Ducournau's film maps mental illness onto a social milieu where a different sort of disorder—virulent misogyny—seems to have infected a populace predisposed to distrusting women and denying them the right to control their own bodies. The fact that these female serial killers' murderous urges and wildly destructive actions can be so easily dismissed as outward signs of their loosening grip on reality only contributes to the unease that comes from watching contemporary horror films in which questions of belief are broached in the absence of both supernatural phenomena and scientific explanations, and in which images of spectacularized human suffering (gouged eyes, impaled torsos, slashed Achilles tendons) substitute for the kind of atmospheric dread or indirect fear that Clarens advocated in his 1967 study.

Not for nothing does Hulu's online release of *False Positive*, a modern-day throwback to *Rosemary's Baby* cowritten by director John Lee and the film's lead, Ilana Glazer, begin with printed text atop a black backdrop informing audiences that its content "may be extra sensitive to some viewers." That brief trigger warning, which immediately precedes production company A24's practically ubiquitous logo slicing into view onscreen, readies us for *False Positive*'s opening image: a flashforward long shot of Glazer's psychologically traumatized character (a New York marketing executive named Lucy) traipsing toward the camera in slow motion as wailing police sirens and flashing lights periodically illuminate a darkening sky (fig. 9.1). Her long hair thrashes wildly in the wind, and her impassive face appears to be coated with blood following what we later learn was a deadly altercation with her unscrupulous fertility doctor. As gynecological horrors go, this is strong, disturbing stuff: a lurid tableau of female suffering and vengeance-seeking front-loaded into a

**Figure 9.1:** A traumatized woman wearing a blood-speckled shirt, later identified as the protagonist Lucy, traipses toward the camera during the opening moments of *False Positive*.

hallucinatory story about madness and maternity that leaves its most shocking displays of violence until the narrative's back end. During the film's penultimate scene, Lucy finally confronts the devilishly goateed Dr. Hindle (Pierce Brosnan) at his clinic only to discover that he has been inseminating patients with his own sperm, vials of which are stored inside a refrigerator that she dutifully smashes to the ground before bashing his face in. Most shockingly, she also finds the female fetus that, unbeknownst to her, had been forcibly removed from her body to make way for male twins.

This latter act of violation—a horrific twist on the medical procedure known as "selective reduction"—is doubly denotative insofar as the infant boys (who represent an extension of Hindle's bloodline) have replaced and taken precedence over the daughter to whom Lucy had expected to give birth. The twins not only deprive Lucy of the mother-daughter bonding of which she had long dreamt; they also metaphorically extend the gendered privilege of the two fathers—including the protagonist's husband, Adrian (Justin Theroux), himself a physician—into the next generation of men who will almost certainly exert control over women's reproductive lives. But the most unsettling aspect of *False Positive*, which concludes with shots of the female protagonist gently putting her tiny reclaimed fetus to her lactating breasts (which dispense milk rather than the motor oil that drips from Alexia's nipples in *Titane*) and magically resuscitating the previously deceased, now-suckling baby girl, is the frequency with which men as well as women—including other pregnant members of Lucy's support group—attribute her increasingly delusional state to "mommy brain."

Also known as "momnesia," that colloquial expression has been widely debated in the popular press over the past decade, with scientists and cultural commentators weighing in on its appropriateness as a catchall description of the biological/neurological and chemical/hormonal changes that might occur during pregnancy or throughout the postpartum period (when sleep deprivation and mental as well as physical fatigue are likely to occur). From memory loss to mood disorders such as depression and a reduced ability to feel empathy, "mommy brain" covers a broad spectrum of cognitive and emotional effects. However, no consensus has emerged within the scientific community as to whether such conditions are strictly maternal outcomes of being "with child" or are evidence of some deeper, more generalized problem endemic to a society of overworked, under-rested individuals. Indeed, the inconclusiveness of scientific findings, with just as many psychotherapists and behavioral specialists speculating that "mommy brain" is *real* as there are naysayers arguing the opposite, means that audiences are likely to experience the same confusion that Lucy does when, at the meetup of expectant mothers, she is informed that childbirth will almost surely bring as much *loss*—of self-control and possibly of gray matter—as it will joy.[5] Regardless, the mental fog in which she (and we) stumble throughout much of *False Positive*'s strangely familiar yet disorienting narrative could be said to blind her (if not us) to the possibility that nearly everything leading up to and including the film's final breastfeeding image (a shot that, in the words of one reviewer, "spells out a metaphor that ought to have been left to suggestion") is a *delusion*.[6] As such, the creeping paranoia that naturally comes from living within a patriarchal society, where men have an "enormous amount of control over what happens to a woman before, during and after her pregnancy," is deflected onto an addled mind that can no longer distinguish between reality and fantasy.[7] In fact, such fantastical elements, coming after we have witnessed Lucy enduring not only a series of experimental IVF treatments but also the cajoling of her own husband to choose male offspring over female, are precisely what link this and other contemporary releases—including those like *Bird Box* (2018) and *Huesera: The Bone Woman* (2022) that have inspired critics to invoke the "mommy brain" metaphor in their online reviews—to an earlier generation of horror films likewise preoccupied with the gendering of belief and disbelief.[8]

As a spokesperson from that earlier generation (and as a cultural historian of the generation before that), Clarens understood the important role that *belief*—the faith or trust that a person places in the existence of something or someone—plays in classic examples of the genre. Be they mad-scientist films revolving around the reanimation of dead bodies or the earliest precursors to today's zombie movies in which voodoo priests, witch doctors, and other practitioners in the "dark arts" cast a convincing spell over their own audiences, the various motion pictures that have been categorized as "horror" since the 1930s often require a suspension of disbelief before the spectator is able to side with the most irrationally minded of souls, including those who started out as rationally minded or scientifically inclined at the beginning of their respective narratives. But Clarens also concluded that many of the moviegoers who were metaphorically coming of age as modern horror fans around the time of his book's publication in the late 1960s not only sought relief from the escalating problems of that period through ostensibly escapist forms of entertainment but also wanted that big-screen entertainment to resemble offscreen reality more closely than it had a generation earlier. In other words, audiences needed something tangibly real in which to believe, a diegetic universe similar to the increasingly turbulent world outside movie theaters, lest they lose their "faith" in the healing powers of those films' supernatural scenarios. Explaining to his readers why he sought to recuperate a genre that had left so many of his colleagues cold, Clarens states, "What seems to put the reviewers off horror films, what prevents them from surrendering their critical resistance, is the frequent—and necessary—depiction of the fantastic."[9]

This prejudice, he argues, is not as apparent in the adjacent spheres of the plastic arts and other visual arts, where one need not "believe in angels and sphinxes" in order to appreciate "a painting by Fra Angelico or Max Ernst." Clarens asks, "Is it indispensable that one be a Christian to read Saint John in Patmos?," extending his study's rhetorical reach into biblical literature, before making the following remarks:

> The flowering of the fantastic in the last century, the period that produced William Blake, Odilon Redon, Gustave Moreau, Gustave Doré, and Robert Louis Stevenson, accompanied the most remarkable strides in the field of science. The more rationalistic a time becomes the more it needs the escape valve of the fantastic. This delicate balance is even more obvious today when the demand for the fantastic (and the horrific) has reached a never before attained height, coinciding with the peak period of scientific technological development.[10]

In that last sentence, the author gestures toward a paradox that was becoming more apparent to readers at the time of his book's publication, and which has further crystallized throughout the intervening years. Indeed, subsequent generations of cinematic horror, leading up to the latest theatrical and streaming releases (films like *Get Out* and *Us*, which have inspired a new legion of fans to celebrate the genre's progressiveness as a vehicle for confronting present-day sociopolitical issues), only strengthen Clarens's claims, even as his distaste for "pornographic gore" seems like a relic from some earlier, bloodless period in cultural production and reception far removed from our own.

Although his book has been said to epitomize "longstanding critical orthodoxy" insofar as it privileges horror movies from the distant past that had the "good taste" to "not show much actual horror" (thus leaving it "primarily to the viewer's imagination"), Clarens was not as prescriptive as he has been made out to be.[11] Nor did he believe that the genre's sole purpose was to instill fear in audiences. He admits that the classic monster movies produced at Universal and other Hollywood studios during the Depression era (e.g., the previously mentioned *Dracula*, *Frankenstein*, and *The Mummy*) "had lost their power to horrify" by the time he set about writing his *Illustrated History of the Horror Film*.[12] More importantly, while he might have exhibited a nostalgic longing for that golden age of cinematic horror, Clarens understood why films were becoming bloodier, less atmospherically suggestive, in the years following *Psycho*'s 1960 release, surmising that "a supremely violent age like ours calls for unprecedented violence in its aesthetic manifestations."[13] Those words, which are especially pertinent to our present-day situation, can help to shed light on why a host of "torture porn" films such as *Saw* (2004), *Hostel* (2005), and *The Devil's Rejects* (2005) sprang up amid the first news reports of prisoner abuse at Abu Ghraib, Guantánamo Bay, and CIA "black sites" nearly two decades ago (as part of the US War on Terror), and why more recent splatter-filled productions such as *The Hunt* (2020)—a "silly horror-satire" about a group of liberal "elites" who kidnap and attempt to kill a group of socially conservative "deplorables" in Croatia—have been prematurely pulled from theaters amid mass shootings and public debates about the handling of hot-button issues in popular culture.[14]

Like Clarens, I do not believe that "people go to horror movies exclusively to be scared." As anyone who has watched Alfred Hitchcock's genre-redefining film (or for that matter *Saw*, *Hostel*, or *The Devil's Rejects*) in a packed or partially filled theater can attest, audiences derive several forms of mental and physical satisfaction from cinematic horror, which might elicit laughter or snickers as frequently as it does screams or shivers, and which serves more than one "purpose" (e.g., allegorically, narratively, politically), as numerous scholars have pointed out. In this book, I have built upon Clarens's and subsequent researchers' writings to explore some of those purposes, explaining in the process why a combined irrational-intersensorial mode of critical-corporeal reflection is needed if we are to glean the paradoxical appeals of horror as a frequently hilarious yet troubling manifestation of imagined and real-world fears. Over the years, several film theorists, including Noël Carroll, Mathias Clasen, Michael Levine, and André Loiselle, have waxed philosophical on the power of fictional representations to generate the kind of negative emotions associated with the genre (e.g., anxiety, dread, revulsion, shock). The genre's sundry pleasures have likewise been taken up by Katerina Bantinaki, Cynthia Freeland, Matt Hills, and other academics with a vested interest in those positively valanced experiences that Clarens had only hinted at decades earlier (when he wrote about the wide "variety of emotion" and high "degree of involvement" that distinguishes horror from other cultural and aesthetic categories).[15] Besides its capacity to entice and repulse in equal measure, one of the central paradoxes of horror, according to these scholars, is its ability to stimulate apparently contradictory feelings even as it foregrounds its own fictiveness through mildly or wildly farfetched scenarios and fantastical beings: the kind of syntactical and semantic "stuff" that requires suspension of disbelief or at the very least some small amount of willful irrationality on the part of spectators. If, as Clarens claims, "we are forced to cheer on, and at the same time be terrified by, the monsters and fiends of horror films," then a more fundamental ingredient—that of *belief*—is required at the diegetic and extradiegetic levels before any such spectatorial realignments take place.

I set out to write this book to consider the broader implications of onscreen and offscreen irrationality within a national context where—in a manner befitting the *Purge* franchise (2013–21)—class divisions have deepened, corporate malfeasance continues to go unpunished, and partisan politics are contributing to a steep rise in senseless hate crimes and violent extremist uprisings across the United States. While much of my analysis in the preceding pages has stuck to textual elements rather than broader contextual concerns, it was written during a calamitous, dramatically drawn-out moment in time that future historians will likely look back at with a mixture of disappointment and sadness (and not only because it encompasses the ongoing COVID-19 health crisis). From those future historians' distant vantage, the period from the Great Recession of 2008 to the January 6 Capitol insurrection of 2021 will surely be seen as one of social inequality and political instability filled with its own horror-like "madness," in the form of angry mobs, dangerous conspiratorial movements, and disingenuous leaders who have somehow managed to gain the electorate's trust amid personal scandals. As such, any present-day discussion of the thematic emphasis placed on belief and disbelief in representative texts, ranging from older cult films such as *Carnival of Souls* (1962) and *Don't Look Now* (1973) to contemporary classics-in-the-making such as *The Babadook* (2014), *It Follows* (2014), and *Saint Maud* (2019), is necessarily informed by the various "crises" that have occurred over the past few years, be they public-health concerns tied to the global pandemic or the equally existential quandaries accompanying the spread of "deepfake" technologies, synthetically simulated "realties," and artificial intelligence (AI) software applications like ChatGPT.

In keeping with the times, I have adopted what might appear to be a counterintuitive, irrational approach to horror throughout this book, posing unconventional questions about its dueling tendencies to entice and repulse audiences while spotlighting several overlooked case studies that have not received the same scholarly attention lavished on many of the aforementioned films. After considering how filmmakers have traditionally relied upon the siloed senses of sight, hearing, and touch to facilitate (if not ensure) characters' conversion from disbelief to belief, I entangled those and other less frequently discussed senses—smell and taste—so that the genre's paradoxical appeals and tendency toward *humor* come into sharper focus. Just as things can be said to smell or taste "funny" (repellently so in horror films), so too can we make what might seem to be weird, ridiculous, or absurdist critical moves—for instance, by "looking" with our ears, "hearing" with our eyes, and holding horror films up to the nose or the tongue in search of those traits of the genre that tend to evade our mental if not physical grasp. Having already explored horror's status as a "body genre" in a previous book devoted to the subject, I have endeavored to flesh out my earlier writing and reveal how motion pictures' physical and sensorial solicitations to the audience—narratively motivated invitations to participate in their various forms of corporeal "play" (as disgusting or terrifying though that might be)—operate in conjunction with the cognitive "work" needed to piece together clues, solve mysteries, discern the killer's identity, or simply follow a conventional yet twist-laden plot as it moves from one gruesome and/or comedic set piece to the next.[16]

The structure, scope, and focus of this book precluded the chance to offer a deeper evaluation of deceptively humorous comedy-horror films. However, from beginning to end I have sought to engage Noël Carroll's foundational work in this area, specifically with regard to the genre's paradoxical appeals, in an effort to balance his *cognition*-leaning approach (which emphasizes the mind) with a *feeling*-based approach (which emphasizes the body).[17] Though he would be the first to remind us that emotions—be they the negatively valanced ones associated with horror (including depression, paranoia, and dread) or the positively valanced ones associated with comedy (including elation, liberation, and happiness)—involve physiological and psychological "feelings," Carroll posits *cognition* as the essential precondition that makes it possible for movie audiences to judge whether something is spine-tingling or rib-tickling (notably, two experiential states that, however metaphorical they might be, draw attention to those audiences' *physical* rather than mental selves). That is, only by making "categorical assessments" of concern-based construals, he argues, can those "psycho-physical agitations" sparked by a genre film ("such as that of feeling our flesh 'crawl'") be translated into a sensible response to onscreen stimuli.[18] Not wishing to dispute these claims, I have sought to supplement them with a slightly more adventurous consideration of the phenomenological aspects of the comedy-horror union, which can be palpably perceived and indeed felt through the body's senses, including that of touch. In the end, it is hoped that the usefulness of such an approach, beyond its hermeneutical value, becomes apparent to readers who might find their own view of the world changed as a result of looking at horror films through other sense organs besides the eyes.

# NOTES

## Introduction

1 Tony Magistrale, *Abject Terrors: Surveying the Modern and Postmodern Horror Film* (Peter Lang, 2005), 64.
2 François Truffaut, *Hitchcock*, rev. ed. (Simon & Schuster, 1985), 269.
3 Stephen Rebello, *Alfred Hitchcock and the Making of "Psycho"* (Dembner, 1990).
4 Joseph W. Smith III, *The "Psycho" File: A Comprehensive Guide to Hitchcock's Classic Shocker* (McFarland, 2009), 176.
5 Linda Williams, "Discipline and Fun: *Psycho* and Postmodern Cinema," in *Alfred Hitchcock's "Psycho": A Casebook*, ed. Robert Kolker (Oxford University Press, 2004), 181.
6 Adam Lowenstein, *Shocking Representation: Historical Trauma, National Cinema, and the Modern Horror Film* (Columbia University Press, 2005), 9–10.
7 Lowenstein, *Shocking Representation*, 9–10.
8 Williams, "Discipline and Fun," 177.
9 Patrick Fuery, *Madness and Cinema: Psychoanalysis, Spectatorship and Culture* (Palgrave Macmillan, 2004), 94.
10 Fuery, *Madness and Cinema*.
11 Peter Hutchings, *The Horror Film* (New York: Routledge, 2014), 61.
12 Hutchings, *Horror Film*, 61.
13 Sven Hroar Klempe, *Sound and Reason: Synesthesia as Metacognition* (Palgrave Macmillan, 2022), 14.
14 Ophelia Deroy, ed., *Sensory Blending: On Synaesthesia and Related Phenomena* (Oxford University Press, 2017).

15 Lawrence E. Marks, "Synesthesia, Then and Now," in Deroy, ed., *Sensory Blending*, 19.

16 Marks, "Synesthesia, Then and Now," 19.

17 Jean-Pierre Ternaux, "Synesthesia: A Multimodal Combination of Senses," *Leonardo* 36, no. 4 (2003): 321–22.

18 Ternaux, "Synesthesia," 321–22.

19 Ternaux.

20 Richard E. Cytowic, "Synesthesia: Phenomenology and Neuropsychology: A Review of Current Knowledge," *Psyche* 2, no. 10 (July 1995), https://journalpsyche.org/files/0xaa34.pdf. See also Richard E. Cytowic, *Synesthesia: A Union of the Senses* (Springer-Verlag, 1989), 5; and Casey Hynes, "Seven Ate Nine: Seeing Is (and Isn't) Believing When You Have Synesthesia," Magazine, August 1, 2013, https://the-magazine.org/22/seven-ate-nine/index.html.

21 Allyson C. DeMaagd, *Dissensuous Modernism: Women Writers, the Senses, and Technology* (University Press of Florida, 2022), 162n7. See also David Howes and Constance Classen, *Ways of Sensing: Understanding the Senses in Society* (Routledge, 2014), 11.

22 DeMaagd, *Dissensuous Modernism*, 9.

23 Caroline A. Jones, *Eyesight Alone: Clement Greenburg's Modernism and the Bureaucratization of the Senses* (Chicago: University of Chicago Press, 2005), 395; DeMaagd, *Dissensuous Modernism*, 9.

24 Howes and Classen, *Ways of Sensing*, 153.

25 Lawrence E. Sullivan, "Sound and Senses: Toward a Hermeneutics of Performance," *History of Religions* 26, no. 1 (1986): 6.

26 Howes and Classen, *Ways of Sensing*, 153.

27 Steven Connor, "Edison's Teeth: Touching Hearing," in *Hearing Cultures: Essays on Sound, Listening and Modernity*, ed. Veit Erlmann (Berg, 2004), 153.

28 Connor, "Edison's Teeth," 153.

29 Tim Ingold, *Perception of the Environment: Essays in Livelihood, Dwelling and Skill* (Routledge, 2000), 261.

30 Thorsten Gieser, "Sensing and Knowing Noises: An Acoustemology of the Chainsaw," *Social Anthropology* 27, no. 1 (2019): 50–61.

31 Gieser, "Sensing and Knowing Noises."

32 Gieser, 50.

33 For an elaboration of the reciprocal relationship between the skin, musculature, and viscera of audiences and those of motion pictures, see Jennifer M. Barker, *The Tactile Eye: Touch and the Cinematic Experience* (University of California Press, 2009).

34 Isabel Cristina Pinedo, *Recreational Terror: Women and the Pleasures of Horror Film Viewing* (State University of New York Press, 1997), 20.

35 Isabel Cristina Pinedo, "Postmodern Elements of the Contemporary Horror Film," in *The Horror Film*, ed. Stephen Prince (Rutgers University Press, 2004), 94.

36 Pinedo, "Postmodern Elements," 95.

37 Pinedo.

38 Pinedo, *Recreational Terror*, 48.

39 Pinedo, 25.

40 Pinedo, 24.

41 David Scott Diffrient, *Body Genre: Anatomy of the Horror Film* (University Press of Mississippi, 2023), 264–66.

42 In one sense, *The Terror* is like *The Horror of Party Beach* (1964), a cheesier drive-in movie from the same period. Directed by Del Tenney, the film features a scene in which a white, pipe-smoking scientist, Dr. Gavin (Allan Laurel), chides his African American housemaid, Eulabelle (Eulabelle Moore), for her "ridiculous" belief in voodoo, telling her that there must be a more "reasonable explanation" for the recent death of a girl besides that of an evil creature "lurking and creeping and crawling around out there."

43 Lanyon writes to a London-based legal practitioner named Utterson that "I saw what I saw, I heard what I heard, and my soul sickened at it." Robert Louis Stevenson, *"Dr. Jekyll and Mr. Hyde," and "An Inland Voyage"* (Bernhard Tauchnitz, 1886), 91.

44 Ken Hanke, *A Critical Guide to Horror Film Series* (Routledge, 2014).

45 Matt Glasby, *The Book of Horror: The Anatomy of Fear in Film* (Frances Lincoln, 2020).

46 James Palmer and Michael Riley, "Seeing, Believing, and 'Knowing' in Narrative Film: *Don't Look Now* Revisited," *Literature Film Quarterly* 23, no. 1 (1995): 14–25.

47 See Vivian Sobchack, *The Address of the Eye: A Phenomenology of Film Experience* (Princeton University Press, 1992); Steven Shaviro, *The Cinematic Body* (University of Minnesota Press, 1993); Julian Hanich, *Cinematic*

*Emotion in Horror Films and Thrillers* (Routledge, 2010); and Adam Daniel, *Affective Intensities and Evolving Horror Forms* (Edinburgh University Press, 2020).

48 Christian Ferencz-Flatz and Julian Hanich, "What Is Film Phenomenology?," *Studia Phaenomenologica* 16 (2016): 40.

## Chapter 1

1 Although photographed in black and white, this opening sequence of the 1964 production of *Witchcraft* might dredge up memories of the opening credits of a color film produced one year earlier: Alfred Hitchcock's *The Birds* (1963), which likewise shows the onscreen text being shredded into "ragged fragments" (as if pecked apart by the titular creatures that appear as black smudges fluttering past the camera). For more information about the possible meanings of this sequence, designed by James S. Pollak, and its similarity to graphic designer Saul Bass's equally austere, typographically slashing contribution to Hitchcock's earlier horror film *Psycho* (1960), see Randy Rasmussen, *"Psycho," "The Birds," and "Halloween": The Intimacy of Terror in Three Classic Films* (McFarland, 2014), 84.

2 Those names include American actor Lon Chaney, Jr., the star of dozens of studio-backed monster movies from the 1940s until his death in 1973, and British film director Don Sharp, who was best known for a number of Hammer-produced horror films that he helmed during the 1960s.

3 Neil Lerner, "Preface: Listening to Fear/Listening with Fear," in *Music in the Horror Film: Listening to Fear*, ed. Neil Lerner (Routledge, 2010), x.

4 Lerner, "Preface," ix.

5 Lerner.

6 Donal Henahan, "Philharmonic: Incarnations of Spring," *New York Times*, March 23, 1984.

7 Those entertainments include the zoetrope, the praxinoscope, and the phenakistiscope, which similarly endowed still images with the illusion of movement.

8 Thomas Elsaesser and Malte Hagener, *Film Theory: An Introduction Through the Senses* (Routledge, 2009), 85–90. An important volume on this subject is Linda Williams, ed., *Viewing Positions: Ways of Seeing Film* (Rutgers University Press, 1995).

9 Carol Clover, *Men, Women, and Chain Saws: Gender in the Modern Horror Film* (Princeton University Press, 1992), 167.

10 Tony Perrello, "A Parisian in Hollywood: Ocular Horror in the Films of Alexandre Aja," in *American Horror Film: The Genre at the Turn of the Millennium*, ed. Steffen Hantke (University Press of Mississippi, 2010), 19.

11 Perrello.

12 Stephen Prince, "Introduction: The Dark Genre and Its Paradoxes," in *The Horror Film*, ed. Stephen Prince (Rutgers University Press, 2004), 4.

13 Paul Mavis, "*Burn, Witch, Burn* (1962): A Classic Witchcraft Shocker You Must See!," Movies & Drinks, October 30, 2019, https://moviesanddrinks.com/2019/10/30/burn-witch-burn-1962-night-of-the-eagle-movie-review/.

14 Mavis, "*Burn, Witch, Burn* (1962)."

15 Douglas Buck, "*Burn, Witch, Burn*," Offscreen.com, March 8, 2020, https://offscreen.com/view/burn-witch-burn-sydney-hayers-1962.

16 AIP was a relatively small film company, run by entertainment lawyer Samuel Z. Arkoff and sales manager James H. Nicholson, more typically associated with teenpics and exploitation fare like *The Ghost in the Invisible Bikini* (1966).

17 Mavis, "*Burn, Witch, Burn* (1962)."

18 John M. Miller, "*Burn, Witch, Burn*," TCM.com, September 28, 2012, https://www.tcm.com/tcmdb/title/69924/burn-witch-burn#articles-reviews?articleId=518300. At the time of its stateside release, a critic for *The New York Times* (July 5, 1962), compared *Burn, Witch, Burn* to an even earlier witchcraft-themed film, calling it "the best outright goose-pimpler dealing specifically with [that subject] since *I Walked with a Zombie*."

19 Aaron Smuts, "Haunting the House from Within: Disbelief Mitigation and Spatial Experience," in *Dark Thoughts: Philosophic Reflections on Cinematic Horror*, ed. Steven Jay Schneider and Daniel Shaw (Scarecrow, 2003), 158–73.

20 Mike's comment is reminiscent of a line spoken by a minor character in Dario Argento's 1980 film *Inferno* who, when asked what he believes in, responds: "Whatever I can see and touch."

21 Jonathan Malcolm Lampley, *Women in the Horror Films of Vincent Price* (McFarland, 2011), 37.

22 Devorah Kalekin-Fishman and Kelvin E. Y. Low, "Introduction," in *Everyday Life in Asia: Social Perspectives on the Senses*, ed. Devorah Kalekin-Fishman and Kelvin E. Y. Low (Ashgate, 2010), 2.

23 Fishman and Low, "Introduction," 10.

24 David Howes and Constance Classen, *Ways of Sensing: Understanding the Senses in Society* (Routledge, 2014), 5.

25 Matthew Milner, "Review: *Ways of Sensing: Understanding the Senses in Society*," *American Historical Review* 120, no. 2 (2015): 568. Notably, Howes and Classen begin their book *Ways of Sensing*—the title of which alludes to John Berger's 1972 book, *Ways of Seeing*—by noting the inordinate amount of attention given by art critics and cultural historians to sight (relative to the other senses, which are not as highly valued in the West). The exalted status of sight as a "'noble' sense . . . associated with both spiritual and intellectual enlightenment," casts in relief the comparatively low standing of smell, taste, and touch, which—as "base" perceptual processes—cannot be so easily detached from the body. As they state, "In a society that emphasizes detachment and objectivity," sight, which "operates at a distance and requires no physical interaction . . . , will likely have a high value and touch may well be viewed with suspicion for its boundary-blurring properties" (1–3).

26 Howes and Classen, *Ways of Sensing*, 3.

27 John Heil, "Seeing Is Believing," *American Philosophical Quarterly* 19, no. 3 (1982): 229.

28 Noël Carroll, *The Philosophy of Horror, or, Paradoxes of the Heart* (Routledge, 1990), 184.

29 Carl Plantinga, *Moving Viewers: American Film and the Spectator's Experience* (University of California Press, 2009), 60.

30 Katerina Bantinaki, "The Paradox of Horror: Fear as a Positive Emotion," *Journal of Aesthetics and Art Criticism* 70, no. 4 (2012): 385.

31 Bantinaki, "Paradox of Horror," 390.

32 Mavis, "*Burn, Witch, Burn* (1962)."

33 Simin Nina Littschwager, *Making Sense of Mind-Game Films: Narrative Complexity, Embodiment, and the Senses* (Bloomsbury, 2019), 37–63.

34 Kier-La Janisse, "*Carnival of Souls*: 'Thinkin' like That, Don't It Give You Nightmares?,'" Criterion.com, July 12, 2016, https://www.criterion.com/current/posts/4143-carnival-of-souls-thinkin-like-that-don-t-it-give-you-nightmares.

35 Littschwager, *Making Sense of Mind-Game Films*, 38.

36 Julie Brown, "*Carnival of Souls* and the Organs of Horror," in *Music in the Horror Film: Listening to Fear*, ed. Neil Lerner (Routledge, 2010), 6, 12.

37 Peter Wilshire, "Dead in the Water? Dream and Reality in *Carnival of Souls*," *Offscreen*, vol. 11, no. 4 (2007), https://offscreen.com/view/carnival_of_souls.

38 Janisse, "*Carnival of Souls*."

39 Littschwager, *Making Sense of Mind-Game Films*, 61.

40 Littschwager.

41 Littschwager.

42 This sequence, lasting approximately four minutes, invites comparisons to another film produced in 1962: Michelangelo Antonioni's *L'Eclisse*. The latter film, one of the touchstones of European art cinema during the 1960s, likewise stars a blonde actress (Monica Vitti) as an emotionally distraught and isolated woman who, fending off the advances of infatuated men, is shown wandering alone through a "vacant urban landscape" against a minimalist soundtrack "punctuated by long stretches of silence and ambient sound." See Michael Croeser, "*L'Eclisse*," Occluded Celluloid, December 24, 2015, https://occludedcelluloid.wordpress.com/2015/12/24/leclisse-michelangelo-antonioni-1962/. Although the Italian filmmaker's work, celebrated as the pinnacle of what might be termed the cinema of social alienation, are "ghost stories of a sort," the critical framework surrounding its reception is considerably different from that of *Carnival of Souls*, which—though "elevated" by the "stunning black-and-white cinematography" of Maurice Prather (whose "unusual compositions" imbue the film with "a look and feel all its own")—is not as technically polished as Antonioni's and did not make inroads into the world's most prestigious, FIAPF-accredited film festivals. See Christopher J. Olson, *100 Greatest Cult Films* (Bloomsbury, 2018), 37.

43 Brown, "*Carnival of Souls* and the Organs of Horror," 17.

44 Brown, 14.

45 Brown.

46 Brown, "*Carnival of Souls* and the Organs of Horror," 14.

47 In this it shares much in common with horror films from the past two decades that are noted for their decidedly unhappy, nihilistically bleak endings, from *Frailty* (2001) to *Wolf Creek* (2005), *The Mist* (2007), *Eden Lake* (2008), and *Sinister* (2012).

48 Bernice M. Murphy, *The Highway Horror Film* (Palgrave Macmillan, 2014), 92.

49 Murphy, *Highway Horror Film*.

50 Tom Weaver, *It Came from Horrorwood: Interviews with Moviemakers in the SF and Horror Tradition* (McFarland, 2004), 40.
51 Mark Parker and Deborah Parker, *The DVD and the Study of Film: The Attainable Text* (Palgrave Macmillan, 2011), 58.
52 Kenneth George Goodwin, "Criterion Blu-ray Review: Herk Harvey's *Carnival of Souls*," Cagey Films, July 27, 2016, https://www.cageyfilms.com/2016/07/criterion-blu-ray-review-herk-harveys-carnival-of-souls-1962/.
53 Clover, *Men, Women, and Chain Saws*, 166; see also Ian Conrich and Laura Sedgwick *Gothic Dissections in Film and Literature* (Palgrave Macmillan, 2017), 53.
54 As I have argued elsewhere, the paratextual features of contemporary home-video releases, including supplement-packed "Collector's Edition" DVDs and Blu-rays, unmask otherwise hidden aspects of motion picture production, presenting viewers and listeners with real-world horrors and terrifying facts that sometimes trump the fiction-based fears to which we are paradoxically drawn. David Scott Diffrient, "A Knowledge of Horror or the Horror of Knowledge? Frightfully Insightful Directors' Commentaries on Blu-rays and DVDs," *Screen* 65, no. 4 (2024): 501–29.

## Chapter 2

1 Steffen Hantke, "'I See Dead People': Visualizing Ghosts in the American Horror Film Before the Arrival of CGI," in *Cinematic Ghosts: Haunting and Spectrality from Silent Cinema to the Digital Era*, ed. Murray Leeder (Bloomsbury Academic, 2015), 182.
2 Hantke, "'I See Dead People.'"
3 Marsha Kinder and Beverle Houston, "Seeing Is Believing: *The Exorcist* and *Don't Look Now*," in *American Horrors: Essays on the Modern American Horror Film*, ed. Gregory A. Waller (University of Illinois Press, 1987), 52.
4 Kinder and Houston, "Seeing Is Believing," 57.
5 Kinder and Houston, 58.
6 James Palmer and Michael Riley, "Seeing, Believing, and 'Knowing' in Narrative Film: *Don't Look Now* Revisited," *Literature Film Quarterly* 23, no. 1 (1995): 16.
7 Palmer and Riley, "Seeing, Believing, and 'Knowing.'"
8 Palmer and Riley.

9 Quoted in Erin E. Benay and Lisa M. Rafanelli, *Faith, Gender and the Senses in Italian Renaissance and Baroque Art: Interpreting the "Noli me tangere" and Doubting Thomas* (Routledge, 2016), 232.

10 Roger Ebert, "*The Exorcist*," RogerEbert.com, December 26, 1973, https://www.rogerebert.com/reviews/the-exorcist-1973.

11 Christopher J. Olson and CarrieLynn D. Reinhard, *Possessed Women, Haunted States: Cultural Tensions in Exorcism Cinema* (Lexington, 2017), 43.

12 Charles Derry, *Dark Dreams: A Psychological History of the Modern Horror Film* (A. C. Barnes, 1977), 104.

13 Ebert, "*The Exorcist*."

14 Kinder and Houston, "Seeing Is Believing," 45–46.

15 Heather Greene, *Lights, Camera, Witchcraft: A Critical History of Witches in American Film and Television* (Llewellyn, 2021), 83, 173.

16 Vivian Sobchack, *The Address of the Eye: A Phenomenology of Film Experience* (Princeton University Press, 1992), 169.

17 Sean Cubitt, *Digital Aesthetics* (Sage, 1998), 35.

18 Cubitt, *Digital Aesthetics*, 36.

19 Here I am reminded of Linda Badley's discussion of "spectral effects" in her book *Film, Horror, and the Body Fantastic*, where she briefly ruminates on the way that motion pictures sometimes draw subtle (or unsubtle) analogies, "essential to the spectator's suspension of disbelief, between cinema spectatorship and being a ghost" (53).

20 Brian Hoyle, *The Cinema of John Boorman* (Scarecrow, 2012), 112.

21 Hoyle, *Cinema of John Boorman*; see also Dennis Schaefer and Larry Salvato, *Masters of Light: Conversations with Contemporary Cinematographers* (University of California Press, 2013), 148–49.

22 Hantke, "'I See Dead People,'" 181, 189.

23 Hantke, 182.

24 Both versions of the film *Exorcist II: The Heretic* are included in Scream Factory's two-disc collector's edition Blu-ray release.

25 "Film: *Exorcist II: The Heretic* Is Heavy Stuff," *New York Times*, June 18, 1977.

26 Todd McCarthy, one of the few naysayers who defiantly supported Boorman's vision at the time of *Exorcist II: The Heretic*'s theatrical release, remarks that the central idea of the film "is that religion and science, so eternally in conflict, might be able to come together in a positive sense

and form a new level of consciousness." See McCarthy, "The Exorcism of *The Heretic*: Why They Had to Destroy This Film in Order to Save It," *Film Comment* 13, no. 5 (1977): 49. And, while this was the director's intention, his use of a generalized, seemingly timeless and mythically enchanted "native African context" to prove that "primitive religions can be just as valid as sophisticated ones and that the two can even be reconciled" could be seen as patronizing and insensitive if not outright racist.

27 Adam Nayman, "The Best Horror Movies of 2021 (So Far)," The Ringer, April 28, 2021, https://www.theringer.com/movies/2021/4/28/22406653/best-horror-movies-2021.

28 Daniel Humphrey, "Gender and Sexuality Haunts the Horror Film," in *A Companion to the Horror Film*, ed. Harry M. Benshoff (John Wiley & Sons, 2014), 51.

29 Humphrey, "Gender and Sexuality Haunts the Horror Film."

30 Barbara Creed, *The Monstrous-Feminine: Film, Feminism, Psychoanalysis* (Routledge, 1993), 36.

31 Robb White, *House on Haunted Hill: A William Castle Annotated Screamplay* (William Castle Productions, 2011).

32 White, *House on Haunted Hill*; emphasis added.

33 Elinor Cleghorn, *Unwell Women: Misdiagnosis and Myth in a Man-Made World* (Dutton, 2021), 20.

34 Cleghorn, *Unwell Women*.

35 Patricia Gherovici, *Please Select Your Gender: From the Invention of Hysteria to the Democratizing of Transgenderism* (Routledge, 2010), 49, 52.

36 Andrew J. Rausch and Charles E. Pratt Jr., *The Cinematic Misadventures of Ed Wood* (BearManor Media, 2015).

37 Christine Cornea, "'So Bad It's Good': Critical Humor in Science Fiction Cinema," in *The Last Laugh: Strange Humors of Cinema*, ed. Murray Pomerance (Wayne State University Press, 2013), 83.

38 Cornea, "'So Bad It's Good.'"

39 Bartłomiej Paszylk, *The Pleasure and Pain of Cult Horror Films: An Historical Survey* (McFarland, 2009), 70.

40 George Ochoa, *Deformed and Destructive Beings: The Purpose of Horror Films* (McFarland, 2011).

41 Ochoa, *Deformed and Destructive Beings*, 84.

42 Murray Leeder, "The Humor of William Castle's Gimmick Films," in *The Laughing Dead: The Horror-Comedy Film from "Bride of Frankenstein" to*

*"Zombieland,"* ed. Cynthia J. Miller and A. Bowdoin Van Riper (Rowman & Littlefield, 2016), 90.

43 Quoted in Leeder, "Humor of William Castle's Gimmick Films," 90.

## Chapter 3

1 Kristina Pia Hofer, "Dirty Sound: The Camp Materialism of *Blood Orgy of the Leather Girls*," in *The Dark Side of Camp Aesthetics: Queer Economies of Dirt, Dust and Patina*, ed. Ingrid Hotz-Davies, Georg Vogt, and Franziska Bergmann (Routledge, 2019), 88–100.

2 Hofer, "Dirty Sound."

3 Vivian Sobchack, *Carnal Thoughts: Embodiment and Moving Image Culture* (University of California Press, 2004), 76; Bernard Perron, "The Survival Horror: The Extended Body Genre," in *Horror Video Games: Essays on the Fusion of Fear and Play*, ed. Bernard Perron (McFarland, 2009), 123.

4 Sobchack, *Carnal Thoughts*, 76.

5 Diane Ackerman, *A Natural History of the Senses* (Vintage, 1990), 6.

6 Andrea Rinaldi, "The Scent of Life," *EMBO Reports* 8, no. 7 (2007): 629.

7 Grady Hendrix, "This Old Grindhouse," Slate, April 6, 2007, https://slate.com/culture/2007/04/grindhouse-nostalgia-is-lame.html.

8 Dennis Schwartz, "Moonshine Mountain," Dennis Schwartz Movie Reviews, August 5, 2019, https://dennisschwartzreviews.com/moonshinemountain/.

9 Angela Ndalianis, *The Horror Sensorium: Media and the Senses* (McFarland, 2012); Larrie Dudenhoeffer, *Embodiment and Horror Cinema* (Palgrave Macmillan, 2014); Xavier Aldana Reyes, *Horror Film and Affect: Towards a Corporeal Model of Viewership* (Routledge, 2016); Lorna Piatti-Farnell, *Consuming Gothic: Food and Horror in Film* (Palgrave Macmillan, 2017); Allan Cameron, *Visceral Screens: Mediation and Matter in Horror Cinema* (Edinburgh University Press, 2021); David Scott Diffrient, *Body Genre: Anatomy of the Horror Film* (University Press of Mississippi, 2023).

10 Jonathan Crane, "Scraping Bottom: Splatter and the Herschell Gordon Lewis Oeuvre," in *The Horror Film*, ed. Stephen Prince (Rutgers University Press, 2004), 150.

11 "Louise Downe," *Chicago Tribune*, January 16, 1972.

12 Herschell Gordon Lewis, *The Wizard of Gore* Blu-ray audio commentary (Arrow Video, 2020).

13 Nicola Jean Evans, "Undoing the Magic? DVD Extras and the Pleasure Behind the Scenes," *Continuum* 24, no. 4 (2010): 590.
14 Evans, "Undoing the Magic?," 596–97.
15 Rob Weiner and A. Bowdoin Van Riper, "Catering to the Cult of Ishtar: *Blood Feast*," in *What's Eating You? Food and Horror on Screen*, ed. Cynthia J. Miller and A. Bowdoin Van Riper (New York: Bloomsbury Academic, 2017), 229; David Scott Diffrient, *Body Genre: Anatomy of the Horror Film* (University Press of Mississippi, 2023).
16 David F. Friedman and Herschell Gordon Lewis, *Blood Feast* Blu-ray audio commentary (Arrow Video, 2020).
17 William Ian Miller, *The Anatomy of Disgust* (Harvard University Press, 1997), 66.
18 Miller, *The Anatomy of Disgust*, 68.
19 Miller, 75.
20 Miller, 67.
21 Miller.
22 Tony Federico and James Phelan, *Paleo Grilling: A Modern Caveman's Guide to Cooking with Fire* (Fair Winds, 2014), 18–19, 161.
23 Federico and Phelan, *Paleo Grilling*, 18–19.
24 Federico and Phelan.
25 Jeremy MacClancy, *Consuming Culture: Why You Eat What You Eat* (Henry Holt, 1992), 159.
26 Michael Newton, *Rosemary's Baby* (British Film Institute, 2020), 28; Gabe Worgaftik, "Ridley Scott Got Elbow-Deep in Sheep Intestines to Make the *Alien* Eggs Move Properly," AV Club, April 2, 2019, https://www.avclub.com/ridley-scott-got-elbow-deep-in-sheep-intestines-to-make-1833746628.
27 Quoted in Andrew J. Rausch, *Gods of Grindhouse: Interviews with Exploitation Filmmakers* (BearManor Media, 2013), 89.
28 Piatti-Farnell, *Consuming Gothic*, 28.
29 John Dieringer, ed., *Horror Caviar: A Cookbook* (A24, 2021).

## Chapter 4

1 Elizabeth Erwin, "How Horror Thwarted 'The Code,'" *Gay & Lesbian Review Worldwide* 22, no. 6 (2015): 18.
2 Xavier Aldana Reyes, *Body Gothic: Corporeal Transgression in Contemporary Literature and Horror Film* (University of Wales Press, 2014), 7, 10–11.

3 André Loiselle, "Buxom Monstrosity: Theatricality and the Ostentatious Body of the Horror Film," *Monsters and the Monstrous* 3, no. 2 (2013): 45.
4 Harmony Wu, "Trading in Horror, Cult, and Matricide: Peter Jackson's Phenomenal Bad Taste and New Zealand Fantasies of Inter/National Cinematic Success," in *The Cult Film Reader*, ed. Ernest Mathijs and Xavier Mendik (Open University Press, 2008), 330.
5 John Sharp and David Thomas, *Fun, Taste, and Games: An Aesthetics of the Idle, Unproductive, and Otherwise Playful* (MIT Press, 2019), 113.
6 Carl Plantinga, *Moving Viewers: American Film and the Spectator's Experience* (University of California Press, 2009), 73, 182.
7 For a rare discussion of the ways that popcorn, soda, beer, and other movie theater concessions shape our material and sensorial relationship to cinema, see Caetlin Benson-Allott, *The Stuff of Spectatorship: Material Cultures of Film and Television* (University of California Press, 2021).
8 I.Q. Hunter, "Trash Horror and the Cult of the Bad Film," in *A Companion to the Horror Film*, ed. Harry M. Benshoff (John Wiley & Sons, 2014), 485.
9 Hunter, "Trash Horror and the Cult of the Bad Film."
10 Jeffrey Sconce, "Explosive Apathy," in *B Is for Bad Cinema: Aesthetics, Politics, and Cultural Value*, ed. Claire Perkins and Constantine Verevis (State University of New York Press, 2014), 32.
11 Less well known, but equally bizarre, is *Wishmaster 2: Evil Never Dies* (1999), a sequel that gives viewers an opportunity to see what would happen to a lawyer's comically contorted body if an imprisoned client's wish that he "go fuck himself" were made possible.
12 John Kenneth Muir, *Horror Films of the 1990s* (McFarland, 2019), 76; Tom Weaver, *Eye on Science Fiction: 20 Interviews with Classic SF and Horror Filmmakers* (McFarland, 2003), 134.
13 Muir, *Horror Films of the 1990s*, 68.
14 Amy McCarthy, "If *The Menu* Makes You Uncomfortable, That's Because It's Supposed To," Eater, November 15, 2022, https://www.eater.com/23458693/review-the-menu-2022-movie-ralph-fiennes-anya-taylor-joy-release-date.
15 Erin Elizabeth, "The Real-Life Restaurant the Movie *The Menu* Was Based On," Restaurant Clicks, August 3, 2023, https://restaurantclicks.com/biz/the-menu-movie-based-on-real-restaurant/.
16 McCarthy, "If *The Menu* Makes You Uncomfortable."

17 McCarthy.
18 B. J. Colangelo, "Be! Aggressive! Three Cheers for the Spirit Squads of Horror," *Fangoria*, June 2, 2021, https://www.fangoria.com/original/cheerleaders-of-horror/.
19 Colangelo, "Be! Aggressive!"
20 Colangelo.
21 Welch D. Everman, *Cult Horror Films: From "Attack of the 50 Foot Woman" to "Zombies of Mora Tau"* (Citadel, 1993), 191.
22 Carrol Lee Fry, *Cinema of the Occult: New Age, Satanism, Wicca, and Spiritualism in Film* (Lehigh University Press, 2008), 155.
23 Joe Zaso and Bryan Thomas Norton, "My Cookies! My Cookies! My Cookies! 40 Years of *Pandemonium*," B&S About Movies, May 1, 2023, https://bandsaboutmovies.com/2023/05/01/my-cookies-my-cookies-my-cookies-40-years-of-pandemonium-by-joe-zaso-and-bryan-thomas-norton/.
24 Laura Wilson, *Spectatorship, Embodiment, and Physicality in the Contemporary Mutilation Film* (Palgrave Macmillan, 2015), 102.
25 Wilson, *Spectatorship, Embodiment, and Physicality*, 104.
26 Erin E. Wiegand, "Who Can Be Eaten?," in *What's Eating You? Food and Horror on Screen*, ed. Cynthia J. Miller and A. Bowdoin Van Riper (Bloomsbury Academic, 2017), 264.
27 Vivian Sobchack, "Bringing It All Back Home: Family Economy and Generic Exchange," in *American Horrors: Essays on the Modern American Horror Film*, ed. Gregory Albert Waller (University of Illinois Press, 1987), 175–92.
28 Sobchack, "Bringing It All Back Home," 175.
29 Tony Williams, *The Cinema of George A. Romero: Knight of the Living Dead*, 2nd ed. (Wallflower, 2015), 123.
30 Quoted in Williams, *Cinema of George A. Romero*, 120.
31 Williams, 124.
32 Bettina Makalintal, "*Swallow* Is Feminist Body Horror About Women, Food, and Control," *Vice*, March 6, 2020, https://www.vice.com/en/article/carlo-mirabella-davis-swallow-starring-haley-bennett-is-feminist-body-horror-about-women-food-and-control/.
33 Michael Gingold, "Review: *Suck*," *Fangoria*, July 23, 2019, https://www.fangoria.com/review-suck/.
34 John Squires, "The Stabby Meal: Paramount and Chain Restaurant Join Forces for *Scream*-Themed Popup Meal!," Bloody Disgusting, February 16,

2023, https://bloody-disgusting.com/the-further/3751780/the-stabby-meal-paramount-and-chain-restaurant-join-forces-for-scream-themed-popup-meal/.

35 Matt Donato, "*Scream VI*: We Sliced into the Stabby Meal and Walked Through the Film's Immersive Experience," Bloody Disgusting, February 27, 2023, https://bloody-disgusting.com/editorials/3752829/scream-vi-we-sliced-into-the-stabby-meal-and-walked-through-the-films-immersive-experience/.

36 Donato, "*Scream VI*."

37 Kartik Nair, "It's (Not) Just Film Studies: On Returning to *Scream*," *Los Angeles Review of Books*, June 1, 2023, https://lareviewofbooks.org/article/its-not-just-film-studies-on-returning-to-scream/.

## Chapter 5

1 Martha Kerr, "Horror Men Talk About Horror," *Modern Screen*, January 1940, 64–65, 68.

2 Kerr, "Horror Men Talk About Horror," 65.

3 Kerr, 68.

4 Jon Towlson, *The Turn to Gruesomeness in American Horror Films, 1931–1936* (McFarland, 2016), 181.

5 Towlson, *Turn to Gruesomeness.*

6 Kerr, "Horror Men Talk About Horror," 65.

7 Kerr.

8 Kerr.

9 Kerr, 68.

10 Kerr.

11 "Deafness as a Public Health Issue in the 1920s and 1930s," NYAM Center for History, June 29, 2016, https://nyamcenterforhistory.org/2016/06/29/deafness-as-a-public-health-issue-in-the-1920s-1930s-part-1-of-2/ (URL no longer available).

12 Octavian E. Robinson and Jonathan Henner, "The Personal Is Political in *The Deaf Mute Howls*: Deaf Epistemology Seeks Disability Justice," *Disability & Society* 32, no. 9 (2017): 1419.

13 John S. Schuchman, "The Silent Film Era: Silent Films, NAD Films, and the Deaf Community's Response," *Sign Language Studies* 4, no. 3 (2004): 232.

14 Anon., "Deafness as a Public Health Issue."

15 Robinson and Henner, "Personal Is Political," 1421.
16 Russell L. Johnson, "'Better Gestures': A Disability History on the Transition from (Silent) Movies to Talkies in the United States," *Journal of Social History* (2017): 8.
17 Johnson, "'Better Gestures.'"
18 Leo Meehan, "*Frankenstein*," *Motion Picture Herald*, November 14, 1931.
19 Peter Hutchings, *Historical Dictionary of Horror Cinema* (Rowman & Littlefield, 2018), 185.
20 Scott Allen Nollen, *Boris Karloff: A Critical Account of His Screen, Stage, Radio, Television, and Recording Work* (McFarland, 1991), 62.
21 Nollen, *Boris Karloff*.
22 Harry M. Benshoff, *Monsters in the Closet: Homosexuality and the Horror Film* (Manchester University Press, 1997), 43.
23 Michael Sragow, "Deep Focus: *The Old Dark House*," *Film Comment*, September 28, 2017, https://www.filmcomment.com/blog/deep-focus-old-dark-house/.
24 Randy Rasmussen, *Children of the Night: The Six Archetypal Characters of Classic Horror Films* (McFarland, 2006), 210.
25 Angela Smith, *Hideous Progeny: Disability, Eugenics, and Classic Horror Cinema* (Columbia University Press, 2011), 120.
26 Smith, *Hideous Progeny*.
27 William Mager, "130 Years of Deaf People and the Moving Image: Coming Full Circle," Watershed, November 29, 2021, https://www.watershed.co.uk/articles/130-years-deaf-people-and-moving-image-coming-full-circle.
28 George William Veditz, "Motion Pictures for the Deaf," *Nickelodeon* (1910): 249–50.
29 Veditz, "Motion Pictures for the Deaf."
30 Johnson, "'Better Gestures,'" 2–3.
31 *The Tingler*, famous for its director's gimmicky, ballyhoo-style reliance on "Percepto" seat buzzers planted in some US theaters during its initial run (in hopes of eliciting audible reactions and physical jolts from his audience), goes so far as to locate mortal risks in the deaf woman's inability to communicate verbally—to talk or, more importantly, to scream: the very thing, Castle tells us during this film's opening scene, that might otherwise have saved Martha's life.
32 V. Renée, "The Sound of Horror: Why Hearing Stuff Is Scarier Than Actually Seeing Stuff," No Film School, November 1, 2013, https://

nofilmschool.com/2013/11/why-hearing-stuff-is-scarier-than-actually-seeing-stuff.

33 Michael Wilmington, "*Hear No Evil* Cast Breaks Shackles," *Los Angeles Times*, March 29, 1993, https://www.latimes.com/archives/la-xpm-1993-03-29-ca-16454-story.html.

34 Chris O'Falt, "*It* Is Loud: For Too Many Horror Movies, Soundtracks Are Scariest Part," IndieWire, September 12, 2017, https://www.indiewire.com/2017/09/it-loud-sound-score-scares-horror-films-1201875236/.

35 O'Falt, "*It* Is Loud."

36 Jon Christian, "How Netflix Alienated and Insulted Its Deaf Subscribers," The Week, January 9, 2015, https://theweek.com/articles/452181/how-netflix-alienated-insulted-deaf-subscribers.

37 Christian, "How Netflix Alienated and Insulted."

38 Christian.

39 For instance, while watching director Michael Reeves's *Witchfinder General* (1968), uploaded onto YouTube courtesy of "Flick Vault," I was aghast to see the parenthetically bracketed word "[laughing]" atop an image of a woman being dragged down a village road by an angry mob, crying every step of the way as they inch closer to the hangman's post on a hill. Occurring during the film's opening scene, prior to its title sequence, this abruptly violent moment sets the stage for what is to come, though anyone viewing *Witchfinder General* with the YouTube captions might presume that its narrative is closer in spirit to *Monty Python and the Holy Grail* (1975) or some other spoof of medieval customs than a brutal, nihilistic account of fearmongering in seventeenth-century England. Notably, the captions provided for the film on Amazon Prime describe the sound coming from the tormented woman as one of "[wailing]" rather than "[laughing]," a far more accurate indication of *Witchfinder General*'s emotional register.

40 Katie Dupere, "Deaf YouTubers Call Out Crappy Captions with #NoMoreCraptions Movement," Mashable, November 11, 2016, https://mashable.com/article/youtube-closed-captioning-nomorecraptions.

41 Dupere, "Deaf YouTubers Call Out Crappy Captions."

42 Gwyneth Peaty, "Power in Silence: Captions, Deafness, and the Final Girl," *M/C Journal* 20, no. 3 (2017), https://journal.media-culture.org.au/index.php/mcjournal/article/view/1268.

43 Peaty, "Power in Silence."

44 Peaty.

45 Although most SDH presentations of horror films feature at least a few parenthetical indications of their musical elements, there are other examples to the contrary besides *Hush*. For instance, Shout Factory's 2013 Blu-ray release of director Tony Maylam's slasher film *The Burning* (1981) has relatively few captions to begin with (besides "[growling]" and "[screaming]," which appear regularly), and none of those communicate anything about composer-keyboardist Rick Wakeman's synth score, which can be heard whenever the disfigured killer Cropsy approaches a potential victim. Additionally, no captioned text accompanies the fast-paced banjo music that plays when several ill-fated summer campers all go canoeing midway through the film.

46 Isabel Cristina Pinedo, *Recreational Terror: Women and the Pleasures of Horror Film Viewing* (State University of New York Press, 1997), 51.

47 Jack Wilhelmi, "*Gerald's Game* Glass Escape Is the Goriest Scene of the 2010s," Screen Rant, January 25, 2020, https://screenrant.com/gerald-game-glass-escape-goriest-scene-2010s/.

48 Tim Underwood and Chuck Miller, eds., *Kingdom of Fear: The World of Stephen King* (New American Library, 1986), 10; see also Paul Wells, *The Horror Genre: From Beelzebub to Blair Witch* (Columbia University Press, 2000), 11.

## Chapter 6

1 Sean Zdenek, *Reading Sounds: Closed-Captioned Media and Popular Culture* (University of Chicago Press, 2015), 6.

2 Zdenek, *Reading Sounds*, 1.

3 Roger Ebert, *I Hated, Hated, Hated This Movie* (Andrews McMeel, 2000), 164.

4 Ebert, *I Hated, Hated, Hated This Movie*.

5 Ebert.

6 Ebert.

7 David M. Turner and Kevin Stagg, eds., *Social Histories of Disability and Deformity: Bodies, Images and Experiences* (Routledge, 2007), 1.

8 Kevin Stagg, "Representing Physical Difference: The Materiality of the Monstrous," in *Social Histories of Disability and Deformity: Bodies, Images and Experiences*, ed. David M. Turner and Kevin Stagg (Routledge, 2007), 19–38.

9 Jason S. Farr, "Attractive Deformity: Enabling the 'Shocking Monster' from Sarah Scott's *Agreeable Ugliness*," in *The Idea of Disability in the Eighteenth Century*, ed. Chris Mounsey (Bucknell University Press, 2014), 181.

10 Dennis Todd, *Imagining Monsters: Miscreations of the Self in Eighteenth-Century England* (University of Chicago Press, 1995), 245.

11 Zdenek, *Reading Sounds*, 1.

12 Ian Cross, "Music and Meaning, Ambiguity and Evolution," in *Musical Communication*, ed. Dorothy Miell, Raymond MacDonald, and David J. Hargreaves (Oxford University Press, 2005), 35.

13 Cross, "Music and Meaning."

14 "Deep Note," JH Wiki Collection, accessed February 2, 2026, https://jhmoviecollection.fandom.com/wiki/Deep_Note.

15 Gary Rhodes, *White Zombie: Anatomy of a Horror Film* (McFarland, 2001), 109.

16 Rhodes, *White Zombie*, 52; Michael Slowik, *After the Silents: Hollywood Film Music in the Early Sound Era, 1926–1934* (Columbia University Press, 2014), 254.

17 The SDH text provided on the Blu-ray release of the postmodern comedy-horror film *Popcorn* (1991) is only marginally better—only *slightly* more evocative or informative. Bookended by the excessively generic subtitle "(music playing)," the film begins and ends with two pieces of music that are in fact radically dissimilar, though the onscreen text that accompanies them elides any differences between a dark instrumental piece (during the opening credits) and an upbeat if macabre pop song (during the closing credits).

18 Despite its failure to provide information about the actual type of music that plays during the opening scenes of *Friday the 13th: A New Beginning* (and which was composed by Harry Manfredini), the Amazon Prime closed captioning for the film is, like that of *Hellbound: Hellraiser II*, instructive, for it showcases the push-pull tension between finite/tensed verbs and nonfinite/present participles, all of which occur in quick succession and are all mixed into a temporally amorphous stew of subtitles. Along with the aforementioned "[MUSIC]" caption, which reappears throughout this film's opening sequence, the following text flashes onscreen: "[THUNDER ROARING]" as well as "[THUNDER ROARS]"; "[LAUGHING]" as well as "[LAUGHS]"; "[GROANING]" as well as "[GROANS]"; and "[GASPING]" as well as "[GASPS]."

19 Matt Glasby, *The Book of Horror: The Anatomy of Fear in Film* (Frances Lincoln, 2020), 27.

20 Murray Leeder, *Horror Film: A Critical Introduction* (Bloomsbury Academic, 2018), 181.

21 James Buhler, "Music and the Adult Ideal in *A Nightmare on Elm Street*," in *Music in the Horror Film: Listening to Fear*, ed. Neil Lerner (Routledge, 2010), 168–86.

22 Buhler, "Music and the Adult Ideal," 181.

23 Buhler.

24 Buhler, 176.

25 Steffen Hantke, "Science Fiction and Horror in the 1950s," in *A Companion to the Horror Film*, ed. Harry M. Benshoff (John Wiley & Sons, 2014), 261.

26 Hantke, "Science Fiction and Horror in the 1950s."

27 Larrie Dudenhoeffer, *Embodiment and Horror Cinema* (Palgrave Macmillan, 2014), 8.

28 Dudenhoeffer, *Embodiment and Horror Cinema*, 9.

29 Jack Halberstam, *Skin Shows: Gothic Horror and the Technology of Monsters* (Duke University Press, 1995), 147.

30 James Marriott and Kim Newman, *The Definitive Guide to Horror Movies* (Carlton, 2018), 218. Reading Marriott and Newman's description, I wonder if they have not seen or simply forgotten about Hideshi Hino's *Guinea Pig: Mermaid in the Manhole* (*Ginī Piggu: Manhōru no Naka no Ningyo*, 1988), which is a bit "soggier" than Jackson's *Braindead*.

## Chapter 7

1 Crane Wilbur, "My Life," *Motion Picture Magazine* 10, no. 9 (1915): 99.

2 Kenneth C. Crain, "Blind 'Spectator' Dies," *Moving Picture World*, May 22, 1915.

3 Crain, "Blind 'Spectator' Dies."

4 Crain.

5 "The Blindness of Not Seeing," *New York Times*, July 15, 1915.

6 "Blindness of Not Seeing."

7 "*The Blind Miner*," *Moving Picture World*, January 20, 1912.

8 Interestingly, another adaptation of Conway's *Called Back*—that of the Thanhouser Company, directed by George Nichols and starring James

Cruze as the temporarily blind protagonist—had been released two years earlier (in 1912), though a reviewer at the time made a point to note that "there are no 'horrors' in the execution" of the drama. This suggests that the film's source material—a popular novel referred to by that same reviewer as a "masterpiece of mystery"—might have lent itself to a grislier treatment than what Nichols and his crew ultimately delivered. See "Thanhouser's *Called Back* Realistic," *Moving Picture News*, June 1, 1912.

9 C. H. Claudy, "Modern Melodrama," *Moving Picture World*, January 13, 1912.

10 Martin F. Norden, *The Cinema of Isolation: A History of Physical Disability in the Movies* (Rutgers University Press, 1994), 30.

11 Norden, *Cinema of Isolation*.

12 James Bordley, "The Blind as Industrial Workers," *Rehabilitation of the Wounded* 80 (1918): 104.

13 "A Film Treatise on Instructing the Blind," *Motography*, April 1912, 163–64.

14 Andrew A. Erish, *Col. William N. Selig, the Man Who Invented Hollywood* (University of Texas Press, 2012), 150.

15 Wolcott Coombs, "A Blind Boy's Interest in Pictures," *Motography*, January 1912, 27–28.

16 Coombs, "Blind Boy's Interest in Pictures."

17 Erish, *Col. William N. Selig*, 153.

18 Ernest A. Dench, "Enjoying the Movies Tho Blind," *Motion Picture Classic*, February 1916, 27.

19 Dench, "Enjoying the Movies Tho Blind."

20 Dench.

21 "*Fall of a Nation* Opens Booking Offices," *Motography*, July 8, 1916.

22 Katherine Anne Avery, "'You Ain't Heard Nothin' Yet!': Audio Description, Spectatorship, and Histories of Access in American Cinema and Media Cultures," master's thesis, University of Iowa, 2022.

23 Gilles Boulenger, *John Carpenter: The Prince of Darkness* (Silman-James, 2003), 232.

24 "Blind See *The Battle Cry of Peace*," *Motion Picture World*, December 25, 1915.

25 "Don't Overlook This Worthy Charity," *New York Clipper*, December 25, 1915.

26 "Don't Overlook This Worthy Charity."

27 "Blind Persons 'See' a 'Movie' Spectacle," *Boston Daily Globe*, December 4, 1915.

28 Katherine Avery, "Now You're Talking! Early Audio Description, Film Spectatorship, and Histories of Access in Early American Cinema," Audio Description Project, September 20, 2022, https://adp.acb.org/docs/Avery%20Term%20Paper%20-%20Now%20Youre%20Talking.pdf (URL unavailable).

29 Avery, "Now You're Talking!"

30 "Don't Overlook This Worthy Charity."

31 Yomota Inuhiko, *What Is Japanese Cinema? A History*, trans. Philip Kaffen (Columbia University Press, 2019), 54.

32 "Don't Overlook This Worthy Charity."

33 "Don't Overlook This Worthy Charity."

34 Isolde Standish, *A New History of Japanese Cinema* (Continuum, 2006), 22.

35 Klaas de Zwaana and Adrian Gerber, "The Battle for Meaning: A Cross-National Film Reception Analysis of *The Battle Cry of Peace* in Switzerland and the Netherlands During World War I," *Early Popular Visual Culture* 14, no. 2 (2016): 168–87.

36 Clarence L. Linz, "Big Vitagraph Subject Shown," *Moving Picture World*, August 28, 1915; see also Henry P. Walthall, "Chats with the Players," *Motion Picture Magazine* (1915): 117. Private screenings of *The Battle Cry of Peace* continued to be held for US congressional leaders through the early spring of 1916, in some cases at the instigation of organizations such as the Daughters of the American Revolution, though President Wilson and members of his administration did not participate, perhaps for political reasons. "Congress to See Battle Cry," *Motography* 14, no. 26 (1915): 1324.

37 "At Leading Picture Theaters," *Moving Picture World*, September 18, 1915.

38 Blackton is quoted as saying, "I do hope and pray that this picture will crystallize the elements that will make for a nation-wide movement which will prevent the horrors of warfare ever being visited upon this country." "Big Opening for Vitagraph Feature," *Moving Picture World*, September 25, 1915.

39 "Big Opening for Vitagraph Feature."

40 "Big Opening for Vitagraph Feature."

41 de Zwaana and Gerber, "Battle for Meaning," 168–87.

42 "Prepare Against Invasion, Is Vitagraph Film Lesson," *Motion Picture News*, July 31, 1915.

43 de Zwaana and Gerber, "Battle for Meaning," 181–83.

44 "The Moving World," *Independent*, October 11, 1915.

45 J. Stuart Blackton, "*The Battle Cry of Peace*," *Motion Picture Magazine*, November 1915, 43–56.

46 de Zwaana and Gerber, "Battle for Meaning," 168–87.

47 "Moving World," 80.

48 W. R. Andrews, "*The Battle Cry of Peace* Is Epic of Patriotism," *Motion Picture News*, July–August 1915, 82.

49 Lynde Denig, "*The Battle Cry of Peace*," *Moving Picture World*, August 21, 1915.

50 W. Stephen Bush, "A Great Patriotic Service," *Moving Picture World*, August 28, 1915.

51 "Battle Cry in Washington," *Billboard*, January 1, 1916.

52 Individuals who were disabled in the line of duty, including soldiers who showed signs of insanity and those who had become addicted to drugs while stationed overseas, were discharged to stateside hospitals by the surgeon general, M. W. Ireland, though "the blind or nearly blind" as well as "deaf or nearly deaf" were not eligible for discharge until they were "functionally able to care for themselves" (by learning how to read lips, for instance). Official US Bulletin, published by the US Committee of Public Information, January 29, 1919, Gilder Lehrman Institute, https://www.gilderlehrman.org/history-resources/spotlight-primary-source/rules-discharging-disabled-veterans-1919.

53 George Henderson and Willie V. Bryan, *Psychosocial Aspects of Disability* (Charles C. Thomas, 2011), 105.

54 R. Bruce Crelin, *The Great War and the Golden Age of Hollywood Horror* (Midnight Marquee, 2021), 13–14.

55 W. Scott Poole, *Wasteland: The Great War and the Origins of Modern Horror* (Counterpoint, 2018).

56 Poole, *Wasteland*.

57 Poole.

58 Fritz Tidden, "The Personal Touch," *Motion Picture World*, September 2, 1922; Avery, "Now You're Talking!," 14–15.

59 "Blind Attend Movie and Weep for *Jazz Singer*," *Times-Picayune*, September 14, 1928.

60 Avery, "'You Ain't Heard Nothin' Yet!,'" 1.

61 Avery.

62 Katie Ellis, *Disability and Digital Television Cultures: Representation, Access, and Reception* (Routledge, 2019), 128.

63 Ellis, *Disability and Digital Television Cultures.*

64 "Blind See *Desert Song*," *Exhibitor*, December 22, 1943.

65 Ellis, *Disability and Digital Television Cultures*, 129.

66 "Audio Description—The Early Development," Described and Captured Media Program, https://dcmp.org/learn/306-audio-description--the-early-development.

67 Joanne Bernardi, *Writing in Light: The Silent Scenario and the Japanese Pure Film Movement* (Wayne State University Press, 2001), 35.

68 Joel Snyder, *The Visual Made Verbal: A Comprehensive Training Manual and Guide to the History and Applications of Audio Description* (American Council for the Blind, 2014).

69 The Audio Description Project's "Mission" statement can be found here: https://adp.acb.org/mission-and-history.

70 Jeffrey Bullins, "Sound over Sight: Depicting Blindness in Horror Films (from a Sound Specialist's Perspective)," in *Lenses on Blindness: Essays on Vision Loss in Media, Culture, Religion and Experience*, ed. Sharon Packer (McFarland, 2023), 33–34.

71 Bullins, "Sound over Sight."

72 Ellis, *Disability and Digital Television Cultures*, 130; emphasis added.

73 Jan-Louis Kruger, "Audio Narration: Re-Narrativising Film," *Perspectives* 18, no. 3 (2010): 232.

74 Kruger, "Audio Narration," 233, 238.

75 Kruger.

76 Kruger.

77 Polish writer-director Bartosz M. Kowalski's horror films, *Nobody Sleeps in the Woods Tonight* (*W lesie dziś nie zaśnie nikt*, 2020) and *Hellhole* (a.k.a. *Last Summer*; *Ostatnia wieczerza*, 2022) are two of many titles currently available on Netflix with multiple AD language options, including one in their native language as well as Spanish and Brazilian Portuguese tracks (but no English-language audio description).

78 https://www.afb.org/blog/entry/standing-ovation-netflix-its-audio-description-announcement.

79 Vernā Myers, "Inclusion Takes Root at Netflix: Our First Report," Netflix, January 13, 2021, https://about.netflix.com/en/news/netflix-inclusion-report-2021.

## Chapter 8

1 Robert Baird, "The Startle Effect: Implications for Spectator Cognition and Media Theory," *Film Quarterly* 53, no. 3 (2000): 15.

2 Baird, "Startle Effect."

3 Casey Ryan Kelly, "*It Follows*: Precarity, Thanatopolitics, and the Ambient Horror Film," *Critical Studies in Media Communication* 34, no. 3 (2017): 236, 237.

4 Kelly, "*It Follows*."

5 Joel Burges, "The Horror of Stagnation; or, the Perspectival Dread of *It Follows*," in *Labors of Fear: The Modern Horror Film Goes to Work*, ed. Aviva Briefel and Jason Middleton (University of Texas Press, 2023), 169–86. See also Mark Binelli, "How *It Follows* Uses Detroit to Explore the Horror of Urban Decay," *Slate*, April 1, 2015, https://slate.com/culture/2015/04/it-follows-how-the-new-movie-uses-detroit-to-explore-the-horror-of-urban-decay.html.

6 Burges, "Horror of Stagnation," 170.

7 Jason Middleton and Aviva Briefel, "Introduction," in *Labors of Fear: The Modern Horror Film Goes to Work*, ed. Aviva Briefel and Jason Middleton (University of Texas Press, 2023), 1, 6.

8 Kelly, "*It Follows*," 241.

9 Kelly, 247.

10 Kelly, 235, 238.

11 Sabine Braun, "Creating Coherence in Audio Description," *Meta: Translators' Journal* 56, no. 3 (2011): 646.

12 Another example of an AD voicer delivering information about visual details several seconds before those corresponding images transpire onscreen can be found in Amazon Prime's streaming version of *Orphan: Kill First* (2022). Near the beginning of this prequel to the 2009 supernatural horror film *Orphan*, an art therapist named Anna (Gwendolyn Collins) walks up the steps of the Saarne Institute (a "two-story, yellow-bricked building with white trimmed windows and topped by a dome with a red roof") and "presses a buzzer" on the intercom next to its front door. The latter action is narrated eight seconds before the actual sound of the buzzing—the first of many instances in which anticipatory cues are granted to blind or low-vision listeners well in advance of the narrated events in this tellingly titled film.

13 For more on this topic, see Jeffrey Andrew Weinstock, "What Is IT? Ambient Dread and Modern Paranoia in *It* (2017), *It Follows* (2014) and *It Comes at Night* (2017)," *Horror Studies* 11, no. 2 (2020): 205–20.

14 Chris Condry, "Small Details You Missed in *Day Shift*," Looper, August 22, 2022, https://www.looper.com/972094/small-details-you-missed-in-day-shift/.

15 Tomris Laffly, "*The Invisible Man*," RogerEbert.com, February 27, 2020, https://www.rogerebert.com/reviews/the-invisible-man-movie-review-2020.

16 Additionally, Samuelson's voice will sound familiar to anyone who has listened to the AD tracks included on the home-video and streaming presentations of such disparate horror films as *Cat People* (1982), *Let Me In* (2010), and *Beau Is Afraid* (2023), as well as episodes of the HBO series *The Last of Us* (2023). Because there are relatively few vocal performers in the growing business of descriptive services, listeners might experience a kind of auditory déjà vu while engaging this accessibility tool, which creates unexpected intertextual linkages across disparate films that would otherwise be invisible to the eye.

17 In their book *Gothic Dissections in Film and Literature: The Body in Parts*, Ian Conrich and Laura Sedgwick discuss the centrality of hair to horror, which is home to hirsute creatures whose "beastliness" is partly conveyed through an excess of a particular bodily growth that, like fingernails, emerge from "old dead cells that have been pushed up and through the skin." According to the authors, "excessive hair . . . can bring into question the boundary that separates human from animal and the civilized from the wild and the monstrous." Although the aforementioned examples of the genre (e.g., *The Ring*, *Cam*) do not explicitly hinge on this theme as obviously as do several classic and contemporary films—from *Dr. Jekyll and Mr. Hyde* (1931) to *Ginger Snaps* (2000)—a similar degree of "excessiveness" can be detected in AD providers' reliance on hair as a metonymic stand-in for either the person on whom it seems to grow on its own or those other identifying features (such as a person's height, weight, size, shape, and skin tone) that are often left unspoken. Ian Conrich and Laura Sedgwick, *Gothic Dissections in Film and Literature: The Body in Parts* (Palgrave Macmillan, 2017), 111, 117.

18 Anna Matamala and Pilar Orero, eds., *Researching Audio Description: New Approaches* (Palgrave Macmillan, 2016).

19 Seymour Chatman, *Coming to Terms: The Rhetoric of Narrative in Fiction and Film* (Cornell University, 1990), 39.

20 See Janet Bergstrom, "Alternation, Segmentation, Hypnosis: Interview with Raymond Bellour," *Camera Obscura* 1–2, nos. 3–4 (1979): 86.

21 Bergstrom, "Alternation, Segmentation, Hypnosis."

22 Gerg Vercauteren, "Narratology and/in Audio Description," in *The Routledge Handbook of Audio Description*, ed. Christopher Taylor and Elisa Perego (Routledge, 2022).

## Coda

1 Carlos Clarens, *An Illustrated History of the Horror Film* (Putnam, 1967), xii.

2 Kylie Cheung, "Sexist Disbelief Is Taking Over the Horror Genre," *Jezebel*, October 10, 2022, https://jezebel.com/sexist-disbelief-is-taking-over-the-horror-genre-1849608771.

3 Cheung, "Sexist Disbelief."

4 Leon Hunt, "A (Sadistic) Night at the *Opera*: Notes on the Italian Horror Film," in *The Horror Reader*, ed. Ken Gelder (Routledge, 2000), 326; Gregory A. Waller, "Introduction to American Horrors," in *The Horror Reader*, ed. Ken Gelder (Routledge, 2000), 260–61.

5 Tomris Laffly, "*False Positive*," RogerEbert.com, June 25, 2021, https://www.rogerebert.com/reviews/false-positive-movie-review-2021.

6 Stephanie Zacharek, "*False Positive* Strives for Elevated Pregnancy Horror but Misses the Mark," *Time*, June 25, 2021, https://time.com/6075258/false-positive-review-hulu/.

7 Zacharek, "*False Positive* Strives."

8 See, for instance, Chrissy Bobic, "Watching *Bird Box* as a Mom Makes It Scary for Different Reasons," Romper.com, December 31, 2018, https://www.romper.com/p/being-a-mom-made-watching-bird-box-impossible-for-me-because-its-scary-in-a-totally-different-way-15579030; and Jonathan Dehaan, "Pregnancy Becomes a Nightmarish Prison in *Huesera: The Bone Woman*," *Nightmare on Film Street*, February 10, 2023, https://nofspodcast.com/review-pregnancy-becomes-a-nightmarish-prison-in-huesera-the-bone-woman.

9 Clarens, *Illustrated History of the Horror Film*, xii.

10 Clarens, *Illustrated History of the Horror Film*, xii.

11 Hunt, "(Sadistic) Night at the *Opera*," 326; Waller, "Introduction to American Horrors," 260–61.

12 Clarens, *Illustrated History of the Horror Film*, xiii.

13 Clarens, xix; see also Jim Kendrick, *Film Violence: History, Ideology, Genre* (Wallflower, 2009), 80.

14 Universal suspended *The Hunt*'s promotional campaign following the mass shooting in El Paso, Texas, on August 3, 2019, and the mass shooting in Dayton, Ohio, on August 4, 2019. The studio then delayed the theatrical release of the film until March 2020, only to shift it to digital platforms once movie theaters were closed due to COVID-19 safety precautions. Simran Hans, "*The Hunt* Review," *Guardian*, March 15, 2020, https://www.theguardian.com/film/2020/mar/15/the-hunt-horror-satire-review.

15 Clarens, *Illustrated History of the Horror Film*.

16 David Scott Diffrient, *Body Genre: Anatomy of the Horror Film* (University Press of Mississippi, 2023).

17 Noël Carroll, *The Philosophy of Horror, or, Paradoxes of the Heart* (Routledge, 1990).

18 Noël Carroll, "Horror and Humor," *Journal of Aesthetics and Art Criticism* 57, no. 2 (1999): 151.

# INDEX

Note: Page numbers appearing in italics refer to figures.


ableism, 50, 168, 201, 225
Abu Ghraib, 298
ACB. *See* American Council of the Blind
accessibility, 83, 169, 195, 236, 247, 253, 255; cinematic and textual, 201, 258; debates, 254; obstacles to, 180; options, 184, 190, 192, 233, 259, 270; socioeconomic, 82; technologies, 189, 250; tools, 29, 80, 278, 282, 287–88, 328n16
Ackerman, Diane, 102
acoustemology, 16
AD. *See* audio description
ADA. *See* Americans with Disabilities Act
Adamson, Al, 126
Adrienne, Amanda, 179
*Adventures of Lucky Pierre, The* (film), 99
affect, 128, 130, 197, 198, 205, 293; theory, 27, 105
AI. *See* artificial intelligence
AIP. *See* American International Pictures
Aldana Reyes, Xavier, 126
Alexis, Nora, 106
*Alice in Wonderland* (film), 5
*Alien* (film), 124
*All Cheerleaders Die* (film), 27, 125, 140
Allensworth, David, 179
*Alley Tramp, The* (film), 113
Amazon Prime, 174, 197, 219, 220; AD services on, 258, 327n12; captioning services on, 195, 201, 206, 207, 210, 215, 216–18, 319n39, 321n18; as content provider, 196
Amenábar, Alejandro, 53
American Council of the Blind (ACB), 248
American International Pictures (AIP), 40, 41, 307n16
*American Niece, The* (film), 226
*American Psycho* (film), 17
American Sign Language (ASL), 179, 184
Americans with Disabilities Act (ADA; 1990), 181, 195
Amicus Productions, 150
*Amityville 3-D* (film), 21–22, *22*, 44
Anderson, Greg, 216
Andrews, W. R., 241
*Anguish* (film), 56
anthology films, 150, 215–16, 249

Antonioni, Michelangelo, 309n42
*Antropophagus* (film), 148
*April Fool's Day* (film), 203–4, *204*
Argento, Dario, 202, 204, 307n20
Aristotle, 127
Arnold, Mal, 120
Aronofsky, Darren, 67
Arrow Video, 191; audio commentary provided by, 99, 114–15, 120; captioning by, 196–98, *198*, 215; Lewis-directed films box set by, 105, 112–15; *Moonshine Mountain* restoration by, 103
artificial intelligence (AI), 281, 300
ASL. *See* American Sign Language
ASMR. *See* autonomous sensory meridian response
*Assignment: Terror* (film), 36
Aster, Ari, 191
*Asylum* (film), 150
*Attack of the 50 Foot Cheerleader* (film), 27, 140
Atwill, Lionel, 165–66
audiocentrism, 38, 199
audio commentary track, 29, 195, 310, 310n54; by Arrow Video, 99, 114–15, 120; *Carnival of Souls*, 60–65; as "earsight," 39; odors and, 114–15; SDH impact kin to, 79–80, 86
audio description (AD), 29, 192, 326n77; on Amazon Prime, 258, 327n12; *benshi* in Japan relation to, 236–37, 247; body language and, 271, 277–82, *279*, *281*; deeper meanings given in, 274–78, *278*, 288; as "directing" the director, 259–61, *260*; early history of, 223–55, 257–58; as "earsight," 39, 254–55, *255*; environment missing in, *267*, 267–68; mistakes, 255, 259, 268–69, 271, 288–89; protocols and practices, 245, 248, 251–55, 258–89; sound effects and, 268, 288; as verbal zoom shot, 260, *260*
Audio Description Project, 248, 250
Audio-Visual Translation (AVT), 251, 287
*Audition* (film), 124
Augusto, Carl, 254
autonomous sensory meridian response (ASMR), 283–84
*Avenged* (film), 179, 202
Avery, Katherine Anne, 232–33, 235, 240, 246
AVT. *See* Audio-Visual Translation
Azzara, Candice, 144

*Babadook, The* (film), 300
*Babysitter, The* (film), 157
Badley, Linda, 311n19
bad taste: as cultural production, 126–27, 131, 132–33, 145; *Hellbound: Hellraiser II* and, 200; inner and outer discourses of, 103; left in one's mouth, 100; two types of, 27, 129
Baird, Robert, 263
Ballin, Albert, 168–69, 173, 174
Bantinaki, Katerina, 49, 299
*Barbarian* (film), 291–92
Barker, Clive, 44, 193, 200, 216
Barker, Jennifer, 305n33
Barrera, Melissa, 156
Barrett, Simon, 216
Barrymore, Drew, 161
Barrymore, Lionel, 24
Barthes, Roland, 287
*Battle Cry of Peace, The* (film), 234–42, *242*, 244, 245, 257, 324n36
Bava, Mario, 124
Bearne, Roland, 191–92, 248
*Beau Is Afraid* (film), 328n16
Beaumont, Charles, 40

Beckley, Tony, 202
belief, 17, 64, 79, 94–96, 294, 299; in belief, 51; delusional, 225, 305n42; in disbelief, 11; disbelief compared with, 20, 24–26, 40–52, 60, 300; disbelief mitigation and, 43–44, 89; embodied, 23, 77; faith and, 18, 19, 69, 71–72, 74, 84, 296–97; gendering of, 292, 296–97; irrational, 40; rightness or wrongness of, 9; sight as pretext for, 3–6, *4*, 23, 26, 48, 68–73, 249; in the supernatural, 4, 5, 15, 42–43, 45, 89, 288; superstition and, 43–44, 47, 72; system, 23, 40; touch as basis for, 4, *4*, 45; unconventional, 36. *See also* skepticism
Bella, Rachael, 285
Bellour, Raymond, 287
*benshi* (Japanese film narrators), 236–37, 247
Benshoff, Harry M., 171
Benson-Allott, Caetlin, 315n7
Berg, Alban, 37
Berger, John, 308n25
Berger, Sidney, 56, 63–64
Bergman, Ingmar, 57
Berman, Shari Springer, 259, 280
Bernstein, Charles, 203–4, 211, 212
Berwick, Wayne, 149, 150
*Better Part, The* (film), 226
Bettinelli-Olpin, Matt, 157, 188, 260
*Bingo Hell* (film), 281
*Bird Box* (film), 296
*Birds, The* (film), 306n1
*Birth of a Nation, The* (film), 232, 237
*Bit* (film), 270
*Black Christmas* (film), 180
*Blackcoat's Daughter, The* (film), 202
*Blackenstein* (film), 81
Blackton, J. Stuart, 234, 237–40, 243–44, 258, 324n38
Blair, Linda, 25, 70, 76, 79
*Blair Witch Project, The* (film), 17
Blatty, William Peter, 70, 78
*Blind* (film), 226
*Blind Basket Weaver, The* (film), 226
*Blind Cattle King, The* (film), 226
*Blind Composer's Dilemma, The* (film), 226
*Blind Deception, A* (film), 226
*Blind Fate* (film), 226
*Blind Fiddler, The* (film), 226
*Blind Justice* (film), 228
*Blind Man's Bluff* (film), 228
*Blind Man's Sacrifice, The* (film), 226
*Blind Miner, The* (film), 226–27
*Blind Musician, The* (film), 226
blindness, 29, 201, 264, 284; AD protocols and, 251–55; *The Battle Cry of Peace* narration and, 234–37, 245; Braille and, 235, 247; as character trait, 172, 323n8; from combat, 220, 254, 325n52; in *Don't Look Now*, 68–69; metaphorical, 50, 58, 221, 240; as plot device, 249; in silent cinema, 226–30, *227*, *228*, 233–34; as socially constructed disability, 258; spectatorship and, 223–24, 230–36, 245–48, 289; as "visible" disability, 168; war and, 224–25. *See also* audio description
*Blind Princess and the Poet, The* (film), 226
*Blind Shall See, The* (film), 226
*Blind Woman's Curse* (film), 220–21
*Blind Woman's Story, A* (film), 229
Blockbuster Video, 253
*Blood and Black Lace* (film), 124
*Blood Feast* (film), 99, 100, 101, 102, 113, 114, 119–20, 122, 202
*Blood Feast 2: All U Can Eat* (film), 99, 120
*Blood Rage* (film), 191

*Blood Red Sky* (film), 281
*Blood Sucking Freaks* (film), 154
Blumhouse Productions, 219, 270
body horror, 197, 244, 293
Bogdanovich, Peter, 17
Boland, Brian, 283
*Boogens, The* (film), 63
Boorman, Imogen, 199
Boorman, John, 26, 72, 76, 311n26
Borch, Gaston, 204
Borja, Joana, 272
Bottaro, Luciano, 3–6, *4*, *5*, 11–12
Bourdain, Anthony, 122
Bourdieu, Pierre, 127
Bradley, Doug, 194
Braille, 235, 247
*Braindead* (film), 216, 322n30
Braun, Sabine, 268
breasts, 74, 112, 126, 141, 295, 296
breath, 121; bad, 117–19
breathing, 16, 88, 89, 184, 194, 213; heavy, 187; labored, 186, 211; metaphorical, 104; sonorous, 85
Brice, Patrick, 153, 258, 270
*Bride of Frankenstein, The* (film), 96, 172, 243
Briefel, Aviva, 265
*Brigadoon* (musical), 121
Briggs, Joe Bob, 124
*Bring It On* (film), 140
*Bring It On 7: Cheer or Die* (film), 140
*Brood, The* (film), 244
Brosnan, Pierce, 295
*Brother Love* (film), 226
Brown, Julie, 59
Browning, Tod, 24, 25, 44, 166, 176
Buck, Douglas, 41
Buckley, Jessie, 292
Buhler, James, 210–11, 212–13
*Bulldog Drummond* (film), 246
Bullins, Jeffrey, 249
Burges, Joel, 265
*Burn, Witch, Burn* (film), 10, 40–43, *41*, *43*, 47, 50–52, 56, 307n18
*Burning, The* (film), 320n45
Burns, Helen, 208
Burstyn, Ellen, 71
Burton, Richard, 72, 76
Bush, W. Stephen, 241

*Cabinet of Dr. Caligari, The* (film), 177, 243
*Cabiria* (film), 237
*Called Back* (film), 226, 227, 228, *228*, 322n8
*Cam* (film), 284–85
Campbell, Georgina, 292
Campbell, Neve, 160, 161
*Candyman* (1992 film), 10, 44
*Candyman* (2021 film), 258
*Cannibal Ferox* (film), 148
*Cannibal Holocaust* (film), 148, 150
cannibalism, 148–51, 153–54; autocannibalistic, 141
captions, 29, 250, 254; Amazon Prime, 195, 201, 206, 207, 210, 215, 216–18, 319n39, 321n18; by Arrow Video, 196–98, *198*, 215; biased, 174; in *The Changeling*, 208–10; deaf actors and early, 173; diegetic, *181*, 183; *Exorcist II: The Heretic* (film), 81–86, *85*; fluidic, 219, 221; in *Hellbound: Hellraiser II*, 193–98, *199*; *House on Haunted Hill*, 91–93, *92*, *97*; humorousness in, *97*; for *Hush*, 184–92, *190*; instructive, 321n18; as interpretative practice, 196, 201–2; of laughter, 182, 191; low standards of, 180–81, 184; missing, 188–89, 192, 216, 219, 320n45; mistakes in, 80, 182; musical, 201–6, *203*, *204*, *206*, 210, 212, 216–17; nonspecific, 202, 206, *206*; onscreen and offscreen environment in, *218*, 218–21;

prefilmic, 89; sound effects, 194, 197, 202, 212; variances of, 91–92, 212–13; of wetness, 96, 98, 221; YouTube, 319n39. *See also* subtitles for the deaf and hard of hearing
*Captive Girl* (film), 72
*Carnival of Souls* (film), 18, 22, 23, 300, 309n42; audio commentary track, 60–65; irrationality of rationality and, 20; perception and, 54–60, *55*; soundtrack, 59
Carpenter, John, 17, 188, 233, 262
Carreras, Michael, 41
*Carrie* (film), 143, 148
Carroll, Noël, 20, 48–49, 96, 299, 301
Cassavetes, John, 93
Castle, William: circus-like atmosphere created by, 238; gimmicks and low-budget approach, 40, 41; *House on Haunted Hill* of, 26, 46–47, 86–94, *92*, 96–97, 191; *The Tingler* of, 87, 96, 176, 177, 238, 318n31
*Castle of Otranto, The* (Walpole), 244
*Catacombs* (film), 37
*Cat in the Brain, A* (film), 133–34
*Cat People* (film), 328n16
*Cave of the Living Dead* (film), 176, 177
*Cellar, The* (film), 63
cemeteries, 34, 36, 94–95
*Cemetery of Terror* (film), 1
CGI. *See* computer-generated imagery
chainsaws, 15–16, 133
Chaney, Lon, Jr., 35
*Changeling, The* (film), 207–10
Chatman, Seymour, 257, 287
Chau, Hong, 136
*Cheerleader Camp* (film), 27, 140, 148
*Cheerleader Massacre* (film), 140
cheerleaders, 27, 125, 126, 139–46, 148
Chendi, Carlo, 3–6, *4*, 5, 11–12
Cheung, Kylie, 292
Christie, Julie, 68
*Christmas Cruelty!* (film), 135–36
Ciccarese, Luigi, 133
*Cinderella* (film), 230–31
"cine-eye" (*kino-glaz*), 38
*Circus of Horrors* (film), 216–17
*City of the Dead, The* (film), 36
clairvoyancy, 25, 43, 68, 69
Clarens, Carlos, 291–94, 296–99
Clark, Greydon, 141–42
Clasen, Mathias, 299
Classen, Constance, 13–14, 47–48, 308n25
Cleghorn, Elinor, 90, 91
Clifford, John, 61–62, 63
*Clinical* (film), 286–87
Clive, Colin, 9
close-ups, 149, 197, 198, 253; of eyes, 41, *41*, 59, 64–65, 199; of faces, 117–19, *118*, *171*, 171–72
Clover, Carol, 38–40, 65, 115, 139
Cocteau, Jean, 57
Cody, Diablo, 142
cognition, 49–50, 252, 263; corporeal, 20, 47, 236; delight of incongruity and, 135; maternal, 295; metacognitive, 12; as puzzle-solving, 220, 301; sight relation to, 15, 249
Cohen, Larry, 129
Colangeli, Otello, 133
Colangelo, B. J., 140–41
Collet-Serra, Jaume, 178
*Color Me Blood Red* (film), 100, 101, 102
comedy, 89, 130, 145, 173, 274; cannibal, 148; comedy-horror mashups, 27, 80, 81, 134, 136, 146, 154, 182, 215, 301, 321n17; parody, 95, 119, 139, 142–44; romantic, 36, 61; sex, 142–43; sketch, 150; teen, 140. *See also* laughter

comics/comic books, 8, 16, 150–52; witches and witchcraft in, 3–6, *4*, *5*, 11–12
*Company of Wolves, The* (film), 67
computer-generated imagery (CGI), 67, 75, 178, 179, 244
*Conjure Wife* (Leiber), 40
Connor, Kevin, 148
Connor, Steven, 11, 14
Conway, Hugh, 227, 322n8
Conway, James L., 63
Cook, Elisha, Jr., 87
cookbooks, 123–24
Cooke, Mervyn, 210
Cooke, Olivia, 275
Cooper, Akela, 281
Corman, Roger, 23
Cornea, Christine, 95
*Corporate Animals* (film), 153
Count Dracula (fictional character), 109, 154, 172
COVID-19, 300, 330n14
Cox, Courteney, 135
Crain, Kenneth C., 223–24
Crane, Jonathan, 106
Craven, Wes, 19, 211, 212
*Creature from Cannibal Creek* (film), 153
*Creepshow* (film), 150–52
Cregger, Zach, 291
Cristiani, Giovanni, 133
Criterion Collection, The, 61–63
Cronenberg, David, 244
Crosland, Alan, 245
Cross, Ian, 201–2
cult movies, 10, 61, 119, 124, 300. *See also* fandom
*Curse of the Mummy's Tomb, The* (film), 37
*Curse of the Werewolf, The* (film), 126
Curtiz, Michael, 176
*Cut* (film), 18
DaCosta, Nia, 258
D'Amato, Joe, 148
Daniel, Adam, 28
Dano, Royal, 255
*Darkened Rooms* (film), 175
*Darkness, The* (film), 254–55, *255*, 258
*Dawn of the Dead* (film), 148, 150
*Day of the Dead* (film), 101
*Day Shift* (film), 274
deaf gain, 80, 186
*Deaf Mute Howls, The* (Ballin), 168–70
deafness, 213, 224, 246, 250, 318n31, 325n52; benevolent medical specialists and, 229–30; *Blind Woman's Curse* and, 219–21; deaf gain and, 80, 186; *The Deaf Mute Howls* and, 168–70; *Exorcist II: The Heretic* and, 81–86, *85*; *Friday the 13th: A New Beginning* and, 217–19; *Hellbound: Hellraiser II* captioning and, 193, 195; "hidden" quality of, 168, 172; Karloff on, 165, 167–68; musical captioning and, 202, 205, 210, 212; as public health issue, 168; representations of, 98, 171–91, *181*; sign language and, 168, 169, 179, 184; unhelpful subtitles and, 92–93. *See also* captions; subtitles for the deaf and hard of hearing
*Death Curse of Tartu* (film), 72
*Deedee's Blind Master* (film), 226
*Deep Blue Sea* (film), 132
deformity, 3, 96, 167, 171–72, 200–201
delusion, 3, 9, 225, 255, 295, 296
*Demonia* (film), 132–33
demonic possession, 26, 54, 179; Clover on, 39; Indian films on, 44; special effects, 71, 75, *75*. See also *Exorcist, The*; *Exorcist II: The Heretic*
*Demons* (film), 18, 39

Dench, Ernest A., 231–32
Denig, Lynde, 241
Deodato, Ruggero, 148
Derry, Charles, 70–71
*Descent, The* (film), 241
*Desert Song, The* (film), 247
*Destined to Be Ingested* (film), 153
Dett, R. Nathaniel, 205
*Devil Bat* (film), 202
*Devil-Doll, The* (film), 172
*Devil's Due* (film), 260–64, 277
*Devil's Messenger, The* (film), 62
*Devil's Rejects, The* (film), 298
De Wilde, Graham, 209
de Zwaana, Klaas, 239–40
disability, 232–33, 250, 289; ableism and, 50, 168, 201, 225; awareness, 39; captioning limitations and, 98; from combat, 240, 243, 325n52; as deformity, 172, 200–201; *Hellbound: Hellraiser II* and, 199–200; in *Hush*, 184; impairment contrasted with, 169; invisible, 173; legislation, 181, 195; as "monstrosity," 200; as object of pity, 225, 229, 235; rights, 168–69, 182; as social construct, 174, 175, 178, 221, 258; studies, 27, 80, 237, 246; tropes/horror subject of, 172, 174, 176, 179, 202, 207, 209
disbelief mitigation, 43–44, 89
disfigurement, 167, 172–73, 200, 216, 244, 320n45
disgust, 42, 101, 103, 106, 107, 109, 111, 114, 121–22, 127, 131, 139, 144–45, 147, 177, 190, 215, 219; enjoyment of, 49; etymology of, 129; moral, 129
dissolves, 8, 64
Dixon, Jill, 35
Dixon, Thomas, Jr., 232
*Doctor's Blind Child, The* (film), 226
Donald, Amie, 281, 282
*Don't Fall Asleep* (film), 93
*Don't Look Now* (film), 26, 52, 67–70, 95, 300
doppelgängers, 77, 81
Douglas, Melvyn, 170
Downe, Allison Louise, 104, 113–14, 115, 123
*Dracula* (film), 10, 25, 43–44, 159, 165, 166, 175, 243, 293, 298
*Dracula* (Stoker), 44; Broadway adaptation, 166
*Dracula's Fiancée* (film), 36
dreams, 20, 63, 73, 265; sequence, 217; waking, 52, 57
Dreyer, Carl Theodor, 62
*Dr. Jekyll and Mr. Hyde* (film), 24, 25, 328n17
*Dr. Terror's House of Horrors* (film), 150
drunkenness, 95, 172, 255
dryness, 86, 90–91, 93, 98, 216, 219
Ducournau, Julia, 98, 124, 293
Dudenhoeffer, Larrie, 214–15
du Maurier, Daphne, 68
*Dumplings* (film), 129
DVD/Blu-ray, 29, 39, 61, 63, 72, 80, 83, 86, 91, 96, 98, 174, 180, 188, 191, 195, 196, 219, 233, 258, 259, 261, 264, 283, 310n54; language options, 253–54; Lewis-directed films box set, 105, 112–15. *See also* audio commentary track; paratextuality
Dwan, Allan, 228

ears, 13, 16, 21, 23, 26–27, 80, 86, 89, 92, 101, 115, 123, 167, 174, 175, 188, 198–99, 217, 220, 249, 258, 267, 292; covering one's, 178, 207; "seeing," 15, 28, 39, 41, 46, 48, 254–55, *255*, 259, 289, 300; targeted by horror films, 38, 103. *See also* hearing; sound effects

*Eat* (film), 153
*Eaten Alive!* (film), 148
*Eating Raoul* (film), 148
Ebert, Roger, 70–71, 148, 199–200, 201
EC Comics, 150, 151, 152
Edeson, Arthur, 171
elevated horror, 27, 131, 191, 309n42
Ellis, Katie, 246–47
Elmore, Brad Michael, 270
emotions, 19, 37, 41, 49, 81–82, 96, 166, 170, 241, 282; contradictory, 131; meta-, 127, 128, 130; mixture of, 59, 152, 191; negative, 20, 70, 281, 299, 301; overwrought, 93; primal, 249
Engineer, Aryana, 178
Englund, Robert, 211, 214
Enos, Mireille, 280
*Eraserhead* (film), 56
Erish, Andrew A., 230
Ernst, Max, 297
Erwin, Elizabeth, 125
eugenics, 172
Evans, Nicola Jean, 115
Everman, Welch D., 142
evil, 18, 26, 40, 45, 68, 70, 73, 76, 79
*Evil Dead* (film), 179
excrement, 122, 134–35
*Exorcist, The* (film), 10, 26, 54, 68, 71–72, 76, 78, 79, 83, 86; critical reception of, 70, 95
*Exorcist II: The Heretic* (film), 26, 71, 73–78, *75*, 80, 95; captions, 81–86, *85*; critical reception of, 72, 79, 311n26
*Eye, The* (film), 67
eyeglasses, 217–18, *218*
eyes, 13, 14, 15, 16, 21, 23–24, 26–28, 38–40, 46, 50–59, 62, 67–71, 74, 80, 85–86, 89, 92, 95, 98, 100, 101, 106, 112, 123–24, 159, 173, 178–79, 198–200, 227–28, 235, 249, 255, 261, 267, 274–75, 287, 292; as center of human subjectivity, 57; "cine-eye," 38; closed/covered, 58, 110, 178, 226, 231; close-ups of, 41, *41*, 59, 64–65, 199; "false," 64; gouged, 132, 294; hearing and, 39, 48, 174, 300–301; of the heart, 223; horror's centering of, 38; sliced, 220

faith, 18, 19, 69, 71, 74, 84, 296–97; superstition and, 43–44, 47, 72. *See also* belief
fake blood, 114, 116, 154
fake fingers, 114
fakeness, 46, 87, 91, 105, 112, 114, 116, 117, 122, 133–34, 280, 300
*Fall of a Nation, The* (film), 232
*False Positive* (film), 292, *294*, 294–96
fandom, 62, 63, 79, 93, 95, 115, 126, 133, 140, 156, 157, 159, 161, 297, 298; cult movie, 10, 61, 119, 124, 300
fantasy, 4, 10, 45, 47, 67, 73, 296
Fargeat, Coralie, 293
Farrow, Mia, 94, 124
*Fatal Games* (film), 145
Federico, Tony, 123
*Feed* (film), 153
Feldman, Corey, 217
Feldstein, Al, 152
Feste, Shana, 280
*Fiend* (film), 36
Fiennes, Ralph, 131, 136
film festivals, 146, 160, 293, 309n42
*Final Destination 3* (film), 67
"final girl," the, 125, 157, 180, 183, 277
fingers, 16, 107, 211, 230–31, 261; Braille and, 235, 247; fake, 114. *See also* tactility; touch
Flanagan, Mike, 179, 180, 183, 186, 189, 190

flashbacks, 69, 77, 151, 209
flavor, 96, 109–10, 114, 119–20, 121, 122, 128–29, 135, 145, 147, 149, 152, 154, 156. *See also* food; gustation; taste
*Flesh and the Fiends, The* (film), 36
Fletcher, Louise, 72, 76
Florey, Robert, 125, 247
Flowers, Christopher, 275, 277
*Fly, The* (film), 244
*Fly II, The* (film), 96
Folk, Robert, 186, 204
food, 27, 89, 112, 118–19, 121, 129, 135, 147–50, 160–61, 275; meat and, 50, 99, 101, 106–7, 111, 114, 120, 122–24, 130, 132, 134, 140, 146, 149, 153, 154, 156–59; in *The Menu*, 136–38, *138*; in *Pandemonium*, 143–45, *144*; *Scream VI* and, 155–58, *156*, *158*; *Suck* and blood as, 154–55, *155*; vegetables and, 107, 111, 123, 143, 145, 146
*Forget Me Not* (film), 245
found footage, 261, 283
*Four Skulls of Jonathan Drake, The* (film), 205–6, *206*
Foxx, Jamie, 274
Fraker, William A., 75–76
*Frankenstein* (film), 9, 25, 36, 165, 167, 170, 172, 175, 243, 293, 298
*Frankenstein* (Shelley), 200, 244
Frazier, Gregory, 247, 248, 249
*Freaks* (film), 176
Freeland, Cynthia, 299
Freeman, Eric, 132
Frees, Paul, 40–41
Freud, Sigmund, 5, 8, 150
*Friday the 13th* (film), 142
*Friday the 13th: A New Beginning* (film), 206, 217–19, *218*, 321n18
*Friday the 13th Part VIII: Jason Takes Manhattan* (film), 158
*Friday the 13th: The Final Chapter* (film), 186, 189
Friedkin, William, 26, 68, 70, 71, 78
Friedman, David F., 120
*From Beyond the Grave* (film), 150
Fry, Carrol Lee, 142
Fulci, Lucio, 132–34, 148, 183, 191
Fuller, Thomas, 67, 70
furrowed brows, 271, 277–81, *279*, *281*, 285, 288

Gabriadzes, Leo, 284
Galindo, Rubén, Jr., 1
Gallagher, John, Jr., 180
*Gallop of Death, The* (film), 226
Garai, Romola, 160
Garland, Alex, 291
Garrison, Lindley Miller, 237
gaslighting, 94, 292
Gayden, Henry, 270
Geiger, Moritz, 28
genitalia, 123, 135, 139
*Gerald's Game* (film), 183, 189–90, *190*
Gerber, Adrian, 239–40
*Get Out* (film), 291, 297
Ghostface, 156–59
ghost glasses, *75*, 75–76, 78
ghosts, 44, 46, 64, 73, 87, 132, 208, 209, 219, 244, 277, 309n42, 311n19; figurative, 161; as imaginary beings, 45, 89; liminality of, 68; long-haired, 286; pre-CGI, 75
*Ghoulies II* (film), 255
giallo films, 81, 161, 191
Gilchrist, Keir, 269
Gilford, Zach, 260
Gillett, Tyler, 157, 188, 260
*Ginger Snaps* (film), 44, 328n17
Ginsberg, Claire, 149
*Girl, the Body, and the Pill, The* (film), 113

Glasby, Matt, 26, 208
Glass, Rose, 216
Glazer, Ilana, 294
*Glory of Light, The* (film), 226
Glover, Crispin, 189
Goldhaber, Daniel, 284
Goldwyn, Samuel, 246
*Golem, The* (film), 243
*Good Little Devil, A* (film), 226
*Gore Gore Girls, The* (film), 27, 106–13, *108*, *113*, 122
*Gothika* (film), 10, 73
*Graveyard Shift* (film), 36
Grayden, Sprague, 283
Great Depression, 10, 72, 125, 166, 191, 298
*Greater Than Art* (film), 226
Greenwald, Robert, 177
Griffith, D. W., 228, 232, 237, 258
*Grimcutty* (film), 281, 282–83
Grissmer, John, 191
Grodin, Charles, 94
*Gruesome Twosome, The* (film), 99, 113, 117, 118, *118*
Guantánamo Bay, 298
Gugino, Carla, 183, 190
*Guiding Light, The* (film), 226
gustation, 12, 27, 48, 65, 100, 110, 119, 122, 129, 135, 139, 147, 199

Hackner, Paul, 178
Halberstam, Jack, 215
*Halloween* (film), 10, 17, 180, 262
*Halloween II* (film), 188
Halperin, Victor, 204
Hammer Films, 41, 126
Hampton, Hope, 245
Hanich, Julian, 28
Hanke, Ken, 25
Hansen, Gunnar, 16
Hantke, Steffen, 67, 75, 214
Harding, Warren G., 175
Harvey, Herk, 18–20, 52, 55, 57, 61–65
Hastings, Reed, 253–54. *See also* Netflix
Hatton, Rondo, 173
*Haunted Hotel, The* (film), 237, 244
haunted houses, 21, 44, 46, 89, 91, 209
*Haunt of Fear, The* (comic book), 150
Hay, William, 200–201
Hayers, Sidney, 40, 42
HBO Max, 212–13
*Head Cheerleader Dead Cheerleader* (film), 125, 126, 139
Headey, Lena, 160
hearing, 11–12, 15–16, 24, 26, 27, 28–29, 40, 46, 47, 53, 59–60, 69–70, 78–89, 92, 98, 100, 101, 111, 116, 163–92, 193–221, 227, 232, 250, 280, 292; aid, 178; eyes and, 39, 48, 174, 300–301; lens, 254; loss, 80, 168, 173, 174, 183, 186, 258; sensory deprivation and, 21–22, *22*; visual expression of impairment in, *171*, 171–72. *See also* deafness; silent cinema; subtitles for the deaf and hard of hearing
*Hear No Evil* (film), 177
*Hearts of the World* (film), 258
Hedley, Jack, 35, 183
Hegel, Georg Wilhelm Friedrich, 27
Heidegger, Martin, 22
Heijningen, Matthijs van, Jr., 271, 280, 282
Heisserer, Eric, 271
Helgren, Jake, 139
*Hellbound Heart, The* (Barker), 193
*Hellbound: Hellraiser II* (film), 44, 193–202, *198*, 218, 321n18
*Hellhole* (film), 326n77
*Hell Night* (film), 39
*Hellraiser* (film), 44

Hendrix, Grady, 103
Henner, Jonathan, 168–69
Hennig, Shelly, 275
*Hereditary* (film), 191
*Her Escape* (film), 226
Herrmann, Bernard, 8, 193, 194, 199, 216
*Her Triumph* (film), 226
*Highgraders, The* (film), 226
hillbilly culture, 103, 118
Hilligoss, Candace, 22, 52, 60, 64
Hills, Matt, 299
Hippocrates, 90–91, 93
*His Busy Hour* (film), 173
Hitchcock, Alfred, 1–3, 6, 8, 37, 67, 119, 157, 298, 306n1
Hodge, Aldis, 279
Hofer, Kristina Pia, 100
Holland, Andrew, 245
Hollingsworth, Tim, 155
Holly, Lauren, 160
home invasions, 179, 187, 270
home video, 29, 62, 65, 79, 80, 82, 83, 85, 86, 105, 112, 116, 174, 182–85, 195, 198, 203, 208, 213, 219, 233, 251, 253, 257–89, 310n54, 328n16. *See also* Arrow Video; DVD/Blu-ray
*Homicidal* (film), 238
homophobia, 127, 139, 269
Hooper, Tobe, 16, 17, 19, 101, 215
*Hopes of Blind Alley, The* (film), 228
*Horror Express* (film), 202
*Horror of Party Beach, The* (film), 305n42
*Hostel* (film), 126, 298
*House on Haunted Hill* (film), 26, 46–47, 86–94, *92*, 96–97, 191
*House That Dripped Blood, The* (film), 150
Houston, Beverle, 68, 70–71
Howes, David, 13–14, 47–48, 308n25
*How to Make a Doll* (film), 121
*Huesera: The Bone Woman* (film), 296
Hulu, 29, 180, 258, 282, 294
*Human Centipede, The* (film), 129, 146–47
Hume, David, 127
humor, 3, 94, 104–5, 112–13, 124, 128, 130, 152, 154, 244, 293, 300–301; of bodily excess, 27, 97, 132–33; carnivalesque, 135; exaggerated, 59, 146; macabre, 86; parody and, 95, 119, 139, 142–44; recurring, 170; unintentional, 51, *97*. *See also* comedy; laughter
Humphrey, Daniel, 79
*Hunt, The* (film), 298, 330n14
Hunter, I. Q., 131
Hunter, Tab, 146
*Hush* (film), 179–91, *181*, 320n45
Husserl, Edmund, 28
Hutchings, Peter, 10–11, 33, 170
hysteria, 46, 86, 87–88, 90–91, 93–97

impairment, 50, 68, 175–77, 186, 192, 213, 225, 228–32, 242, 245, 246, 249, 251, 257, 259, 284, 287; disability contrasted with, 169; visual expression of hearing, *171*, 171–72
implants, 64; cochlear, 179
intersensoriality, 27, 28, 48, 101, 121, 134, 145, 151, 221, 233, 249, 288, 299; synesthesia and, 12–16, 29, 47, 111
intersubjectivity, 28, 47, 74
intertextuality, 36, 81, 141, 157, 264, 269, 328n16
*Intolerance* (film), 232
*Intruder* (film), 186, 208–9
*Invisible Man, The* (1933 film), 243
*Invisible Man, The* (2020 film), 258, 278–80, *279*
*Invisible Ray, The* (film), 172

*Iron Rose, The* (film), 34
irrationality, 6–9, 11–16, 18–21, 23, 27, 29, 40, 46, 47, 90, 93, 288, 292, 299–300
Ishii, Teruo, 219
*I Spit on Your Grave* (film), 39
*It* (film), 178, 270
*It Comes at Night* (film), 270
*It Follows* (film), 89, 264–71, *267*, 288, 300
iTunes, 196
*I Walked with a Zombie* (film), 307n18

Jackson, Peter, 216
Jackson, Samuel L., 132
Jackson-Cohen, Oliver, 279
Jacobs, Devery, 280
Japanese film narrators (*benshi*), 236–37, 247
*Jaws* (film), 37
*Jazz Singer, The* (film), 245–46
*Jennifer's Body* (film), 142
*Jigsaw* (film), 280
Johnson, Russell L., 169, 175
Johnstone, Gerard, 281
Jolie, Angelina, 160
Jolson, Al, 245–46
Jones, Amy Holden, 124
Jones, F. Richard, 246
Jones, James Earl, 77, 79
Judd, Ashley, 160
jump scares, 202, 209, 263
*Just for the Hell of It* (film), 117, 121
Jusu, Nikyatu, 259

Kalekin-Fishman, Devorah, 47
Kalinak, Kathryn, 210
Kane, Carol, 143
Kanopy, 81, 91–92, 174, 182, 191, 202
Kant, Immanuel, 28, 127
Kaproff, Dana, 202–3
Karloff, Boris, 23, 165, 166–68, 169–70, 172
Kaufman, Lloyd, 150
Kelly, Casey Ryan, 264, 266
Kent, Charles, 241
*Kentucky Fried Movie, The* (film), 150
Kerr, Martha, 165–67
Khan, Sofian, 153
*Killer Klowns from Outer Space* (film), 154
Kinder, Marsha, 68, 70–71
King, Joe, 150
King, Joey, 280
King, Stephen, 36, 150, 178, 190
*King Kong* (film), 72
*kino-glaz* ("cine-eye"), 38
Kolster, Clarence, 171
*Konga* (film), 93
Krasinski, John, 179, 191
Kress, Frank, 107
Kruger, Jan-Louis, 251–53
Kusama, Karyn, 142

*Lady of the Lighthouse, The* (film), 226
Lam, Karen, 140
Lambert, Mary, 124
*Land of the Dead* (film), 241
Langenkamp, Heather, 20, 214
Laser, Dieter, 147
*Last Cannibal World* (film), 148
laughter, 7, 33, 49, 51, 87, 157, 168, 207, 298; captioned, 182, 191; of horror, 94–96; maniacal, 211, 212, 213; purgative, 130; sarcastic, 199; shared, 128
Laughton, Charles, 9
*Lazarus Effect, The* (film), 219
Lee, John, 292, 294
Leeder, Murray, 96, 209
Legrand, Alistair, 286
Leiber, Fritz, 40
Leigh, Janet, 1, 2, 157
*Le manoir du diable* (film), 244
Lenzi, Umberto, 148
Leonard, Brett, 153

Leonetti, John R., 258
Lerner, Alan Jay, 121
Lerner, Neil, 37, 210
*Let Me In* (film), 328n16
Levine, Barry, 248
Levine, Michael, 299
Lewis, Herschell Gordon, 27, 99–124, 150, 202
Lewton, Val, 2
*Lie, The* (film), 280–81
*Lighthouse by the Sea, The* (film), 245
liminality, 21, 43, 49, 56, 68, 75
Lindsay, Vachel, 169
Liszt, Franz, 204
Littschwager, Simin Nina, 52, 53, 57
*Living Venus* (film), 99
Loiselle, André, 126, 299
*London After Midnight* (film), 25
*Lost Highway* (film), 56
*Lost Note, The* (film), 226
*Love at First Bite* (film), 136
Lovecraft, H. P., 234
*Love Is Blind* (film), 226
*Love Witch, The* (film), 81
Low, Kelvin E. Y., 47
Lowe, Alice, 293
Lowenstein, Adam, 2–3
Lubitsch, Ernst, 228
Lugosi, Bela, 9, 25, 44, 94, 165–66
Lynch, David, 56
Lytton, L. Rogers, 241

MacClancy, Jeremy, 123
magic, 3, 4, 36, 42, 52, 114, 115–17, 244
Mailes, Charles Hill, 245
makeup, 71, 143, 152, 166–67, 170, 258; prosthetics and, 64, 83
*Malevolence* (film), 63
Mamoulian, Rouben, 24
Mane, Tyler, 188
Manfredini, Harry, 217, 321n18
*Maniac* (film), 41
*Man's Best Friend* (film), 226
*Man Who Collected Food, The* (film), 153
*Mark of the Vampire* (film), 24, 25
Marks, Lawrence E., 12–13
Martelli, Carlo, 35, 37
Marvel, David, 173
masculinity, 136, 139; toxic, 291–92
masks, 16, 45, 114, 157, 166, 179, 186, 188, 270; death, 215; hockey, 218; ski, 274
masochism, 119, 152; sado-masochist, 81
Mason, Hilary, 68
Massey, Raymond, 170
Matania, Clelia, 68
Matheson, Richard, 40
Mathieson, Muir, 216
Matlin, Marlee, 177
matricide, 7
Maxim, Hudson, 240, 242
*Mayhem* (film), 157
Maylam, Tony, 320n45
Mayne, Judith, 57
McCarthy, Amy, 136–37
McCarthy, Todd, 311n26
McCrann, Charles, 148
McDowell, Malcolm, 154
McGowan, Rose, 160–61
McGraw, Violet, 282
McLean, Greg, 258
meat. *See* food
*Meateater, The* (film), 148
Medak, Peter, 207
*M3GAN* (film), 281–82
Méliès, Georges, 244
*Melody of Love, The* (film), 226
*Men* (film), 291
Mena, Stevan, 63
Mencken, H. L., 169
Menghini, Santiago, 272
*Menu, The* (film), 20, 131, 136–38, *138*, 139

metafiction, 18, 39
#MeToo, 153, 278, 291
*Microwave Massacre* (film), 146, 149–50, 158
Middleton, Jason, 265
*Midnight Mystery* (film), 175
*Midsommar* (film), 241
Migliore, John, 153
Miike, Takashi, 124
Miller, Allsion, 260
Miller, Jason, 72
Miller, Jeff, 126–27
Miller, William Ian, 121–22
Mirabella-Davis, Carlo, 153
Miramax, 159–60
misogyny, 125, 140, 291
*Mist, The* (film), 36, 309n47
Mitchell, David Robert, 88, 264, 268, 289
Monière, 179
Monroe, Maika, 265
*Monster Walks, The* (film), 93
*Moonshine Mountain* (film), 103, 117–19, *118*
Moore, Eva, 170, 173
Moreau, David, 270
*Moro Witch Doctor* (film), 72
Morris, David Burton, 148
Moss, Elisabeth, 278
*Motel Hell* (film), 148, 150
*Mother!* (film), 67
*Mountain of the Cannibal God* (film), 148
mouthfeel, 130, 149
mouths, 112, 129–31, 135, 139, 145, 147, 150, 156, 157, 159, 160, 219, 276, 285; mindful, 138; open, 51, 59, 75, 77, 109, 117–18, 170, 194, 281
movie posters, 34, 67, 142, 145
Muir, John Kenneth, 134
*Murders in the Rue Morgue* (film), 125
Murnau, F. W., 177
Murphy, Bernice M., 60–61
Mussorgsky, Modest, 204
Myers, Verna, 254
*Mystery of the Wax Museum* (film), 176

Nair, Kartik, 159–61
*Nanny* (film), 259
nausea, 99, 101, 112, 119, 122, 129, 135; odor and, 151; vomit and, 26, 130, 219
Nayman, Adam, 78–79
Neff, Miles, 248
Netflix, 29, 174, 179, 180–82, 184–85, 191, 219, 248, 253–54, 258, 266, 270, 274, 285, 326n77
Neumeyer, David, 210
neurodiversity, 39, 234
neurology, 12, 13, 47, 70
neuroses, 89, 170, 243
*New York Ripper, The* (film), 81, 183, 191
*Next of Kin* (film), 98
Nicholson, Jack, 23
*Night Gallery* (film), 249
*Night Has a Thousand Eyes* (film), 25
*Nightmare on Elm Street, A* (film), 19, 93, 180, 203, 211–12, 214, 217, 218
*Night of the Demon* (film), 10, 42
*Night of the Eagle*. See *Burn, Witch, Burn*
*Night of the Living Dead* (film), 17, 36, 265, 291
*Nobody Sleeps in the Woods Tonight* (film), 326n77
*No One Gets Out Alive* (film), 272–74
*Nope* (film), 98
Norden, Martin F., 179, 229
North, Wilfrid, 234, 258
*Nosferatu* (film), 177, 243
Novak, B. J., 155
Nyong'o, Lupita, 160

Obama, Barack, 250
occultism, 24, 43, 68, 142

Ochoa, George, 96
ocularcentrism, 65, 230, 254, 275; in film theory, 23, 38, 57, 100, 199; in horror films, 38, 249
odor, 135, 145; audio commentary track and, 114–15; body, 117, 119; good or bad, 101–3; imagined, 116; molecules, 102; nauseating, 151; noxious, 104, 118; olfaction and, 12, 27, 48, 65, 99–124, 199; qualifiers, 122
offal, 99, 101, 110, 119, 122–24
*Offerings* (film), 129
Ohmart, Carol, 46, 86
Ojeda, Michael, 179
Okuno, Chloe, 216
*Old Dark House, The* (film), 170–73, *171*, 182, 188, 191
olfaction, 12, 27, 48, 65, 99–124, 199
*Omen, The* (film), 34, 142
*One Flew Over the Cuckoo's Nest* (film), 72
opening credits. *See* title sequences
*Open Water* (film), 48
*Orphan* (film), 178, 327n12
*Orphan: Kill First* (film), 327n12
Ortega, Jenna, 155
*Others, The* (film), 53, 56
*Ouija* (film), 275–78, *278*

Palmer, James, 26, 67, 69
Paltrow, Gwyneth, 160
Palud, Xavier, 270
*Pandemonium* (film), 27, 139, 141, 142–45, *144*, 146, *146*, 148–49
paranoia, 60, 296, 301
*Paranormal Activity 2* (film), 283
paratextuality, 29, 34, 61, 62, 64, 115, 116, 259, 310n54; intertextuality and, 36, 81, 141, 157, 264, 269, 328n16; movie posters and, 34, 67, 142, 145
Paré, Jessica, 154
parody, 95, 119, 139, 142–44. *See also* comedy
*Passion of Joan of Arc, The* (film), 62
patriarchy, 148–49, 150–51, 153, 159, 161, 296; abusive, 152; bourgeois, 148; embodied, 60; white supremacist, 149
Peaty, Gwyneth, 183–84
Peele, Jordan, 98, 291
*Peeping Tom* (film), 39, 40
*Penitent, The* (film), 226
perception, 13, 40, 47, 57, 69, 74, 117, 129, 130, 225; auditory, 264; dialectic of, 28; visual, 13, 23–24, 51
Perkins, Anthony, 1, 144
Perkins, Stephanie, 270
Perkins School for The Blind, 234–35
Perrello, Tony, 39
Perryman, Lou, 214, 215
*Pet Sematary* (film), 124
Pfänder, Alexander, 28
*Phantasm* (film), 34
*Phantom of the Opera, The* (film), 158, 243
Phelan, James, 123
phenomenology, 27–28, 46, 69, 74, 100, 101, 105; of comedy-horror, 301; of senses, 198
Phillips, Wendell C., 168
Piatti-Farnell, Lorna, 124
*Pieces* (film), 101
Pierce, Jack, 167
Pinedo, Isabel Cristina, 17–20, 189
*Pizza* (film), 44
*Plan 9 from Outer Space* (film), 94–95
Plantinga, Carl, 127–28
Plato, 127
pleasure, 17–18, 81, 107, 115, 123, 138, 139, 180, 239, 299; guilty, 126; negative, 7, 15, 48–49, 101; sadistic, 191
plot twists, 53, 142

point-of-view (POV) shot, 38, 54, 262
Polanski, Roman, 41, 94, 124
*Polish Vampire in Burbank, A* (film), 154
*Poltergeist* (film), 176
*Polyester* (film), 102
*Pom Pom Girls, The* (film), 142
Poole, W. Scott, 243–44
*Popcorn* (film), 18, 80, 182, 321n17
*Possession* (film), 124
*Possession of Nurse Sherri, The* (film), 126
postmodernism, 19–20, 188, 321n17
poverty, 266
POV shot. *See* point-of-view (POV) shot
Poynter, Rikki, 182, 184
Prather, Maurice, 63, 309n42
premonitions, 69, 257
*Prevenge* (film), 293
Price, Vincent, 46, 86, 87, 89
Prince, Stephen, 40
pronouns, 253, 259, 261, 263, 270, 275
proprioception, 13, 16
prosthetics, 64, 83
psychiatrists, 5, 14, 20, 58; representations of, *6*, 6–7, 9–11, 44, 46, 72–74, 79, 87, 89, 134, 286
*Psycho* (film), 1–5, 9, 10, 11, 19, 37, 40, 119, 144, 157, 159, 241, 298; as protoslasher, 39; psychiatrist representation in, *6*, 6–7; title sequence of, 306n1
Pulcini, Robert, 259, 280
*Pumpkinhead* (film), 36
*Purge, The* (film), 299
puzzle films, 53, 193, 220

*Quiet Place, A* (film), 179, 191
Quinn, James W., 25
Quinn, John, 140
*Quo Vadis?* (film), 237

*Rabid* (film), 244
racism, 72, 127, 179, 269, 291, 312n26
Randel, Tony, 194
Rasmussen, Randy, 172
Rathbone, Basil, 165, 166
rationality, 4, 6, 8–10, 17–21, 42–46, 50, 69, 72–73, 76, 147, 292, 296, 297; belief and, 40; instrumental, 19; limits of, 18, 23, 45. *See also* irrationality
*Raven, The* (film), 167
*Raw* (film), 124, 293
Rawlinson, Herbert, 227
*Ready or Not* (film), 20, 157
*Rear Window* (film), 67
Redner, Gregg, 210
Reed, Carol, 62
Reeves, Michael, 319n39
Reid, Storm, 279
Reizenstein, Franz, 216–17
*Repulsion* (film), 41, 153
*Return of the Living Dead* (film), 34
Reubens, Paul, 139
*Revenge* (film), 20, 293
*Revenge of the Cheerleaders* (film), 142
Rhodes, Gary, 204–5
Richman, Charles, 240, 241
Riesenfeld, Hugo, 204
Riley, Michael, 26, 67, 69
*Ring* (1998 film), 285
*Ring, The* (2002 film), 285–86
Rin Tin Tin, 245–46
*Risen Soul of Jim Grant, The* (film), 226
Robinson, Octavian E., 168–69
Roden, Claudia, 123
Rodlo, Cristina, 273
Rodriguez, Oz, 258, 280
Roeg, Nicolas, 26, 52, 68, 70
*Roe v. Wade*, 292
Rogers, Bill, 108
Romero, Eduardo, 173
Romero, George A., 17, 101, 148, 150, 152, 265
*Rosemary's Baby* (film), 93, 124, 153, 291, 294

Ross, John, 282
Roth, Matthew, 153
Rothafel, Samuel Lionel, 238
Rousselle, Agathe, 293
*Ruins, The* (film), 241
*Run Sweetheart Run* (film), 280

Sager, Ray, 104–5, 111, 117
*Saint Maud* (film), 216, 300
Sarandos, Ted, 253, 254. *See also* Netflix
Sarsgaard, Peter, 280
Satan, 25, 45, 77, 93, 142
*Satan's Cheerleaders* (film), 27, 141–42
Savini, Tom, 152
*Saw* (film), 126, 298
Scheler, Max, 28
Schoenberg, Arnold, 37
Sconce, Jeffrey, 128, 131, 142
Scott, George C., 207
Scott, Ridley, 124
*Scream* (film), 139, 140, 157, 159–61, 180
*Scream 4* (film), 135
*Scream VI* (film), 17, 20, 153, 154–61, 188; "Stabby Meal" fast food tie-in with, 155–56, *156*
screenwriting, 88–89
*Scum of the Earth* (film), 113
SDH. *See* subtitles for the deaf and hard of hearing
séances, 208, 209
*Seeing Is Believing* (film), 226
*See No Evil* (film), 249
Selig, William N., 230
senses. *See* hearing; sight; smell; taste; touch
sensory deprivation, 21–22, *22*, 249
*Sentinel, The* (film), 249
*Serbian Film, A* (film), 126
serial killers, 2, 3, 25, 45, 69, 106, 109, 111, 116, 135, 179, 183, 191; female, 293
*Serpent, The* (film), 226
*Seven Footprints to Satan* (film), 175
sexism, 90, 139, 152, 153; misogyny and, 125, 140, 291. *See also* patriarchy
sexual assault, 135, 160, 187. *See also* #MeToo
sexual harassment, 137, 160
sexuality, 3, 56, 81, 90, 107, 126, 131, 265, 285, 293; comedy and, 142–43
sexual objectification, 140
Sharp, Don, 35, 306n2
Sharp, John, 127
Shaviro, Steven, 28
Shaw, Vinessa, 286
*She-Devils on Wheels* (film), 100, 117
Shelley, Mary, 200, 244
Sherriff, R. C., 243
Shim, Iris K., 280
Shipka, Kiernan, 179
Showalter, Elaine, 93
Shyamalan, M. Night, 53, 57, 259
Siegel, Kate, 179
sight, 12, 14, 31, 45, 47, 51–54, 56, 58, 65, 80, 86, 100, 101, 115, 131, 188, 192, 226, 230–36, 247, 248, 252, 258, 261, 272–74, 277, 308n25; cognition relation to, 15, 249; combined with other senses, 46; with ears/hearing, 15, 28, 39, 41, 46, 48, 254–55, *255*, 259, 289, 300; limitations of, 26, 64, 288; as pretext for belief, 3–6, *4*, 23, 26, 48, 68–73, 249; primacy of, 67, 69, 76; reflection and, 55, *55*, *171*, 171–72; restored, 227, 229, 232; second, 68, 72, 76; sensory deprivation and, 21–22, *22*; sight-based hermeneutics and, 15, 48; temporary loss of, 22, *22*. *See also* blindness; eyes; vision
sign language, 168, 169, 179, 184
*Silence, The* (film), 179, 254, 258

silent cinema, 25, 29, 165, 170, 177–78, 204, 244–45, 287; actors, 168, 231; blindness in, 226–30, *227*, *228*, 233–34; deaf viewers of, 173; intertitles in, 169, 174; musical accompaniment to, 246; special effects in, 76; spoken narration of, 236–37, 247; touch and, 227, *227*
*Silent Hill* (film), 36
*Silent Movie* (film), 142
*Silent Night, Deadly Night Part 2* (film), 132
*Silent Night, Deadly Night 3: Better Watch Out!* (film), 205
*Silent Night, Deadly Night 4: Initiation* (film), 98
Simón, Juan Piquer, 101
Six, Tom, 146, 147
*Sixth Sense, The* (film), 53, 56, 57
Skarsgård, Bill, 178
*Skeptic, The* (film), 73
skepticism, 21–22, 25, 42–43, 45, 46, 50, 58, 59, 60, 69, 73, 79, 87, 90, 96, 184
skin, 16, 24, 46, 103, 112, 132, 183, 249, 305n33, 328n17; animal, 100, 101; artificial, 282; color, 251, 285, 286; conductance, 49; flayed, 100; melted, 25; oily, 117; removed, 189–90, 199, 214; as sensing organ, 48, 115; virtual, 215. *See also* fingers
slasher films, 2, 39, 45, 80, 98, 129, 134–35, 139, 145, 155, 179, 182, 186, 191, 206, 208, 262, 264, 266, 270, 320n45; endurance of, 141; final girl and, 125, 157, 180, 183, 277; formulas of, 141; gaze structures of, 40; homages to, 141; laughter in, 191; meta-, 19, 126, 212, 293; nostalgia for, 140; parodies of, 142; soundtracks of, 219
Slater, Tom, 247
*Slayer, The* (film), 186, 204
slime, 26, 86, 96, 111, 122, 131, 144, 151, 188, 214, 215
Sloyan, Samantha, 180
*Slumber Party Massacre, The* (film), 124
smell, 13–16, 21, 26, 46, 47, 128, 129, 131, 144–45, 198, 216, 300, 308n25; olfaction and, 12, 27, 48, 65, 99–124, 199. *See also* odor
"Smell-O-Vision," 102
Smith, Albert, 238
Smith, Angela, 172
Smith, Dick, 26, 71
Smothers, Tom, 139
*Snow White and the Seven Dwarfs* (film), 247
Sobchack, Vivian, 28, 74, 101–2, 148, 150
Soderbergh, Steven, 292
Sole, Alfred, 27, 141, 144
somatosensation, 12
*Someone Inside Your House* (film), 259, 270–71
*Something Weird* (film), 99, 116
*Son of Frankenstein* (film), 166, 167
Sorvino, Mira, 160
*So Speaks the Heart* (film), 226
*Soul to Keep* (film), 179
sound effects, 71, 177, 181, 185, 211, 218, 220, 258; AD and, 268, 288; captioned, 194, 197, 202, 212; contextualizing, 268; tactile, 147
Spacek, Sissy, 143
Spalding, Harry, 35
special effects, 5, 26, 63, 86, 99, 101, 122, 133, 152, 178, 228, 244; demonic possession, 71, 75, *75*; in *The Gore Gore Girls*, 110, 112–13; reflection and, 55, *55*, *171*, 171–72; in silent cinema, 76. *See also* makeup; trick photography

*Species* (film), 67
spectral effects, 311n19
spectrality, 42, 46, 58, 68, 75, *75*, 208, 228
Spencer, Octavia, 188
*Spider Woman Strikes Back, The* (film), 173
Spiegel, Scott, 208
Spielberg, Steven, 37
*Spirit Camp* (film), 141
splatter films, 99, 106, 119, 121, 202
"Stabby Meal" (fast food tie-in), 155–56, *156*
startle effects, 4, 264; false, 263
*Star Wars: Episode VI—Return of the Jedi* (film), 203
St. Clair, Malcolm, 245
Stefaniuk, Rob, 154
Stevenson, Robert Louis, 24
Stoker, Bram, 44, 166
Stoller, Lucia, 160
Stovall, James, 250
*Strange Case of Dr Jekyll and Mr. Hyde* (Stevenson), 24
*Stranger Things* (TV series), 89
strangulation, 133, 152, 188
Stravinsky, Igor, 37
Stuart, Gloria, 170, 173, 188
*Stuff, The* (film), 129
subtitles for the deaf and hard of hearing (SDH), 29, 62, 174–75, 183–84, 189–90, 193–221, 258, 320n45, 321n17; audio commentary impact kin to, 79–80, 86; Eurocentrism of, 82; in *Exorcist II: The Heretic*, 82–86, *85*; in *Hellbound: Hellraiser II*, 197–99, *198*; *House on Haunted Hill*, 91–93, *92*, *97*; layering of, 209; mistakes, 80, 182, 185, 203; music and, 201–6, *203*, *204*, *206*, 216–17; omissions, 188, *190*, 197; pedagogical value of, 185, 210; as textual "skin," 215; as transcription, 81, 84, 86, 89, 96, 98, 182, 185–87, 195
*Suburban Roulette* (film), 113, 117
*Suck* (film), 17, 154–55, *155*
Sud, Veena, 280
superstitions, 43–44, 47, 72
*Suspiria* (film), 202, 204–5
Sutherland, Donald, 68
Sutton, Travis, 179
*Swallow* (film), 153
*Swinging Cheerleaders, The* (film), 142
Synder, Joel, 248–49, 250
synesthesia, 12–16, 29, 47, 111

tactility, 27, 48, 70, 86, 100, 122, 130, 147, 199, 227, 230; Braille and, 235, 247
*Tales from the Crypt* (comic book), 152
*Tales from the Crypt* (film), 150, 249
Taliaferro, Mabel, 230
talking books, 247, 248
Talmadge, Norma, 241
Tamblyn, Amber, 286
*Targets* (film), 17
taste (aesthetic), 101; Ebert on breaches of, 148; "good," 298. *See also* bad taste
taste (sensory), 26, 115, 120, 121, 300, 308n25; aftertaste, 129; of blood, 106–9, *108*; buds, 129, 135, 144, 145; in *The Gore Gore Girls*, 111–13, *113*, 122–23; imagined, 150; masculine and masochistic, 125–61; sensory deprivation and, 21; smell bond with, 121; sound inducing, 14, 111; synesthetic tendencies and, 12–15. *See also* gustation
*Taste of Blood, A* (film), 100, 101, 108, 109
Taylor-Joy, Anya, 137
telekinesis, 143

Tenney, Kevin S., 63
Ternaux, Jean-Pierre, 13
*Terror, The* (film), 23, 305n42
*TerrorVision* (film), 39
testicles, 123
*Texas Chain Saw Massacre, The* (film), 15–16, 17, 19, 101
*Texas Chainsaw Massacre 2, The* (film), 214, 215
texting, 157, 180, 181, *181*
texture, 100, 111, 122, 144, 145, 150, 151, 190
*Thankskilling* (film), 134–35
*Them* (film), 270
*There's Someone Inside Your House* (film), 258, 270–71
Theroux, Justin, 295
Thesiger, Ernest, 170
*They/Them* (film), 270
*Thing, The* (1982 film), 17
*Thing, The* (2011 film), 247, 257, 271, 280, 282
*Things Heard & Seen* (film), 259, 280–81, *281*
*13 Ghosts* (film), 238
*Thirteenth Chair, The* (film), 175
*This Stuff'll Kill Ya!* (film), 119
Thomas, David, 127
*Through Darkened Vales* (film), 228–29
THX "Deep Note," 203
*Tides of Retribution, The* (film), 226
*Tingler, The* (film), 87, 96, 176, 177, 238, 318n31
*Titane* (film), 98, 293, 295
title sequences (opening credits), 34, 36, 43, 81–82, 149, 182, 197, 306n1, 319n39; hypnotic quality of, 41; music of, 216–17, 321n17
tongues, 14, 48, 103, 105, 106, 107, 115, 119, 123, 128, 134, 145, 152, 154, 300; animal, 100, 102, 120; receptor cells of, 129; violence directed toward the, 132, 159. *See also* taste (sensory)
*Torture Garden* (film), 150
torture porn, 126, 298
touch, 12, 13, 15, 16, 21, 26, 47–48, 69, 115, 145, 198, 215, 275, 300, 301, 307n20, 308n25; as basis for belief, 4, *4*, 45; Braille and, 235, 247; enhanced sense of, 184; lexicon of, 122; seeing through, 70, 235; silent films and, 227, *227*; touchscreen, 254. *See also* tactility
Tourneur, Jacques, 42
*Toxic Zombies* (film), 148
trailers, 34, 67
trauma, 52, 74, 77, 78, 79, 191, 260, 278, 280, 281, 283, 292; bodily, 134; *False Positive* and, *294*, 294–95; familial, 209; unending, 180; war-related, 243
*Trick* (film), 46, 47
*Tricked into Happiness* (film), 226
trick photography, 75, 228; ghost glass, *75*, 75–76, 78
Trump, Donald J., 153, 299–300
Turner, David M., 200
*Two Faces of Dr. Jekyll, The* (film), 176
*Two Thousand Maniacs!* (film), 100, 119, 121

*Umma* (film), 247–48, 253, 280
uncertainty, 52, 53, 56, 59, 63
*Unfriended* (film), 284
*Uninvited, The* (film), 75
Universal Monsters, 2, 43, 125, 166, 170, 258, 293, 298
*Unsane* (film), 292
*Us* (film), 291, 297
Usherwood, Amy, 282

*Vamperifica* (film), 136
*Vampires vs. the Bronx* (film), 258, 280

vampirism, 10–11, 24–25, 43–44, 109, 154–55, 270, 274
Van Dyke, W. S., 245
Van Sloan, Edward, 25, 44
*Varsity Blood* (film), 139, 145
*Vault of Horror, The* (comic book), 150
*Vault of Horror, The* (film), 150
Veditz, George William, 173–74
vegetables, 107, 111, 123, 143, 145, 146
Verbinski, Gore, 285
Vernon, Jackie, 149
Vertov, Dziga, 38
*V/H/S 94* (film), 215–16
*Videodrome* (film), 39
*Virgin Cheerleaders in Chains* (film), 140
vision, 26, 28, 38, 57, 68, 69, 100, 167, 201, 225, 228, 232, 242, 245, 246, 254, 258, 266, 284; low, 29, 50, 191, 226, 247, 250, 252–53, 264, 327n12; obscured, 217; persistence of, 56; prosthetic, 64; technologies of, 74; 20/20, 272. *See also* blindness; eyes; sight; visuality
*Visit, The* (film), 259
visuality, 12, 13, 23–24, 27, 29, 37–38, 48, 51, 65, 111, 172–73, 177, 187, 192, 225, 236, 251–52, 258–59, 262, 271, 287–89; haptic, 214–16; in *Witchcraft*, *35*, 35–36. *See also* eyes; sight; vision
vomit, 26, 130, 219; nausea and, 99, 101, 112, 119, 122, 129, 135, 151
von Sydow, Max, 72, 76
*Voodoo Woman* (film), 72
*Voyage to the Planet of Prehistoric Women* (film), 269

Wagner, Richard, 177, 204
*Wait Until Dark* (film), 249
Wakeman, Rick, 320n45
Walas, Chris, 96
Wallfisch, Benjamin, 178
Walpole, Horace, 244
Walter, Dick, 209
war: *The Battle Cry of Peace* and, 234–42, *242*, 244, 245, 257, 324n36; real-world horror of, 241–43, *242*; trauma related to, 243; World War I, 229, 231, 237, 242–43, 244, 254; World War II, 166
"Washed-Up Witch" (comic), 3–6, *4*, *5*, 11–12
Waters, John, 102
Waters, Marilyn, 119
Weary, Jack, 266
Weaving, Samara, 157, 161
Weber, Jimmy, 153
Webern, Anton, 37
Weinstein, Bob, 159–60
Weinstein, Harvey, 159–61. *See also* #MeToo
Welles, Orson, 42
Wells, H. G., 278
*Wes Craven's New Nightmare* (film), 19, 212
wetness, 21, 86, 92, 134, 147, 175, 188–89, 213–14, 217–18, *218*, 220; aural qualities of, 215; captioned language of, 96, 98, 221; dryness and, 86, 90–91, 93, 98, 216, 219; haptically felt, 216
Whale, James, 167, 170, 171, 182, 191, 243
Whalen, Geoffrey O., 236, 242
Whannell, Leigh, 258, 278
*When a Stranger Calls* (film), 202–3, *203*
*When the Blind See* (film), 226
White, Ted, 189
*White Zombie* (film), 202, 204–5
*Who Is Killing the Cheerleaders?* (film), 140

Wiegand, Erin E., 148
Wiene, Robert, 177
*Wife's Battle, A* (film), 226
Wilbur, Crane, 223
Williams, Allison, 282
Williams, Caroline, 214, 215
Williams, John, 37
Williams, Linda, 306n8
Williams, Sharon, 68
Williams, Tony, 151
Williamson, Kevin, 160
Wilmington, Michael, 177
Wilson, Laura, 147–48
Wilson, Woodrow, 224, 241, 243, 324n36
Winstead, Mary Elizabeth, 257
*Wishmaster 2* (film), 315n11
*Witchboard* (film), 39
*Witchcraft* (film), 34–37, *35*, 40, 72, 306n1
witches and witchcraft, 94, 142; *Burn, Witch, Burn* and, 10, 40–43, *41*, *43*, 47, 50–52, 56, 307n18; in comic books, 3–6, *4*, *5*, 11–12; in film, 7, 10–11, 34–37, *35*, 40, 72, 306n1
*Witchfinder General* (film), 182, 319n39
*Witchtrap* (film), 25, 26
*With the Eyes of the Blind* (film), 226, 227, *227*
*Wizard of Gore, The* (film), 100, 101, 105, 106, 114–17
*Wolcott Coombs* (film), 229, 231
Wolfkind, Sara, 283
*Wolf Man, The* (film), 10, 36
*Woman in the Window, The* (film), 67
Wood, Edward D., Jr., 94–95
Wood, Robin, 151, 265–66
World War I, 229, 231, 237, 242–43, 244, 254
World War II, 166
Wright, Joe, 67
*Wrong Bottle, The* (film), 226
*Wrong Turn* (film), 241
Wu, Harmony, 127
Wynorski, Jim, 140
Wyss, Amanda, 211, 214

*X-Ray Fiend, The* (film), 244

*Yōkai Hantā: Hiruko* (film), 44
*Young Frankenstein* (film), 249

Zdenek, Sean, 195–96, 201
*Zombie* (film), 148
Zombie, Rob, 188
zombies, 49, 53, 148, 150–51, 179, 205, 296
zoom shots, 87, 89, 133, 134, 262; "verbal," 260, *260*
Żuławski, Andrzej, 124